The Philosophy and Politics of Freedom

Richard E. Flathman

The University of Chicago Press
Chicago and London

RICHARD E. FLATHMAN is professor of political science at The Johns Hopkins University. He is the author of numerous books, including *The Practice of Political Authority*, published by the University of Chicago Press.

The University of Chicago Press, Chicago 60637
The University of Chicago Press, Ltd., London

96 95 94 93 92 91 90 89 87   54321

Library of Congress Cataloging-in-Publication Data
Flathman, Richard E.
  The philosophy and politics of freedom.

  Bibliography: p.
  Includes index.
  1. Liberty. 2. Liberty—Philosophy. I. Title.
JC585.F554 1987   323.44   86-16128
ISBN 0-226-25316-3
ISBN 0-226-25317-1 (pbk.)

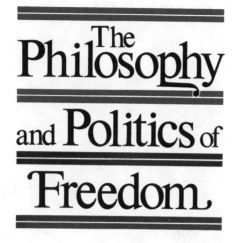

The Philosophy and Politics of Freedom

For my mother and the memory of my father

Contents

Political philosophy cannot be expected to increase our ability to be successful in political activity. . . . But the patient analysis of the general ideas which have come to be connected with political activity—ideas such as nature, artifice, reason, will, law, authority, obligation, etc.—in so far as it succeeds in removing some of the crookedness from our thinking and leads to a more economical use of concepts, is an activity neither to be overrated nor despised.

Michael Oakeshott

Acknowledgments

Ungrateful as it may be, I must begin by dissenting from a view of the theorist to whom these reflections are most heavily indebted. Thomas Hobbes is famous for the pronouncement that obligation is thralldom. My ingratitude in this regard is compelled by gratitude itself, by my appreciation for the help and support I have received throughout the preparation of this work. No thralldom here.

Both early and late versions of the work met with vigorous, critical responses in graduate seminars at Johns Hopkins. Special thanks to Michael Briand, Thomas Eagles, Bonnie Honig, Norma Moruzzi, and David Mapel. Faculty colleagues at Hopkins continue to sustain an intellectual atmosphere distinctively supportive of political theory and related modes of reflection. As usual, conversations with Nancy Hartsock, George Kelly, John Pocock, Jerry Schneewind, David Sachs, and—more recently, but to my great pleasure and profit—Bill Connolly, have been especially valuable. I have also enjoyed generous support, both financial and otherwise, from Dean Sigmund Suskind and Dean George Fisher, and cheerful secretarial assistance from Catherine Grover, Evelyn Scheulen, and Evelyn Stoller.

When the manuscript was about half finished I directed a National Endowment for the Humanities Seminar for College Teachers on the topic of political freedom. This was an unusually rewarding experience, for which thanks to the NEH and especially to the superb group of scholars and teachers who participated in the seminar. Particular thanks to Steven Delue, James Knauer, Arthur Poskocil, and Peter Steinberger, each of whom provided acute comments on draft chapters.

I was privileged to spend 1983–84 at the Center for Advanced Study in the Behavioral Sciences. It is a pleasure to add my voice to the chorus of praise for this incomparable institution and to express my appreciation to the Center, the John Simon Guggenheim Memorial Foundation, and the Mellon Foundation for financial support during my tenure as a Center Fellow. For reasons that any present or past fellow will understand, I hesitate before the attempt to distinguish among the valuable experiences of this memorable year. I must, however, thank Larry Becker and Paul Brest for any number of ideas and for detailed comments on my work and Dorothy Brothers for kindnesses well beyond excellent typing.

Parts of the book have been presented at Reed College, Harvard University, Balliol College, Oxford, at meetings of several professional associations, and at a conference on "The Making of Modern Freedom" sponsored by the Liberty Fund and held at Washington University in St. Louis. In each case I have benefited from comments and discussion. Materials from chapters 8 and 9 have appeared in Alphonso J. Damico, ed., *Liberals on Liberalism* (Totowa, N.J.: Rowman and Littlefield, 1986), and are reprinted by permission.

I completed the book while holding a Visiting Senior Research Fellowship at St. John's College, Oxford. I am deeply grateful to the president and fellows of St. John's for a stimulating and highly agreeable five months. Particular thanks to Leslie Macfarlane for warm hospitality and much excellent conversation.

In addition to colleagues already mentioned, all or part of the manuscript was read by the late Stanley Benn, John Burke, John Charvet, Arthur DiQuattro, John Gray, Robert Goodin, J. David Greenstone, Felix Oppenheim, Quentin Skinner, the late Elaine Spitz, and William Weinstein. The weaknesses that remain are of course my responsibility, but the work would be far poorer if I had not had the thoughtful criticisms and suggestions of these fine scholars. I want especially to thank David Sachs for saving me from any number of blunders and John Charvet for his deep but always friendly disagreements.

The two scholars who read the manuscript for the University of Chicago Press helped me to a better understanding of my own position and made a number of valuable suggestions.

My largest debt is to the large and excellent literature on the subject of freedom. Although I have steadily disagreed with proponents of "positive" theories of freedom, and with a number of writers firmly in the "negative" tradition of thinking about it, my views have shifted substantially as I have considered and responded to their often powerful arguments. If I have been less assiduous in recording my borrowings from theorists with whom I generally agree (most especially Maurice Cranston and Felix Oppenheim), I hope they will find that I have not otherwise misused their ideas.

Introduction

Negative, situated, elemental. Prosaic though they are, these terms will serve as insignia of the views about freedom presented in these pages. Because the pages are more numerous than the list of insignia might predict, a prefatory gloss on them may be of use to the reader.

Part I advances a modified version of the negative conception of freedom that derives most clearly from Thomas Hobbes. For purposes of moral and political thought, our subject should be understood as freedom and unfreedom of action. Actions are taken by persons ("agents") who adopt and hold beliefs, form desires and interests that are influenced by their beliefs, frame intentions to act to satisfy their interests and desires, and attempt to act on their intentions. Agents and their actions are free insofar as their attempts to act are not prevented by the actions of other agents, unfree insofar as they are so prevented. In the absence of attempted actions, there is nothing of which freedom or unfreedom can be predicated (there is nothing that is "freedom-evaluable").

For several centuries, negative conceptions of freedom and unfreedom have been contrasted with and opposed to positive accounts (the "negative-positive" terminology, although unfortunate, is so well established in moral and political philosophy that the least cumbersome course is to continue to use it) according to which conditions such as those I have listed are necessary but not sufficient for freedom. On the latter views, in order to be free, agents must maintain various further characteristics such as rationality, an internally harmonious self, autonomy, various moral virtues, and the like. Agents who lack these characteristics, and actions that do not manifest them, are therefore unfree.

There is one respect, however, in which this contrast is diminished by the argument that "freedom" is a predicate of actions and by the intimately related thesis that freedom is "situated." On some formulations of the positive conception of freedom, agents lacking the characteristics just mentioned are unfree because overcome by passions or desires. Reason, autonomy, virtuous dispositions, and so forth are understood as opposed to, and as means of controlling, brute forces that dwell in the pre- or a-social (and hence unsituated) recesses of the self. Persons lacking the former characteristics are therefore vulnerable to being "enslaved" by the latter forces.

As advanced here, the argument that agency, action, and hence freedom and unfreedom are situated involves the claim that these concepts (as with all others) are part of a public, shared, mutually meaningful language and hence presuppose some form of the further elements of sociality that Ludwig Wittgenstein and other philosophers have identified as necessary to language. Otherwise put, the present situated version of the negative conception of freedom is part of a philosophical anthropology intended to account for the facts (among innumerable others) that the agents to whom freedom and unfreedom are attributed make sense of themselves, of one another, and of one another's actions. If there are human beings or human behaviors that are privatized in the deep sense suggested by talk about enslaving passions and desires, neither the human agents nor their behaviors are freedom-evaluable. In this respect, the present version of the negative view of freedom substantially reduces the conceptual distance between negative and positive conceptions of it.

It may therefore be thought that the theory presented here is in fact a version of the positive theory of freedom. In another and (I argue) historically more important dimension of positive theories, however, there remains a wide gulf between them and my modified negative conception. In this second dimension, rationality, autonomy, and virtue are essential to freedom because they are elements of morally defensible conduct and of morally commendable character. From Rousseau through Kant and Hegel to later neo-Hegelians, proponents of positive theories have sought to moralize the concept or idea of freedom. Perhaps responding to a cultural tendency to celebrate freedom, they have moved from the proposition that freedom is a moral and political good or a moral and political right to the quite different proposition that persons and actions are free only to the extent that they are morally good and their actions morally right. Moreover, because they have thought that qualities essential to morally good character and conduct can be developed and sustained only in a society or a culture that itself has certain quite elevated characteristics, they have promoted, in part in the name of freedom, quite definite social and political principles and rules, institutions and practices. They too adopt a situated theory of freedom (or rather they first advanced such a theory, the notion of situatedness being of Hegelian and perhaps Rousseauian provenance), but in an insistently moralized form, not in what I call the generic, morally indeterminate Wittgensteinian form advanced here.

These themes and contrasts lead to the third of my insignia (and to Part III of this work), the notion that freedom is elemental. But before outlining this progression I must say a further word about situatedness and issues that arise concerning it (about Part II of this work).

It might be thought (a) that action which is situated in the sense I have sketched is *therefore* unfree or (b) that the forms situatedness in fact takes in modern societies are incompatible with or at least severely and pervasively restrictive of freedom. If so, the thesis that freedom is necessarily situated is tantamount to the view that freedom is an impossibility or that there can be little or no freedom in modern societies.

These are haunting but elusive possibilities. As to (a), religious thinkers have given intelligible expression to the thought that the societies of this world or this life are incompatible with the true freedom of the City of God; even so, I argue, there can be no cogent secular formulation of a freedom-sociality antinomy. Many societies, perhaps including the societies I am considering here, may in fact be unfree or largely unfree, but this must be a contingent and an in principle remediable fact about them, not a necessary truth. In arguing for this view in Chapter 5, I begin with a brief discussion of Hobbes and Rousseau, both of whom can be interpreted as entertaining but rejecting the possibility that humankind gave up its freedom when it left its original, presocial condition. Hobbes seems to have regarded this idea as coherent but to have rejected it on the ground that as a practical matter freedom would not be reliably available outside of a politically organized society. I then take up Rousseau's far deeper objection that this idea of presocial freedom is incoherent, and I draw on Rousseau for the rudiments of a theory of generic sociality of the kind I introduce in Chapters 1 to 4. The remainder of the chapter develops this theory further, primarily through a construal of the later philosophy of Wittgenstein. In terms of thesis (a), these discussions dissolve rather than refute the notion that situatedness is incompatible with freedom. Situatedness, rather, is a condition of freedom-evaluability and hence of both freedom and unfreedom.

This conclusion brings me to thesis (b), a claim about the extent to which and the ways in which social arrangements in Western modernity exclude or narrowly restrict freedom of action. Whereas Hegel believed that the Idea of Freedom was conclusively realized in modernity, numerous later but recognizably Hegelian thinkers claim that the forms of sociality distinctive of Western modernity are pervasively antagonistic to it.[1] They attempt to articulate the idea that modernity is deeply at odds with itself. Although officially committed to individual freedom, and having destroyed premodern and arguably freedom-restricting beliefs, arrangements, and practices, the most admired of modern Western societies subject their members to an encompassing array of controls. The conflict between appearance and reality, profession and practice, they claim, is at the bottom of the *angst* prevalent in these societies.

Except in a sense briefly discussed at the end of this introduction, this is not a work in empirical political sociology and I do not attempt to assess the evidence that there are structural or other deep and pervasive constraints on freedom in modern Western societies. The most sweeping and disturbing of such claims, however, rest less on empirical evidence than on underdefended assumptions. Freedom is equated with a form of individual autonomy requiring fully critical attitudes toward all social conventions and expectations, all norms and rules. Modern Western societies are condemned as arenas of unfreedom because they do not sustain a mode of individuality that is and must be purely supposititious. My critique of these views will not tell us whether unfreedom is in fact widespread in this or that society, but it may disqualify certain unsettling suspicions and facilitate more fruitful inquiries about the incidence and distribution of freedom.

Chapter 7, which in some respects is transitional between Parts II and III, takes up questions about the place of rationality in the theory of situated negative freedom and considers, in the perspective provided by the discussion of rationality, questions about coercion. I argue that rationality is a necessary feature of agency and action and hence of freedom-evaluability. But I claim that a minimal or weak form of rationality is sufficient for this purpose. My argument proceeds from cases of valued freedoms, for example, religious confession and various kinds of association, in respect to which modern Western societies reject the idea that agents must show that their choices are correct and are cautious about the idea that such choices must be defensible or even defended. Of course more robust forms of rationality are valuable in many ways, particularly in sustaining freedoms against coercive interferences. A society that values freedom will promote rationality in order to promote and protect freedom. But valuing and promoting should not be confused with requiring. Salient features of modern Western societies are best understood, as I think Hobbes understood them, as valuable in part because they diminish the necessity of rationality for freedom, sustain freedoms of individuals who may be no more than minimally rational in many of their activities and perhaps autonomous in none of them.

Chapter 8 advances a general argument for freedom of action as a high-order human good and contends that there is and should be a heavy burden of justification on those who propose interferences with it. (I label the presumption the General Presumption in Favor of Freedom, or GPF.) This argument is naturalistic in that it is grounded in salient features of human beings and their circumstances and in appealing to the likely consequences, for such persons in those circumstances, of treating freedom of action as a high-order good. The characteristics of human beings I adduce are those that make for agency, above all the tendency to form desires and interests, ends and purposes, and to attempt to act to satisfy and to achieve them. The circumstances are both natural and social. On the one hand, action is ordinarily required to achieve ends. Whether the humanly useful substances of nature are plentiful or scarce, whether human relations are competitive and conflictful or cooperative and harmonious, human endeavor is ordinarily required to benefit from them. On the other, desires and interests, ends and purposes, vary from person to person and group to group. Although often complementary, some combinations of desires are intrinsically incompatible with one another, and others are practically and circumstantially so.

In negative terms the argument is naturalistic and consequentialist in avoiding claims about intrinsically, rationally, or historically necessary goods or values (including notions such as the intrinsic dignity of persons, the respect owed to all persons as such, and the like). Although general, the argument is culture-specific. The features of human beings and their circumstances to which it appeals may or may not be characteristic of all or of a very wide range of human societies, but the discussion here is limited to societies in which the characteristics are already regarded as legitimate, as without shame or stigma. Where such legitimation has not occurred, my generalizations, even if in some sense true, would not support GPF. Or rather, to adduce those generalizations in support of GPF would be to argue against the grain of the culture to which the argument was addressed. I do argue for legitimation (for what I call, perhaps tendentiously, the Liberal principle, or LP, the principle that it is a prima facie good for persons to form, to act upon, and to satisfy or achieve, desires and interests, ends and purposes), but these arguments are against ascetical and related views that are already on the defensive in modern Western societies. In short, my argument for LP and GPF presumes that at least tacit acceptance of something akin to them is already widespread. This means, I hope, that the argument has a certain commonsensical quality.

Chapters 9 and 10 address, in a moderately skeptical spirit, questions left open despite general acceptance of the arguments of Chapter 8. LP identifies no more than prima facie goods, GPF states no more than a presumption and burden of justification. Instances of the goods that LP identifies and of the freedom that GPF privileges can conflict with one another. In addition, those goods and that presumption can and do conflict with other highly esteemed and widely held values in societies that endorse LP and GPF. Neither LP, GPF, nor the combination of them can resolve these conflicts. In addition, there are questions about the conditions, over and above endorsement of LP and GPF, necessary or at least strongly contributive to the efficacy of LP and GPF. What must be the case if freedom of action is to be more than a piety and better than a cover for class, caste, or other injustices in the distribution of effective freedoms? In Chapter 9 I take up arguments that certain freedom*s* deserve and require protections beyond what is accorded by LP-GPF, deserve and require the stronger standing and protections of *rights* that hold against all conflicting or competing considerations. In Chapter 10 I consider further arguments to the effect that, empirically and causally, certain social and political arrangements are necessary to a reliably available array of freedoms of action.

Although tempted by the antinomian view that conflicts among freedoms of action and between such freedoms and other values should be resolved circumstantially, I endorse practices and arrangements that accord rights to an inventory of freedoms. I also endorse a number of John Rawls's conclusions concerning the freedoms that now deserve the special standing of rights. But I argue against Rawls's contractarian mode of reasoning for these conclusions and against his view that political philosophy must itself supply a determinate inventory of rights that invariably take precedence over all other considerations. Against his and other rigorist views, I argue that rights can and should be adopted, interpreted, and implemented on the basis of reasoning (intuitionist reasoning) of a kind continuous with the reasoning that supports LP and GPF.

In Chapter 10 I present a related criticism of theories that purport to identify the empirical but necessary conditions of an adequate array of effective freedoms. Every society that values freedom develops understandings concerning the conditions that contribute to its availability and all such societies implement those understandings through arrangements and institutions. But just as it is implausible to think that there is one ranking of freedoms that all societies should adopt, it is equally implausible to think that there is one set of conditions necessary to effective freedom. If it were the task of a theory of freedom to establish claims of this sort, attempts at such a theory would be doomed to failure.

Having discountenanced the excessive ambitions of some theorists of freedom, I proceed to advance a very general thesis of my own, one that is implicit in much of the argument of the book and that takes the argument to its limit in ways that I now try to indicate. The thesis is represented by the third of the insignia already mentioned, namely, that freedom is an elemental feature of moral and political life.

By "elemental" I intend two apparently conflicting but complementary claims: (1) freedom-evaluability and freedom itself are *suppositions* in modern Western societies; (2) they are also widely *valued* features of those societies. It is ordinarily assumed that persons are agents engaging in action. Members of these societies think and act *from* these assumptions; the assumptions are explicitly or self-consciously invoked, defended, or qualified only in the face of definite evidence that they do not hold concerning particular persons in specific circumstances. Attention focuses not on freedom-evaluability or on freedom, but on more differentiating features of persons, of their actions, and of the consequences of their actions. If an action is unwelcome or objectionable, the presumption against interference with it may become the focus of attention and may be rebutted. But this is not, or very often is not, the first or even an early response. Tolerance and forbearance, accommodation and compromise, attempts to educate, persuade, and otherwise influence, are not merely possible alternative responses but the generally endorsed alternatives. Or rather, the attempt to prevent unwelcome or objectionable actions is regarded as an alternative to the usual, the matter-of-course ways of responding to them. Freedom-evaluability and freedom are elemental in the sense of being taken for granted as elements in a great deal of what goes on in society.

At the same time, freedom and freedom-evaluability are widely and strongly (if for the most part implicitly) valued. Agency and action are normal not only in a statistical but in a normative sense. They are prominent elements in the concept of a normal as opposed to an abnormal, subnormal, or defective person. When encountered, moreover, abnormality in these respects is regretted and if possible remedied or ameliorated. Expressions of regret and attempts at amelioration evidence the value placed upon freedom-evaluability. Of course interferences with freedom occur and can sometimes be justified, but it is at least equally important that such justifications are expected, that failure to provide them is a breech or an offense.

The thesis that freedom is elemental is implicit in the other main conclusions I have summarized; the thesis is therefore correct if or to the extent that those conclusions are warranted. I end this introduction with a few comments concerning the standing of those conclusions as I understand it.

My conclusions are based on interpretations and elaborations of an array or constellation of concepts and ideas that are salient in our moral and political thinking. It would of course be idle to pretend that these concepts and ideas are univocal or that analyses of them could be correct, interpretations warranted, and elaborations convincing in some unequivocal or indisputable sense. Nor is there any metatheoretical or methodological principle or procedure that could underwrite my claims. Rather, those claims stand or fall on the arguments I give for them and on the ways those several arguments do or do not extend and complement one another so as to accumulate toward an integrated and enlightening account. I proceed on the assumption that the concepts and ideas I discuss are, in Ludwig Wittgenstein's phrase, "somethings," not "anythings" or "nothings," hence that theorizing about them is not make-believe, hence that we can deploy the notion that there are better as opposed to worse accounts of those "somethings." My claim is that my accounts are improvements upon those that I argue against and that they accumulate to the view that freedom is elemental in the societies I am discussing.

Of course the "somethings" that I discuss are not what they are, do not have the characteristics and connections with one another that they have, apart from thinking in and about them. It is equally idle to think that further thinking in and about them should or could leave them entirely as they are. Freedom is no longer the same something it was for me when I began these reflections, and if these or similar reflections are considered by others freedom will almost certainly not remain the same something for them that it was before they considered them.

There is, however, a difference between thinking that aims to clarify and elaborate upon concepts and ideas and thinking that presumes an understanding of them and sets out to preserve or to change them. Of course this distinction cannot be categorical; the first kind of thinking cannot help but affect what it thinks about and the second cannot help but take much of what it thinks about as it "finds" it. Moreover, the distinction is in part between differing intentions and purposes, and these are typically mixed, uncertain, and only partly understood by those who act on them. The distinction is nevertheless important. This is not because either of these modes of thinking is superior to the other by some criterion independent of both, but because they respectively require partly different kinds of evidence and argumentation.

I have tried to show that my account of freedom is superior to negative freedom accounts that do not include the elements of situated agency and action, and superior to positive freedom theories that insist upon autonomy, rationality, virtue, and the like. I have also advanced a general argument for the value of freedom and an analysis of rights and their connections with freedom. If I have shown that these analyses are superior (to the available alternatives) by the criteria appropriate to the first kind of thinking distinguished, proponents of alternative views who are engaged in this kind of thinking should give those views up. But my arguments do not discredit alternative views understood as proposals to protect or to change freedom and the ideas with which it is interwoven.

My claim that freedom is elemental in modern Western societies can be viewed as abbreviating my reasons for these conclusions. That claim implies that much in social life is left open, left to be settled, unsettled, and settled and unsettled anew, by the continuing flow of actions and interactions among individuals and groups. As a generalization, members of a society in which freedom is elemental *require* of one another no more than the mutual acknowledgment of agency expressed in acceptance of what I have called LP and GPF. Whether they believe, expect, or hope that this stance or outlook will lead to something further and in their view more elevated than agency and freedom of action, they regard it as the appropriate basis for much of social life among themselves and they think that departures from it must be justified in the light of the considerations that make it appropriate. That this is the appropriate understanding, that departures from it need to be justified, is itself one of the few things that is settled in such a society.

The views I argue against are more or less sweeping challenges to this understanding. Over a narrower or wider range, questions that the understanding leaves open are to be closed, matters that are to be settled locally, circumstantially, and tentatively are to be resolved globally, authoritatively, and into the indefinite future. Of course a society in which freedom is elemental may include ideals and aspirations that soar well above freedom. Members of such a society may hope for, encourage, and delight in one another's successes in attaining to these ideals; they may be disappointed and saddened when their hopes are dashed, distressed when their efforts come to nothing. And for various purposes there may be more definite requirements and prohibitions that are enforced by sanctions much stronger than expressions of disappointment and disapproval. But the ideals and the requirements, certainly efforts to pursue the former and enforce the latter, are vulnerable to challenges that could no longer be mounted on the views I argue against.

These remarks help to explain my comment that the thesis that freedom is elemental takes the argument of this book to its limit. That thesis draws the most general conclusions supported by my account and elaboration of freedom. Insofar, then, as my reflections are in the first of the two modes of thinking that I distinguished, those reflections reach their limit with the claim that freedom is elemental.

How far is insofar as? My remarks in this introduction emphasize the aspects of this work that are most clearly in the first of the two modes of thinking, an emphasis that I believe is faithful to the predominant characteristics of the discussions they introduce. As I have said, however, the distinction between the two modes of thinking is never categorical, and in any case no one who reads what follows will think that it is strictly maintained in these pages. I have already introduced a principle that I label "liberal," and at various later junctures I further indulge my predilections by using the terms "liberal" and "liberalism" to characterize and to endorse a number of the ideas I discuss. I claim that my account of freedom is correct whether it is an account of a something that can plausibly be called liberal. But it would be self-deception to deny that my account is influenced by my own views about how freedom should be understood and about the place it ought to have in moral and political life.

Further defense of these views will have to be postponed to a future work in which I hope to present a more explicit and systematic formulation of liberalism than I attempt here. But I must guard against misinterpretations that might be made of my last remarks. This work is concerned with prevalent understandings of concepts and ideas relating to freedom, with a large and prominent subset of the concepts and ideas at work in modern Western societies. Those understandings are consonant with ideas that can plausibly be called liberal. Thus if my account is correct, we can also say that, at the level of ideas, the societies I have discussed are (what their members and others often—albeit in quite various tones of voice—call them) liberal societies. Of course it does not follow that these societies are, again at the level of ideas, liberal in their understandings of other ideas. More important, it does not follow that these societies are adequately or satisfactorily liberal in their arrangements, practices, and activities.[2]

If the ideas I have discussed played no role, or no more than a marginal role, my account of freedom in modern Western societies would be mistaken. But it is consistent with that account that departures from and violations of the understandings be numerous and widespread and that the ideas I have discussed be invoked largely in objections to departures and violations from and of them. If there were no violations, the understandings might well cease to be normative, might recede further into the background assumptions of society. If the understandings were honored exclusively or even primarily in the breech, they would be available, if at all, primarily as bases for criticisms of society. Between these limiting extremes there are a wealth of possibilities and combinations of possibilities. Because I have not attempted the kind of investigation necessary to determine which among these possibilities actually obtain, I ought perhaps to remain silent on the question. But you don't need a political sociologist to know that, at the level of events, freedom in self-declared liberal societies is too often minimal rather than elemental. On the view of political philosophy that informs these reflections, what little of a practical character I have to say about this situation concerns how *not* to go about the task, at once urgent and perennial, of improving upon it.

Part One

Analyzing Freedom

I

Kinds of Freedom

A baby emerges from the womb. Nothing apart from itself is moving it, but it moves nevertheless. It is self-activated, possessing what Aristotle called *energeia*.

Some of the baby's movements go unimpeded. It extends its legs, twists and turns. Other movements encounter obstacles.

Does a case like this give us the conditions necessary to our notions of freedom and unfreedom; the conditions sufficient to those notions? Of course we use the words "free," "freely," and "freedom" where there is neither self-activation nor a genuine possibility of obstacles to movement. Free-falling objects and branches swaying freely in the breeze are not self-activated; the notion of an omnipotent God excludes the possibility of effective obstacles; accounts of ghosts and creatures of science-fiction often achieve their distinctive flavor by denying or severely qualifying this possibility; a cloud-free sky, a complexion free of blemishes, does not depend literally or straightforwardly on either condition.

Just because of these characteristics, the latter uses of "free" and its cognates and counterparts are sharply and strikingly different from uses concerning ourselves and higher-order animals. Such uses render uninteresting if not pointless the contrasts we draw between freedom and unfreedom in our lives.

The two conditions with which I began do seem to be necessary elements in our concept of our own freedom and unfreedom. Are they jointly sufficient to that concept? A prominent account of freedom, which forms the conceptual foundation of a moral and political theory of recurrent appeal, answers this question in the affirmative.

Thomas Hobbes portrayed not just human beings but all higher animals as *self*-activated in a very strong sense. Impulses that originate within these creatures are the necessary and (given their physical makeup and certain very general features of their environment) sufficient conditions of their movements. He contended that these creatures should be said to be free just insofar as their movements are unimpeded by forces or obstacles external to themselves, unfree just insofar as those movements are effectively impeded or prevented. Information about the two conditions is all that is needed, indeed is all that can properly be employed, in discourse about their freedom and unfreedom.

Hobbes's account has served as a starting point for much subsequent discussion in moral and political philosophy. Friendly critics, who think the account is correct in its essentials but in need of amendment, have observed that the notion of acting involves such attributes as intentionality and purposiveness, and they have incorporated distinctions between mere movement and action on the one hand and mere obstacles versus impediments knowingly and intentionally placed or left on the other. These amendments do complicate, as against Hobbes's often highly mechanistic account, the concept of agents or actors to whom human freedom can be attributed. For example newborn infants, although not likely to be confused with a waving tree-branch, are not regarded as experiencing the same kind of freedom and unfreedom as mature persons. The intention of these friendly critics is nevertheless to stay close to Hobbes's account.

Less friendly critics have urged far-reaching alterations and additions. On their view we cannot say that a person is free unless we have criteria for deciding which impulses, which intentions and purposes, ought to be or are worthy of being pursued. Freedom is achieved only if the persons in question distinguish good and bad, right and wrong, worthy and unworthy conduct. In addition, the persons to whom freedom is attributed must employ such distinctions in choosing more or less extended or encompassing plans of action. Finally, on some theories of freedom the chosen courses and plans of action must actually be good, right, or worthy and the criteria by which this is decided must themselves be correct or at least justified criteria. The conditions of saying that a person is free have been greatly complicated by comparison with Hobbes's rudimentary account.

Perhaps we can deal with the differences among these accounts by using the simple device I have already introduced, the notion that there are "kinds" of freedom. If we set aside tree branches and cloud-free skies, the following list identifies, in terms of their characteristic conditions and elements, the different "kinds" of freedom that can be extracted from the discussion to this point. Self-activated movement plus the possibility of obstacles to that movement give us freedom$_1$, and unfreedom$_1$, or "freedom of movement." Intentional or purposive action plus the possibility of impediments deliberately placed or left by other intentional and/or purposive agents are the elements of freedom$_2$ and unfreedom$_2$, or "freedom of action."[1] Intentional and/or purposive action taken in the more or less rational pursuit of an intelligently (and at least in that sense independently) conceived plan or project that is consonant with norms or principles that the agent believes to be justified, plus the possibility of impediments deliberately placed or left by other intentional or purposive agents, are the conditions of freedom$_3$ and unfreedom$_3$, or "autonomy." These same conditions plus the proviso that the action is taken to satisfy, and in fact satisfies, norms or principles that are authoritative in the agent's community, give us freedom$_4$ and unfreedom$_4$, or "communal freedom." These same conditions again plus the requirement that the authoritative norms and principles be certifiably worthy of endorsement give us freedom$_5$ and unfreedom$_5$, or "fully virtuous freedom." (For convenience of reference a somewhat modified version of this list is given in the Appendix.) We would expect controversy over how these kinds of freedom should be evaluated, but the several kinds are importantly distinct and each of them can be seen to have an established place in our thought and action. The point is not to give one among them priority but simply to keep them distinct so that thought and action about them can proceed in a clearheaded manner.

Such conceptual pluralism or latitudinarianism has been powerfully resisted by the major writers on the topic of freedom. Consider the most familiar philosophical controvery concerning freedom, that between advocates of negative and positive conceptions. Roughly, proponents of theories of negative freedom recognize freedom$_1$ and freedom$_2$, sometimes freedom$_3$. They strongly deny that freedoms$_{4-5}$, which are the favored and the characteristic notions of theorists of positive freedom, are kinds of freedom at all. The requirement that the agent's action satisfy some criterion or norm (other than being the agent's action), and that the norm itself be worthy, it is argued, confuses freedom and unfreedom with such quite different things as virtue and vice. A conception that imposes these further requirements disallows perfectly familiar and intelligible attributions of freedom. More serious, it encourages a host of restrictions on freedom in the name of freedom itself, thereby creating both conceptual conundrums and moral and political enormities. Critics of negative theories of freedom, in their turn, contend that freedoms$_{1-2}$, perhaps even freedom$_3$, allow of saying that a person is free or has acted in freedom despite being in the grip of, despite being "enslaved" by, impulses, passions, and desires that are harmful to the agent or to arrangements that the agent does or should value. Because freedom and slavery are incompatible, a theory that produces or allows such a result cannot be accepted.[2]

A somewhat less dogmatic response to my list of five kinds of freedom and unfreedom allows that there are such distinctions but argues that no one of the distinguished kinds can stand alone. The several kinds of freedom are a part of a larger, encompassing, and normatively more attractive concept, one of full or perhaps genuine freedom. For example Franz Neumann (1957), contributing to a tradition that is foreshadowed by Aristotle and is powerfully expressed in Machiavelli, Rousseau, and Hannah Arendt, argued that the "negative" or "juridical" elements in freedom (stressed by theorists of my freedoms$_{1-2}$) and the "cognitive" elements (stressed by theorists of my freedoms$_{4-5}$) must be supplemented by a "volitional" component that is most satisfactorily expressed by certain theories of political democracy. In its fullest or most complete form, our conception of freedom unites several complementary elements or moments and takes on a specifically political character. Partial notions such as freedom$_1$ and freedom$_2$ are intelligible to us. But they are intelligible because (only if?) we have the full or complete conception and are able to grasp the partial notions as elements thereof.

If any of these contentions are correct, we may be obliged to reject the claim of MacCallum(1967) and Feinberg (1980, esp. the first essay) that there is a serviceable distinction between conceptual and normative questions about freedom. There is no single concept of freedom that we can hold constant as we debate normative questions such as the rank that should be assigned to freedom among other perhaps competing desiderata. Freedom is an "essentially contested" concept that cannot be elucidated or construed apart from a larger pattern of argumentation concerning the moral and political issues in which freedom is implicated. To achieve agreement concerning what freedom is and is not would be to achieve consensus concerning a wide array of moral and political issues.

It is certainly false to say that there is nothing settled, that there are no agreed points, concerning the concept of freedom. "Freedom" is a concept in nontechnical English, one governed by rules that we know as competent speakers of our language and that inform and constrain our uses of the concept. We are not in the position of having nothing more than a term or signifier (an "articulate sound" as John Locke would say) and needing to construct a concept from the ground up. Were we in the latter circumstance, the disputes I have been mentioning would not be disputes at all but mere sets of stipulations with no intelligible relations to one another.[3]

MacCallum's now familiar triadic analysis (1967), moreover, seems to me to provide a perspicuous identification of important parts of what we share as competent speakers. Theories of human freedom that have no place for agents, for obstacles, or for objectives pursued are vulnerable to powerful objections. Their proponents must show either that they in fact encompass those elements or that there is good reason to alter our shared concept of freedom.

But MacCallum's analysis, valuable as it is, gives us no more than a framework in which to think about freedom. Major conceptual questions that it insistently leaves open, questions about the range over which the "term variables" (agents, obstacles, objectives) can move, are at the center of cogently conducted but heated disputes among competing theories of freedom. However we resolve such questions as whether a person's action or course of action must satisfy a normative criterion, or a worthy normative criterion, in order to be free, it is clear that the putative ends or purposes must be intelligible as such, that is, as possible ends or purposes. As Benn and Weinstein put the matter, "it is apposite to discuss" whether an action is free "only if . . . [the end it pursues] is a possible object of reasonable choice; cutting off one's ears is not the sort of thing anyone, in a standard range of conditions, would reasonably do, i.e., 'no one in his senses would think of doing such a thing' (even though some people have, in fact, done it). It is not a question of logical absurdity; rather, to see the point of saying that one is (or is not) free to do X, we must be able to see that there is some point in doing it" (1971, 194–211, 310). As the example makes clear, what counts as a reasonable choice, what is regarded as intelligible, varies from society to society and may be a matter of dispute within a society or culture. The conceptual point, however, is well-taken.

The position in respect to freedom, then, appears to be of a kind familiar to students of a number of the concepts salient in political and moral practice. As with justice, rights, authority, and obligation (among others) we share enough about freedom to allow mutually intelligible use of the notion and enough to dispute cogently concerning it. But it has proven difficult to arrive at a systematic analysis that is generally or even widely acceptable. Quite well-defined accounts, each of which finds support in and from what we share, have been in competition for more than two centuries.

Can we improve upon this position? It should not be taken for granted that we can. Despite close attention from powerful and well-instructed minds, on central questions the theory of freedom has been at something of a stalemate for a considerable period. The competing positions are supported by argumentation that has the marks of pertinence and plausibility. Perhaps the best that we can hope for (no small thing) is clarification and improved comprehension of alternative understandings.

The springs of philosophical hope, however, have been replenished (at least in my own case) by comparatively recent work concerning language and meaning, action, agency and personal identity, and philosophical and empirical psychology. Done largely by investigators not directly concerned with the topic of freedom, studies in these areas seem to promise fresh perspectives on issues about freedom. As is frequently the case, they do so in part by calling attention to unexamined assumptions common to the competing positions.

Many writers in the negative-freedom tradition, to take a salient example, tend to think (or at least are said by their critics to tend to think) of self-activation in terms of passions, desires, interests, and the like, conceiving of these as mental or even physical (neurophysiological) states or events occurring within and moving the agent's body. The agent is held to be free if the resulting movements are not effectively impeded from outside. Proponents of the theory of positive freedom agree that self-activated movement is sometimes directly prompted by such inner forces, but they are unwilling to regard such movements as free. On their view, freedom obtains only to the extent that inner forces are controlled by reason (or some analogue thereto such as judgment exercised by the agent's higher or better self) expressing itself in deliberately chosen and defended criteria, norms, rules, and laws. If there prove to be agents incapable of controlling the causal effects of their own passions and desires, other agents, frequently conceived of as possessing status or authority in a political society or community, make freedom possible by supplying the wanted discipline. In this way the norms of conduct said to be conceptually necessary to freedom come to be understood as external to agents, a circumstance that proponents of negative theories of freedom regard as the very paradigm of unfreedom.

We can begin to evaluate this dispute by asking questions such as the following: Is there such a thing as an objective, a purpose, an interest, or even a passion or desire, that can be *acted* upon (not to say achieved, attained, or satisfied), entirely without reference to criteria or norms or rules that have interpersonal standing? Contrariwise, is there such a thing as a norm or rule (in any sense beyond an observer-detected regularity) that has not been accepted, subscribed to, or in some manner internalized by those whose conduct it actually governs? On the first question there is indeed reason to think of emotions such as fear and fright, joy and delight, longing and pining, as sheer happenings, as unchosen, undeliberated occurrences. We can study the conditions under which they occur in ourselves and others and, given the knowledge that such study affords, we can arrange our affairs so as to increase or decrease the probability that we will experience them. There is no further sense in which we do, or could, choose to have them or not. Moreover, for all practical purposes "having them" consists in the occurrence of (what Wittgenstein termed) certain "natural" or "primitive" expressions in certain "characteristic circumstances." These expressions and circumstances can be misdescribed in the sense that we can unwittingly make verbal mistakes in identifying them and we can deliberately misdescribe them in order to mislead others. But there is no other sense in which we can be mistaken or make mistakes concerning them.[4]

But even if having emotions is passive in these ways, is it plausible to regard evaluating the emotions we have, and acting on those evaluations, in the same manner? I experience fright, but do I not decide or judge whether the events that frightened me were dangerous or threatening and do I not (or at least can I not) choose to act one way rather than another in response to those events and my evaluation of them? Or more exactly, is it not the case that I *act* in response to those events and my emotions only if I choose one action as opposed to others? Of course such evaluations and choices are mine, are made by me. But they are neither passive nor personal in the same strong sense as emotions and passions (cf. Aristotle 1953, chap. 2, sec. 5). To begin with, they are the evaluations and choices that they are, each of them is *this* as opposed to some or any other evaluation or choice, by virtue of satisfying the criteria that govern *our* use of the concepts in which they are expressed and by which they are identified. These criteria do make reference to, do require the presence of, certain types or classes of circumstances, characteristics, or conditions. But the tie between the criteria and the conditions is not as close as with the concepts that identify passions and emotions. To substantiate my statement or claim that I had a frightening experience (as opposed to my having experienced fright), I have to show that something occurred which in fact put me or some other person or creature in some kind of danger. The "natural expressions" and "characteristic circumstances" mentioned above are the necessary and ordinarily the sufficient conditions of experiencing fright. By contrast, my claim to have had a "frightening experience" must be warranted by pointing to events that are or could plausibly be regarded as dangerous or threatening. Others can dispute the adequacy of the evidence that I adduce. Nor will just any evidence whatsoever, any consideration I choose to advance, count as justification for my saying that I "fled from," "stood up to," or "acted courageously in the face of" my fright. Many different things are relevant to supporting such claims and there is commonly room for cogently conducted dispute concerning the evidence adduced.

In this connection we may note further arguments, forcefully presented in social psychology, in theories of acculturation, socialization, and learning, and in the sociology of knowledge and belief, according to which the evaluations that persons in fact form and the actions they in fact take must be at least partially understood and explained in terms of beliefs and values, norms and expectations, shared among the members of communities, societies, and polities, cultures and civilizations. Philosophical psychologists in their turn have argued that this not only is but must be the case, and theorists of agency and personal identity have drawn on such argumentation in contending that the creatures who populate prevailing theories of freedom (roughly, those who are said by negative theories to be free but who must be called unfree by the criteria of positive formulations) could not be agents and could have no identities.

These arguments remain controversial in important respects, and in any case their bearing upon this or that theory of freedom needs to be worked out in detail. I will be giving them closer attention in later chapters. Even in the crude forms I have used, however, it is undeniable that the arguments sharply challenge understandings embedded in prevailing theories of freedom. If action involves evaluations and decisions that are public in the ways indicated, proponents of the theory of negative freedom (at least as described by their critics) would have to conclude that freedom (for human beings) is not only unknown but an impossibility. All action would be informed and hence in some measure constrained by considerations external to the agent. But the same reasoning implies that what theorists of positive freedom regard as a leading class of cases of unfreedom, namely, agents controlled by their passions, is and must be an empty class. If action is never an unmediated result of impulse, emotion, or passion, then there can be no case of action that is "enslaved" or unfree in this sense. Further, insofar as human action is norm- or rule-governed, to that extent it satisfies what is at least a necessary (and perhaps—when fully explicated—the sufficient) condition of freedom for the positive theorist.

It is possible, in short, that the dominant alternative theories of freedom are committed to an understanding of agency and action that renders freedom impossible for the first and inescapable for the second; unfreedom necessary for the former and impossible for the latter.

A similar suggestion emerges if we focus on the notion of a norm or rule as it has figured in leading versions of the negative and positive theories. Hobbes is famous for the argument that subjects or citizens are at liberty just insofar as their Sovereign has not promulgated laws or commands requiring or forbidding modes of conduct. Freedom consists of the absence of rules; their presence is a sufficient condition of unfreedom. Although modified in various ways by later proponents of negative conceptions of freedom, this view has been prominent in the negative-freedom tradition throughout its history. Proponents of the theory of positive freedom take a sharply contrasting position. On their view, free conduct conforms to norms; therefore norms requiring and forbidding conduct, so far from preventing freedom, are necessary to it. Here again there is reason to think that the competing theories in fact share a single misunderstanding, namely, an exaggerated view of the effects—whether for or against freedom—of rules. Writers otherwise as diverse as Oliver Wendell Holmes, Jr., the later Wittgenstein, and Michael Oakeshott have urged that rules, that is, general and prospective guides to conduct, can do neither as much to agency and action as theorists of negative liberty suggest nor as much for it as proponents of the theory of positive freedom contend. Even rules that form a "strict calculus" (Wittgenstein) take the agent by the elbow, not by the throat. Theorists of negative freedom underestimate the extent to which human conduct must be rule-governed in order to be intelligible; proponents of theories of positive freedom underestimate the extent to which the most precisely formulated norm or rule, the most tightly integrated system of norms and rules, leaves scope for variations in conduct.

These and related possibilities are examined in the chapters that follow. To borrow James Madison's language in *The Federalist* 10, I propose to extend the sphere in which argumentation about freedom has been conducted; to extend argumentation to include considerations from the literatures mentioned above. In doing so I may bring about no more than an increase in the number of philosophical "factions." But this result may also "dissipate the force" of those factions and it is at least possible that it will contribute to "the equalization and assimilation of opinions and passions" that have been in contention in respect to freedom.

I will not, however, take my cues from the ardent and probably negative-liberty theorist Madison. Rather, I will initially look to the suggestive notion of "situated freedom" bequeathed to us by Hegel, implicit in most versions of the positive theory of freedom, and elaborated explicitly and self-consciously in later recognizably Hegelian thought. This strategy partly reflects what seems to me to be the current philosophical ascendancy of positive theories: it examines well-developed versions of that theory and attempts to determine whether their ascendancy is deserved. In this perspective my conclusion will be that the best versions of that theory contain vitiating defects. As I have begun to suggest, however, I will also argue that the notion that freedom is "situated" is separable from the characteristically "positive" aspects of the theory and contributes importantly to remedying difficulties commonly and in some measure correctly attributed to "negative" theories.

2

Freedom and Desire

For Hobbes, persons are free if their movements are unimpeded by forces and obstacles external to them. By external Hobbes means literally outside of the physical limits of the person's body. Hobbes was prepared to recommend a considerable variety of interferences on the grounds that the movements in question are contrary to the interests or harmful to the well-being of the person. The most dramatic example in his thought is suicide. Those prepared to attempt this act thereby demonstrate (to Hobbes's satisfaction) that they are *non compos mentis* (Hobbes 1971, 116–17). They also license the intervention of other parties to prevent their attempt from succeeding. But Hobbes's disapproval of suicide did not lead him to regard those who attempt it as therefore unfree. Nor did he justify efforts to prevent suicide (or any other movement or action) as contributions to the freedom of the persons disposed to it. Movements or actions that find their origins within the spatiotemporal entity that is a person's body, however ill-considered, are the movements or acts of that person. Persons are free or unfree depending exclusively on whether their movements and actions are impeded or prevented by some force or obstacle physically external to their bodies.

According to Charles Taylor, Kant accepted the root idea that to be free is to act undirected and unimpeded by forces alien to one's person. On this interpretation, a formula such as "to be free is to be uncontrolled by forces alien to the self" will hold for both Hobbes and Kant; for classical statements of both the negative and the positive theories of freedom. (Of course Kant should not be classified as a positive theorist in his political philosophy.) But Kant transformed Hobbes's idea of the self or agent of whom freedom and unfreedom can be predicated. The self that is eligible for freedom and unfreedom does not find its locus in the contingent, transitory, and thus merely phenomenal entity that is its body. Rather, it is constituted by the timeless, extensionless, "noumenal" operation that is its rationality. This self is free only if it acts on laws or maxims that are chosen or laid down or dictated by its own rationality. Specifically, the impulses and desires, passions, inclinations, and interests that energize Hobbes's agents are alien to this self and the self must gain control over them if it is to achieve freedom. Action, or rather physical movement, prompted by mere impulse or desire is unfree. Laws and maxims that control and direct such movements are necessary to freedom.

For now I pass over with no more than this comment exegetical questions raised by this interpretation of Kant's thought. There is reason to think that Taylor's account holds for Kant's understanding of autonomy versus heteronomy but not for Kant's understanding of freedom versus unfreedom. According to the alternative interpretation to which I allude, for Kant freedom is a predicate that we cannot deny of ourselves as human agents; its opposite is not unfreedom but being determined. Autonomy and heteronomy are further properties which, empirically, characterize agents who we must suppose to be free in order to raise the question whether they have achieved and maintained autonomy or fallen into heteronomy. Later we will see that this distinction and related distinctions, such as between being free and having achieved or failed to achieve various further attributes such as good character, responsibility, authenticity, and the like, are not adequately respected in post-Kantian versions of the positive theory of freedom.

If we waive these objections for now, the Kant just described above presents us with a radical version of the notion of an inauthentic self and of actions or movements which are, despite taking their origin and their character from within the self as conceived by Hobbes, alien to the true or real or higher self, to the self as it should be and should be understood. These notions sharply alter the content of the idea that to be free is to be uncontrolled by forces alien to the self.

Taylor agrees with Kant that Hobbes and the utilitarians (who he interprets as for the most part following Hobbes in the negative freedom tradition) have an inadequate conception of the self and, therefore, of human freedom. In Taylor's summary formulation, their conception makes it "impossible to say that our freedom was ever thwarted by our own compulsions, fears, obsessions, or to say that freedom widens with heightened awareness or awakened aspirations. And these are not the only things that we feel inclined to say in our pre-philosophical reflections about life; . . . We have to be able to distinguish compulsions, fears, addictions, from those of our aspirations which we endorse with our whole soul, not just by some quantitative criterion, but in a way which shows these latter to be more authentically ours" (1979, 156–57).

These remarks echo views which, in various formulations, are familiar to readers not only of Kant and Hegel but also of Rousseau, Green, and Bosanquet, Hobhouse, Laski, and Cole, and recent writers otherwise as diverse as A. J. M. Milne, Benjamin Gibbs, and Hannah Arendt, Harry Frankfurt, John Charvet, and H. J. McCloskey. So-called "springs of action" such as passions, desires, and interests are compatible with freedom only to the extent that they are controlled and directed by Reason, Judgment, the Will, or some other higher-order process, agency, or faculty. Although eschewing the radical metaphysical dualism of Kant's distinction between the phenomenal and the noumenal, these writers posit a self divided between lower and higher, inauthentic and authentic elements and insist that persons attain to freedom only if or only to the extent that the higher controls or governs the lower.

Abstracting from the important differences among these writers, we can regard the position they share as forming one end of a continuum of views concerning the relationship between freedom and desire. If we indulge another simplification and let "desire" stand for the whole array of sources of, or impetuses to, movement and action (passions and emotions that are not part of desires, interests, etc.), we can say that for these writers desires (or some among our desires) are a source of unfreedom.[1] Freedom can occur only if these "forces" are overcome by some higher or otherwise more estimable agent or agency.

I

Assessing the merits of this view is a primary purpose of this and the following two chapters. First, however, it behooves us to notice that the other "end" of the continuum I have just posited is not occupied by the Hobbesian or utilitarian view as sketched above. On that view, desires set actors into movement or action and questions about freedom and unfreedom concern whether the resulting movements or actions are impeded or prevented by agents or agencies external to the actor. At least implicit in this view are understandings about action and about why freedom-of-action matters, understandings that are so vital that they must be regarded as part of the position's conception of freedom and unfreedom. Desires are the activating or energizing agencies in human affairs; someone who lacked them entirely would be an object or subject, not an agent or actor; those who have them only intermittently or weakly are torpid, flaccid, and aimless. As Hobbes put it in a famous passage in *Leviathan*, "a man who has no great passion . . . but is, as men term it, indifferent; though he may be so far a good man, as to be free from giving offense; yet he cannot possibly have either a great fancy, or much judgment. For the thoughts are to the desires, as scouts, and spies, to range abroad, and find the way to the things desired; . . . as to have no desire, is to be dead: so to have weak passions, is dullness" (1959, chap. 8, par. 16). With comparatively minor changes in terminology the same views are to be found in Locke and Hume, in Bentham, James Mill, and in classical utilitarians generally. Life consists in having and acting on desires; the good life, a life of "felicity" as Hobbes called it, consists in more or less regular and more or less reliable success in satisfying the desires one has and acts upon.

On this view, neither the application nor the significance of freedom and unfreedom are separable from desires. A person lacking desires would not be an agent of whom either freedom or unfreedom could be predicated (except in the sense of freedom$_1$, and unfreedom$_1$). And freedom, which is the absence of obstacles and impediments to action, takes its value from the fact that those who enjoy it are therefore able to and more likely to succeed in acting on and in satisfying their desires (albeit they are not therefore guaranteed of either because inabilities or incapacities of their own or natural circumstances may prevent them from doing so).

Positive theorists from Kant forward have treated Hobbes's view as the quintessential version of the negative conception of freedom and have directed their attacks against it. Because desires themselves are or can be a source of unfreedom, the formula "externally unimpeded movement or action on or out of desires" cannot be an adequate account of freedom. But recent proponents of negative conceptions of freedom have argued that Hobbes's theory is at best a very imperfect version of the negative view. They have further argued that positive theorists have compounded what in any case are serious mistakes by forming their views in opposition to Hobbes's.

As with much else in the recent literature, this revisionary negative conception took its impetus from (or at least can helpfully be understood in the light of) the essays of Isaiah Berlin. In the well-known Introduction to *Four Essays on Liberty* Berlin accepts the criticism that the original (1958) version of his *Two Concepts of Liberty* made too close a connection between "liberty" and "desire." In the 1958 essay he had treated "liberty as the absence of obstacles to the fulfillment of a man's desires" (1969, xxxviii). Although Berlin did not stress the point I have been discussing, on the formulation just quoted from him having desires is a necessary condition of a person being free or unfree. As with Hobbes, it is in effect made a conceptual truth that someone who has no desires would not be eligible for these predicates. But Berlin's reason (or rather the one he first gave in his 1969 introductory essay) for rejecting his 1958 formulation does not focus on this Hobbesian feature of his earlier position. Instead, he launches an eloquent attack on a quite un-Hobbesian view, which he takes to be implied by the terms of his 1958 statement, namely, that freedom could be as effectively increased "by eliminating desires as by satisfying them; I could render men (including myself) free by conditioning them into losing the original desires which I have decided not to satisfy" (ibid.). In an attempt to avoid this unacceptable Stoic implication, he alters his account to read as follows: "freedom consists in the absence of obstacles not merely to my actual, but to my potential choices—to my acting in this or that way if I choose to do so" (ibid., xl).[2] On this view (which Berlin goes on to reformulate several times, using a somewhat disconcerting variety of terms and metaphors), it is conceptually of no consequence to my freedom whether I actually do or might conceivably develop a desire to do X or Y or Z. My freedom or unfreedom depends exclusively on whether other human agents or agencies deliberately or at least knowingly place obstacles in the path of actions that *could* be chosen by me. That I actually make such a choice may affect whether I feel free or regard myself as free, but it has no bearing on whether I am in fact free.

Berlin was mistaken in thinking that the Stoic view is implied by his 1958 formula. "Freedom is the absence of obstacles to acting on or satisfying actual or likely desires" does not imply that the reduction or elimination of desires will increase freedom; it implies, rather, that if desires are reduced or eliminated questions of freedom and unfreedom will arise about me less frequently or not at all. On this definition the perfectly Stoic person would be neither free nor unfree. (If the 1958 formulation is taken to be Hobbesian the point can be put empirically and rather more dramatically. In the extreme case of the *perfectly* Stoic "person," one self-divested of all desires, we would be talking about a corpse. And the person with few and only weak desires, that is, Hobbes's indifferent man, would be someone to whom neither freedom nor unfreedom would matter.) This point, which concerns the conditions under which questions about either freedom or unfreedom *can* arise, will require substantial further attention below.

Later in the 1969 introductory essay, however, Berlin restates the difficulty with his 1958 view in a way that expresses, or at least anticipates, a fundamental conceptual contention of recent proponents of "Pure Negative Freedom."[3] "If a man is too poor or too ignorant or too feeble to make use of his legal rights, the liberty that these rights confer upon him is nothing to him, but it is not thereby annihilated" (1969, liii). Whatever may be the case concerning the actual or the actually likely desires of the poor, the ignorant, and the feeble, their having legal rights means that others are legally barred from placing certain kinds of obstacles before them. More emphatically, even if the poor, ignorant, or feeble come to have contempt for their legal rights, come to regard them as part of their misfortune and actively to seek their abolition, it will remain the case that they are (legally) free to take the actions protected by those rights.

This is the point insisted upon by J. P. Day (1970, 1977), William Parent (1974), Hillel Steiner (1974–75), and Michael Taylor (1982). Steiner's formulation is representative: "I can . . . be free to do actions which I do not want to do. It is not unintelligible—on the contrary, it makes perfect sense—to assert that 'I am free to do A, i.e., am not prevented from doing A, though I have no desire to do so'" (1974–75, 35). It is perfectly intelligible to say that I am legally unfree to sell heroin despite having no desire, to me no practically conceivable desire, to do so, and legally free to sell the inexpensive watch bequeathed to me by my father despite having a strong aversion to the idea of doing so. Freedom and unfreedom concern, exclusively, the question whether I am or would be prevented by others from doing X. The Hobbesian thesis I have been considering confuses the question whether I am free or unfree with the quite different matter whether I *feel* free or unfree. Having no desire to sell heroin, I am not made *to feel* unfree by the laws against doing so. If I have no desire to sell the aforementioned watch, the fact that I am legally at liberty to do so will hardly enhance my estimate of my freedom. But my feelings or other subjective judgments in these or any other regards are neither here nor there to the question whether I *am* free or unfree. The "impure" Hobbesian version of the negative freedom theory, as well as all those versions of the positive theory that treat desires as sources of unfreedom, commits an *ignoratio elenchi*. Except in the sense of feeling free or unfree, desires have nothing whatever to do with freedom and unfreedom.

What are we to make of Pure Negative Freedom? In its most un-compromising formulations, that is, Steiner's, Parent's, and Michael Taylor's, the constructive account of freedom that it offers limits unfreedom to cases in which B makes it physically impossible for A to do X by depriving A of what Steiner calls the necessary physical components of one or more actions that A would otherwise be capable of performing. Insofar as some B does so, A is therefore made unfree to perform that or those actions. Otherwise, A is free to perform any and all actions which she has the ability or capacity to perform. (And if A is, in her own right as it were, incapable of doing X, she is just that, i.e., incapable, not unfree.)

Waiving for a moment questions about their use of "action," there is no doubt that instances which this analysis picks out are typical cases, perhaps paradigm cases, of unfreedom. Secondly, the severe, schematic quality of this view is at least initially attractive because its steadfast dismissal of the subjective elements or conditions of freedom holds out the promise that the theorist of *freedom* can stay out of the philosophical quagmire that is the theory of desires and other motives to and reasons for action. Its lean conception of agency and action permits a stripped-down and manageable theory of freedom. Thirdly, as we will see in Chapter 7, this promise is partly fulfilled in that writers of this persuasion have helped to clarify topics such as threats and offers, intimidation and seduction, manipulation and deception, and the bearing of these modes of intervention and interaction on freedom and unfreedom. Finally and most immediately, the distinction be-tween feeling free and being free is of undeniable importance. One can certainly be mistaken as to whether she is or is not, was or was not, free to do X; to equate feeling free with being free would create in a far worse form the difficulties that Berlin was trying to avoid when he abandoned his original formulation of the relationship between desire and freedom.

For these reasons, Pure Negative Freedom will require attention at various later junctures. The position, and particularly the insistence of its defenders that being free has nothing to do with desires, is neverthe-less unacceptable. A short way to indicate why is to say that it confuses freedom$_1$ and freedoms$_{2-5}$. It makes unimpeded *movement* a sufficient condition of human freedom. But the subject matter of the theory and practice of human freedom is not movement, it is action. Of course movements of the bodies of human actors are components in most human actions. This is why obstacles to such movements are typically also obstacles to human freedom. But—to begin with the obvious—

A's movements are not made unfree if B physically prevents A from falling because B has been pushed by C or because B has slipped on a banana peel; A is no more made unfree by B's action than B is made free to fall by C's push or by the discarded peel. At a minimum we have to distinguish between self-originated movement and movement brought about by the operation of forces external to A's body that affect A without A's consent or encouragement. But this distinction, which is at least implicit in the theory of Pure Negative Freedom, is not sufficient to distinguish movement from action. We also have to attend to the "whys" of A's self-moved movements, to the causes or considerations, internal to A, that set A to moving or to acting. Parts of A's body are caused to move by a very large number of biochemical, neurophysiological, and psychological events over which A has little or no control. These are movements of A's body, but they are not actions that A takes.[4] If B interferes with these movements, B may harm, injure, or even kill A and may thereby make A incapable of acting at all or incapable of taking some number of actions. But B does not make A unfree (except, again, in the sense of unfreedom$_1$).

It is a simplification (or an inflation of "desire") to subsume the entire array of considerations that lead to action under the term "desires." But because desires in a more differentiated sense are within the class of such considerations (and because the proponents of Pure Negative Freedom also exclude passions, interests, objectives, purposes, beliefs, intentions, reasons, and all other "subjective factors" from their analysis of human freedom) a theory of being free that excludes them cannot reach, except coincidentally, the subject matter that it purports to theorize. Exactly what place "desires" should have in a theory of human freedom remains to be determined. But they cannot be excluded from such a theory.

II

Pure Negative Freedom is a behaviorist theory in the generic sense that it does not concern itself (*qua* theory of freedom) with *why* self-moving agents move or attempt to move. Given observable self-movement or an observable tendency to self-movement, questions about freedom are answered exclusively in terms of the further observable fact that impediments or obstacles do or do not prevent the movements.[5] By contrast, theorists of ordinary or "impure" negative freedom and theorists of positive freedom are antibehaviorist; they agree that we must distinguish action from mere movement and further agree that doing so requires attention to "why" questions, to questions about desires, beliefs, intentions, purposes, reasons, and other "subjective" factors. But this perspective also identifies a chief difference between theorists of ordinary negative freedom and theorists of positive freedom. That difference concerns the range of "whys" these two schools of thought respectively regard as compatible with the conclusion that A did X in freedom. Large subclasses of "whys" that theorists of negative freedom regard as components of action and hence compatible with freedom are regarded by theorists of positive freedom as forces that impel movements and hence incompatible with freedom. In particular, a more or less encompassing class of desires is treated in this way. In a manner reminiscent of a narrower species of behaviorism, theorists of positive freedom regard many desires as stimuli that yield or produce responses—responses that can and must be explained without use of subjective concepts such as "reason," "intention," "purpose," and "choice." Although such desires operate within the spatiotemporal limits of the person, they are forces which, in some sense, compel movements the person would otherwise not make or obstacles that prevent movements that the person might otherwise make. Because they compel or prevent, they "enslave" the agent at least as effectively as forces imposed or obstacles placed or left by other persons. The theory of freedom must concern itself with desires not because desires are components in actions that may be free or unfree depending on what others do, but because desires are a source of unfreedom. Having rejected the Pure Negative Freedom view that desires are irrelevant to the theory of freedom, we must consider the positive freedom view that desires are incompatible with freedom. I begin by returning to passages already quoted from Charles Taylor.[6]

We saw that for Taylor, and for Taylor's Kant, control over "alien" forces is, as with Hobbes and theorists of Pure Negative Freedom, a defining feature of freedom. But since the forces that must be controlled operate within as well as without the self as Hobbes had described it, it follows that we need criteria for distinguishing the true or authentic self from the gross, psychophysical, spatiotemporal entity of Hobbes's thought.

Taylor agrees with Hegel that Kant failed to provide criteria adequate for this purpose. In Taylor's view, the abstract rationality of Kant's noumenal realm leaves the selves that are constituted by it "characterless and . . . without defined purpose, however much this is hidden by such seemingly positive terms as 'rationality' and 'creativity'. These are ultimately quite indeterminate as criteria for human action outside of a situation which sets goals for us, which thus imparts a shape to rationality and provides an inspiration for creativity" (1979, 157). Anxious to escape the force of the psychophysical agencies that set Hobbesian and utilitarian selves in motion, Kant emptied rationality and the self of all content and hence made freedom impossible. If Hobbes, Hume, and Bentham left the self possessed and driven by ugly but real demons, Kant turned it into an abstractly attractive but literally and figuratively disembodied entity so ghostly as to be incapable of action.

Taylor's phrase "a *situation* which sets goals for us" introduces a key notion in an alternate understanding that he and others have wanted to put in place of the formulations of Hobbes and Kant. This is a complex notion that will concern us frequently in what follows. Let us first note Taylor's contention that the views of Hobbes and Kant, despite the great differences between them, share a deep defect, one which presents itself as the idea that freedom is a kind of "self-dependence." "This cast of thought, which sees freedom as self-dependence, has . . . been a common basis underlying . . . the modern notion of freedom. It is common to the original 'negative' conception of classical liberalism from Locke to Bentham, to Rousseau's conception of obeying only oneself, to the Kantian notion of autonomy and its successors, right up to the Marxian idea of the realm of freedom . . . though the subject of this [last] freedom is . . . generic, not individual man." Although the differences among the several formulations of the idea are important, "it is arguably this general conception itself, equating freedom and self-dependence, which generates the dilemma" central to the theory of freedom. Taylor argues that this is because none of the versions of this conceptualization leave room for the notion of a "predicament which sets us a certain task or calls for a certain response if we are to be free." From the perspective of the quest for freedom, Hobbes and Kant define the agent's situation exclusively in terms of forces and obstacles to be evaded, cleared away, or overcome. Taylor thinks that this view implies an ideal, one that he sometimes calls "liberation," and he argues that such freedom would be achieved in a circumstance in which the very possibility of obstacles had been eliminated. Thus "full freedom would be situationless." Predictably, Taylor goes on to contend that for this very reason it "would be empty. Complete freedom would be a void in which nothing would be worth doing, nothing would deserve to count for anything" (1979, 156–58).

In its broadest terms, Taylor's objection to "self-dependence" articulates a pervasive theme in post-Kantian thought. In F. H. Bradley's metaphysical but generically familiar language, it is the theme that the isolated, atomic, or self-subsistent individual "is a delusion of theory"; "man is a social being; he is real only because he is social" (1927, 174). To understand individuals and their actions we must grasp the historical, cultural, and social settings in which they are what they are and do what they do. This imperative must govern us whether we are concerned with the most complex, refined, and elevated ratiocination or the basest, simplest, and least reflected impulse or inclination. The passions, interests, and desires of Kant's phenomenal realm are historical and cultural every bit as much as the maxims and judgments constitutive of the noumenal sphere.

Owing to the contemporary ascendancy of this understanding, there is an at least initially puzzling quality to the attacks of positive theorists on self-dependent individualism. Crudely stated, these attacks look rather like a case of flogging a philosophical corpse. If it is settled that individuals and individual actions are social through and through, then the Hobbesian and Kantian doctrines discussed above are of no further philosophical interest. They will figure in histories of the theory of freedom but not in contemporary attempts to theorize about freedom.

As with Hegel and Marx, Green and Bosanquet, however, contemporary proponents of the theory of positive freedom such as Milne, Taylor and Charvet, Arendt and McCloskey believe that the notion of self-dependent individuals remains with us. If it has been largely or at least officially banished from metaphysics and the philosophy of language and meaning, it continues to work its mischief in moral and political philosophy. Perhaps metaphysical individualism has been interred. But as evil spirits are wont to do, the demons that energized that philosophical monostrosity maintain worldly habitations. Most particularly, one or more of them reside in the theory of negative freedom. Critics are not flogging a corpse, they are exorcising real demons from live bodies.

As I have already anticipated, I will be arguing that the witches have once again outwitted the priestly doctors. The notions of self-subsistence and self-dependence are most clearly to be seen in the theories of positive freedom that officially condemn and insistently combat them. In developing this theme, I first take the modest step of asking how the thinkers most frequently accused of propagating an atomic individualism might respond to their detractors.

A first point, which I think holds for Kant as well as for Hobbes and the classical utilitarians, concerns the charge that on their view a life of full freedom would be empty in the sense of devoid of value or significance. For the writers just mentioned, this suggestion would be without sense. For Hobbes and the classical utilitarians, human beings just are desiring, interest-seeking, end-pursuing creatures. The significance of their lives consists in, is given by, experiencing, pursuing, and satisfying or failing to satisfy desires and interests. Life would not lose its significance in a "situation-less" or "predicament-free" condition in which all obstacles to satisfaction had disappeared, but it would for a person who ceased to experience desires and interests. The substance or content of Kant's view is of course entirely different. For him Reason, not passion, desire, interest, or any comparable notion, is the essential, the constitutive, feature of the human species. Here again, however, it makes no sense to say that a life of full freedom, a life governed by Reason, would be empty of value. Reason is the constitutive element of the very concept of significance. A life governed entirely by Reason would be the most significant conceivable life.

There is a further preliminary point in respect to Hobbes and the classical utilitarians. Abstractly, it may be an implication of their (or any) insistently negative conception of freedom that freedom would be maximized in the entire absence of obstacles or impediments. In fact, however, this possibility plays no role in Hobbes's thought and little or no discernible role in the thought of the classical utilitarians. The persons who figure in these theories struggle to achieve and maintain such degrees of freedom as they can in a world that is and will of certainty remain rife with obstacles and impediments. Nonhuman nature itself places no end of difficulties in their paths. In part for this reason, as persons pursue their interests and desires they inevitably come into conflict with one another. True, freedom and its significance are ultimately self-dependent in the theoretically deep sense that for these writers agents are self-moving; they are also self-dependent in the further, more mundane sense that freedom depends heavily on the individual's own efforts to fend off or overcome the interferences of others. But in the world we know there is no prospect of a circumstance devoid of predicaments that set tasks and call for certain responses from those seeking to achieve and maintain freedom. It would perhaps not be too much to say that it is because we inhabit such a world that freedom is important. It is important because we are passionate, desiring, interest-seeking creatures whose efforts to satisfy our passions, desires, and interests can easily be frustrated by our human and extrahuman environment.[7]

These last preliminary remarks help to open up deeper questions. If all known instances of human action are situated, if they occur in a setting largely comprised of competing, conflicting, and hence mutually comprehending and influencing agents (and if all questions about human freedom concern human actions or attempted actions), then as a practical matter self-dependent or situationless freedom is unknown. Official or programmatic doctrines of Hobbes and Bentham appear to deny this and hence raise the specter of a situationless and an empty freedom. But any very close attention to their thought shows that specter to be no more than that, shows that questions about emptiness or insignificance do not in fact arise. In this perspective, objections such as Taylor's are concerned not with practical normative questions but with the conditions under which normative questions can arise. Such objections are responses not to the normative conclusions that negative theorists have in fact drawn but to confusions in official doctrines concerning persons and actions.

III

Taylor allows that the utilitarians intended to situate action in the sense that they aimed to describe and analyze it as it actually occurs in the world of ordinary experience. From Hume and Bentham forward, the major utilitarians prided themselves on the empirical and scientific character of their theorizing. They were insistent that moral, political, and legal reasoning must be grounded in facts about human nature and about the consequences of human actions. It would not be implausible to say of classical utilitarianism that it presents a conception of human activity which "sees it as a response called for by a situation which is ours in virtue of our condition as natural and social beings. . . ." (Indeed, given the insistently teleological character of utilitarianism, it is perhaps not implausible to say that these utilitarians had a conception of free activity as, to finish Taylor's sentence, "in virtue of some inescapable vocation or purpose" [1979a, 160].)

Why, then, should we regard the utilitarians as theorists of an unsituated or self-dependent individualism? The answer to this question brings us back, after a series of excursuses, to the matter of desires and their relationship to action and to freedom. Numerous recent critics of utilitarianism contend that its conception of human activity is "reductive" and "mechanistic." The utilitarians "do . . . place free activity within nature, since it [the activity] is one possible output of a natural system." But we cannot accept their views without incurring the unacceptable cost of "adopting a definition of freedom as the unchecked fulfillment of desire" (Taylor 1979a, 160).

Why is this definition unacceptable? For theorists of positive freedom it is, finally, unacceptable because human beings as we know them have desires that they should not have at all or should not satisfy. They have desires that are, in themselves or in their satisfaction, vulgar, debased, stupid, harmful, destructive, cruel, vicious, and the like. Recognizing this, and thinking as we do that freedom is a good thing, we can hardly accept the definition in question. Freedom could be taken to mean the unchecked fulfillment of desire only if all actual (all possible?) desires were worthy of fulfillment.

Why is the definition "finally" unacceptable for this reason? I have two grounds for stating the matter this way. The first and most positive of these is that the reason just stated seems to me to be the governing consideration in most versions of the theory of positive freedom.[8] Wanting to praise freedom, theorists of this persuasion restrict the concept to actions that they judge worthy of praise. I will be arguing for this interpretation of the theory when I take up the relationship between freedom and virtue. The second reason is that theorists of positive freedom often write as if a quite different (albeit at least apparently related) consideration governs their thought. They argue not that (some) desires are unworthy in the sense that the objects of the desires should not be pursued but that (some) desires are coercive or enslaving. Whatever we may think of the object of the desire, to be moved by it is to be coerced or compelled. The familiar objection that utilitarianism is "reductive" and "mechanistic" is, indirectly, an expression of this argument. Utilitarianism reduces human beings to mechanisms powered, nay driven, by internal forces. Its conception of human beings has no secure place for intentionality, intelligence, reflection, and deliberate choice. But positive theorists think that utilitarianism is nevertheless correct in at least one important respect, namely, that the "springs of action" which are its preoccupation *are* mechanical in character. Insofar as human beings are moved by (certain classes of) desires, to that extent they are compelled or driven and are not free. While insistent that utilitarianism presents a radically incomplete understanding of human beings as they can be, should be, and sometimes are, theorists of positive freedom endorse what they take to be the utilitarian account of the only springs of action that utilitarians recognize. It is precisely because utilitarians have a *correct* understanding of (some) desires that they are mistaken in thinking that persons activated by those desires are in that respect free. On this view, the utilitarian (and negative freedom) criterion of freedom is correct, but it is not and could not be satisfied by human beings as utilitarians understand and endorse them. Human beings achieve freedom by breaking the control that (some) desires exert over them.

Of course both of these reasons for rejecting the definition of freedom as the fulfillment of unchecked desire are normative. Each of them advances a certain ideal for human beings and identifies freedom with the achievement of that ideal. Moreover, the ideals frequently coincide at least in the sense that the desires that are coercive turn out to be the very desires that are vulgar, debased, and destructive, while those that are not coercive are at least normatively acceptable. It is nevertheless important (as important as it is difficult) to keep the arguments separate. The question whether a desire compels or enslaves is an issue in philosophical psychology and the theory of action. The answer to it depends not at all on whether the object of this or that desire is morally, aesthetically, or in any other way worthy or admirable. (It might be added that if we truly are enslaved by our desires, telling ourselves that our masters are debased or vicious teaches a lesson—namely, to despise ourselves more deeply—that is perhaps not likely to prepare us for freedom.) It is to this question that I now turn.

Charles Taylor presents his version of these views through a series of distinctions the first and most encompassing of which is between "opportunity" and "exercise" concepts of freedom. Freedom as "the unchecked fulfillment of desire" is an opportunity concept; agents are free in the sense that others leave them the opportunity to pursue their desires. It is unsatisfactory because it does not require the agents said to be free to have "exercised control" over themselves. That other agents and agencies provide or leave opportunities for and to the agent may be a necessary but it is not a sufficient condition of the agent's freedom. Freedom is achieved only when agents exercise control over their use of those opportunities.

I have suggested that the subject of predications of freedom (except freedom$_1$) is action and I will be further suggesting that the subject of "unfreedom" (except unfreedom$_1$) is actions attempted but externally impeded or prevented. If so, it would seem that Taylor is correct although for a reason other than the ones he explicitly gives. The concept of action itself (as distinct from movement, response, or behavior) involves the notion of exercising control. We need an exercise concept of freedom because instances of freedom are instances of a wider class, namely, actions, all of the members of which presuppose agents who exercise control over themselves.

Of course Taylor and other proponents of positive freedom agree that actions are the subject matter of freedom. But in significant measure the agreement here is merely verbal. There is sharp disagreement concerning the range over which the concept of action properly applies. We can begin to identify the disagreement by reverting to the notion of Pure Negative Freedom. Charles Taylor's "opportunity" concept of freedom is Michael Taylor's Pure Negative Freedom amended so as to treat what might appear to be actions as no more than movements. Agents energized by certain types of desires are not acting, they are merely moving. They do not exercise control over their movements. They are not compelled to move or prevented from moving by agents or agencies (forces) external to themselves, but they are compelled or prevented nevertheless. Because freedom is the absence of compulsion, they are unfree.

It is of course undeniable that there are failures of self-control; that human beings who are neither compelled nor prevented by external agents or agencies nevertheless move or fail to move, behave or fail to behave, in a self-controlled manner. The most dramatic instances of this phenomenon, those associated with severe forms of psychosis (especially those instances that thus far cannot satisfactorily be explained by neurophysiological disorders) are among the most mysterious and unsettling features of human experience. Nor is there anything approaching consensus concerning less astonishing but nevertheless disconcerting phenomena such as compulsions and obsessions, so-called akratic behaviors, or even deeply habitual conduct and seemingly unreflective conformity with rules. All of these involve qualification of agency; more or less lack of control by the agent over behaviors and over movements of the body. And all of them tempt us to say that the agent is unfree or only imperfectly free.

We can certainly agree that the more extreme instances of psychosis and genuine compulsions and obsessions are incompatible with the predication of freedom. These and the other types of cases just mentioned will be discussed at greater length in the following chapters. There is a question, however, whether we should say that hysterics and catatonics, kleptomaniacs and acrophobics, are *unfree*. Perhaps it would be more perspicuous to say, as we usually do in cases of ordinary physical disabilities, that persons suffering these disorders are unable or incapacitated and hence that questions about freedom and unfreedom arise about them only after and to the extent that their incapacitating defects have been remedied. But however we construe and deploy the essential distinctions between ability and freedom, inability and unfreedom, we must not assimilate acting from ordinary, commonplace desires and interests to the statistically and normatively extraordinary and abnormal behaviors of catatonics and compulsives.

There may be instances in which otherwise normal persons are "overcome" or "taken over" by desires. Perhaps there are persons who are so continuously "overwhelmed" by their desires that we are justified in using the metaphor of "enslavement" to describe their condition. Perhaps Hobbes and the utilitarians inflated the concept of desires and exaggerated both the incidence and the significance of desires in human action. But if correctives are in order in these and related respects, if we need a more differentiated analysis of action and of freedom, it is implausible to equate, as theorists of positive freedom tend to do, large classes of desires as such with lack of control and unfreedom.

IV

In the view of Charles Taylor, John Charvet, H. J. McCloskey, as well as the nineteenth-century theorists of positive freedom, the negative or opportunity concept of freedom has been associated with an empirical and a philosophical psychology featuring (exclusively or primarily) desires and feelings that are "brute" and "first-order" and with an understanding of evaluations as purely "compositional." Proponents of "exercise" concepts of freedom, by contrast, while recognizing that such desires, feelings, and evaluations are all too prevalent in human affairs, distinguish them from "import-regarding" and "second-order" desires and feelings and from "contrastive" evaluations. "Brute" feelings and desires simply well up. They are to be discussed in the passive voice. There is no sense in which the agent chooses them, and the agent can be mistaken about their occurrence or their character only in the sense of making witting and unwitting mistakes of labeling. They are mere occurrences in the agent's experience. As the foregoing language suggests, Taylor likens them to, perhaps thinks of them as, sensations: for instance, "the stab of pain I feel when the dentist jabs into my tooth, or the crawling unease when someone runs his fingernail along the blackboard" (Taylor 1979b, 187). But the "notion that we can understand *all* our feelings and desires as brute . . . is not on" (ibid., 188; emphasis added). Rather, "our emotional life . . . [is] made up *largely* of import-attributing desires and feelings," (ibid.; emphasis added), of desires and feelings that are distinguished not just by "throbs, *elans*, or tremors" but by their "significance for me"; by the fact that they "meet important, long-lasting needs, represent a fulfillment of something central to me, will bring me closer to what I really am, or something of the sort" (ibid.).[9] We can experience these desires "mistakenly" in further and stronger senses than those I mentioned above, we can "repudiate" them, and we can struggle, sometimes successfully, to rid ourselves of them.

Because it involves the use of criteria for assessing the value or significance of desires, the notion"import-attributing" posits a more complex self or agent than do brute desires. The self is more than a passive Humean theater of experience; it is an active agent that judges or assesses its experience by standards neither given by nor derivable from any item or element in that experience itself. In traditional language, the self is characterized not merely by consciousness but by self-consciousness or reflexive consciousness. Or in the language familiar from the history of positive conceptions of freedom, there is a distinction between the lower and higher self (or higher selves).

This more complex conception of the self is also presupposed by the further distinctions between first- and second-order desires (between mere desires and—as Harry Frankfurt calls them—desires about desires [1971]) and between "compositional" and "contrastive" evaluations. As a practical matter both brute and import-attributing desires sometimes conflict in that the agent cannot, or cannot simultaneously, act on both or all of the desires she experiences. In order to act, the agent must form a "desire about her desires," must form an evaluation of the conflicting desires and arrive at a judgment as to which among them should be pursued and as to when and how to pursue them.[10] The simplest of such evaluations, which Taylor thinks are the only ones that utilitarianism can and theories of negative freedom do recognize, are purely compositional. The conflicting desires are regarded by the agent as qualitatively commensurable and are evaluated exclusively in terms of their "weight" or "score" on a single scale or metric of value. Courses of action are arrived at by a purely quantitative procedure that "composes" the conflicting items into units which (are designed to?) maximize the good or value which the metric calibrates. Thus the self who makes such evaluations, while not necessarily capable of qualitative judgments in any strong sense, must have a certain overview of at least tolerably encompassing stretches of experience, must be capable of differentiating among and aggregating and disaggregating elements in that experience, and must conceive of and act upon courses of action of some duration.[11] Accordingly, such agents must have an identity that itself perdures through considerable stretches of experience.

Agents capable of "contrastive" evaluations must have further characteristics and capacities, and pass additional tests. Desires evaluated contrastively "are described [by the agent] as noble or base, integrating or fragmenting, courageous or cowardly, clairvoyant or blind, and so on. . . . Each concept of . . . the above pairs can only be understood in relation to the other. No one can have an idea what courage is unless he knows what cowardice is" (Taylor 1976, 283). Evaluating in the contrastive mode, then, requires command of a conceptual system of some complexity. The items to be assessed *cannot* be experienced or understood particularistically, and the relations among them *must* be understood in a more or less closely specified and established manner. These modal cannots and musts, moreover, are normative, indeed typically moral, in character. To understand them is to know what, morally speaking, one cannot do and must do and it is to know that failure entails self-criticism (self-reproach, guilt or shame, remorse) and justified criticism by others (rebuke, blame, punishment). The agent must succeed in integrating and harmonizing her thoughts, her actions, and indeed her feelings. And as we will have occasion to emphasize below, this means that she must harmonize herself with the other agents who, together with herself, make up the community of which she is part.

We have, then, an ascent from a self that is no more than the locus of individual brute desires that move "it" (i.e., "its" body) this way or that to a higher self that forms and acts more or less steadily upon integrated and harmonized import-attributing desires and contrastive evaluations. This is an ascent to a self that exercises control over itself; it is an ascent from a self that is unfree through a self capable of no more than an impoverished freedom to a "responsible self," to a self which, to the extent that it does not suffer external compulsion, has achieved full or genuine or significant freedom.[12]

In company with Charvet, McCloskey, Milne, Frankfurt, Dworkin, and Rousseau, Taylor urges his distinctions and argues for this ascent as essential not merely to an adequate philosophical psychology but to a satisfactory theory of freedom. There are brute desires and merely compositional evaluations. There are or could be (Rousseau had no doubt that there were) human beings who do not exercise control of their brute desires and hence do not ascend above them or above compositional evaluations. Insofar as any of us are moved by brute desires and merely compositional evaluations, we are unfree. Human beings moved exclusively by such desires and evaluations are categorically or unqualifiedly unfree.[13]

V

Brute, first-order desires are remarkably reminiscent of entities prominent in the doctrine of David Hume and in the doctrines of those of his empiricist heirs known as the emotivists. In this perspective it is not surprising that "actions" taken to satisfy such desires are presented as little more than uncontrolled responses to stimuli or even direct consequences of psychological forces operating within the "actors" who experience them. Again, the notion of purely compositional evaluations cannot but remind us of the Benthamite idiom in which evaluations involve no more than a weighing up of such quantities as pain or pleasure, satisfaction or dissatisfaction. Like a balance, the agent comes down in favor of the course of "action" that promises the most of whatever she desires.

I suggest that these are supposititious entities and notions. The desires and evaluations that figure in human action, that is, the desires and evaluations that answer to our ordinary, established concepts "desires" and "evaluations" (and the persons who form, make, and act upon them), are more complex than these accounts recognize. To adopt Taylor's terminology, *all* desires are import-attributing. And if there are evaluations that are purely quantitative, the least that we must say is that quantitative evaluations are more intricate than Taylor's discussions suggest. If I am correct on these points, it would follow that human beings do *act* to satisfy desires and to implement quantitative evaluations. It would also follow that the question whether those actions are free or unfree could not be settled exclusively by reference to the desires or evaluations that inform and motivate them.[14]

As already noted, the distinction between first- and second-order desires is necessary to accommodate the fact that we act in the face of conflicts among our first-order desires. On the accounts under consideration, some second-order desires are quite uncomplicated, quite unprepossessing entities. The agent experiences conflicts among first-order desires and forms a further desire which, as an existential fact, resolves the conflict by propelling the agent toward satisfaction of one of the first-order desires. In the simplest cases this is not a reflective or deliberative process and notions such as "correct" and "mistaken," "wise" and "stupid," "right" and "wrong"—and hence "praiseworthy" and "blameworthy"—have no application to it.

But the same accounts recognize second-order desires that allow of at least some such assessments. These second-order desires are more than a mere strengthening or intensification of one or more of the conflicting first-order desires. The agent surveys her occurrent first-order desires and assesses their importance to her. This process requires a criterion or standard that is not implicit in, and is not a mere intensification of, the conflicting first-order desires themselves. The criterion employed for this purpose can be incorrectly applied. Thus it becomes possible to say not only that the agent made a decision or choice but that her choice was well or badly made, right or wrong, and the like. Accordingly, if the agent is not impeded from acting on her choice we can say that she enjoys freedom—albeit no more than an impoverished freedom. Further, because the criterion is not given by the properties of first-order desires themselves, it transcends such desires and can be employed to assess a diversity of them as they are experienced by the agent in various circumstances through time. Thus it becomes possible to assess not merely particular choices but the on-going performance of the agent. The agent herself, and others familiar with her, can judge whether she has been consistent or inconsistent, prudent and thoughtful or impulsive and heedless, intelligent or stupid.

When we reach second-order desires formed by making such compositional evaluations, we have arrived at phenomena that are more plausibly regarded as part of action rather than as mere stimulus-response or cause-movement patterns. Hence we have also arrived at agents who have an identity that continues through time and at agency the quality of which allows of moral or other normative assessment. It is not clear, however, that we have reached a person rather than a "wanton," a self who "exercises" control over her life. Hence it is not clear that we have yet satisfied the conditions necessary to being a free person or to warranted talk of human freedom.

If we have not attained to these heights, the explanation lies in the fact that the evaluations thus far considered are merely quantitative compositions of brute desires. In short, we have arrived at nothing better than the understanding of human beings said by its positive theory critics to be presented in utilitarianism.

If we leave aside the historical question of what various utilitarians did or did not hold, the first question that arises here concerns use of the concept "desire" to talk about the kinds of occurrences thus far considered. We have seen that there are sensations, passions, and emotions that are unchosen and hence passive in the sense under discussion. We do not elect to have sensations such as pain and itching, or emotions such as fear and anger. As Wittgenstein said, the agent does not stand in an epistemic (much less a choosing or judging) relation to the pain she experiences. "I know that I am in pain" is not right or wrong, it is nonsensical (Wittgenstein 1953, I, 246). In most if not all instances, desires involve emotions and possibly sensations as well. Consider how the *OED* entry for the noun "desire" begins. "1. The fact or condition of desiring; that emotion which is directed to the attainment or possession of some object from which pleasure or satisfaction is expected; longing, craving, a wish." The entry continues in a manner that treats some desires as consisting in part of sensations: "2. Physical appetite, lust." "Fact" and "condition" in the first entry could be taken as endorsing the view that desires are unchosen, passive, merely experienced. In their turn, notions such as "appetite," "craving," and "lust" seem to acknowledge the familiar view that (some) desires are powerful forces by which we are overtaken, taken over, and even overcome. Talk of brute desires evidently refers to these characteristics.

Among several complications to be noted here is the fact that all desires are transitive in the sense of requiring an object. Desires are *for* something that is independent of the desire itself in that it (the some-thing) may exist or not whether anyone desires it. As the *OED* has it, a desire is an emotion "directed to the attainment of some object." In this respect desires are importantly distinct from sensations such as pain, a sweet or sour taste, a tingling, and so on. The latter are produced by a cause that is independent of the sensation, but the sensation is not "directed toward" its cause. Desires are also distinct from "pure" emotions such as fear and anxiety, pride and shame. There is something (difficult to identify in the case of anxiety) that is independent of these emotions, and the emotion can be said to be directed toward that something. But the emotion is not directed toward the attainment of the something. (It is not necessarily directed toward achieving or establishing any specific relationship between the agent and the something. There are deeply established regularities here such as the agent wanting to escape from that which she fears or wanting to conceal that of which she is ashamed. I disagree, however, with the view that there is an internal relationship between the emo-tion and the response to it. It is not only the foolhardy who confront what they fear, not only the shameless who deal with their shame in part by being open about its sources.)

A desire, then, is a more complex phenomenon than an emotion. It is a whole or composite of which emotions are commonly a part but which also includes the objects of the emotion. A second complexity in the notion of desires is that a desire involves an expectation that attaining or possessing the object of the desire will yield pleasure or satisfaction and that the agent directs (or has a disposition to direct) her conduct toward attaining the object and hence experiencing the pleasure or satisfaction. I suggest just below that these features of desires put into question the idea that an emotion itself can direct the agent to its object, the idea that there can be a direct relationship, one unmediated by reflection, deliberation, or at least choice on the agent's part, between the emotion and its object. But let us take seriously a possibility that may be suggested by such familiar expressions as "being overcome by desire"; let us provisionally allow that there may be instances in which an emotion picks out its own object and moves the agent toward its attainment. Allowing these assumptions still leaves the notion of expectation in a problematic, or rather a mysterious, condition. Expectations are based on experience and, in all but the most mechanistic of associational theories, on reasoning. The agent has learned or come to believe from experience, or from experience plus reasoning, that attaining a particular object yields pleasure or satisfaction of a certain kind. An agent lacking such knowledge or belief could not form an expectation. Thus from the fact that the concept of an expectation is integral to the concept of a desire it follows that reductive-mechanical accounts of desires cannot be correct.[15]

An implication of the foregoing analysis is that certain phenomena that are sometimes treated as desires and actions on desires (and that appear to support reductive-mechanical accounts of desires) should be conceptualized in some other way. Examples from human life would be the first occasions on which a neonate finds and sucks its mother's nipple or an infant (or even a fetus) moves its body so as to stimulate its genitals in a manner that yields pleasure to it. If expectation is based on experience, the neonate, fetus, or infant (even if consciousness is attributed to them) cannot *expect* that (the first instances of) its movements will yield pleasure and hence, on the above analysis, cannot be said to experience desires. The usual alternative conceptualization of these phenomena would be, I suppose, the one most commonly used of nonhuman animals, namely, "instinct"; it is instinctual for the neonate to "seek" the nipple or to move in ways that stimulate its genitals. Presumably this conceptualization could yield to, perhaps in some quarters has already been replaced by, a biochemical analysis. The neonate or the infant is characterized by consciousness. As with higher-order but nonhuman animals as distinct from plants and insects, it is aware of, not merely casually influenced by, its environment. But it is not yet characterized by self- or reflexive consciousness. Its responses to its environment and to processes that occur within itself are not directed by evaluations that it makes on the basis of knowledge it has acquired or beliefs it has previously formed. It has no conception of itself or its purposes that figures in its responses and that is itself subject to modification in the light of its experience.[16]

If we cleave to the concept of desires in such cases it may be because of the continuities, some of which are so evident as to be undeniable, others of which have been seductively but, for me, quite deniably announced by Freud, between the earliest of infant behaviors and the conduct of maturing and mature human beings. Among children, adolescents, and adults, the hungry and the lustful sometimes pursue food and sex with—as we might put it—a singlemindedness that is at least reminiscent of the earliest passages in infant behavior. Given that the infant has by a continuous progression become an adult, and given that we commonly say that such adults are satisfying desires for food and sex, it is perhaps understandable that we attribute desires to neonates and fetuses and that we sometimes think of the desires of adults in strongly reductive-mechanical terms. But if an analysis so unremittingly mechanical as to exclude knowledge and belief and hence expectation does hold for some adult movements or responses, my account of desires commits me either to denying that those behaviors are brought about by desires or to differentiating sharply between or among differing concepts of desire. Whatever may be the merits of mechanical analyses, what seems undeniable is that the food and sex seeking of even the hungriest and most lustful of the adult population are instances of desiring as I have analyzed that notion and do involve expectations and directedness based on experience and reasoning. The desires that are integral to such actions may sometimes be so powerful as to be all but irresistible; in a vital respect they are nevertheless learned, chosen, and deliberately pursued, not brute, determined, or determining. If we say that those who act on such desires are unfree, we are either confused about "desires" or using "unfreedom" to express disapproval of their actions.

The foregoing remarks about desires set the stage for the more important questions that arise about "wantons," about nonimport-attributing first-order desires, and about second-order desires that express purely compositional evaluations of conflicting first-order desires. Let us allow that there are first-order desires that are brute in all respects save that they involve the element of knowledge or belief necessary to form the expectation that attaining a particular object will yield pleasure or satisfaction. Given such an expectation, the emotion or sensation itself directs the agent's movements toward attaining the object of the desire. Talk of being overcome by or in the grip of desires, particularly when concepts such as lust and craving are employed in that talk, seems to imply such a process. The agent doesn't reflect about or evaluate the desire, doesn't deliberate whether or even how to go about satisfying it, doesn't form an intention to pursue its satisfaction in *this* as opposed to some other manner, and doesn't make a decision or choice to act on such an intention. The agent, as we might once again put it, displays mere or simple consciousness, not complex-, self-, or reflexive consciousness. If we simply assume that there are instances of this sort, it is undeniable that these are not instances of actions and that there are cases in which desires and desiring do play a part in what is undoubtedly action.

Theorists of positive freedom concede both of these points but do not recognize the implications of either for the theory of human freedom. Second-order desires, desires about desires, second-order volitions comprise desires partly formed by agents who evaluate their first-order desires in the course of deciding whether and if so how to act in the attempt to satisfy them. Moreover, such evaluations are said to be conditions of saying that a person is free. These views tacitly accept the distinction between having an emotion or sensation and acting on it and they make that distinction integral to the theory of freedom. The difficulty with the position (as examined thus far) is that it treats instances (if any) of responses or movements or behaviors that are caused by desires without the mediation of action as instances of unfreedom. Insofar as persons are "overcome by" desires, they are said to be unfree. This analysis will be unobjectionable if we are prepared to regard mechanically caused but causally unobstructed movements of tree branches as unfree and/or if we assign no significance to the differences between freedom$_1$ and unfreedom$_1$ on the one hand and freedoms and unfreedoms$_{2-5}$ on the other. But if we regard those differences as important to thinking about human freedom we will say not that such responses or movements are unfree (or free) but that questions of freedom and unfreedom do not arise about them. (We will say that they are not "freedom-evaluable"; cf. the notion that "performative" utterances are not "truth-evaluable.") On this view, persons (if any) who are overcome by desires are not agents or actors of whom freedom or unfreedom can be predicated; they are the patients or subjects of forces over which they have no control. If Baker intervenes to disrupt the desire-instigated sequences that produce Able's movements or behaviors, Baker's interventions do not free or liberate Able, they help to create the conditions under which questions about freedom and unfreedom can arise about Able. Baker's interventions do not force Able to be free; at most they contribute to creating conditions under which Able can be said to be free or unfree.

The distinctions I have just invoked may also be relevant to "purely compositional" evaluations and the second-order desires and second-order volitions they are said to yield. These desires about desires do not simply well up or overtake those who experience them. Their formation involves a comparative assessment of two or more conflicting first-order desires. Here again, however, surprising credit is given to rather crude psychological doctrines for which Charles Taylor in particular has otherwise shown little or no sympathy (indeed of which he has been one of our most acute critics). In a discussion reminiscent of the least subtle passages in Bentham and James Mill, Taylor seems to allow that in some of our acting we somehow abstract out the quantities of pleasure or pain to be expected from competing first-order desires, compose those quantities into second-order desires, and, like a balance, come down on the side of the weightiest of the latter. Of course Taylor credits the empirical reality of such operations or processes in order to discredit them (and theories that endorse them) as instances of human freedom. But if we take his descriptions at all literally we are once again presented with occurrences that fail to qualify as actions. Once the expectations that form a part of each desire have been formed and the quantities of pleasure abstracted and composed, the agent's responses take place in a robot-like fashion. If we encountered an instance that fit this pattern we would, or at least we should, say not that it was a case of human unfreedom but a case to which neither "freedom" nor "unfreedom" (except freedom$_1$ and unfreedom$_1$) have any application.[17]

To summarize the discussion thus far, I have entered two main types of objections to positive freedom treatments of desires and actions on desires. The first is that they misrepresent desires and certain modes of evaluation in ways that make them appear to be brute and mechanical. The second is that they treat (putative) instances of mechanical movements and responses as unfree, thereby wrongly assimilating them to the proper subject matters of predications of freedom and unfreedom, namely, action and attempted but prevented or impeded action. The first of these objections is the contention that theorists of positive freedom have accepted too much from the reductive-mechanical theories to which they are otherwise opposed. The second objection presents a more general challenge. If the objection is well founded, criticisms of utilitarianism and other allegedly reductive-mechanical theories are neither here nor there concerning the choice between negative and positive theories of freedom. If theorists of Pure Negative Freedom and other theorists of negative freedom have treated mechanical movements and responses as free, they have made a mistake that is the other side of the coin of the mistake of treating them as unfree. In this respect none of these theorists has reached the subject matters of human freedom and unfreedom and hence their observations have no bearing on how those subject matters should be theorized. Put another way, my second objection accuses theorists of positive freedom of making what is in fact a rhetorical move against the theory of negative freedom, a move that takes its apparent plausibility from what is (in Gilbert Ryle's sense) a category mistake. They tie the theory of negative freedom to a psychology, both philosophical and empirical, with which it properly has no connection and to which, actually, it has and has had no more than contingent connections. Because that psychology deals in movements and responses, there is an apparent plausibility, provided by the availability in our language not only of unfreedom$_1$ but of unfreedom in the sense of tree branches physically prevented from swaying in the breeze, to the assertion that they are unfree. By tying the theory of negative freedom to this psychology, and by themselves illicitly assimilating movement to action, theorists of positive freedom make it appear that at least some of the instances that theorists of negative freedom call instances of freedom are in fact instances of unfreedom. If my second objection is well founded, this appearance is false.[18]

3

Freedom and Virtue

The two main theses of the previous chapter are (1) that the subject matters of human freedom and unfreedom are, respectively, action and attempted but prevented action and (2) that desires are an integral part of some if not all action. From (1) it follows that performances which are not actions, e.g., movements and behaviors, are neither free nor unfree; questions about freedom and unfreedom arise about them only in the sense of freedom$_1$ and unfreedom$_1$. Accordingly, theories that construe human behaviors and movements as unfree or as instances of an impoverished freedom commit a category mistake. From (2) together with (1) it follows (a) that actions of which desires are components are freedom- and unfreedom-evaluable but also (b) that the question whether such actions are free or unfree is not answered by the fact that they include desires. Thus (1) and (2) together disqualify one of the two main lines of argument for a positive theory of freedom. Desires do not compel or enslave; they include such elements as beliefs and expectations, deliberation and reasoning, decision and choice. These elements of action become part of human performances by virtue of the fact that desires are components of those performances. We do not need a positive theory of freedom to protect freedom from the tyranny of desires.[1]

This reasoning greatly enhances the plausibility of the negative conception of human freedom. Crudely, agent A forms and attempts to act upon and to satisfy desires. If other agents do not prevent A's actions, A is free; if others prevent those actions, A is unfree. This picture has a strong claim to our allegiance now that the suspicion cast on it by the idea that desires compel and enslave has been at least partly disqualified.

As already suggested, however, the argument that desires compel and enslave has been no more than one source of support for positive theories of freedom. Even if we had entirely disposed of that argument we would have left untouched what I earlier said was "finally" the most important basis of the positive theory, the contention that acts and the agents who perform them cannot be called free unless they satisfy more emphatically normative criteria. With qualifications involving the notion of "forcing to be free," most positive theorists accept the idea that freedom is a predicate of actions, not of mere movements or behaviors. (They have rarely if ever accepted, or considered, the idea that movements and behaviors are not freedom-evaluable.) But that a performance is an action, even that it is a successful action in the sense of not being prevented by others, is no more than a necessary condition of freedom. Actions and the actors who take them are free only if, in addition, they are morally or otherwise right, good, virtuous, or some such. To show that desire-initiated performances are actions, and to show that a particular attempted action was successful in the sense just employed, is insufficient to show that the action or its agent was free.

I proceed as follows. In the present chapter I discuss leading versions of the second argument. My objectives are to identify their main contentions, sort out the differences among them, and begin the process of assessing the merits of those contentions and differences. In the following chapter I attempt a more systematic critique of the argument in its strongest forms. Because those forms include admixtures of the thesis that desires and other "inner forces" enslave those who experience them, my criticism will require further and wider consideration of that thesis.

I

The best-developed versions of the thesis that equates freedom with virtue, at least in the post-Hobbes literature that makes freedom a central concern of morals, politics, and moral and political philosophy, are in Rousseau, in Kant and later Kantianisms, and in Hegel and nineteenth-century Hegelian thought. If I may use "virtue" and "virtuous" as stand-ins for the whole array of moral concepts, these writers can be said to argue for a strong, indeed for a conceptually necessary, connection between freedom and virtue. Agents and actions who and which are not virtuous are therefore either unfree or have achieved no better than an "impoverished" freedom. And as the notorious phrase "forced to be free" reminds us, for some of these writers virtue sometimes appears to be a sufficient, not merely a necessary, condition of freedom. Stated in more general terms, these writers agree that we cannot properly predicate freedom of agents or actions unless they satisfy criteria over and above those which distinguish action from movement and behavior and action from attempted but prevented action. Thus they agree that the negative theory, as found in Hobbes and the utilitarians, is entirely inadequate.

Despite these points of agreement, there is the sharpest controversy between these schools of thought about freedom. Leaving aside Rousseau (who is regarded as an ally by both Kantians and Hegelians but whose thought is quite differently interpreted by the two schools), the controversy is given the form it retains to this day by Hegel's attack on what he took to be Kant's doctrine.

For reasons at least suggested by my endorsement of the notion that freedom is "situated," the Hegelians have the better of *this* controversy. That is, the Hegelian position presents the case for a positive theory of freedom in a more plausible form than does the Kantian. Accordingly, my brief discussion of the controversy will be from the Hegelian perspective as I understand it on the basis of Hegelian criticism of Kant and Kantianism. I will then try to show that this most plausible version of the positive theory is unsatisfactory and I will go on to argue for a situated but negative theory. This procedure is not likely to be well received by Kantians, but I hope that in carrying it through I can make it seem less arbitrary than may be suggested by this schematic anticipation.

As interpreted by Hegel and later Hegelians, Kant attempted to show that freedom (or autonomy) and morality are mutually dependent or interwoven concepts, concepts inextricably bound together by (practical) Reason. Human beings are free just insofar as they act on the imperatives of Reason rather than on the urgings of desire. The imperatives of morality are also the imperatives of Reason. In deciding whether an act is morally right, the agent is to formulate the principle or maxim implicit in the doing of that act and is to subject that maxim to the highest test of practical Reason, that is, to the test "can the Maxim be universalized without contradiction; can I (on my own behalf and on behalf of all rational agents) will the maxim as a universal law of conduct?" The maxims that pass this test constitute the categorical rules of moral life, the rules that all rational creatures must follow without exception. And because following these rules is acting on practical Reason, discharging the duty to do so (for its own sake) is to be free. Actions that violate or that only coincidentally conform to those rules are immoral or amoral, nonrational, and therefore unfree (heteronomized). Combinations such as "immoral freedom" and "freely done but immoral" are incoherent.

As indicated, something like this identification of, this conceptually necessary relationship between, freedom and the morally correct, between unfreedom and the morally objectionable, is an objective of all positive theories of freedom. Nor is Kant the only writer who has attempted to establish such a strong connection through a doctrine about Reason or Rationality. The Hegelian and neo-Hegelian criticisms that I am about to take up proceed from sympathy for Kant's most general objectives (certainly from sympathy for his objective of refuting and discrediting Hobbesian and utilitarian doctrines) and for his conviction that Reason is the key to understanding freedom, morality, and the relationship between them. Why then is Kant's version of the theory of positive freedom so sharply criticized and so thoroughly rejected?

We have already encountered Charles Taylor's dismissal of the "abstract rationality" invoked by Kant and later Kantians. Kantian moral agents are (or would be if there were any) "characterless and . . . without defined purpose." Despite the "seemingly positive" quality of notions like "rationality" and "creativity," these "are ultimately quite indeterminate as criteria for human action or mode of life. They cannot specify any content to our action outside of a situation which sets goals for us, which thus imparts a shape to rationality and provides an inspiration for creativity" (1972a, 157).[2] These remarks echo passages in Hegel, in Green and Bradley, and in Bosanquet. Hegel: "Kant's philosophy is a high one in that it propounds a correspondence between duty and rationality. . . . [But] we must notice here that this point of view is defective in lacking all articulation. The proposition: 'Act as if the maxim of thine action could be laid down as a universal principle' would be admirable if we already had determinate principles of conduct. . . . In Kant's case, however, the principle itself is still not available and his criterion of non-contradiction is productive of nothing, since where there is nothing, there can be no contradiction either" (1942, add. no. 86, par. 135, pp. 253-54). In Paragraph 135 of *The Philosophy of Right*, Hegel puts the criticism more sharply. Kant's doctrine reduces to "an empty formalism" that can be given content only by bringing in material from "the outside." And if such alien material is imported into the system of reasoning, the system itself provides no criterion for judging its worth. Thus "any wrong or immoral line of conduct may be justified" (ibid., 89-90).[3]

T. H. Green is, characteristically, more generous in his recognition of the elevated character of Kant's objectives. But he hastens to insist on the truth in Hegel's criticisms. "I have already tried to show how the self-distinguishing and self-seeking consciousness of man, acting in and upon those human wants and ties and affections which in their proper human character have as little reality apart from it as it apart from them, gives rise to a system of social relations, with laws, customs and institutions corresponding; and how in this system the individual's consciousness of the absolutely desirable . . . finds a content or object which has been constituted or brought into being by that consciousness itself as working through generations of men; how interests are thus supplied to the man of a more concrete kind than the interest in fulfillment of a universally binding law because universally binding, but which yet are the product of reason, and in satisfying which he is conscious of attaining a true good, a good contributing to the perfection of himself and his kind" (1964, 152-53). Gentler in tone (and more convoluted!), Green nevertheless insists that it is in actual, historically developed and developing "systems of social relations" that notions such as "desirable," "good," and "interest," "law," "duty," and "bindingness" take on meaning sufficiently definite to inform and to guide conduct. And the "rational perfection" of self and of kind to which he refers, which in his view is what freedom in the only finally defensible sense is about, cannot occur apart from such a system.

Bradley: "Everybody knows that the only way to do your duty is to do your duties; that general doing good may mean doing no good in particular, and so none at all, but rather perhaps the contrary of good. Everybody knows that the setting out, whether in religion, morals, or politics, with the intent to realize an abstraction, is a futile endeavor; and that what it comes to is that either you do nothing at all, or that the particular content which is necessary for action is added to the abstraction by the chance of circumstances or caprice. Everybody suspects . . . that the acting consciously on and from abstract principles means self-deceit or hypocrisy or both"(1927, 152-53).[4] Duties, Bradley is famous for arguing, are attached to, are inconceivable apart from, "stations," which are features of organized social and political life. Kant's attempt to transcend these concrete historical entities, to identify a "pure" or formal notion of right and duty that will control thought and action regardless of such circumstantial factors, is empty in itself and a chief source of harmful delusions.

Bosanquet reiterated these objections and applied them to Kantianisms of his own day. "The essence of the matter is that the pure will directed towards good for the sake of good, having no real connection with any detailed conduct, may be alleged . . . in support of any behavior whatever, and out of this may spring the whole sophistry and hypocrisy of 'pure intention'"(1899, 263-64).

II

As objections to Kantianism as Hegel and these Hegelians understood it, these criticisms are well-taken. If we understand reason as a process or activity rather than a faculty, reasoning clarifies, assesses, and adjusts relationships among concepts and the facts, ideas, statements, and so forth expressed in and through concepts. Although we can reason about reasoning (as Kant did, as the passages quoted do, and as I am presently trying to do), here as elsewhere our reasoning works with and on "materials" given to it. Having concepts of reason and reasoning in our language, our history, and our culture, we can distinguish, combine, make inferences from, draw conclusions about reason and reasoning. Having concepts of duty, of justice, and of courage, and presented in our experience with phenomena to which these concepts have come to apply, we can reason about our duties to the starving of Ethiopia, about the justice of using gender distinctions in the life insurance industry, about whether Martin Luther King, Jr., was a courageous man. But our reasoning about such matters would get no foothold, would have nothing to work with and hence no work to do, apart from "data" which it assembles, construes, reconstructs, and assesses. Perhaps Hegelians such as Green and Bradley exaggerated the extent to which such "data" develop in and take their character from the traditions, languages, and practices of distinct social and political associations; perhaps they underestimated the extent to which whole civilizations and even all of humankind have arrived at (or could "constructively" develop and agree upon) a single conception of duty to kin, or of bravery as opposed to foolhardiness or recklessness. But they were certainly correct that reasoning takes its concerns and the criteria of its successes and failures from more or less settled, patterned, even organized human social life. Our culture is accustomed to applaud the sentiment that reason and reasoning are at the apex of and ought properly to govern the activities of humankind. But reason and reasoning themselves, if I may shift from Hegelian to Wittgensteinian images, are something, not anything or nothing. As with Wittgenstein's brake-lever, they can be such only as a part of the "mechanisms" of more or less organized social life (Wittgenstein 1953, I, 6). In short, reason and reasoning are situated.

Whether these criticisms apply to Kant himself, their force and their significance for the theory of freedom can be appreciated by considering some of the more recent writing mentioned in the previous chapter. A major restatement of the Hegelian view is provided by Alasdair MacIntyre's recent *After Virtue* (1981). Owing to the abstract and empty character of Kant's conception of reason, MacIntyre argues, the Kantian attempt to refute Hume succeeded rather in enthroning a subjectivism more virulent than any Hume ever imagined. Kant's true heirs are Kierkegaard and Nietzsche, Ayer, Stevenson, and the "emotivist culture" which is accurately described by these (in most quarters) notorious theorists. I have argued elsewhere that MacIntyre's sweeping intellectual history is seriously misleading and that his account of modern culture is conceptually confused and empirically mistaken (Flathman 1984a). But his claim that views of a recognizably Kantian provenance bring subjectivity and arbitrariness into the theory of freedom acquires credibility from a number of recent discussions.

Consider the arguments of Gerald Dworkin (1970) and Harry Frankfurt (1971). Both take up complexities and puzzles that arise because our desires are multiple and frequently in conflict with one another. How are conflicts resolved so that both aimless, random movement and paralysis are avoided, and directed action occurs? Dworkin, whose main concern is to clarify the distinction between "acting freely" and being coerced, deals with this question by distinguishing between different senses in which my desires are "mine," in which I genuinely or authentically "possess" them. When the armed robber says "Your money or your life" I form a desire to give her my money. The process by which I "acquire" the desire is clear and there is no doubt that I experience, and in this sense "have," that desire. But I do not "identify" with the desire. I am aware that I have it and it is likely that I will form and act upon an intention to pursue its object. But it does not "please" me to do so. Alternatively, I may resent the duty to care for my aging parents or the obligation to pay my taxes and I may have to be induced or coerced or even compelled to do so. In one sense of "want" or "desire" I do not want to do these things; I want not to do them. Yet I "identify with" the reasons for the moral principle or the reasoning that supports the legal obligation. The desire to meet these requirements is "mine," is possessed by me, in a different and a stronger sense than my desire to meet the demand of the robber or my desire to evade the duty or the obligation. We cannot equate freedom with doing what I want or with acting on my desires, because wants and desires are at work in all of these very different cases. But acting freely is nevertheless acting on desires; it is acting on desires with which I identify, which are mine in this stronger sense.[5] Thus Dworkin concludes that "A does X freely if A does X for reasons which he doesn't mind acting from" (1970, 381).

The obvious question is what criterion, if any, this "identification with," this "doesn't mind acting from," must satisfy. Dworkin offers no answer to this question. The agent either does or does not have an "attitude" of "resentment or aversion" to acting for or on certain reasons. If on balance she finds that she identifies with the reasons for doing X (even if she is coerced or compelled into doing it), she does X freely. If not, then she does X unfreely. Dworkin does think there is a "normal" set or range of such attitudes and that we have difficulty understanding persons whose attitudes are substantially or significantly "aberrant" by comparison with that normal set. But if the attitudes are genuinely "theirs," if like Thrasymachus they really do regard ordinary morality as "a subtle scheme enabling the powerful to enforce their rules" (ibid., 382), then they act freely when they violate moral norms, act unfreely if compelled or coerced to conform to them. And if we could imagine a creature who did not "possess" any desires in this stronger sense, "who saw every action of his as arising from a new desire" no more and no less authentic than any other, then we would have imagined a creature "whose liberty we could not infringe. Just as one cannot force open a door that swings freely on its hinges one cannot force a man whose will swings willingly in any direction" (ibid., 383).

In the respects most pertinent at this juncture, Frankfurt's argument is closely analogous to Dworkin's. He too stresses the variability in our uses of "want" and "desire," and his "wantons" are very much akin to Dworkin's free-swinging seekers of transient satisfactions. We once again begin with a multiplicity of frequently conflicting wants and the question of how directed, nonrandom action can nevertheless occur. As we have seen above, for Frankfurt such action requires desires about desires. But forming such second-order desires is not sufficient to bring about "effective action"; A can want or desire X, including at the second-order level, and yet do nothing to act on that desire. Desires become effective only if, as with Dworkin's authentic desires, they engage the agent's "will," only if the agent forms a "volition" to act on this rather than that, these rather than those desires. But the "person" as opposed to the "wanton" does yet more than this. The "person" forms "second-order volitions," that is, volitions about which of her first-order volitions *should* govern the ongoing flow of her conduct. The person "cares about" her will, cares about which of her desires-cum-volitions predominate in her acting. She may not succeed, or may succeed only in part, in maintaining the sovereignty of her second-order volitions. Frankfurt distinguishes, for example, between "willing" and "unwilling" drug-users (1971, 8). Both desire drugs, both may form first-order volitions such that they in fact take drugs, and both may form second-order desires according to which they rank their desire for drugs lower than other of their first-order desires. But only "persons" form the second-order volition to make their will not to take drugs rule over their desire and their will to take them. If such a person nevertheless takes drugs, she is an "unwilling" user of them; her second-order will, which is the locus of her personhood, is defeated by desires and first-order volitions that she would rather be without or would rather hold in check. The wanton, by contrast, is a "willing" user, a creature lacking the ability to be "unwilling" and hence lacking the possibility of those distinctive satisfactions that are part of disciplining oneself and achieving the quality of life and character that one really cares about.

Frankfurt's second-order volitions are evidently much akin to Dworkin's notion of desires that are "mine" in the strong sense that I regard them as embodying my identity or character. They are strongly felt, more or less settled and continuing attitudes of mine. But Frankfurt makes yet more explicit than Dworkin that these attitudes or dispositions need satisfy few if any criteria other than emotional duration and intensity. "In speaking of the evaluation of his own desires and motives as being characteristic of a person, I do not mean to suggest that a person's second-order volitions necessarily manifest a *moral* stance on his part toward his first-order desires. It may not be from the point of view of morality that a person evaluates his first-order desires. Moreover, a person may be capricious and irresponsible in forming his second-order volitions and give no serious consideration to what is at stake. Second-order volitions express evaluations only in the sense that they are preferences. There is no essential restriction on the kind of basis, if any, upon which they are formed" (1971, 13n.6). Consistent with this last phrase, it also emerges that there is nothing final, nothing conclusive or dispositive about *second*-order volitions. Second-order volitions, as the terms themselves imply, are "higher" than the first-order variety. This presumably means that, in addition to being stronger and longer-lasting, they collect a number of first-order desires and wills into more encompassing categories and subsume such desires and wills under the criteria that define those categories. But there is nothing to prevent a plurality of and conflict among these higher classes of desires. "[A] person may have, especially if his second-order desires are in conflict, desires and volitions of a higher order than the second. There is no theoretical limit to the length of the series of desires of higher and higher orders; nothing except common sense and, perhaps, a saving fatigue prevents an individual from obsessively refusing to identify himself with any of his desires until he forms a desire of the next higher order. The tendency to generate such a series of acts of forming desires, which would be a case of humanization run wild, also leads toward the destruction of a person" (1971, 16).

In Kantian terms the ascent Frankfurt imagines would presumably be to, would finally be halted by, the achievement of genuine universality. That is, distinct but mutually compatible classes of volitions would be rationally delineated and the maxims that identified those classes would therefore be such that the agent could without contradiction will that she and all other persons form and act upon those volitions whenever an occasion for doing so presented itself. In this perspective we can say that Frankfurt and Dworkin retain a Kantian notion of persons. By comparison with wantons and Dworkin's aimless wanderers, persons are not merely victimized by the sheer continuing flow of the desires they chance to experience. Persons are more complex creatures who are capable of imposing control (or at least of forming the aspiration to impose control) over their desires. Frankfurt and Dworkin also retain remnants of Kant's attendant idea that persons subsume particulars under higher principles or maxims and act on the latter. But it is manifest that the Kantian belief that these latter operations are and must be operations of reason, that "persons" are necessarily rational, plays little or no role in their formulations. Rampant "humanization" is, more likely than not, bridled not by reason but by "identification," by "decisive commitment," by acts of the will. "When a person identifies himself *decisively* with one of his first-order desires, this commitment 'resounds' throughout the potentially endless array of higher orders. . . . The fact that his second-order volition . . . is a decisive one means that there is no room for questions concerning the pertinence of desires or volitions of [yet] higher orders. . . . The decisiveness of the commitment he has made means that he has decided that no further question about his second-order volition, at any higher order, remains to be asked" (1971, 16).

These volitions not only constitute the person (the person's distinctive identity), they are constitutive elements in the person's freedom.[6] Frankfurt claims that such terminations or arrests are not arbitrary. But this claim (which directly precedes the sentences just quoted) could hardly be said to take support from the remarks that follow it or from the other passages I have quoted. These accounts resonate with the views of those writers whom MacIntyre regards as having drawn the inescapable implications of Kant's formal and empty rationalism. The content of the "higher" and "governing" principles of conduct comes not from reason but from some non- or extra-rational source.

There is of course nothing exceptional about theories of the self and of the bases of conduct that are at once complex and even hierarchical in structure but that emphasize non- or extra-rational elements and components. What is striking about the views I have been discussing is the strong connection they attempt to make between such an account of the self and the theory of freedom. As we have seen, Hegel and Green conceded that Kant's theory of freedom is elevated, even noble, in its aspirations. They did so because Kant attempted to wed freedom to morality and to rationality. We might say that Kant's higher self deserves to be free because it is a rational and moral self. More accurately, perhaps, freedom being a good, it is right to wed it to a self that is itself good, right to disjoin it from selves that are not themselves good. The doctrine that the higher self is eligible for, is a possible subject of, the predication of freedom, and that the lower self is necessarily unfree, takes an at least initial plausibility from the understanding that the freedom of the higher self will issue exclusively in the morally right and that the "freedom" of the lower self will issue exclusively in the amoral and immoral. But when Frankfurt says that the higher self may form itself in a "capricious and irresponsible" manner, that "there is no essential restriction on the kind of basis, if any, upon which" it forms itself, (even) this plausibility is destroyed. The Hegelian and the original Kantian reason for restricting "freedom" to the actions of the higher self (and the at least implicit justifications for preventing the actions of the lower self and for compelling actions consonant with the higher self) disappears. Accordingly, the doctrine presents itself as arbitrary and its implementation as tyrannical—or, if this is a distinction—unqualifiedly paternalistic.[7]

III

None of the foregoing would come as a surprise to Hegel or to the Hegelians discussed earlier. On their view, theories that begin with abstract and individualist notions such as will, commitment, authenticity, and personhood can acquire content only through subjective and arbitrary processes. Moral thinking that is not historically and sociologically concrete at its very foundations deprives itself of the possibility of rationality and objectivity. Attempts to build a theory of genuine, moralized freedom out of abstract elements necessarily end in the kind of nonrationality or irrationality exemplified by the views of

Dworkin and Frankfurt. The essential linkages between freedom and virtue can only be forged by a theory that understands reason as immanent in social and political life in its historical actuality. The vital task of such a theory, accordingly, is to discern the rationality and morality implicit in evolved social practice and to employ that rationality in distinguishing genuine freedom from the capricious and licentious behaviors of those who have understood their own social practices (and hence themselves) incompletely or otherwise inadequately. Successful completion of this task is the only way to realize the noble Kantian project of rationalizing and moralizing freedom.

The best-rehearsed objection to this view, already implicit in the Kantian doctrine against which it is a reaction, is that it is unavoidably relativistic and hence ideological in Karl Mannheim's sense of endorsing and to that extent protecting the understandings, practices, and arrangements that happen to have become established in this or that society or culture. Having rejected the possibility of principles or criteria the validity of which is independent of specific times and places, this view is without resources for any very deep or fundamental assessment of the historically and sociologically actual. Of course societies, cultures, and civilizations are complex entities. At any moment in time they include anachronistic residues from previous periods, inappropriate borrowings from other places, and elements produced and sustained by the unwitting misunderstandings and the perversities of contemporary members. The theorist who has grasped the distinctive and essential character of a society is thereby positioned to detect, expose, and at least to that extent supply the remedy for incongruities and incoherencies. But because the only criteria pertinent to assessing the society are themselves given by its own most basic features, neither the theorist nor anyone else can attain critical purchase or leverage on those features. Platonic, Kantian, Marxist, or any other attempts at more radical assessments are misbegotten.

Hegelians and other historicists and conventionalists have responded to this objection in a number of ways. Hegel's own response contained two distinctive and crucial elements. First, the vantage point provided by location at a later point in historical time permitted members of successor cultures to discern the inadequacies in the beliefs and arrangements of their predecessors and the *comparative* superiority of their own. Second, because the dialectical progression of History had reached its culmination in the unqualifiedly Rational and hence Necessary arrangements of Hegel's own place and time, his own culture was finally and *absolutely* superior. Neither of these views was intended as a criticism of earlier peoples or less evolved peoples of his own day; they had done and do as they must and hence as well as they could and can. Nor was it praise of himself or his mature contemporaries; he and they simply had the good fortune to appear on the historical scene at its final and most favorable moment. But he contended that these judgments of his were objectively correct and hence that anyone who dissented from them or acted in ways inconsonant with them made identifiable and correctable errors. Thus critical tasks remained to be performed, but for the first time they could be carried out in a manner at once internalist in the sense of relying entirely on considerations integral to the culture itself and Rational or Objective in the sense that neither those considerations nor the pattern or gestalt that they formed were liable to coherent objection or so much as the possibility of improvement. Thus the charge that his views were relativistic or a manifestation of conservative bias was philosophically jejeune. Indeed the very concepts of relativism and conservatism were to be stricken from serious thinking.

We will see that these of Hegel's doctrines, despite their widespread rejection by later Hegelians, are by no means extraneous to the theory of positive freedom. But let us note first that if adopted in anything like the uncompromising form of my summary they would mark the end of philosophy as well as of history. The oppositions and antinomies that had motivated and organized Occidental philosophical reflection— reality versus appearance, knowledge versus belief, truth versus falsity, right versus wrong, the beautiful versus the ugly—were all decisively and finally resolved and there remained only—as we might put it—the need to *police* thought and action so as to enforce the former of each pair against the latter. The entirety of human affairs would form a kind of *Rechtsstaat* governed by a "law" that excluded the very possibility of appeal. In a later but recognizably Hegelian idiom, philosophy as well as politics would be replaced by the administration of things.

It would therefore be surprising if later *philosophers* were congenial to Hegel's claim to have achieved such finality. Hope for, the aspiration to, and even the claim that they themselves had brought philosophy to its conclusion is encountered among later Hegelian (and some non-Hegelian) thinkers; to my knowledge none have been prepared to adopt the radically self-limiting ordinance that would be constituted by entire subscription to Hegel's system. The various ways in which later Hegelians have stopped short of doing so are of consequence for the theory of freedom, and present purposes will be advanced by considering some salient recent instances.

On Hegel's view, genuine and worthy freedom is found in unequivocal form in the activities of those members of modern states who understand and intentionally act in consonance with the laws, customs, and norms that (as grasped and displayed in their thought and action) embody its reason. In the distinctions I set out in Chapter 1, Hegel's conception is a historicized and communalized version of freedom$_5$. In Hegel's system Freedom = Virtue = knowing and intentional conformity with the norms, the *nomoi*, of one's community.[8] In Charles Taylor's terms, true freedom is freedom$_5$ "situated" in the deeply communitarian sense that agents choose their actions because they are consonant with community norms that they know to be worthy of acceptance.

But what if one thinks, as Marx did and as contemporary communitarian writers such as MacIntyre, Robert Nisbet, and—to a more qualified extent—Charles Taylor and John Charvet do, that one's own community and virtually all of modern culture or civilization have gone seriously or even horribly astray? What if, in other words, one follows Hegel in being historicist and communitarian and in adopting a situated positive conception of freedom but rejects Hegel's belief not only that History has culminated in one's own time but that History is necessarily progressive?

Consider once again MacIntyre's argument in *After Virtue*. He is a historicist in the sense of contending that we can understand the present only as an outcome of the past from which it evolved, and he is a communitarian in his insistence that genuinely virtuous conduct is possible only in a community characterized by articulated and integrated communal norms with which individual members identify and which are the bases of their conduct. But he is convinced that modern Western societies have lost such communality and have disintegrated into a fragmented, atomistic, and "emotivist" individualism in which virtue in anything more than a corrupted bourgeois sense of skill in pursuing primarily selfish objectives is all but unknown. Genuine virtue, and hence freedom,[9] can be reestablished only if we level the ruins of the large, bureaucratically organized nation-states that we inherited and create small, intimate communities in which commonality, fellow-feeling, and mutual concern can develop anew.

In the perspective of Hegel's thought, an obvious question about MacIntyre's argument is how these communities can be (or can be known to be) more than subjective and capricious in character. Hegel's contention that the mature nation-states of his day embodied Reason and Freedom, not mere collective will and license, rested squarely on his philosophical historiography and his claim that History's dialectical progression had moved from contingency and subjectivity to Necessity and Objectivity and hence to Rationality. Rejecting this claim, and yet insisting on historicism and communalism, MacIntyre's communities would seem to have no better foundation than Hegel could discover in communities as understood and proposed by Rousseau. "[A]s Fichte did later, . . . [Rousseau] takes the will only in a determinate form as the individual will, and he regards the universal will not as the absolutely rational element in the will, but only as a 'general' will which proceeds out of this individual will as out of a conscious will. The result is that he reduces the union of individuals in the state to a contract and therefore to something based on their arbitrary wills, their opinion, and their capriciously given express consent; and abstract reasoning proceeds to draw the logical inferences which destroy the absolutely divine principle of the state, together with its majesty and absolute authority." This misunderstanding, Hegel goes on to say, informed the French Revolution—with the consequence that "the experiment ended in the maximum of frightfulness and terror" (1972, par. 258, p. 157).

Of course my use of Hegel's criticism is unfair to MacIntyre's understanding and intention (as unfair as Hegel's criticism almost certainly was to Rousseau). The loss of a rational basis for resolving moral and political disagreements is MacIntyre's deepest complaint against modernity, and it is his explicit objective to regain or reestablish that desideratum. But he concedes that he has thus far achieved no more than a sketch, identified no more than the bare form, of an adequate conception of rationality (MacIntyre 1981a, esp. 242). What is more important, it is not easy to see how, consistent with his historicism and communalism together with his rejection of Hegel's historiography, he *could* develop a conception of rationality that would bear the burdens his theory places on it. Lacking the Objectivity and Necessity purportedly provided by Hegel's History, the rationality of any particular community would all but certainly (i.e., apart from a series of quite astonishing coincidences) differ from the rationality of other communities. And given that these communities share a planet, this in itself would make available to members of any given community the conceptual and ratiocinative wherewithal for cogent dissent against the conception that informed and governed its practices. Of course such dissent might not develop. Processes of socialization, education, and habituation might produce a consensus so entire and so deep-going as to exclude it. Or the dissent might be marginal and easily suppressed or effectively managed by those who share in the consensus. But these are, in a Hegelian sense, no more than contingencies. They provide nothing better than a morality (*moralität*) as distinct from an ethic (*sittlichkeit*); no better than a "happy consciousness" as opposed to a community of agents who grasp and act on the Idea of Reason and Freedom as embodied in their culture. We may have to rely upon such contingencies, but recognizing this does not warrant us in pretending they are something which they are not.

In short, Hegel's thought forms what he himself claimed, an integrated system the parts of which are not only complementary but mutually necessary. If we eliminate a major element such as his philosophical historiography, Hegel's major contentions and conclusions lose their support. More important here, the historiography supplies an element of a kind generally agreed to be necessary to a positive theory of freedom. Without it or some functionally equivalent substitute for it, we have no reason to think, no grounds on which to claim, that our judgments about virtue (and hence about freedom) are at once substantive and objective or rational.

Let us pause at this juncture and recapitulate the views thus far considered concerning freedom and virtue. It is agreed among the thinkers discussed that a strong conceptual and theoretical linkage between these notions is required if we are to avoid the absurdity of leaving the honorific term "freedom" available to characterize agents and actions that are or ought to be sharply disapproved. It is also agreed that this linkage can be more than merely "elevated," can amount to more than a mere piety, only if the theory of freedom is an integral part of a developed theory of virtue. Thirdly, it is agreed that the moral theory must provide nonarbitrary, intersubjectively valid, grounds for its distinctions between virtue and vice. If the theory is not objective or rationalist in this sense, "freedom" will remain at the disposal of anyone prepared to assert, on whatever ground or none at all, that an action is virtuous. The linkage between freedom and virtue will compound and deepen rather than diminish or resolve disagreement and conflict concerning freedom. These points of agreement, together with corresponding criticisms of negative conceptions of freedom and of positive conceptions that lack a developed moral theory or are accompanied by a subjectivist moral theory, constitute the common and unifying features of what deserves to be called the classical theory of positive freedom.

Agreement among proponents of the classical theory breaks down over the question of what will satisfy the requirement of rationality or objectivity. Hegel and later Hegelians agree that a theory must be substantive, not "pure" or formal à la Kant, and they further agree that this means that the theory must be historically and sociologically "situated." Hegel's doctrine of the historically necessary rationality of the modern state purports to provide a situated and yet objective ethics which demands the allegiance of all maturely rational agents and which therefore settles, at the theoretical level (at the level of the idea), all questions about freedom. But the rejection of this doctrine, and the failure to achieve a functional equivalent for it, leaves the classical theory of positive freedom vulnerable (by its own canons and criteria) to powerful objections. Having made the virtuousness of agents and their actions a necessary condition of their freedom, but lacking an account of virtue that is at once substantive, general, and generally accepted, proponents of the theory are unable to deliver their promised improvement on the merely pious character of Kantianism.

IV

From the perspective of any of the more robust forms of metaethical skepticism, this difficulty is of course irremediable. If one believes that moral evaluations and judgments are necessarily subjective, one will also believe that the quest for a successful (by its own criteria) positive theory of freedom must fail. Thus metaethical skepticism has been an important component in a number of versions of the negative theory of freedom. If questions of freedom are to be rationally or intersubjectively or perhaps scientifically manageable and decidable, they must be kept separate from questions about virtue. Whatever else we might think of it, the classical positive theory of freedom sinks the topic of freedom in the philosophical swamp that is moral or ethical theory.

We cannot, however, adopt a deep or thoroughgoing metaethical skepticism and nevertheless deal with freedom as that concept is ordinarily understood and used. To take such a position, for example, the emotivist position of A. J. Ayer in *Language, Truth, and Logic*, would denature "freedom" and disable the attempt to theorize about it. Freedom is itself a good, "freedom" a normative concept. To deny or to bracket these facts (as theorists of Pure Negative Freedom attempt to do) is to lose contact with the subject one purports to be discussing. Thus it is not open to us to dismiss later Hegelian attempts at a theory of positive freedom on the ground that they seek to integrate theories of freedom with more general moral theories.

As already indicated, moreover, I agree with the Hegelian view that theories of freedom and of morality must be "situated" sociologically and historically. Although I will continue to interpret this notion in a Wittgensteinian rather than a Hegelian manner, I understand it to mean that a genuinely "pure" or formal moral theory is an impossibility. But I also agree with the qualified skepticism implicit in Taylor's view (shared in one form or another by most later Hegelians) that Hegel's historicized but nevertheless necessary ethical objectivism is "close to incredible" (Taylor 1979a, 69). A posteriori necessary and synthetic moral truths are no more available to us than the a priori variety. It follows from this view together with the rejection of emotivism that neo-Hegelian versions of the classical positive theory of freedom require serious attention. Considerations examined thus far diminish (as compared with Hegel's own soaring aspirations) the philosophically plausible objectives of such theories but they do not disqualify this mode of theory as such. I proceed by examining Charles Taylor's version. My primary conceptual objective will be to show that Taylor makes the wrong *kind* of connection between freedom and virtue. But I also argue that Taylor's normatively communitarian understanding of virtue is morally objectionable in ways that are deepened by his misunderstanding of the relationship between freedom and virtue.

We must note at the outset that Taylor's is a qualified version of the classical positive theory. He fully accepts the opposition or incompatibility between freedom and desire only in respect to brute desires and merely compositional evaluations of such desires. It is basic to his position that "Freedom is important to us because we are purposive beings" and that "attributions of freedom make sense against a background of more and less significant purposes" (1979b, 183, 192). Import-attributing desires that do not also involve what he calls contrastive evaluations are not likely to embody or express the highest or the most significant of our purposes. Theories that do not make this distinction, that lump all unimpeded actions under an undifferentiated concept of freedom, are therefore crude and unsatisfactory. Nevertheless, there is no doubt that Taylor ranks import-attributing desires much more highly than the brute variety and regards action on them as purposive. When unimpeded, such action deserves to be called free.

Such freedom, however, is "impoverished" (Taylor 1979a, 192); it lacks the "significance" that makes rich or genuine freedom important to us. Agents and their actions are fully, richly, significantly free only if they satisfy further conditions.

The first of these further conditions, and the one about which Taylor is most explicit and insistent, is that those to whom rich and significant freedom is attributed must achieve and maintain what he calls "responsibility for self." What does this mean and what implications does it carry for the theory of freedom? In negative terms, it means that it is not enough that the person form and act on a string or sequence (however long and unbroken) of desires and evaluations each of which, taken alone, is import-attributing (or even contrastive) in character. Rather, the self which persists over time must attend to and exercise continuing control over the flow or unfolding of desires and evaluations and must see to it that they stand in a mutually coherent, an integrated, relationship. Language that is prominent in recent antiutilitarian moral and political philosophy expresses at least a part of Taylor's thought in this regard. Freedom requires not merely an array or collection of ends and purposes each of which is meritorious by some criterion but "projects" (Williams 1981, esp. "Persons, Character and Morality") and even "life plans" (Rawls 1971, esp. sec. 63) that encompass and integrate substantial stretches of the life-history of the person. It requires persons of "character" and "integrity" whose day-to-day decisions and actions are governed by a strongly settled sense of what they stand for and against, of what is and is not consonant with their understanding of themselves. Someone whose several desires and evaluations (however meritorious by other standards) are mutually contradictory, conflicting, or even significantly disjunctive manifests a failure of responsibility for self, is readily victimized by the shifting currents of circumstances and events (like Frankfurt's wantons), and is, if not unfree, enjoying no more than the "impoverished" freedom already mentioned.

This condition moves Taylor from what I called freedom$_2$ to freedom$_3$. It also appears to entail at least a weak or modest version of freedom$_4$, that is, an understanding according to which full, significant freedom requires satisfaction of a standard of judgment that transcends the criteria employed in choosing any one of the particular ends, purposes, and actions that the individual pursues and takes. In order to say that a person is fully free it must be the case that more or less extensive, more or less encompassing sets or combinations of her choices and actions satisfy the criterion of mutual consistency and coherence.

This injunction is susceptible of a variety of interpretations—interpretations which carry quite different implications for the theory of freedom. On a narrow, minimal interpretation of its demands they would be satisfied by anyone who steadily formed and acted on import-attributing desires and compositional evaluations. On this view, the requirement would add nothing to the criteria implicit in the very notions "import-attributing" and "evaluation." (The all-too consistent consistency of utilitarianism?) Assessing "import" and making "evaluations" entails identifying, classifying, and arriving at comparative rankings of interests and desires, objectives and purposes. Anyone who performs these operations with so much as the minimal rationality assumed by theories of "economic man" and "rational choice" would maintain a degree of consistency and coherence in sets of their choices and actions. Such a person, for example, would not violate the so-called principle of transitivity, that minimal requirement of instrumental rationality which specifies that a person who prefers A to B and B to C therefore must prefer A to C. At what might be regarded as the other extreme of a spectrum of interpretations, the requirement would be satisfied by nothing less than the Platonic philosopher-king or the fully self-conscious modern Hegelian citizen whose thoughts and actions perfectly mirror the unqualified coherence of embodied Reason.

It is not clear precisely what, precisely how much, is required by responsibility for self as Taylor employs the concept. But it is clear from Taylor's criticisms of the utilitarians and of Kantian formalism that he intends something more substantive than the first of the interpretations I sketched. The coherence, the rationality, must be substantively normative, not merely formally consistent. Of course it does not follow that he is therefore driven all the way to a Platonic or Hegelian view. It does follow that attributions of a more than impoverished freedom require assessment, by whoever is making the attributions, of the merits of the choices and actions of the person or persons to whom freedom is ascribed. It will emerge that this assessment must be made, at least initially and in most cases finally, in terms of norms established in the community in which the subject of those attributions is "situated." At least in these respects, I argue, Taylor's theory forges conceptual connections among freedom, virtue, and community. As with Hegel, it thereby makes both the theory and the practice of freedom conditional upon the theory and practice of virtue in a community. A person who does not know how to be virtuous by the standards of her community cannot attain to a more than impoverished freedom (can attain to significant freedom only by accident?), and a theorist who does not command the norms of virtue established in some community cannot so much as identify instances of freedom.

A large part of Taylor's argumentation for these conclusions is presented through his notion of strong, qualitative, and contrastive evaluations. Desires evaluated in this way "are described as noble or base, integrating or fragmenting, courageous or cowardly, clairvoyant or blind, and so on. But this means that they are characterized contrastively. Each concept of one of the above pairs can only be understood in relation to the other. No one can have an idea what courage is unless he knows what cowardice is. . . . And of course . . . the contrast may not just be with one other [concept], but with several" (1976, 283; see also 1977, 104–5, 107–8). In the mode of contrastive evaluation the conflict between or among the competing desires is more than contingent and it cannot be resolved by appeal to or by the occurrence of merely contingent considerations. A conflict between the desire to buy a new suit and to buy a new coat can be eliminated by receiving a gift of money which allows one to buy both. But the conflict between acting courageously in the face of danger and the desire to avoid injury and pain by running away cannot be so resolved. Contingencies may remove the danger and get me off the hook for the moment. But "it is an essential part of being courageous that one eschews such craven acts" whenever one is tempted by them. If I do not understand this, and do not commit myself accordingly, then I am not courageous. "Being cowardly doesn't compete with other goods by taking up the time and energy I need to pursue them, and it may not alter my circumstances in such a way as to prevent me pursuing them. The conflict is deeper; it is not contingent" (1976, 285; see also 1977, 107–10).

Taylor recognizes that the agent can define and characterize her circumstances so as to avoid contrastive evaluations. For example, she might describe her choice as between the injury and pain she will suffer if she intervenes in a mugging and the pleasure she will feel if she gets to the theater before the curtain goes up: or perhaps as between the pain and injury of the victim of the mugging and that which she will suffer if she comes to her assistance. Utilitarianism, according to Taylor, encourages us to think in these ways.

In Taylor's view, then, contrastive evaluations are not imposed on us. As a logical or conceptual matter it is open to us to live by a purely "utilitarian" calculus that has no place for strong, contrastive, evaluations. And it appears that persons who live such a life can be said to achieve and to maintain a kind of freedom.

Such a life and such a freedom, however, is impoverished. The price of avoiding contrastive evaluations is a self devoid of moral character and incapable of, or at least failing in, responsibility for itself.[10] Taking responsibility for our selves, exercising responsibility in the shaping and conduct of our lives, consists in grasping the nettle of contrastive evaluations (rather than "copping out" in the manner in which Taylor thinks utilitarianism teaches us to do). Our selves and their characters are formed in making and acting steadily, dispositionally, on such evaluations; and the shape our selves and our characters assume as we reach maturity is largely given by the pattern of evaluations that has come to be more or less settled for us. A responsible self, a self who has attained to fully significant freedom, is one who exercises control over this process.

Three aspects of this argument should be emphasized. First, the contrastive evaluations Taylor has in mind are moral or at least normative in character. We do develop settled inclinations and dispositions in respect to many matters that are no more than narrowly prudential or even mere matters of taste; we may follow Dworkin and Frankfurt and regard these dispositions as forming part of our personal identities and even our characters. Some of them, moreover, can be described contrastively. I may be adventurous as opposed to circumspect concerning diet, preferred entertainments, and travel; I may be outgoing and gregarious rather than diffident and narrowly selective in personal relations. As Taylor's examples indicate, these are not the dimensions of character that he wants to connect to freedom. In company with his predecessors in the history of the theory of positive freedom, Taylor wants to moralize freedom. He does so by connecting it conceptually and hence criteriologically to the language of moral evaluation and judgment.

The second aspect that needs emphasis returns us to the notion of situatedness. As with Hegel and MacIntyre, the standards of moral judgment that Taylor proposes are communal in standing and character. Despite the prominence of the concept "self" in his discussions, talk of the agent exercising control over her dispositions and character should not be taken as an endorsement of the theory of freedom as self-dependence. Oppositions such as "courageous-craven" are established in any number of communities, any number of languages. But to know that *these* particular acts are craven is to command criteria that are established in the community in which one is thinking and acting. And to develop a disposition to avoid such acts is usually (though not necessarily) to subscribe to, to endorse, those criteria. To develop and to act steadily on such a disposition is usually to identify with one's community. It does not follow that the genuinely free person invariably accepts the norms of her community; indeed Taylor argues eloquently that the genuinely "responsible" person is critical of the deepest norms of her community. But there is a powerful tendency in Taylor's argument to understand "free activity as grounded in the *acceptance* of our defining situation. The struggle to be free . . . is powered by an affirmation of this defining situation as ours" (1979a, 160; see also 161–62).[11]

We are presented, then, with a strongly communalist or communitarian version of freedom$_4$. It is a condition of rich or significant freedom that the agent steadily and by cultivated disposition acts in conformity with the norms of her community. Freedom that is genuinely worth having is deeply situated indeed. A question that immediately arises about this position concerns its implications for unfreedom. If freedom is situated, does it follow that unfreedom is unsituated? This is the third aspect of Taylor's theory that I want to stress. I take it up below by way of completing my exposition of Taylor's version of the positive theory of freedom. In the next chapter I argue that his treatment of the distinction between freedom and unfreedom, his tendency to align that distinction with a contrast between situated and unsituated action, displays an unacceptable aspect of his theory of freedom.

Before considering unfreedom, however, we must ask whether Taylor's concept of freedom, like Hegel's, is freedom$_5$; whether he requires not merely character and conduct that conforms to some norm or satisfies some standard but character and conduct that satisfy a standard itself known to be *worthy* of acceptance. There is of course a sense in which as a practical matter this question often cannot be raised. The set of beliefs and values, prescriptions and proscriptions, that make up the norms of a community just are the criteria of worthiness in that community. In this descriptive-logical or perhaps anthropological sense of "norms," there are no criteria apart from community norms by which the worthiness of those norms could be assessed. If the members of a community employ a criterion to assess some of their rules and arrangements, beliefs, values, and practices, they thereby show that the criterion they are employing *is* a community norm. Or at least those who employ the criterion show that they are proposing that it be accepted as among the community norms. And if they do not win substantial assent to their proposal the evaluations they make by using the criterion will not be accepted. Thus by virtue of being communitarian, Taylor's position employs a version of freedom$_5$. Or more precisely, by virtue of its communitarianism Taylor's theory merges freedom$_4$ and a version of freedom$_5$.

There is an undeniably important understanding here and we will have occasion to discuss it again when we consider what "unfreedom" and "unsituatedness" might mean in Taylor's theory of freedom. But explicating the meaning of the concept "established community norm," which is all my previous paragraph does, will not itself tell us the extent to which communities are or should be characterized by established norms. Nor will such an explication prevent us from comparing the norms of our community with those of some other community (actual or imagined) and asking whether our norms should be changed. There are two further normative and theoretical levels on which Taylor can be said to treat community norms as self-certifying. Both are responses to the questions we first encountered in discussing Hegel and MacIntyre and that arise again in respect to Taylor's theory.

In Taylor's view, not only significant freedom but human well-being and indeed a distinctively human form of life are possible only in some form of community—probably a community more encompassing than the nuclear family (1979d). This thought informs his skepticism about that notion of "liberation" to which I alluded earlier, liberation being "a word that reappears today in every conceivable context" (1979a, 157) and that betrays not merely a possibly justified antagonism toward or disaffection from the arrangements of this or that actual community but the misunderstanding that freedom could be situation-less without being empty.[12] Yet more generally, he assaults "atomism" and the notion of largely or entirely self-sufficient individuals who relate to one another and to society exclusively as holders of rights against one another (1979d). Freedom and much more depend upon a community formed by duty-defining norms that have the allegiance of community members. The concept of a community, and hence of community norms, certifies itself at least in the sense that it is a constitutive feature of human freedom and well-being. Those who understand this will be preserved from the individualist fantasies that have frequently been at the root of sweeping forms of antinomianism. Perhaps they will also be less disposed to cavil over imperfections, alleged or real, in the norms that have developed in this or that actual community. Specific norms can and sometimes should be questioned, criticized, and modified. Sometimes entire communities go horribly wrong and should be remade. It would be altogether wrong to suggest that Taylor is recommending uncritical accommodation to any sort of norms or any sort of community whatsoever. But as a practical matter, albeit one ultimately grounded in the most fundamental propositions of moral and political theory, the fact that the norms *are the norms* will mean that there will be much to be said for accepting them. The tautology with which I began this discussion of community norms coincides with a deep and substantive truth about human affairs.

In the light of these considerations, how can the members of a community assess its—and hence almost certainly their—norms? What criteria are available to them for this purpose? Is it possible to distinguish between freedom$_4$, taken to mean actions that are intended to and that do in fact conform to a community's conception of virtuous conduct, and freedom$_5$, taken to mean actions that are intended to and do in fact satisfy norms that are demonstrably worthy of acceptance?

These questions are familiar to us from our discussion of Hegel and it will be useful to examine them in light of Taylor's studies of and indebtedness to that thinker.

As with MacIntyre, Taylor's theory of fully significant freedom is recognizably Hegelian in being both historicist and communalist. Such freedom requires the satisfaction of norms that have evolved, could only have evolved, out of historical experience. This historical experience is the experience of more or less organized communities. Norms of human conduct can be understood and acted on only in the light of the concrete historical experience of which they are a product or a result. The idea of a norm (for example a Kantian imperative or a natural right) that is worthy as such, worthy apart from the historical experience in and through which it evolved, is a misunderstanding.

We have seen that Hegel thought that Historical Experience had been progressive. Looking back on it in its entirety (as he thought he had succeeded in doing), he convinced himself that it had culminated in norms and understandings that were Rationally Necessary. These culminating norms and understandings were therefore self-certifying in the strongest possible sense. Whereas all previous systems of norms could be assessed from the perspective provided by further experience, in respect to the culminating norms the notion of further experience, experience in and with a further and better set of norms, and hence of a perspective in any sense apart from the norms from which to assess them, is excluded.

As already noted, Taylor regards this "historicized ontology" of Hegel's as "close to incredible." He rejects entirely the possibility of a set of community norms that are immune to cogent, pertinent criticism. Despite his historicism and his communitarianism, he insists upon the possibility that those familiar with a community's norms can and should subject those norms to critical scrutiny. He trenchantly practices such criticism on norms and understandings which, according to his own account, are all too well established in societies of his own time. His biting criticisms of utilitarianism, of rights-oriented, atomistic individualism, of freedom as self-dependence, are all assaults on conceptions that work a powerful influence in modern moral and political practice.

Given Taylor's rejection of Kantian transcendentalism, of utilitarianism, of natural rights and natural-rights theory, and of Hegel's Historical Objectivity, how are such critical assessments possible? What standards are we to employ in making them? Despite the disagreements I have noted, Taylor's doctrine is influenced by and reminiscent of Hegel's. Critical reflection is not a process of assessing community norms by some standard or criterion external to or independent of them. Assessing communal norms is first and foremost, though not exclusively (see Taylor 1982b), a process of grasping, clarifying, and perhaps adjusting relationships among the multiplicity of beliefs and values, conventions and rules, practices and institutional arrangements, of which the community in question has come to consist. It therefore requires immersion in and sensitive attention to the detail of community history and practice. It is continuous with those processes through which individuals seek to understand the array of their own desires and interests, beliefs and expectations, and attempt to discern and to contribute to consistency and continuity, coherence and integration, among them. It involves an attempt to articulate what is already present, perhaps in inchoate form, in day-to-day thinking and experience (see esp. Taylor 1977).

Thus Taylor opts for a mode of evaluation that seeks the coherence immanent in social practice. Norms are worthy of allegiance, one might say are possible objects of critically reflective allegiance, if they hang together sufficiently to allow the members of the community to understand them and to act in a consistent and integrated manner in following them (to allow them to discern and pursue their intimations?). Norms are unworthy if they are inconsistent, disjunctive, and make mutually incompatible demands. And just as coherence theories of truth are usually taken to imply the possibility of a multiplicity of true theories concerning a given class of phenomena, so what we might call Taylor's coherence theory of virtue implies the possibility of a multiplicity of worthy systems of community norms. At the community level, Taylor's theory implies a pluralism as deep, perhaps as ineliminable, as the pluralism insisted upon, only now at the individual level, by proponents of the theory of negative freedom such as Isaiah Berlin (see Taylor 1977, 1982a).

But the pluralism is not without limit. Although rejecting Hegel's notion of the Rationally Necessary, Taylor follows him at least some distance in the quest for general criteria of assessment. Norms must be genuinely and quite deeply coherent. For example, a community of persons that was utilitarian in a thorough-going way would display a good deal of consistency and continuity; there would be many circumstances in which its members could find practicable guidance in its principles and rules. At its foundations, however, utilitarianism is confused in ways that will defeat anyone who tries to follow its counsels. Thus it is a general truth that utilitarian communal codes, if any, are unworthy of acceptance. Yet more generally, Taylor allows that a useful perspective can be gained by making comparisons among the norms of several communities. Just as individuals attempting to exercise control over their desires can learn from the self-evaluations made by others, so the members of a community can better assess their own norms if they have familiarized themselves with the practices and arrangements of communities other than their own. Such comparisons are instructive only if they are based on detailed knowledge of the several communities compared; facile, high-flying characterizations and assessments such as those retailed by structuralists, structural-functionalists, and other political and social scientists are as useless, as empty, as the Kantian tests and standards of rationality and morality (see Taylor 1967, 1971, 1973). If so grounded, such comparisons contribute to an understanding of, a "clairvoyance" concerning, the norms of one's own community. When present, such insight provides the only kind of warrant of worthiness and unworthiness that is available to us. Fully significant freedom requires such warranted judgments. Fully significant freedom is freedom$_5$.

I return now to the question of unfreedom. Dispositions and conduct consonant with worthy community norms are necessary conditions of rich or significant freedom. If persons act steadily on such dispositions, if they consistently attempt such conduct; and if (as one would expect in an independent community governed by such norms) they are unhindered or unimpeded by other agents and agencies, then those persons are free. Does it follow that persons who steadily violate or flout such norms, whose dispositions and conduct are consistently wrong or evil by the standards of such norms, are therefore unfree? The logic of Taylor's schema suggests an affirmative answer to this question. This suggestion, moreover, is reinforced by the fact that Taylor at least appears to adopt the traditional positive freedom view that preventing persons from violating worthy community norms contributes to the freedom of those persons. "A man who is driven by spite to jeopardize his most important relationships, in spite of himself, as it were . . . is not really made more free if one lifts the external obstacles to his venting his spite. . . . Or at best he is liberated into a very impoverished freedom" (Taylor 1979b, 192).

In fact, however, concepts like wrongdoing, evil, and wickedness, although at least implicit in his notion of contrastive evaluations, have little prominence in Taylor's writings about freedom. Why is this? Taylor employs a trichotomy consisting of persons who are richly or significantly free, persons who have attained to nothing better than an impoverished freedom, and persons who are unfree. Those falling into the first category are persons whose dispositions and actions are virtuous by the critically examined standards of the community in which they think and act. Those in the second category are characterless types (such as utilitarians) who may form import-attributing desires and make compositional evaluations but who have no settled dispositions or continuing plans and projects that guide and integrate their conduct. The unfree, I suggest, are more akin to, more a continuation or accentuation of, the characteristics of the second group than they are the opposites of the first. Of course harm and evil results from their shortcomings. But it is misleading to say that this is because such persons are evil or wicked by disposition, intention, or choice. It is not that they are unfree because they are evil, it is rather that evil results because they are unfree. This view can be stated in language with an impressive lineage in theology and theological ethics as well as in moral philosophy. Evil is not a quality or property in its own right, it is an absence, a negation, of other qualities. In Taylor's version of this position, it is the absence of those qualities and characteristics that are necessary to virtue and hence to significant freedom. Owing to his account of the necessary conditions of full or genuine freedom, the negational or privative prefix in the concept of unfreedom negates or denotes the absence of much more than it does in the theories of freedom he contends against. It is therefore to be expected that the process of negating the negation, the process of making the unfree free, will require much more than the mere lifting of external obstacles. It will require no less than integrating the individual into a community characterized by a coherent set of norms.

In Taylor's own language, this position can be described as treating unfreedom as a kind of unsituatedness. Of course harm and evil can only occur in communities. This is because it is only by the norms of some community that consequences are harmful or evil. But they occur because some persons in the community are not attentive or responsive to its norms. Such persons are self-dependent and unsituated in much the same sense as those who are moved by brute, unevaluated desires. They do not choose and act on the basis of evaluations informed by community norms, they respond to desires and impulses that well up within themselves. The difference between persons who cause or bring about evil and those who are merely, one might say regrettably but innocuously, unfree is that the latter chance to experience desires that move them in ways which contravene established community norms. The former live impoverished lives and enjoy no more than an impoverished freedom. The latter, equally contingently but now harmfully and perhaps tragically, damage others and the community. The community can, perhaps should, tolerate the former. It may be that the community has no choice but to tolerate a certain number of people of the former kind and a certain amount of behavior of the former kind on the part of all of its members. Communitarianism should not be equated with totalitarianism. But no community can tolerate evil (and remain a community). A community must "force its members to be free" to the extent of inducing them to abide by its basic norms (or it must find ways to insulate itself from the effects of their unfreedom).

4

Is the Positive Theory of Freedom a Theory of Freedom?

Major elements and contentions of leading versions of the positive theory of freedom are now available for assessment. The distinctive features of the conception as I have discussed it thus far can be summarized in eight sets of propositions concerning the conditions of freedom and unfreedom.

1. If I generally and by reflective, cultivated, and integrated dispositions attempt to act in conformity with the certifiably worthy norms of my community, and if other agents do not impede or prevent my attempts at such actions, I am fully, richly, significantly, free.

2. If I attempt to act as in (1) but am occasionally impeded or prevented by other agents or agencies, I am unfree in those cases. In a more generalized sense, however, I am a free person, a person capable of and for the most part enjoying fully significant freedom.

3. If I generally attempt to act on unintegrated or weakly integrated import-attributing desires and compositional evaluations, and if I am not impeded or prevented in those attempts by other agents or agencies, then I have attained to a subjective, thin, or impoverished freedom.

4. If I regularly or at least sometimes attempt to act as in (3), but on some of those occasions am impeded or prevented as in (2) and (3), my impoverished freedom is qualified in those cases. But if the interferences induce me to reconsider my desires and evaluations, if they enhance my capacity for and inclination to reflective, integrated dispositions as in (1), they contribute to the possibility of a rich and significant freedom on my part.

5. If I a moved by "brute" desires or impulses, and my movements are not prevented by other agents or agencies, I am unfree.

6. If I am moved and unprevented as in (5), and if my movements have consequences that are indifferent to community norms and values, my unfreedom is regrettable but may be, from a community standpoint, tolerable.

7. If I am moved and unprevented as in (5), and the consequences of my movements violate community norms and values, there is a case for inducing, possibly for forcing, me to an at least tolerable freedom, perhaps to an impoverished freedom, and preferably to a full and rich freedom.

8. If I am moved as in (7), and my movements are prevented, the preventing agents or agencies have not compounded my unfreedom (which is already entire), they may have contributed to my freedom, and they have protected the freedom of others in the community and perhaps contributed to the achievement of other community values. (Owing to the Kantian elements in his thought, T. H. Green would not accept [7] or [8])

A major difficulty is with the acceptance by positive theorists of radically subjectivist or emotivist accounts of desires and of behaviors set in motion by them. Kant viewed all desires as nonrational and heteronomizing; Hegel and nineteenth-century Hegelians assaulted what they called mere subjectivity and caprice; contemporary writers such as Milne and McCloskey, Dworkin and Frankfurt, Charvet and Taylor credit the reality of desire- or interest-impelled behaviors in which intentionality, deliberation, judgment, and rationality play little or no role. Although differing in their estimates of the acceptability and/or the means of eliminating or controlling these phenomena, none of these theorists question the essentially Kantian picture of human agents liable to be propelled or driven by extrarational, "brute," but internal desires. And with something of an exception in the cases of Dworkin and Frankfurt, all of them contrast this driven self with a rational, deliberative self that aspires to and sometimes attains genuine freedom.

In respect to this feature of the positive theory, I will first add to my earlier criticisms by arguing that endorsement of it goes badly with the argument that freedom involves knowing, intentional, reflective conformity with communally established and contrastively defined moral norms. This, as it were, internal criticism of the most plausible versions of the positive theory will then open out into an attempt to see the issues about desire, virtue, and freedom in a wider perspective.

The difficulty in question presents itself most plainly when we consider the last topic discussed in the previous chapter, namely, the account of unfreedom and the character of the distinction that positive theorists draw between freedom and unfreedom. Recall that the norms which are of greatest concern to positive theorists are said to be formulated contrastively. Justice is contrasted with injustice, courage with cowardice, generosity with selfishness and mean-mindedness, loyalty with faithlessness. Most generally and familiarly, the notion of acting in an expected, proper, or virtuous manner is contrasted with acting wrongly, improperly, immorally. When brought to the theory of freedom, this allegedly contrastive view creates the following expectation: just as genuine freedom requires approved, proper, virtuous conduct, so impoverished freedom and unfreedom involves acting in a disapproved, improper, immoral manner.

In fact, however, this expectation is disappointed. On the accounts of license, of impoverished freedom, and of unfreedom, that are before us, these concepts, together with such concepts as improper, immoral, and wrong, cowardice, dishonesty, and selfishness, stand in a negational or privative, not a genuinely contrastive, relationship with "freedom," "proper," "brave," "generous," and so on. Cowardice, dishonesty, and selfishness are not qualities in their own right that contrast with bravery, integrity, and generosity, they are the absence of bravery, integrity, and generosity. It is true that we cannot understand cowardice apart from courage or bravery, but the reason is not that the set of dispositional characteristics distinctive of cowardice contrast with a different set distinctive of bravery; it is that cowardice is the absence of the characteristics of bravery. To say that we understand cowardice by contrast with bravery is parallel to saying we understand an empty glass by contrast with a full one, not to saying that we understand a glass of water by contrast with a glass of orange juice or whiskey.

Of course this "absence" cannot be merely that, cannot be a void or nothingness. Behaviors do occur and they need to be identified and explained. But there is a moral or normative void. In place of the particular characteristics that constitute bravery, generosity, and so on, there are a- or non- or pre-moral desires and impulses. Or in the negative terms that predominate in this literature, there is a more generalized deficiency. In Taylor's language it is lack of responsibility for self; in Frankfurt's it is the absence of higher-order volitions; in Bradley it is failure to understand one's station and its duties; in Hegel it is lack of grasp of the Idea as embodied in one's culture; in Kant it is falling short of autonomy of the noumenal self. And in all of these cases it is at bottom the failure adequately to control the brute, the merely phenomenal, merely subjective and capricious, merely first-order volitions and desires that well up in the person who chances to experience them. It is failure to act as opposed to be moved, failure to become an agent as opposed to a subject or patient.

The difficulty is that concepts such as selfish, dishonest, cowardly, and unjust, properly understood as concepts of moral or more generally normative evaluation, in fact have no application to the creatures to whom these qualities are attributed. There is no belief or intentionality, no reflection, evaluation, or judgment, no deciding or choosing. The movements of such creatures are sheer happenings. They are situated only in the sense that they occur in, as a part of, a field of causal forces. Others may welcome or regret the outcomes or consequences of the movements and may attempt to intervene in the field of forces in order to change those outcomes. And the creatures themselves, if they achieve a measure of "liberation" from their "unfreedom," may arrive at similar assessments and may act rightly or wrongly on them. Until they do so, there is no room for the notion that such creatures have committed any sort of impropriety, done any sort of wrong, should be blamed or punished. Cowardice and dishonesty, injustice and disloyalty, are no more than behaviorist notions; like a hermit crab, the "coward" retreats from threatening forces; like the cowbird, those who are faithless abandon their dependents and associates. Why they do so is a question for the ethnologist, if not for the biophysicist or biochemist.

It follows that unfreedom and impoverished freedom are also behaviorist notions. Schematically: conduct that is morally or normatively satisfactory in displaying the communally established virtues is a necessary condition of rich, genuine, freedom; the partial or entire absence of such conduct itself demonstrates (is the criterion of) morally unsatisfactory behavior; the absence of such conduct is explained or understood as the partial or entire failure to control impulses and desires; the partial or entire absence of such control is impoverished freedom or unfreedom. Thus "morally satisfactory," "virtuous," and "rich, genuine, freedom" are attributes of conduct that is situated, intentional, purposive, and rational. The subject matter of these predications is human action. "Morally unsatisfactory," "unvirtuous," and "impoverished freedom" and "unfreedom" are characterizations of behavior that is inadequately situated and inadequately intentional, purposive, and rational (or entirely lacks these characteristics). The subject matter of these predications is behavior or movement.[1]

There are phenomena in the human realm for which analyses such as these are appropriate. I reconsider this topic below, taking up possibilities such as mental illness, compulsions and obsessions, so-called *akrasia* or weakness of will, habitual behavior, and so forth. But in respect to the familiar run of human desires and evaluations, this argument, in addition to being mistaken in ways indicated in Chapter 2, creates incoherence in the larger theory. The asymmetry between free action satisfying contrastively defined norms, and unreflected and unchosen movement that is unfree, is a conceptual impossibility. It has to be part of the notion of "contrastive evaluation" that both courage and cowardice, both justice and injustice, both generosity and selfishness, be in the realm of reflected, chosen action. It is part of understanding "courage" that I know how to be cowardly and how not to be cowardly, and that I know that the former is virtuous and admirable, the latter unvirtuous and shameful. Of course I might nevertheless act in ways that others regard as cowardly without recognizing that I am doing so. In fact I am inattentive, negligent, or careless, but I create a yet worse impression that may have to be corrected. There may even be cases in which I am causally moved in ways that others mistake for cowardice on my part. Projecting from their past experience with me they might too hastily attribute to me self-awareness or intentionality or choice when those qualities are in fact absent from my behavior. But these possibilities do not and cannot warrant the view that *cowardice* is merely behavioral and hence "unfree," as positive theorists attempt to construe the latter concept. As someone who commands "courage" and thus far can act courageously, I also command "cowardice" and thus far can *act* in a cowardly manner. Claims that I have not in fact done so must be supported in each case by evidence about that case. Given the view that courage is reflective and dispositional, and given that courage stands in a contrastive relationship to cowardice, one cannot categorize cowardice as an unreflective, nondispositional response to some stimulus or as a movement brought about by causal forces. The concepts are interwoven more tightly and elaborately than this analysis allows. To separate them by a gulf as wide as the distinction between reflected, dispositional, or chosen action on the one hand and movement caused by unevaluated desire on the other is to render them unintelligible.

Nor is it plausible to think that one could avoid making contrastive evaluations and live a life consisting of unevaluated responses to brute desires (or even purely compositional evaluations of first-order desires). Certainly it is implausible to think this of persons living in a society or culture that gives prominence to the concepts in which contrastive evaluations are formed and expressed (and hence gives bite to the criticisms the positive theorists tacitly level against the unfree). The question of how to identify or describe an action, of *what* action it was or would be, is not one that we are at liberty to decide as we see fit. If in fact I act in a way that my society has denominated cowardly or unjust, I cannot annul that characterization by telling a story about the desires I have experienced. If contrastive evaluations are salient in the system of concepts and moral norms of a culture, the idea of living a life in that culture without making such evaluations is simply not credible. Positive theorists credit the possibility of such radically unsituated lives in order to discredit theories of freedom which, on their interpretations of them, work exclusively with that possibility. But they do more than merely credit the possibility. They build it into the very structure of their theories in the form of their account of unfreedom. The results have even less to recommend them than has thus far appeared.

I

I have suggested—and in Chapter 5 will argue—that the distinction "situated" versus "unsituated" has no application to human action. Some actions could be said to be more deeply situated than others if it is meant that the agent is more or less self-conscious about the norms of her community and/or more or less intent on conforming to them; or that community norms are more or less clearly articulated, integrated, and established. But all acting is situated at least in the sense that all actions are the actions that they are by virtue of the public language and shared norms of some community or other. If we connect this view to the doctrine that freedom is situated and unfreedom unsituated we get the result that the expression "unfree human action" is a contradiction in terms. Freedom becomes a corollary of, necessarily comes along with, standing as a human agent. We are unfree only if or only insofar as we fall short of or fail to maintain our human capacity for action. If unfreedom is unsituated, the unfree are un- or less-than-human.

If we mean by freedom what Kant and others have called metaphysical freedom, this result is neither unprecedented nor absurd. But this metaphysical freedom is not more than a supposition of what (on the interpretation I alluded to earlier) Kant called autonomy and what many writers have called moral and political as opposed to metaphysical freedom. In the language I am using, metaphysical freedom is a condition of the capacity for action. When this capacity is present, the question whether or to what degree an agent achieves moral or political freedom arises but remains to be answered. Capacity for action is a condition of the predication of either freedom or unfreedom.

If we are talking about moral and political freedom and unfreedom, the result that "unfree human action" is a contradiction in terms is an absurd result. It renders unintelligible the whole notion that some human *agents* are free and others unfree, some *agents* more free than others. And it makes pointless the history of disputation over whether or to what extent human agents should or should not be free.

How can we recognize that human action is situated and yet avoid this absurdity? I propose a modified version of the conceptualization familiar from the history of the negative theory of freedom. Both "free" and "unfree" are predicates of human action and hence of situated phenomena. The question whether action is free or unfree is the question whether a human agent is impeded or interfered with in attempts at action. Freedom is attempted action that is successful in the sense that it is not impeded or prevented by other human agents or agencies, unfreedom is attempted action that is impeded or prevented by other human agents or agencies.

Although directly in conflict with positive theories as I have been construing them, this conceptualization opens up an alternative construction of positive arguments, one that is less dramatic in its implications but a good deal more plausible. The conceptualization suggests that the unsituated unfreedom that is so prominent in discussions from Hegel to Taylor is in fact an incapacity for action and should be called unfreedom only if we are thinking of what I have just called metaphysical unfreedom or what I have all along been calling unfreedom$_1$. Unsituated unfreedom is the condition of persons who, in general or in certain respects, do not have or are unable to make use of such capacities as to reflect, to deliberate, to form, act upon, and to revise and hold back from acting on, intentions and purposes; to follow or refuse to follow norms, rules, and instructions. Pursuing this alternative construction will be assisted if we also reconsider the argument of MacCallum and others that the distinction between negative and positive theories of freedom is without application to moral and political freedom. Because of its bearing on the treatment of freedom, desire, and virtue by Hegel and later Hegelians, I proceed by examining Joel Feinberg's recent version of the argument that there is a single concept of freedom that incorporates the elements of both negative and positive conceptions of freedom.

II

The notion that positive freedom is importantly distinct from negative freedom takes its plausibility from a fact that looms large in the views I have been considering, namely, that we can be unconstrained by "external" forces and yet be unable to carry out certain patterns of actions or achieve certain goals and purposes. But this plausibility disappears, Feinberg contends, when we recognize that constraints can be both internal and external and both "positive" and "negative" in character. Hobbes and others in the negative-freedom tradition focus on external, positive constraints such as "barred windows, locked doors, and pointed bayonets," and theorists of positive freedom urge attention to internal positive constraints such as brute desires and obsessions and compulsions. We must also recognize external negative constraints such as the lack of money, power, or other necessities for successful action, and internal, negative limitations such as the lack of ability, character, will, knowledge, and so forth. In Feinberg's words, freedom from negative constraints is the "absence of an absence, and therefore the presence of some condition that permits a given kind of doing. The presence of such a condition when external to a person is usually called an opportunity, and, when internal, an ability" (1980, 6).

When these several kinds of constraint are acknowledged, "there is no further need to speak of two distinct kinds of freedom. . . . A constraint is something—anything—that prevents one from doing something. . . . Thus, there can be no special 'positive' freedom *to* which is not also freedom from" (1980, 6–7). Feinberg follows Isaiah Berlin to the extent of allowing the possibility that a person might attain freedom from some hated constraint without having "formed a project on which the agent plans to act" and hence not yet involving consciousness of freedom to act in a particular manner. But he regards such cases as atypical (ibid., 5). Thus the main concerns of positive theorists can be accommodated within a single concept of freedom. Achieving the qualities of self and character that these theorists prize can be understood not only as overcoming internal positive constraints such as compulsions but also as freeing oneself from the constraints imposed by the lack of such character, by the absence of certain abilities.

As I proceed I will argue that Feinberg unduly extends the notion of constraint and thereby distorts our thinking about freedom. But if we follow him in understanding "constraints" to encompass such notions as limitations and incapacities, and if we think of the latter in contrast with abilities, capacities, and opportunities, he provides a more parsimonious conceptualization than the negative-positive dichotomy.[2] If we combine this conceptualization with my objections to the distinction between situated and unsituated freedom, the task of theorizing about freedom assumes a different shape and character than that to which we have been accustomed. Most notably, the task ceases to be choosing between allegedly dichotomous, mutually incompatible theories. There are a considerable number and variety of characteristics and circumstances that contribute to or detract from freedom. What matters from a practical standpoint is the ways in which these combine and interact in particular action settings. What matters from a theoretical perspective is to identify, to order, and to assess the recurring kinds of characteristics and circumstances that create and constrain opportunities for action.

I adopt this conceptualization and use it to widen my discussion of positive theory arguments that certain kinds of "internal" forces "enslave" the persons who experience them. There are certainly forces that limit the possibilities of human action and there is much that occurs in human affairs that appears to support views such as Taylor's and Feinberg's. But positive theorists have misdescribed the phenomena that concern them and have exaggerated their significance for the theory of freedom. Developing this argument will help to reduce my list of five kinds of freedom and unfreedom and allow me to coordinate the remaining items on that list with the MacCallum-Feinberg thesis that there is a single concept of freedom.

III

If we leave aside limits imposed by what are widely accepted at any given time as the largely unalterable natural conditions of all human life, it would by now be difficult to deny that there are illnesses and disorders, commonly characterized as mental, that severely narrow (as against what have come to be our expectations) the range of actions possible for those who suffer those illnesses and which grossly distort their in some respects action-like performances. In some cases these limitations and distortions are so striking that others come to think of such human beings not as agents but as subjects, and to regard their performances not as actions but as movements or behaviors. These arresting and deeply unsettling phenomena provide a starting point for wider consideration of the thesis that factors "internal" to human beings render them unfree.

It will be instructive to notice at the outset the view taken of even the most extreme forms of mental illness by radical critics of the notion such as Michel Foucault, R. D. Laing, and Thomas Szasz.[3] Although differing from one another in important respects, these writers share the view that talk of mental illness is an expression of ideological thinking. They believe that such thinking, despite employing allegedly scientific—and hence morally and politically neutral—concepts such as "illness," "normal," and "well-adjusted," puts these concepts to repressive moral and political purposes.

Whatever else we may think of these critiques, they have two connected implications or consequences that are pertinent to present concerns; they situate the performances, both of those said to be mentally ill and of those who respond to them as such, in a social and political setting and they give a definite foothold to the concepts of freedom and unfreedom as those concepts have been used by proponents of the negative theory of freedom. Very palpable external restraints are placed on those characterized as mentally ill, and those who place the constraints justify doing so with the claim that the "patients" violate established community norms and expectations and are dangerous to others as well as to themselves. On the assumption that the "patients" are in fact agents engaged in action, the imposition of these restraints easily warrants the conclusion that the patients have been made unfree.

This critique is indeed radical—radical in the fashionable sense of going to the roots. Its most radical aspect, however, is not its challenge to notions such as illness, normality, and good adjustment. The content of these has shifted about a good deal historically; it is less than surprising to be told that their uses in any culture or society reflect its dominant beliefs and values. Much deeper-going is the claim that persons judged to be, say, in a catatonic state, are nevertheless actors or agents engaged in action in the sense in which I have been using that term. This claim proposes a transformation of our concepts of agency and action and much of what depends upon them.

I do not say this to endorse any one of the diverse accounts of the protean phenomena that nowadays get called mental illness. Although skeptical about much of what is said concerning, and unsettled by much of what is done in the name of, this variegated conceptualization, I am not competent to pass on the intricate questions that make up the controversies concerning it. But it is, as I said, "by now difficult" to say that someone judged to be in a catatonic state is acting as opposed to moving, or perhaps behaving. It is difficult to say this because the concept "catatonic" (or less technically and more generally, "psychotic" or "insane") defines an outer limit of the widely received, I think it is fair to say the established, understanding of "action." We conceive of the movements of catatonics as the effects of some kind of force or forces (the exact "kind," of course, is a matter of wide and intense disagreement) that they are unable to control. Thus we do not hold them morally or legally responsible for the consequences of movements that occur when they are in that state, we sometimes feel justified in removing them from society, and we believe that they need the assistance of others—who often employ powerful countervailing forces such as drugs, electrical currents, surgical knives—if they are to regain or to achieve the capacity for action.

I cannot assess the observations and interpretations out of which this understanding has been built. Certainly I cannot assess the large bodies of theory that attempt to render the observations and interpretations intelligible and that inform the numerous and often mutually incompatible practices that have developed concerning the mentally ill. My timorous venturing just across the borders of this (to me) dark territory is in the hope of achieving much more modest purposes. I seek to provide an anchor or to establish a benchmark for a discussion of internal sources of unfreedom, one that will hold for or not be deeply contested by readers less radical than Foucault, Laing, and Szasz. If we agree to some sense in which a human being who is in a catatonic, schizophrenic, or hysteric condition is unfree because of "internal" forces, we can use that agreement to discipline examination of other alleged but more disputed instances of internally caused unfreedom. More specifically and polemically, I have presented the foregoing remarks as preparation for suggesting that positive theory arguments about unfreedom involve either a conceptual mistake that is the other side of the coin of the mistake made by Foucault, Laing, and Szasz or a proposal for a conceptual transformation that would be at least as far-reaching, in a quite different direction, as the implicit proposals of these theorists. To anticipate, Foucault, Laing, and Szasz attribute agency, and hence the capacity for moral and political freedom (and responsibility), to persons regarded by most of us as incapable of it. Positive theorists deny agency and hence freedom to persons regarded by most of us as not only capable of but in fact exercising freedom in the very instances in question.

As a preliminary to presenting this argument, I reiterate a conceptual point already made. If widely received opinion about psychosis is correct, and if positive theorists are also correct to extend the same or a strongly analogous analysis to a further range of cases, the appropriate inference would not be that those for whom the opinion or the analysis holds are unfree; it would rather be that questions about freedom and unfreedom arise about them only if we are thinking of freedom$_1$ and unfreedom$_1$. Such persons do not satisfy conditions requisite to predication of freedoms$_{2-5}$ and unfreedoms$_{2-5}$. Putting the matter this way, it seems to me, sharpens the edge of the following question: Is this the appropriate way to think about those who would like to be cooperative, and forgiving but are persistently selfish, obstinate, and vindictive? Is it the way to regard those who agonize about their overeating, their smoking, their poor work habits, but who, perhaps despite every assistance and encouragement from family, friends, and fellow-workers, do not succeed in breaking these habits or reversing these tendencies?

In the hope of addressing these questions in an orderly manner, I posit a continuum moving from individuals entirely lacking in control over forces internal to them to those with control so complete as to be able to eliminate such forces. Anchoring one end of this continuum are the psychotics I have been discussing. Setting aside views such as Foucault's and Laing's, it is part of a widely influential understanding of such persons that they are so incapable of "responsibility for self" that they can be said to be unfree only in the sense of unfreedom$_1$. There is *energeia* or self-activation and of course there can be impediments and obstacles to the movements produced. But questions about freedoms$_{2-5}$ and unfreedoms$_{2-5}$ arise about such persons only in the sense that others might attempt to cure their illnesses and thereby render them capable of moral and political freedom and unfreedom.

The other end of the continuum I am positing is occupied by creatures familiar enough in imagination and even belief but hard to come by empirically. Some conceptions of gods and goddesses, perhaps of angels, saints, and holy persons in certain religious traditions, are expressions of this ideal. In the more worldly (but far from mundane) realm of secular (or apparently secular) thought, this notion has been expressed in the ideal of a human life of fully self-critical, entirely presuppositionless, judgments and actions, an ideal that has been the aspiration of hubristic philosophers from Plato to Jürgen Habermas.

This continuum might be thought of as moving from entire unfreedom to perfect freedom. But this would be a mistake on several counts. In respect to the psychotic it would confuse unfreedom$_1$—and hence a lack of capacity for freedoms$_{2-5}$ and unfreedoms$_{2-5}$—with unfreedoms$_{2-5}$. In respect to gods and god-like philosophers it would either confuse omniscience with omnipotence or make the Stoic's mistake encountered earlier, namely, *equating* freedom and control of self. Most generally, and most importantly for the theory of human freedom and unfreedom, it would be to ignore such facts as that freedom in one respect often conflicts with freedom in another and that the value we place on freedom varies depending on the importance we assign to the actions we are free to take and the objectives we are free to pursue. Someone not far removed from the psychotic on the continuum might be free in ways very important to her or might have relatively few goals and objectives and hence might rarely experience the necessity of choosing among actions all of which she is free to do. On the other hand, because not even the most god-like of philosophers can be in two places at one time, entire control over their internal forces would not make their freedom "perfect" or "full." It makes good sense to talk of more and less freedom, but the notion of complete, or full, or perfect freedom is a misunderstanding.

A person's location on the continuum, then, may be relevant to assessing her freedom but it cannot itself settle that assessment. With this proviso in mind, let us consider a few of the large number of "stages" that might be singled out between the psychotic—call this position (a)—and the god-like philosopher. Leaving aside undoubted cases of organic disorders (such as epilepsy) and addictions that are agreed to be at least in part neurophysiological or biochemical, a next stage (b) might be occupied by persons suffering obsessions, phobias, and compulsions. Here again the ordinary uses of these terms attribute to the compulsive such characteristics as being "in the grip of" or "overcome by" some inner force. The kleptomaniac "cannot help herself"; when surrounded by the cornucopia of goods displayed in a supermarket or a department store her best efforts are not enough to prevent her from slipping items into her purse or under her coat. The acrophobic simply cannot maintain composure at the top of the Eiffel Tower. If she is so foolish as to ascend, she will all but certainly panic and do harm to herself unless restrained.

In certain respects, then, notions like "phobia" and "obsession" overlap with "psychosis" and "insane." The reflection, deliberation, intention formation and revision, the choosing, deciding, explaining and justifying, the adapting to changed circumstances and accommodation to other persons, the following of rules, routines, and recipes, the making and correcting of mistakes—none of these components of "ordinary" or "standard" action and acting are present in those aspects of the phobic's or the compulsive's life in which the phobia or the compulsion holds sway. (Of course the compulsive or phobic, just as with the psychotic, may be the very paradigm of the ordinary or standard agent or actor in some or much of her conduct.) For these reasons, the responsibility of compulsives and phobics, and the appropriateness of blaming and praising, punishing and rewarding them for the specifically compulsive and phobic behaviors, is minimal if not nonexistent. Because these abnormalities are often quite specific and coexist with ordinary capacity for action in other respects, we expect those who suffer them to take such precautions as they can against their occurrence and their effects. But when they do occur our role is to help and to sympathize, not to blame or punish.

Here again, then, we can make good sense of the notion of inner forces taking control of, even (if we remember that it is metaphorical) enslaving, human beings. Nor is there reason to doubt that persons who suffer compulsions and obsessions would like to be freed of or from them. But this too is unfreedom$_1$, at most the aspiration to freedoms$_{2-5}$. In respect to her obsessions and phobias, the genuine compulsive or phobic is incapable of action and hence of freedoms$_{2-5}$ and unfreedoms$_{2-5}$. To relate to her on any other assumption, for example to accuse her of inadequate responsibility for self or to read her lectures about her failings of character, would be either stupid or cruel.

The movement of my continuum toward its appointed termination with the god-like philosopher could proceed in a wide variety of ways or through a considerable diversity of "stages." One perhaps not implausible sequence would be the following: (c) habits in the at least mildly perjorative sense in which we say that smoking and pot-taking are habits; (d) a wide variety of so-called akratic behaviors, cases in which a person fails to act in the manner or in pursuit of the end or goal that she herself identifies as right or best by criteria that she herself endorses; (e) habits in the benign or even favorable usage of theorists such as Edmund Burke and Michael Oakeshott; (f) the purely preferential and instrumental but perhaps exquisitely calculated choices of some utilitarianisms and of classical and neoclassical economic theories; (g) character traits or settled but principled dispositions à la Aristotle and such contemporary writers as Bernard Williams and Charles Taylor; (h) the casuistries, firmly practical, elegant in formulation, and deeply grounded in an elaborate system of reflections, of the scholastic moralist; (i) the thoughts and actions of the philosopher who would be divine if only she hadn't suffered the indignity of being created mortal.

I comment briefly on some of these (most particularly habits and the moderately technical notion of *akrasia*) just below. But I will assume that the idea informing the progression from stage to stage is at least as available and as intuitively clear to readers of this book as are the notions of psychosis and obsessions, compulsions and phobias. For present purposes what is needed is not a detailed explication of these familiar notions but rather consideration of the bearing, if any, of the similarities and differences among them on theories of freedom and unfreedom.

It appears to me to be the Hegelian and the neo-Hegelian view that unfreedom, or no better than a thin, insignificant freedom, prevails until we reach (e) or even (f) on this continuum and that rich, fully significant freedom is a possibility only for those who have arrived at least at stage (g), perhaps at (h) in this sequence. (Note that in principle a person could be at various stages in respect to the several dimensions or aspects of life. At least this could be true up to [h] or [i].) If I am correct about this, two now familiar ways of interpreting this view emerge from my previous discussions. One of these is that the view equates freedom with various other values or ideals such as virtue, good character, authenticity, and the like. Those at stages (c) through (e) or (f) fall short of their own or their community's ideals in various ways and to various degrees. As we move from (f) or (g) toward (i), the degree and quality of freedom increase along with the extent to which the individual achieves (so far as she is not prevented from doing so by others) whatever ideals are in question. The second interpretation is the one I have been considering and that led me to posit the continuum. Movement along the continuum is not calibrated in terms of more or less virtue, higher or lower levels of achievement of valued objectives or states. Rather, it is from little or seriously inadequate control over inner forces to entire control over them. On this second interpretation, persons at stages (c) through (f) are treated as remarkably similar to psychotics in respect to their psychoses and obsessives in respect to their obsessions. Those who eat too much, work inefficiently, live fragmented, disorganized lives, have poor relationships with others, above all persons who are cowardly, selfish, unjust, illiberal, and the like are said to be in the grip of or overcome by some sort of internal but alien force. It is in this sense, it is for this reason, that they are unfree or enjoy no more than an impoverished freedom.

At least in respect to Charles Taylor, both of these interpretations are partly correct. Freedom is a kind of virtue and virtue is knowledge of self-in-community that makes possible rational control of action. Unfreedom is a kind of vice or evil when vice is an absence or failure of knowledge of self-in-community and of self-command which leaves the individual at the mercy of the irrational and nonrational forces that lurk in the subhuman recesses of the self. In a manner at least reminiscent of earlier versions of the theory of positive freedom, neo-Hegelian arguments combine these two doctrines.

If we exclude ordinary desires and compositional evaluations on the grounds presented in Chapter 2, and if we set aside psychosis and compulsions for the reasons discussed in this chapter, the plausibility of the second doctrine is left to depend on those occurrences in human affairs that we would place at stages (c), (d), and possibly (e) on my continuum. In both (c) and (d) and perhaps in (e), certain of the elements that are prominent in our ordinary notion of action are thought to be very little in evidence or perhaps missing altogether. In the case of habits in the at least mildly pejorative sense expressed by talk of having the habit of smoking, the elements alleged to be missing are critical self-consciousness, deliberation, rationality, and even decision and choice. There are those who invariably reach for a cigarette as they swing their legs out of bed in the morning, on the appearance of a cup of coffee, in the course of starting their cars, answering their telephones, beginning lectures to their classes, and so forth. Their smoking in these and other circumstances is as if by rote or by the numbers. They pause for not so much as an instant. There seems to be no evidence of their asking themselves whether they want to smoke, should smoke, have already smoked enough that day, would do better to save their remaining cigarettes for later, or anything of the sort. In the more inclusive case of (d), which on some interpretations would in fact encompass (c), there may be reflection, an abundance of self-examination and criticism, ambivalence, dissonance, hesitation, vacillation, agonizing, and so forth. The akratic, in short, may give an appearance very different from the person "locked into" a habitual mode of behavior. Here the missing or inadequately represented element is more like Harry Frankfurt's "will" to act on the conclusions of one's deliberations, to implement one's "choices" in the sense of the results of one's deliberations. For all of her agonizing and self-castigation about past failures, despite her elaborate preparations, strategies, and scheming, the akratic cannot resist the cigarette, the rich dessert, the nasty comment about a colleague, the putting herself first. If the habitual smoker is "in a rut," of which she may no longer be aware and from which she does not try to escape, the akratic is aware of her deficiencies and failings but fails to correct or overcome them. In both cases, perhaps for different reasons or by different psychological mechanisms, it appears that the persons are controlled by some force or forces that are alien or at least inauthentic. Hence they are unfree. It also appears that they could be made free, or that their freedom could be enhanced, if other agents or agencies would remove them, even if forcibly, from their rut or would prevent them from acting in ways that they themselves may regret and even despise.

We do frequently talk in ways that seem to warrant such conclusions about habitual and akratic conduct. I will comment on these forms of

speech in a moment. But we should first note some additional characteristics of each of these modes, characteristics that support quite
different conclusions about them. Habitual conduct is properly contrasted with decisions reached and choices made as the more or less
direct or immediate conclusion of reflection and deliberation. It is
"matter of course" in the sense that the conduct occurs without critical
reflection about its propriety or desirability when the agent finds
herself (or thinks she finds herself) in the kind of circumstance or
situation in which it has previously served. The person does not, in
Hannah Arendt's phrase, "stop to think" (1981, 2:78; see also 88–9)
There is no turning inward, no consideration of alternatives, no seeking of further information or advice. Nevertheless, even the most
settled, the least reflective of habitual behaviors are only "robot-like,"
not the movements of robots. Even the monotonous, the dreary
regularity with which Able, a member of my car pool, lights up as she
settles into the back seat each morning is broken if she hasn't seen to
having cigarettes and matches in her purse. Nor is Able literally a
"smoking machine"; her deadly instrument moves irregularly from
hand-to-hand and hand-to-mouth, she puffs rapidly and then slowly,
exhales first in my direction and then in that of another sufferer, she
flicks her ashes sometimes on the floor, sometimes out the window,
occasionally in the ashtray. These depressing sequences, moreover,
are learned and practiced. Able knows how and how not to smoke. She
conceives of herself as smoking in a sophisticated manner. There are
many ways in which she would "not be caught dead" smoking. The
angle at which she holds her head and her arm, the manner in which
she holds the cigarette in her yellowing fingers, the ways in which she
uses her inhaling and exhaling to punctuate her speech and to express
her mood, all of this is ritual. If it is a ritual by now performed largely
or even entirely without deliberation, if it is thoughtless in numerous
senses of that word, it is nevertheless replete with intentionality and
with purposiveness and it manifests choice and decision throughout.
Although repeated many times each day by Able, and many times
each day by millions of other human beings, each of these repetitions is
a chosen, an enacted, performance, one that differs from every other.

Owing to these characteristics, each of these habitual performances
is subject to evaluation. Each of them can be carried out elegantly or
inelegantly, smoothly or awkwardly, efficiently or wastefully. More
important for present purposes, as with any and all habits, the habit
itself (taken to be the ensemble of actions that constitutes having the
habit of smoking) is subject to evaluation as a good or a bad habit.
Perhaps my morning companion no longer asks herself this question.

Perhaps she hasn't asked herself this question for years. But at some point in her life history, at some level of self-consciousness, Able asked and answered it. Her habit developed because she repeatedly answered some formulation of the question in the affirmative. Having become satisfied with her answer, she has since had no more occasion to continue to ask it than a dispositionally courageous person has to ask herself whether she should be a coward. But any one of a wide array of events or occurrences might prompt her to ask it again. And if Able doesn't ask it, or asks it but comes to what others think is the wrong conclusion concerning it, she is subject to criticism. If those who know her are convinced that the habit has become so "deeply ingrained" that it is genuinely difficult for her to reconsider it or to consider it in an open-minded, balanced, manner, they may be sympathetic, patient, and gentle with her. They may decide that the habit has come to occupy so central a place in her life that it is better not to bring the matter up at all. But the same assessment, if combined with the view that smoking is a very bad habit indeed, that it is deeply harmful to herself or to others, may convince others that they are justified in employing measures so severe that they deprive Able of freedoms she had previously been enjoying (the same freedoms that will continue to be enjoyed by persons whose habits are judged to be good).

According to Amalie Rorty and other recent students of akrasia, akratic behavior is itself habitual (Rorty 1975, 193–212; Elster 1978). It differs from habits such as I have just discussed in that it typically occurs when there is a conflict among two or more of a person's habits. On this account of the phenomenon, the Able of my car pool is a likely candidate for akrasia. Her habit of smoking coexists with a variety of others such as attending to her health and her good physical appearance, seeking the approval of others and avoiding actions distressing or annoying to them, being frugal about her money, and so forth. She took up smoking before it came to be thought harmful to health, when it was considered fashionable by all but the unfashionably ascetical or puritanical and even a mark of liberation on the part of a woman, and before her government had come to appreciate its potential as a source of revenue. As changes occur in these regards, Able's habit of smoking will increasingly conflict with other of her dispositions and inclinations and she may decide that it would be better if she "kicked" it. Not smoking may become what Rorty calls her "preferred judgment," continued smoking an "*akratic* alternative" to that preferred judgment. If she nevertheless continues to smoke she will in that respect become an *akrates*. Despite her sincere belief that she should not smoke, her concerted efforts to act on that belief, and her regret and perhaps even self-disgust at her failure to do so, her smoking continues unabated.

Traditional analyses of akrasia support the view that the akrates is unfree. For Socrates, a person who takes an action or follows a course of action that is wrong or less attractive than available alternatives is either ignorant of what she is doing (doesn't realize the consequences of her action or doesn't appreciate that it falls under a principle she rejects) or under some kind of compulsion. Plato simplified this view by treating all wrongdoing as a result of ignorance of the good. As Rorty points out, however, these analyses, and even Aristotle's more plausible view that akrasia is explained by mistakes of fact or of practical reasoning, "explain" the phenomenon by denying its existence. Their explanations do not explain akrasia, they explain it away. My smoker Able is by now well-informed about smoking. She knows the grim statistics about lung cancer, heart disease, and emphysema; she is intensely aware of the disapproval of others; she keeps accurate account of the money she spends on cigarettes and adverts frequently to the other pleasures she must therefore forego. In other regards, morever, she maintains a close and effective discipline over her conduct. Although fond of rich desserts, she ends her meals with black coffee in order to remain trim and to save money; although intensely disliking her boss, she never permits herself so much as the mildest criticism of her. In most respects she is a paradigm of the "responsible self."

Of course there is weakness here, weakness that may deserve understanding and sympathy on the part of friends and acquaintances that would never occur to them in respect to other aspects of Able's conduct. Moreover, Able may talk about her smoking in ways which, if taken literally, suggest more than mere weakness. For example, she may say that she "can't help" smoking, or that it is "impossible" for her to stop doing so. These and many related locutions, which are characteristic of persons experiencing akrasia, might seem to support the view that the akrates is unfree.

The most serious difficulty with this analysis can be seen by noting that the akrates herself, despite using language that suggests unfreedom, continues to describe her smoking as mistaken or regrettable at least in the sense of not being the most desirable or best or right thing for her to do. Rorty argues that this does not mean that akrasia always involves conduct of a deeply or seriously mistaken kind; conduct that is immoral or seriously harmful to the agent or to others. On her analysis, the concept applies even if the akrates has no more than a mild preference for some alternative pattern of conduct.[4] But as the traditional term "weakness of will" suggests, akrasia involves some sense of shortcoming or deficiency, some at least mildly negative or critical self-assessment. Weakness and shortcoming, however, are not unfreedom. If the akrates were unfree, such self-criticism would be out of place. I cannot at once be unfree and *make* a mistake. If I am unfree in a particular respect I cannot *act* in that respect and hence I am not subject to criticism, by myself or by others, in that respect. (Of course I might be subject to criticism for past actions that led to my present unfree condition.) It is a condition of the applicability of "mistake," "criticism," and a whole host of evaluational concepts that I am an agent engaged in action.

Statements that appear to claim unfreedom should be understood, rather, as expressions of a two- or perhaps a three-fold regret, but a regret that is at least partially qualified. (i.) Able regrets her continued smoking; there is an obvious alternative, one that she genuinely and sincerely prefers. (ii) She regrets the fact that she allows herself to be influenced by considerations—the anticipated pleasure of the cigarettes, the comradely support of other smokers—over which she could exercise control if she made a sufficient effort. (iii) She regrets earlier decisions and actions that established her habit of smoking and that make her susceptible to the continuing influence of considerations such as in (ii). But the regret is qualified or partial, not entire. From early in the history of her habit Able genuinely enjoyed smoking and she continues to do so. The cigarettes do taste good to her, do give her other pleasurable sensations; she enjoys the ritual, likes to discuss the differences among brands with other smokers, finds satisfaction in the thought that, unlike earlier generations of women, members of her generation are at liberty to smoke if they see fit. If she gave up smoking her sense of achievement would be qualified by regret over the loss of these pleasures. The considerations that influence the partially regretted action are not alien or external or inauthentic to her. They influence her, they have weight with or for her, because of beliefs, inclinations, and preferences that are among her characteristics as a person. She may succeed in changing herself in these respects, but until she does so her smoking remains an action that she takes.[5]

I suggested that positive theorists exaggerate the significance, for the moral and political theory of freedom, of the idea that desires, interests, inclinations, and so forth "enslave" the agent. There is no denying that something like this notion is frequently encountered outside of the pages of philosophical works. My argument that positive theorists exaggerate the significance of the notion is in two stages. I concede, *arguendo*, that "enslavement" occurs in cases of psychoses and obsessions and compulsions. But I contend that these are cases of freedom$_1$, and hence are relevant to moral and political theory only insofar as it is possible to cure psychosis and addiction and hence make those who have suffered them eligible for predication of freedoms$_{2-5}$ and unfreedoms$_{2-5}$. To put this thesis somewhat differently, in the cases in which the language of brute and alien forces, and hence absence of agency, is appropriate, talk of "enslavement" is metaphorical and the "enslaving" forces should not be assimilated to the desires and interests that operate at stages (c) through (e) or (f) on the continuum I have posited. Secondly, I contend that talk of "enslavement" in respect to stages (c), and (d) is inappropriate; these stages— and more obviously (e) and (f)—should be understood in ways that leave agency largely if not entirely intact. Taylor is correct in his sometimes implicit thesis that notions such as making a mistake remain available in the cases that concern him, and hence he is also correct that freedoms$_{2-5}$ and unfreedoms$_{2-5}$ can be predicated of the actors in such cases. But he is mistaken in his view that evidence of the kinds he considers is sufficient to justify saying that those agents are unfree if we are thinking of unfreedoms$_{2-5}$.

In the light of these reflections, it appears that the versions of the positive theory of freedom I have examined combine, in an inappropriate manner, the two views that I suggested as ways of interpreting it. These theorists *are* working with an ideal of virtue or authenticity or integrity or good personal adjustment. They value and hope for persons whose actions are deliberately chosen to satisfy norms and principles that those persons correctly believe to be morally and otherwise worthy. And they are disposed to say that actions which do not meet these criteria are unfree. But they are unwilling to adopt in an unvarnished form the position that equates freedom and virtue or freedom and authenticity, unfreedom and vice or unfreedom and inauthenticity. Hence they seek plausibility for their uses of "freedom" and (especially) "unfreedom" by treating actions that are not morally or otherwise worthy as compelled by inner forces. I suggest that this move, although seeming to find support from certain ordinary modes of speech, misinterprets the locutions that appear to support it and leads to incoherence in the theory of freedom.

If we recur now to Feinberg's schema, it is evident that the foregoing remarks are primarily concerned with constraints of the internal, positive variety. Not only obsessions and compulsions but unevaluated desires, passions, habits, and so forth are treated by positive theorists as forces preventing the agent from acting as she should and as compelling untoward or inadmissible "actions." So understood, their discussions give an apparent plausibility to the argument that such persons are unfree.

The same passages to which I have been responding support the interpretation that the positive theory equates freedom with ideals of virtue and character. To see this, we need do no more than shift our focus to Feinberg's category of constraints that are internal but negative. In this perspective, those persons whom positive theorists regard as unfree (in ways that negative theories of freedom cannot accommodate) lack the qualities of character that are necessary conditions of proper action. Just as a person who is suffering from the negative external constraint of lack of money cannot buy a new car, so persons who lack the qualities that positive theorists celebrate cannot act in a proper manner. By implicitly adopting Feinberg's notion of negative, internal constraints, they connect freedom with virtue without explicitly using an unvarnished version of the position that assimilates freedom and virtue.

My objection to the positive theory, then, is at three levels. In respect to psychotics, genuine compulsives, and the like, I allow that there is no action or agency and hence a kind of unfreedom. But this is unfreedom only if we are thinking of unfreedom$_1$. Questions about freedoms$_{2\text{-}5}$ do not arise about psychotics and compulsives. The second and third levels of my objection concern habitual actions and actions taken to satisfy evaluated passions, desires, and interests, objectives and purposes, evaluations that positive theorists disapprove and that the agent herself may regret in the qualified senses discussed above. I contend that such actions are the agent's own. The evaluations and choices that prompt them are authentic to the actor as she is and as she understands herself and should not be regarded, in Feinberg's language, as positive, internal constraints that compel movements or behaviors on the agent's "part." In the absence of external, positive impediments or constraints, these actions, however objectionable, are freely done, are done in freedom.

The third level of my objection can be put by stressing the respect in which the second objection is in effect conceded by positive theorists. When actions are called base as opposed to noble, cowardly as opposed to courageous, mean as opposed to generous, spiteful or vindictive as opposed to understanding, forgiving, or magnanimous, the actor is *criticized* and *blamed*. Such criticism abandons the view that the person in question was compelled by internal or any other forces. To save the notion that the actor is nevertheless unfree, a conceptual move is made that can be described in any one of three interrelated ways: in a vocabulary that equates freedom and virtue; by using "freedom" to refer to my kinds of freedom$_{4-5}$; as a readiness to treat the absence of virtue or good character as a negative, internal constraint that allows the agent to act but prevents her from acting in a noble, courageous, generous, understanding, forgiving, or magnanimous fashion.

Having separated this move from the positions criticized at my first two levels, how should we assess it? It will help to note again the difference between freedom$_4$ and freedom$_5$. As introduced in Chapter 1, freedom$_4$ requires that the plan of action followed by the actor satisfy the criteria that purportedly inform the actions in question. This formulation does not specify *who* is to make the judgment whether the actions taken in fact satisfy those criteria. Most important, it does not specify whether (for purposes of assessing the freedom or unfreedom of the act and the actor) that judgment is to be made by the actor herself or by other parties. By contrast, freedom$_5$ clearly posits some species of interpersonally defensible judgment concerning the worthiness of the agent's objectives and hence excludes the possibility that the agent's own judgment, as such, could be conclusive.

In respect to freedom$_4$, the move that I am discussing takes plausibility from the fact that the agent who acts habitually says or shows that she partially regrets her action because it does not fully satisfy the criteria that she accepts and aims to satisfy. Able aims to have cordial, harmonious relations with Baker and she partially regrets it when her actions produce tension and ill-feeling. Thus she criticizes herself for not having fully satisfied her own objectives. The language of freedom and unfreedom appears to obtain a foothold in this setting. Able does not want to disavow responsibility for the outcome, does not want to "cop out" or "pass the buck" to someone else. Yet something stands between her and her objectives. Because of this feature, it is not inconceivable that she would say of herself that she would be more free if that something were removed or brought under control.

I have argued, however, that if such talk is taken literally—whether by the agent herself or by other parties—it is incoherent. A person cannot at once, that is in respect to one and the same act or failure to act, claim that she was unfree and that she has *made* a mistake. Persons who talk themselves into such an incoherence in respect to their own conduct are either confused or, more likely, suffering from a more or less serious case of that mode of self-deception that existentialists call *mauvaise foi* (or perhaps it is deception of others and should be called, less esoterically, bad faith). Persons who interpret such talk on the part of others in this literal-minded way either misunderstand it (perhaps because they accept a certain theory of freedom) or are taken in by it.

The position of positive theorists is yet less plausible if we assign to other parties the judgment whether Able's actions serve Able's own objectives or meet her own criteria. Let us focus on cases in which Able is, on balance, satisfied with her actions but Charlotte and Dorothy, although raising no questions about Able's objectives, conclude that her actions in fact disserve those objectives and betray inadequate responsibility for self. For example, Able aspires to good relationships with her academic colleagues but frequently publishes sharply critical analyses of their scholarly work. Some at least of Able's colleagues resent this practice and are cool to her because of it. Charlotte and Dorothy attribute Able's conduct to jealousy and personal insecurity and urge Able to seek counseling so as to better understand and control her inclinations. They argue that following this course would enhance Able's freedom.

Able admits to a degree of jealousy of some of her colleagues and to insecurity about her own professional standing and achievements. She even allows that she would be happier if she were rid of these feelings. But she contends that the actions in question conform to the norms of academic life as she understands and accepts them and that she takes the actions for this reason. The resentment and cool relationships are the fault of her colleagues' failure to understand collegiality at its best.

Pressed by Charlotte and Dorothy, Able may be induced to claim that she is "free" to alter her practice out of deference to the feelings of colleagues. She may also contend that her colleagues are equally "free" to adopt her understanding of collegiality and thus to appreciate rather than to resent her practice. I suggest, however, that even such talk on Able's part would be an inappropriate concession to an unfortunate misconception held by Charlotte and Dorothy. The issue is not whether Able or her friends are free; that issue is already settled, indeed tacitly acknowledged to have been settled. Rather, the issue is whether she or they are justified in their respective views concerning the norms that do and/or that should inform and govern academic life. The freedom of Able and her friends is a supposition of the disagreement between them concerning this normative issue. In attempting to transform the normative issue into a question about Able's freedom, Charlotte and Dorothy patronize—that is, insult—Able. If Able is a patient (or perhaps a charitable) as well as a clear-headed sort, she will explain this distinction to Charlotte and Dorothy. If they persist in their views despite her explanation, she will be presented with a choice between sympathizing with their incapacity and resenting their obnoxious conduct.

We can now set aside as irrelevant the differences between freedom$_4$ and freedom$_5$. Questions about the worthiness of Able's projects and objectives presuppose Able's freedom to choose and to pursue them. If she were unfree in these respects, the projects and objectives would not be *hers* and criticism of her would be misdirected. Given that she has chosen and pursued her projects and objectives, any number of issues can be raised about the merits of her choices and actions. To treat these as issues about freedom is to confuse the question whether Able is free with the quite different matter of the merits of Able's use of whatever freedom she has.

In sum, the concepts of freedom and unfreedom encompass my kinds of freedom$_{1-3}$. Persons or other creatures characterized by no more than freedom$_1$ are as yet neither free nor unfree by the criteria of freedoms$_{2-3}$, that is, by the criteria of the only kinds of freedom that can be thought of as moral and political in character. My supposed freedoms$_{4-5}$ and unfreedoms$_{4-5}$ are not kinds of freedom and unfreedom at all. They are made to appear as such (and positive theories are made to appear to be theories of freedom) by equating (confusing) freedom with abilities and virtues or unfreedom with the absence thereof (that is, with internal, negative constraints). All instances of freedoms$_{2-3}$ and unfreedoms$_{2-3}$ are situated as opposed to "brute," and most if not all such instances are situated in further respects that remain to be explored.

I conclude this chapter by explaining my earlier assertion that positive theories of freedom make the wrong kind of connection between freedom and virtue. Questions about virtue and vice, good and evil, right and wrong, are of course importantly related to freedom and unfreedom. To begin with, in our culture freedom is itself widely regarded as a good and various particular freedoms are regarded as especially valuable and important. Whether and why this should be the case will be our concern in later chapters. If we simply accept the fact for now, for this reason the question whether an action is right or wrong, good or evil, virtuous or unvirtuous, often cannot be decided apart from, independently of, whether it is or will be done in freedom or in the exercise of a particular freedom. If Mr. Harding in Trollope's *Barchester Towers* had thought Eleanor's (supposed) willingness to marry Mr. Slope had been coerced or even manipulated, his readiness to accommodate himself to that arrangement would have diminished or disappeared. Although he despised the match itself, his belief that his daughter was acting in freedom was important in convincing him that he ought to accept it. If a despicable racist harangue is regarded as an exercise of freedom of speech, our estimate of the importance of that freedom convinces many that the act should not only be allowed but protected. In short, the freedom or unfreedom of actions is itself sometimes a consideration in our moral and other evaluations of those actions. In addition, actions and proposed or attempted actions typically raise further moral or normative questions, questions about which our thinking may be influenced but is seldom settled by the fact that they are or would be done in freedom. Let us assume that Mr. Harding was right to respect his daughter's freedom and that we are right to protect the racist's speech. Let us further assume that Eleanor and the racist have a right to act as they see fit in these regards. It may nevertheless be that Eleanor would have been wrong to marry Slope and that the racist would be wrong to give her speech. The moral good that is freedom, even the good that is a freedom protected by an established right, coexists and often conflicts with other moral goods. If we tried to assess these actions without attending to the fact that freedom is involved (as Dr. Grantly was disposed to do and as opponents of racism sometimes do) our identification of the issues before us would be incomplete and prejudicial. But we might recognize and attach great significance to these features of the actions and yet conclude that other considerations, other values in question in the circumstances, should properly take precedence. For example, we might desist from any active attempt to prevent the actions and yet think less well of the agents for persisting in them.

As against theorists of Pure Negative Freedom, theorists of positive freedom are therefore correct in thinking that the theory of freedom is an integral part of the more general theory of morality. Questions about freedom are typically moral questions. But these theorists make the wrong kind of connection between freedom and other moral concepts. By making the question whether an action is done in freedom equivalent to the question whether it is virtuous, by equating freedom and virtue, they lose the independence of the concept and the value of freedom and they distort and simplify moral issues. On their construction, the moral good of freedom and of particular freedoms cannot conflict with the moral goods with which freedom is equated. If the racist is morally wrong to hold and to express her views, she is *therefore* unfree in doing so. As we have seen, on the "enslaved by desires" dimension of the positive theory, it follows that the racist cannot be criticized or blamed for the particulars of (what appears to be her thought and action but in reality is) her behaviors. At most we can criticize her for the train of failures of responsibility for self that have left her in the grip of such vile impulses. Setting this consequence aside, we now see that it is impossible for us to conceptualize the issue posed by her proposed speech as involving a conflict between (genuine) freedom and other moral values. Quite apart from anything we may or may not do, the racist is already unfree (or enjoying no better than an impoverished freedom); hence there can be no such conflict (or the conflict will be easily resolved against the impoverished freedom). Difficult and vitally important moral and political questions disappear.

Of course this or that theorist of positive freedom might well reach correct substantive conclusions about any number of moral issues. The theory of positive freedom might be regarded as a theory of freedom in the powerfully moralized sense of a theory that tells us who *ought to be* free to do what. But equating "freedom" with "morally virtuous (or otherwise right or proper) action" conceals an important part of what is at issue in the judgments that the theory urges on us. We are conceptually blinded to the fact that the judgments propose limitations on freedom itself. Not knowing what is at issue, we are in no position to assess the merits of proposed resolutions of it. In the name of wedding freedom to reason and morality, the positive theory diminishes our ability to deal intelligently with moral issues involving freedom.

Part Two

Situating Freedom

5

Situating Freedom

My chief purpose in Part II is to elaborate, defend, and detail the implications of the thesis that freedom and unfreedom are situated. I begin by pursuing somewhat further the relationship between freedom and morality as discussed in the previous chapter. Implicit in my concluding objection against positive theories of freedom is the claim that the views I have thus far advanced leave the major moral and political questions about freedom unanswered. Those views do not tell us how to rank the value of freedom in comparison with other moral and political values, they do not tell us who should be free to do what under what circumstances, and they do not tell us how to achieve and maintain the freedoms we value or how to combine various freedoms with one another or with other desiderata. True, I adopted the assumption that freedom is itself a moral good and that certain classes of freedom are further, more particular goods. But as a moral as opposed to an empirical sociological proposition the defense for this assumption remains to be given. In particular, it is not provided by the primarily conceptual arguments that I have thus far advanced. Rather, an intended effect of my discussions has been to hold such questions open; to fend off what I have argued are ill-advised strategies for closing such questions by construing the concept of freedom in a certain fashion.

But this view of the foregoing chapters might well be disputed. It might be contended that positions I have taken have quite definite and quite substantial normative implications.

One formulation of this objection needs to be mentioned only to be acknowledged as well taken. If I regarded freedom as of little or no value or significance, had no concern with how it is construed and understood, the foregoing discussions would be sterile exercises. Having arrived, at least tentatively, at an understanding of what freedom is and is not, and valuing freedom so understood, I have thought it worthwhile to assess alternative views and to argue against them where I find them unsatisfactory. In this sense the positions I have taken are certainly not morally neutral. (But it is one thing to take a moral position, another to defend it.)

The more interesting and important form of the objection focuses on my claim that the subjects of the predicates "freedom" and "unfreedom" are human actions and attempted but prevented actions; and, more particularly, the attendant notion that freedom and unfreedom are therefore situated. I have suggested, and will now be arguing, that situatedness involves such elements as shared language, common traditions and beliefs, norms and rules that are more or less settled among persons who make up a community or association, institutions and practices invested with some species of legitimacy or authority. Actions take their identifications and much of their character from these features of the situations in which they occur. To say this, to make situated actions a feature of the use of the concept of freedom, is to say that actions are influenced, limited, and perhaps directed by elements external and possibly alien to the agents who take them. This move might be taken to imply heteronomization in Kant's sense and it certainly seems to exclude the possibility that entire or unrestricted freedom (as negative theorists have construed "freedom") could be achieved.

A version of this line of thought, albeit not precisely in the form of a normative objection to situatedness, is familiar from the thought of resolute state-of-nature theorists such as Hobbes and Rousseau. There is an important sense in which the Hobbesian and Rousseauean states of nature are presented as at once unsituated and as states of entire freedom. In Hobbes's thought the latter understanding is expressed through his notion of the "right of nature" that entitles all those in the state of nature to do whatever they deem necessary to satisfy their interests as they see them (1955, chap. 14). Freedom is entire in the sense that, prudential considerations apart, there is nothing that any agent must or ought not do. Rousseau's view is more insistently unsituated and more deeply amoral or premoral. Criticizing Hobbes for attributing social characteristics and understandings to creatures in an allegedly presocial condition, Rousseau contends that Homo sapiens in their natural state are entirely devoid of moral (or any other) conceptions (1950, 193–95, 197–98, 201–3). The idea of justifications for their behavior, even in the primitive form supplied by Hobbes's right of nature, is simply not available to them. Their freedom (which of course could be identified and discussed as such only by persons who have left the state of nature) is my freedom$_1$.

Neither Hobbes nor Rousseau approved of the conditions they called the state of nature. But both of them took the idea seriously in the sense that they thought it necessary to justify the features of human life that differentiate the state of society and political society from the state of nature. They shared the view that the question "Why should human beings give up the morally entire freedom of the state of nature, why ought they submit to the limitations inherent in social and political situatedness?" is the most fundamental of moral and political questions. And while they both argued (although for quite different reasons and with substantively different conceptions of situatedness in mind) that human beings should accept social and political arrangements, we can easily imagine them objecting that my claim that situatedness is a condition of talk about freedom begs those very questions.

In this and the following chapter I attempt to take versions and levels of this objection seriously and to rejoin to them. I say "attempt" because familiar formulations of the objection, in addition to involving assumptions that are necessarily conjectural, deeply counterfactual in respect to our actual experience of ourselves, and hence hard to assess, seem to call into question features of our thinking that are integral to thinking itself. For these reasons, in the end my response to the apparently deepest forms of the objection is less to meet or to refute them than to dissolve them by denying their coherence. But this cannot be done directly or briskly. As Wittgenstein (on whose work I will be making increasingly heavy reliance as I proceed) shows by his philosophical practice, we have first to understand why these objections have seemed powerful; why it has seemed essential that we get behind or beneath the merely social or conventional and ground our understandings and our assessments of them in something more substantial and more secure. In this chapter I begin with the explicitly political and moral argument of Hobbes, take up Rousseau's rejoinder that Hobbes's position is incoherent, and, with pauses along the way to comment on normative matters, attempt to improve on Rousseau's position by appeal to the less conjectural and more detailed arguments of Wittgenstein's later philosophy. In the following chapter I take up views that seem to retain force even if one accepts the arguments of the present chapter.

I

For Rousseau the freedom of the state of nature might not be practicable or viable but it is of certainty conceptually and rationally nonmoral. For this reason it is unworthy. If (contrary to fact) we had the option of returning to that condition, we should reject it in order to achieve the kind of freedom befitting our potential as human beings. By contrast, for Hobbes the freedom of the state of nature is worthy in conception—indeed is the only kind of freedom there is—but empirically or practically illusory. As we have seen, Hobbes was disposed neither to dismiss nor to demean self-engendered and unimpeded movement of the kind that Rousseau regarded as amounting to no better than an animalistic freedom. In Hobbes's view the difficulty is rather that self-moving and legally and morally unconstrained human agents so often collide and conflict that their freedom, though "morally" entire, is destructive of peace, of security, and hence of itself. Hobbes urges human beings to submit to the restrictions of organized social and (more especially) political life not so as to achieve more elevated or noble impulses and dispositions and hence a morally higher freedom but to reconcile freedom with peace and security and hence with itself. We exchange our unqualified but mutually destructive natural freedom for the bounded but vastly more secure and reliable "liberties of subjects."

Hobbes's argument for the rather thin situatedness he advocated is empirical and instrumental, not conceptual, mundane, and prudential, not moralizing. For all of its strident insistence, it is even made with a certain tinge of regret over the unfortunate fact that human beings and their world are such that the state of nature and its freedom are untenable. Situatedness is no more to be posited, stipulated, or assumed than it is to be celebrated as a good in its own right. It is to be understood and coolly accepted as a necessary means to ends and purposes given prior to it. It is by no means a condition necessary to our concept of freedom. On the contrary, our recognition that situatedness is necessary to the practical realization of freedom shows (to Hobbes's satisfaction) that the latter concept is logically prior to and independent of the former. We know what freedom is and why we want it and we situate ourselves in political society in order (among other things) to get it. Thus Hobbes would regard the position taken here as logically and conceptually mistaken and as confusing an end pursued with a means of pursuing it. Because in his judgment the means are indispensable to the end, and because Hobbes in fact confronted arguments that we should be forced to be righteous or good, not forced to be free, we do not find him objecting to the moral, political, or other normative implications of these mistakes. But materials out of which to form such an objection are available in his argument and it is tempting to permit ourselves the anachronism of imagining his fervent response to Rousseau and Kant and especially to Hegel and later Hegelian proponents of the positive theory of freedom. Because I have endorsed important aspects of his thinking about freedom, it is imperative that I show that he and other proponents of the negative theory are mistaken concerning the conceptual points just discussed (and that this mistake can be remedied without giving up the essentials of the negative theory).

We can begin by returning to the distinction between freedom$_1$ and unfreedom$_1$ and my claim that Rousseau would regard (if he employed the terminology) the freedom possible in his state of nature as freedom$_1$. This distinction (the distinction, not merely the terminology) has no clear or secure place in Hobbes's official conceptualization. He refuses to differentiate between the freedom of action and the freedom of movement.[1]

Hobbes's theory nevertheless provides compelling evidence for the importance of this distinction. Why *should* human beings accept the authority of political society? How can Hobbes himself conceive of and develop arguments for this imperative? What is he assuming about his fellow human beings when he addresses imperatives and arguments (these or any other) to them? The entire exercise takes its sense from an implicit distinction between purposeful, deliberately chosen actions that are defensible by some standard and mere movements which cannot be avoided and which "arise not for deliberation." In slightly different terms, the whole idea that the "liberties of subjects" are *preferable* to the freedom of the state of nature presupposes agents who make and act upon these distinctions. It presupposes the distinction between freedom$_1$ and freedom$_2$, and agents who make that distinction and apply it to themselves and to others.

The next step in my response to Hobbes was taken by Rousseau when he objected that Hobbes illicitly attributed social characteristics to creatures who he (Hobbes) claimed were in an entirely pre- or non-social situation or circumstance. Having conceptions of any sort becomes possible only after a series of accidents has brought numbers of human beings, who in their natural state scarcely recognize one another as of a distinct kind, into more or less steady and patterned contact with one another.[2] The advent of social relationships leads (in a manner that Rousseau regards as unabatedly mysterious) to the development of language and hence of the ability to make, to remember, and to communicate various distinctions.

On this view, situatedness in the sense of an at least minimal sociality is a necessary condition of the formation of anything that could be regarded as a conception. It *seems* also to be an implication of the view that situatedness in this sense is a sufficient condition of those conceptions I found implicit in Hobbes's theory of freedom. In yet more forceful terms, it appears to be a necessary truth that situatedness and the conceptualizations it yields includes the distinctions between action and movement and between freedom$_1$ and freedom$_2$.

Rousseau's discussions of these points might be called mock-empirical or mock-historical in character. Cast in the "state of nature" idiom, they present themselves as an account of two states of affairs and of the transition from the one to the other. In fact, of course, Rousseau knew that he had no empirical evidence about the state of nature or the "earliest" states of sociality. He says we should "begin . . . by laying facts aside" and enter instead into "conditional and hypothetical reasonings, rather calculated to explain the nature of things, than to ascertain their actual origin" (1950, 198).[3] In later jargons, his discussions might be called a priori, conceptual rather than empirical, an exercise in descriptive metaphysics, or the like. If we set aside the distracting talk about the state of nature, and particularly if we also follow Rousseau's lead in making the focus of our attention the fact that human beings are language-using creatures, we can put Rousseau's suggestive and—in my view— essentially correct understanding of situatedness and its significance on better foundations and into a less confused form. But first I must return to the normative concerns that motivated my discussion of Hobbes and Rousseau and enter some qualifications to and some cautions concerning the foregoing discussion.

II

In terms of those normative concerns the conclusion I want to take is that the notion of situatedness is neutral to normative issues about human freedom. If situatedness is a condition of all thinking about human freedom, then it is presupposed by or implicit in all of the contending positions that are in dispute about such issues (or in all positions save those that are so deeply confused as to be manifestly untenable). Sustaining this conclusion, however, requires distinctions that I have thus far left aside. One of these is between what I will call the generic notion of situatedness and various more particular and normatively more substantive conceptions of sociality delineated by social theorists and marked by oppositions like organic versus mechanical, *gesellschaft* versus *gemeinschaft*, contract versus status. In addition, we must make the following distinctions: (1) between societies in which the notions of action as opposed to movement and freedom$_2$ as opposed to freedom$_1$ are explicit and self-consciously recognized and those in which they are no more than implicit; (2) between societies in which they are widely recognized and those in which they are recognized only by a minority or an elite; (3) between societies that both recognize and assign normative importance to these notions and those that recognize them but attach positive importance to them in respect to some classes or groups among their members but no importance or negative importance in respect to other classes or groups. I begin with the last set of differentiations.

The implicit-explicit distinction, although controversial, is familiar from the large historical and social scientific literature that employs terms such as barbarian versus civilized, primitive versus advanced, underdeveloped versus developed, traditional versus modernized. Writers from Herodotus and Aristotle to contemporary students of comparative political culture have used one or more of the first of these terminological pairs to designate human associations that, despite being "social" in Rousseau's minimalist sense, display no recognition or self-conscious awareness of the distinctions between action and movement and freedom$_2$ versus freedom$_1$. Insofar as the members of these associations have a conception of themselves it is as creatures or even things entirely controlled by nature, by gods or spirits, or by some other force or forces utterly superior to themselves. If the idea of action as opposed to controlled movement were articulated it would be alien and perhaps threatening. These notions are nevertheless implicit in the activities of these members. Unlike subhuman animals, they form, communicate, and act upon beliefs, maintain and hold one another to norms and standards. Arrangements of theirs (for example, religious ceremonies or rituals) are inexplicable except on these suppositions. Yet it would be misleading to say that they "have," or think in terms of, these notions.

We need not go beyond theorists already mentioned to find the further distinctions between general and only partial recognition and/or positive valorization of action and of freedom$_2$. Aristotle's citizens both have and value these notions, but in Aristotle's view numerous members of his own highly civilized society, those human beings who are "slaves by nature," are no more than "animate instruments" (1953, bk. 1). Aristotle held the same view, in only slightly qualified form, of all women, and Rousseau followed him to the extent of thinking that women should be socialized so as to diminish or even to eliminate their tendency to think of themselves in these terms. Women are evidently capable of a certain apprehension of the concepts of free will and self-improvement, but their grasp of them is defective and insecure. If they act on their imperfect understandings they harm themselves and society. John Stuart Mill found these particular views of Aristotle and Rousseau repugnant, but he embraced the idea that societies develop from a nonage in which the notions of action and freedom have actual, deserved, or desired place, if any, exclusively within a narrow elite to a maturity in which they are and should be paramount in the self-conceptions and aspirations of the entire adult population.[4] And of course mention of progressive if somewhat patronizing nineteenth-century views such as those of Mill (we could add Hegel, Marx, Spencer, and numerous others) can hardly fail to remind us of both earlier (for example, Plato's) and later (for example, B. F. Skinner's) projects grounded in contempt for these notions and aiming to eliminate them from the thought and action of all but the Managers of the ideal society.

Of course all of the views referred to are sharply controversial. But their salience and the continuing disputes concerning them should be enough to warn us off what might otherwise be tempting inferences from the Rousseauean account of situatedness. Let us briefly consider one undeniably attractive possibility. If sociality in the minimal sense that marks the termination of the Rousseauean state of nature itself yields the concepts of action and of freedom$_2$, we might think that a yearning for freedom is at least implicit in the thinking and aspirations of all human beings. Having acquired a conception of themselves as agents rather than subjects or patients, and having learned that the interests and desires, objectives and purposes that manifest and embody their agency can be frustrated by other agents and agencies, human beings, we can be certain, will value freedom$_2$. Agency and freedom$_2$ are concepts that one cannot grasp or comprehend without also valuing the phenomenon they identify.

In Chapter 8 I try to show that something like the propositions just stated should form a vital part of the *argument* for valuing agency and freedom$_2$. Nor am I disposed to deny that versions or variations of that argument have been persuasive to large numbers of human beings or that a yearning for freedom has been and remains widespread. It hardly needs to be said that this yearning has been satisfied all too rarely; that situatedness has been and is very far indeed from a sufficient condition of a remotely satisfactory measure of actual freedom. More important in our context, the views I briefly rehearsed make it plain that many would contest not only the claim that all situated human beings *should* enjoy a substantial measure of agency of freedom$_2$ but also the conceptual thesis that situatedness itself yields a grasp or command of these concepts. And while there is nothing to be said for the views that there are human beings who are barbarians or slaves by nature and that more than half of humankind is incapable of securely grasping the concept of agency, we have reason to believe that people who hold such views can find means of *making* something ominously akin to them true of the unfortunates who fall under their domination. We know that the capacity for agency can be destroyed by disease, injury, and by the damage inflicted by various drugs. It at least appears to be true that all too similar effects can be produced by less crudely physical interventions and manipulations. Indeed understandings of and arguments concerning the *kinds* of situatedness appropriate to human life have been among the devices employed for these purposes. It is therefore wrong to say that situatedness is a sufficient condition of actually having the concepts of agency and freedom$_2$; and it would be worse than naive to draw optimistic normative inferences from the reasoning that substantiates the claim that situatedness is a necessary condition of having those concepts. Situatedness in Rousseau's minimalist sense is a necessary condition of assigning positive value to freedom. It follows that it is also a necessary supposition of theorizing about freedom. But it is not a sufficient condition of having these concepts in any explicit or self-conscious form and it is certainly not a sufficient condition of valuing agency and freedom.

My last remarks are intended as further support for the claim that insistence on situatedness does not prejudge the resolution of normative issues about freedom. In particular, they are intended to support my assertion that we can endorse a notion of situatedness without thereby embracing a positive conception of freedom. But there are other and at least initially more plausible formulations of this objection, and to deal with them we must take up the distinction between generic and particular conceptions of situatedness.

Situatedness in Rousseau's minimal or generic sense involves shared language and hence (the "hence" is part of Rousseau's thought and will be defended from another perspective below) some number of beliefs and values held more or less in common, certain norms or standards of conduct and legitimate and illegitimate expectations, and shared institutions or arrangements in which actions occur and through which a degree of cooperative interaction more or less regularly takes place. But this generic conception does not specify the particulars of the shared language; the number, subject matter, or content of the beliefs and values or norms and standards; the complexity, stability, or salience of the institutions and arrangements. Of course, empirically there are no generic societies or associations. Every actual society consists of a particular language or set of languages, beliefs and values of specific content, and so forth. Empirically, we confront not a distinction between situated and unsituated human life but societies and associations with a variety of definite characteristics. Comparative analysis of actual societies and associations, moreover, has led various social theorists to think of situatedness or sociality as increasing or decreasing, enlarging or diminishing, thinning, thickening, or deepening by various criteria or along various dimensions. The classical sociological distinctions I mentioned earlier can be understood in this way. Durkheim's mechanical solidarity, Tönnies' *gemeinschaft*, and Maine's status society, all involve more, more substantial, and more deeply established beliefs, values, and the like, than does organic solidarity and than do a *gesellschaft* or a contract society. If situatedness is necessary to conceptions of agency and freedom, it might be thought (as Rousseau and Durkheim if not Tönnies and Maine certainly thought) that an increase in or deepening of situatedness by these or other criteria is more favorable to those conceptions, or favorable to more satisfactory versions of those conceptions. More plausibly, perhaps, it might be thought that differing conceptions of situatedness produce, or are conducive to, differing conceptions of freedom.

These speculations, especially the last, take plausibility from the fact that proponents of the main competing conceptions of freedom have tended to favor sharply different modes or species of sociality. We have already encountered the strong association between "deeper," more communitarian conceptions of society and the positive theory of freedom. Proponents of the negative theory, by contrast, have promoted individualistic, *gesellschaft*-type understandings and arrangements. If Rousseau, Bradley, and Charles Taylor are clear examples of the former tendency, Hobbes is once again the leading example of the latter. Although favoring political absolutism in the sense of a government with unlimited authority to act as the Sovereign judges necessary, Hobbes was a thoroughgoing individualist who opposed limitations on conduct save those necessary to maintain peace and security. The picture is more complicated in respect to later theorists of negative liberty such as Bentham and Constant, Mill and Berlin, but it would undoubtedly be a distortion to portray any of these writers as enthusiasts for mechanical solidarity or anything approaching a *gemeinschaft*.

As a matter of empirically grounded social theory, and particularly

theory that issues in moral and political recommendations and prescriptions, I am inclined to think that there is good reason for the latter
sympathies and tendencies of thought. Certain cultural, social, and
political forms, especially those that are regarded as deeply situating
human conduct, while not themselves excluding individual freedom,
are inhospitable or unconducive to a number of freedoms that should
be highly valued. But there is nothing direct, certainly nothing necessary, about these connections. There is nothing contradictory or incoherent about combining a negative theory of freedom with a preference for deeply situating, strongly communitarian arrangements. This
would be true even if the association between communitarian-type
societies and limitations on individual freedom were much closer and
more direct than it is. Commitment to the negative theory of freedom
entails nothing about the value of freedom by comparison with other
values. A proponent of that theory might allow that communitarian
arrangements systematically subordinate freedom to equality or
fraternity or social justice and yet favor such arrangements. Such a
person need only insist that arrangements which serve these other
values do not *therefore* also serve freedom. (Bentham is a clear case of
a theorist who insists on a negative conception of freedom but who
ranks other goods—especially security of person and property—much
more highly than freedom. Indeed Bentham is a clear case of a theorist
who employs a negative concept of freedom as part of an antifreedom
argument.) Again a theorist of negative freedom who valued freedom
highly might favor communitarian arrangements on the ground that
they diminish obstacles to action and hence maximize, at least by
comparison with actually available alternatives, freedom itself. Finally, a proponent of the positive conception of freedom might argue
for an individualistic, even an anomic society, on the ground that the
genuinely worthy beliefs, values, and patterns of conduct necessary to
true freedom develop only, or best develop, where authoritative cultural norms and social and political institutions are at a minimum.

To sum up this last stretch of discussion, the claim that situatedness
is a postulate necessary to theorizing about freedom implies nothing as
to how moral and political questions about freedom can or should be
answered. This conclusion is reinforced by the more detailed and
sophisticated account of situatedness to which I now turn.

III

" 'I set the brake up by connecting up rod and lever.'—Yes, given the
whole rest of the mechanism, and separated from its support it is not

even a lever; it may be anything, or nothing" (Wittgenstein 1953, I, 6; hereafter cited as *PI*). This passage can be taken as a synecdoche for much of Wittgenstein's argument in the *Investigations*. Apart from the "mechanism" that consists of such Wittgensteinian elements as language-games, agreements in judgment, established conventions and rules and techniques for interpreting and applying them, shared or widely accepted propositions, characteristic patterns of thought and action, and the like—apart, that is, from life in something like a society—our experience of ourselves, of one another, and of the world we inhabit could be "anything or nothing." Life situated in such a "mechanism" is a condition of life that has meaning for those who live it.

The significance of Wittgenstein's contentions for our purposes can be appreciated by considering some of the views against which they— as distinct from Rousseau's analogous views—were a reaction. Throughout the *Investigations* Wittgenstein is arguing against theories which claim that meaning and meaningfulness are dependent on social situation only in unessential or even superficial respects. Most of these theories tacitly concede that there is some sense in which, in Wittgenstein's words, "meaning is in language." Their task, accordingly, appears to be the same as Wittgenstein's, namely, to explain how this can be, how seemingly arbitrary sounds and signs—that vary widely from time to time and place to place—can bear meaning. But this appearance is deceptive. If we construe "language" broadly, the proposition that meaning is *in* language can serve as a kind of abbreviation of Wittgenstein's theory. In the theories he mainly attacks, by contrast, language is no more than a vehicle or medium by or through which meaning may be recorded and communicated. Meaning is not *in* language in the strong sense that without language there would be no meaning. Meaning is *in* something antecedent to or independent of language. We grasp, apprehend, or otherwise acquire meanings apart from language and then we contrive signs and sounds that we make to stand for those meanings. At least logically and in all likelihood temporally, there is first meaning and only later language. Language is derivative of, secondary and even epiphenomenal to, meaning. Thus the fact that natural languages in the sense of Greek or English or Chinese are social phenomena, in that they are shared among those who speak them, does not show that meaning or meaningfulness is essentially social in character.

In the discussion immediately surrounding the brake-rod-lever passage Wittgenstein is attacking versions of such theories according to which meaning resides in extralinguistic entities that are initially (again in a logical and in the first instances a temporal sense) perceived and identified apart from language. The word "lever" *means* a particular object (or class of objects) of experience. If I use the word "lever" meaningfully I am aware of that object and I employ the word to refer to or to stand for it. Of course the particular combination of sounds or signs that make up "lever" acquires meaning only when I or someone else uses it to stand for the object. But the choice of "lever" is perfectly arbitrary; any mark or sound would do as well. More important, meaning or meaningfulness is not dependent on language. The meaning or meaningfulness resides in, is constituted by, the object itself. We might even say that the "I," the experiencing subject or agent, is unessential. True, if neither I nor anyone else had experienced the object there would be no one for whom it was meaningful and no one who would have occasion to adopt a word to stand for it. But the object, which *is* the meaning, would or could just as well nevertheless exist. It is obviously a condition of meaningful experience that there be human beings who have such experiences; it is a condition of meaningful human language that there be human beings who have experiences and who mark them by language. But given these conditions, the meaning of the experiences and the language used to mark it is constituted by the objects experienced and marked. The locus, the substance or essence, of meaning is not in language and it is certainly not in the community of human beings who share language. Rather, it is in the extralinguistic world. Human beings (and presumably various nonhuman creatures as well) have the good fortune of inhabiting a world replete with distinct, distinguishable, and hence meaningful entities. They also have the good fortune of being able to discern and distinguish those entities. They do not create meaning by contriving language, they invest such language as they choose to contrive with meanings that they appropriate, ready-made as it were, from the non- or extra-linguistic world. If God or nature had been mechanically inclined, there might have been brakes, rods, and levers. If so, human beings (and perhaps other creatures) would be capable of experiencing them as such, that is, as distinct, recognizable objects or entities. If a human being (or another creature capable of making and remembering what Locke called "articulate sounds") did so, and if for some reason she decided to mark that experience with the sounds or signs "brake," "rod," and "lever," those markers would acquire the meaning they now in fact have.

On some versions of this object-word or name-thing theory of language it is alleged that there is no special difficulty about interpersonal communication. Language took its beginnings from single-handed linguistic creations. Individual persons assigned names of their own contrivance to objects that they personally experienced. And each of us can create new words in this same manner. But once I have created a word I can teach it to others. I simply call their attention to the object and indicate that I use a particular word to stand for it. They understand what my word means and hence are in a position—if they so choose—to use the word in the same way that I do. This process of "ostensive teaching" (As Wittgenstein calls it [*PI*, I, 6]) can be repeated for an indefinitely large number of words, among an indefinitely large number of persons, and over any number of generations. Through it, words that began as personal and idiosyncratic become public and common. With the passage of generations a great many of the objects that make up the world that human beings inhabit are named and later generations learn and accept much of the vocabulary invented by their predecessors. This vocabulary becomes sufficiently extensive and customary to constitute not merely language (as opposed to a collection of meaningless sounds and marks) but *a* language in the sense of French or German and *the* language of entire peoples.

Of course Wittgenstein agrees that languages are public. Nor does he deny that many of the particulars of French, German, etc., their orthographies, vocabularies, distinctive verb structures, and so forth, developed and achieved customary status through historical processes that could have eventuated differently and that may, in their continuation, yield large-scale changes in many of the characteristics of these languages. Indeed his account, not being founded on the notion that words name objects the characteristics of which are known apart from language, is much more open to variability and change in language than are the accounts against which he is arguing. What he denies is that language *could* be individual or personal in the sense I have been discussing and could have become public by a historical and hence contingent process. Language is necessarily, essentially, public.

The basic elements of Wittgenstein's argument for the necessarily public character of language are present in his objections to the object-word theory that I have been discussing. But we can better appreciate his argument if we follow him in considering a variation on the object-word account that directly and explicitly challenges the view that some language, however it began, has become genuinely public. The variant in question (of which there are a number of versions) follows the object-word or thing-name account in holding that the meaning of a word is given by some extralinguistic entity for which the word stands or to which it refers. Its challenge to the shared, public character of language resides in its denial that one person can know the referents of another person's words. On some versions of the theory this difficulty presents itself in respect to "things" such as emotions and sensations that occur within the agent who experiences them and hence are not directly accessible to others. For example, I use the word "headache" to refer to pain that I am suffering. You cannot feel *my* headache. Hence you cannot know to what my word "headache" refers. In fact you too may have headaches and you too may use the word "headache" to refer to them. (God might know that this is the case.) But you cannot *know* that my word "headache" refers to the same kind of pain as does your word (and the reverse). We may suppose that we have this knowledge and we may act successfully on this supposition. But because the phenomenon to which my word refers is inaccessible to you (and the reverse), and because the meaning of words *is* their referent, you cannot know the meaning of my word (and I cannot know the meaning of your word). Language, or at least those parts of language that refer to states or events internal to the person who uses it (whose language it is), is necessarily private.

It is easy to see how the theory that these aspects of language are private can be extended to all of language. A premise sufficient to effect such an extension is that words which seem to refer to objects that are mutually accessible (stones, trees, etc.) in fact refer to images, percepts, sense data, or some other phenomena that are internal in the same way as sensations and emotions. If my word "tree" refers to an image or a sense datum in my mind, you can once again do no more than make suppositions about its meaning. On this view language ends as well as begins in experience that is not only personal but private. The idea that we do, or that we might some day come to, share a language (and all that depends upon it) is simply an illusion.

These theories of language and meaning have an obvious and an obviously important bearing on our present concerns. They support an understanding of action as meaningful (as a something rather than an anything or a nothing) despite not being situated in any sense beyond being located in a field of experience that is intelligible to the agent whose action is in question. If the word-object theory in the first form discussed is correct, an actor could identify herself and could discriminate among her various actions on the basis of nothing more than self-observation. If she entered into interactions with other persons she might observe herself taking actions that she could not take if she were isolated from others. And if those others had come to share her language through the process of mutual ostensive teaching, these actions and interactions might have the added dimension that is mutual meaningfulness. In these ways social dimensions would become a part of her understanding of herself and her actions. But these social dimensions would not be a necessary part of her self-understanding as an actor taking actions; they would be a necessary part of the meaning of only those of her actions that in fact involved her in interactions with other persons, and meaningfulness would be mutual only insofar as language had in fact come to be shared between or among them. If "necessarily private" versions of the word-object theory are correct, social dimensions in the sense of mutually meaningful action could enter into self-understandings either not at all or only in respect to those parts of language that refer to "external" phenomena.

Thus if these accounts of language and its meaning were correct they would support deeply atomistic understandings of action. They would support Hobbes's understanding of action in the state of nature (not surprising since Hobbes offers us an early version of the object-word theory of language). They would also support Humean and emotivist theories of that subclass of actions taken (according to these theories) as a direct, an unmediated, result of brute passions and desires. If the actor experiences a distinct and recognizable passion or desire, and if that passion or desire produces a distinct and recognizable action on the part of the actor, the conditions of meaningfulness have been satisfied. In identifying (naming) the desire and the action, the actor may employ language that (on the not-necessarily-private version of the object-name theory) she shares with others—even that she has learned from others; but for the purpose of accounting for the meaningfulness of her experiences this feature is nonessential. Thus whether it is impossible for others cogently to object to the action (as emotivists hold), or whether such objections are possible (as Taylor and MacIntyre contend), there is no difficulty about saying that such occurrences fall not only into the category "action" but into more differentiated categories that identify actions of particular kinds. Meaningful action that is radically unsituated, whether rare or commonplace, whether welcome, deplorable, or indifferent, is a conceptual possibility. Quite clearly, then, the adequacy of these theories is a matter of some moment.

Wittgenstein attacks these theories of language and meaning from a number of directions, his several lines of argument converging to show that they and everything that depends upon and follows from them is untenable. In the discussion leading to the brake-rod-lever passage he writes as if a major assumption of the object-word account is justified. The assumption is that an individual can create language that is meaningful to herself by inventing words and using them to stand for objects she has experienced. His initial attack is on the further and (apparently) more problematic proposition that she can make such language meaningful to others by ostensive teaching. He assumes that B (who is to learn the meaning of one or more of A's words) does not yet know any of A's language and hence that A cannot use words in teaching. A turns instead to a procedure very much like that which she herself followed in inventing the word for herself. Her attention had focused on a distinct object and she had invented a name to stand for it. To teach B the word, she uses gestures such as pointing to call B's attention to the object while pronouncing the word. The idea is to get B to make the same association between object and word that B herself makes, thereby learning the meaning of the word.

It is worth emphasizing immediately that nonverbal actions are thus assigned a vital role in the theory. The theory is not an object-word theory but an object-action-word theory. There is an important respect in which Wittgenstein has no objection to this modification of what appeared to be the theory. He himself puts acting "at the bottom" of language (Wittgenstein 1969, 204; hereafter cited as *OC*). On the assumptions of the theory he is criticizing, however, appeal to actions such as pointing and demonstrating is illicit and shows the theory to be untenable. The theory itself provides no reason for thinking that the meaning of such nonverbal communicative devices will be any clearer than the meaning of the words they are supposed to teach. If A points or otherwise calls B's attention to an object that she (A) has singled out and to which she has given the name "stone," B might take her gestures to single out not the "entire" object that A has in mind but some feature of it such as its color, shape, location, hardness, and so forth. Or B might think that A is pointing past or through the stone to something beyond or beneath it. B might even take what A intends as pointing to be some altogether different signal, for example a warning or a supplication. Just as with words themselves, in the absence of an understood "mechanism" in which they have an established place and use, ostensive communications "can be variously interpreted in every case." For the object-word theory, our successful use of these modes of communication (which of course Wittgenstein himself does not for a moment deny) is as much in need of explanation as our successful use of words.

There are numerous additional difficulties with object-word theories taken as an account of anything like the languages that we in fact employ. They are implausible in the extreme concerning so-called logical words such as "and," "or," "if," and "then," concerning negatives, privatives, and demonstratives; in their most philosophically influential versions they depend on a notion of "simple" or "atomic" entities that cannot be cogently explained, much less defended. But let us leave these points aside and consider instead Wittgenstein's argument that the objection to ostensive teaching applies just as decisively against the assumption that A herself can create language for her private use by picking out objects and assigning names to them. In considering this argument we confront the deepest and most uncompromising sense in which, according to Wittgenstein, all meaning is situated.

As noted, in passages discussed thus far Wittgenstein allows, *arguendo*, the assumption that A herself knows the referent, and hence the meaning of the words she invents for her own use. But how does she know this? We are tempted to say "Of course she knows. She herself identified the object and assigned the word to it." The very fact that the process of assigning the word is purely arbitrary seems to exclude the possibility that anything could go wrong with it, that any sort of mistake could be made in carrying it out.

As Anthony Kenny points out, Wittgenstein has frequently been interpreted as allowing the (initial) assignment or definition but raising the question whether A will later remember the definition correctly (Kenny 1973). On this view, A can successfully create language for herself but there is reason to doubt that she can successfully use it into the future. Having nothing to test her memory against, the objection goes, there is no way for her to be sure that her later uses of her words will stand for the same objects as those to which she initially assigned them. Thus for all she knows (can know), her entire "language" alters continuously as she uses it.

Kenny seems to me to be correct, however, in arguing that the difficulty Wittgenstein sees with the "necessarily private" version of the object-action-word account of meaning is deeper, or earlier, than this. Wittgenstein says: "I speak, and write the sign down, and at the same time I concentrate my attention on the sensation—and so, as it were point to it inwardly. —But what is this ceremony for? For that is all it seems to be! A definition surely serves to establish the meaning of a sign. . . . But 'I impress it on myself' can only mean: this process brings it about that I remember the connexion *right* in the future. [Emphasis in the original. Note that "right" is emphasized, not "remember."] But in the present case I have no criterion of correctness. One would like to say: whatever is going to seem right to me is right. And that only means that here we can't talk about 'right' " (*PI*, I, 258).[5] The deeper problem, then, is not with memory. It is that there is no criterion of "correct" or "right" and hence nothing to remember correctly or incorrectly. Or as Kenny formulates the point, the measure or criterion of correctness and that which it measures or tests are one and the same (1973, 191–95). This is why whatever seems correct is correct; it is also why claiming that the word has been used correctly is like claiming that one copy of the morning newspaper has substantiated reports in another copy of the same paper (*PI*, I, 265), why I cannot show that I know how tall I am by putting my hand on the top of my head (*PI*, I, 279), and why my left hand can't give money to my right hand. "[J]ustification consists in appealing to something independent" (*PI*, I, 265), and the account in question does itself out of that possibility.

These arguments show that many views and much controversy concerning human freedom are untenable and confused because concerned with an impossibility. Hobbes imagined human beings who inhabit a meaningful world and live lives meaningful to themselves despite being so radically unsituated, so atomized and privatized, that one person's thoughts and actions have no meaning to or for any other person. Hume and Ayer, Taylor and MacIntyre, think they have identified human beings at least a part of whose experience—that part which involves sensations, emotions, and desires and hence much if not all of morals and politics—is unsituated in this radical sense. Hobbes seems to have found this notion attractive and to have wanted to maintain at least a measure of privacy of this radical sort. Rousseau was apparently ambivalent about it and the freedom he took it to involve but he concluded that it could be eliminated and that it would be better for humankind if such privatism were overcome and a deeply situated and more "positive" freedom achieved. Hume and Ayer thought such privatism inescapable and busied themselves with dispelling the illusion that there is an alternative to it. Taylor and MacIntyre, while thinking such a privatism all too real and all too prevalent, regard it as a lamentable consequence of specific and alterable historical and cultural developments that must be reversed if significant human freedom is to be regained. In short, controversy swirls about the alterability and the desirability of "something" that Wittgenstein shows to be an impossibility. If human thought and action—and hence human freedom and unfreedom—are meaningful (if they are *thought*, *action*, *freedom*, *unfreedom* as opposed to anything or nothing) they are not and cannot be private or unsituated in the deep sense these writers have in mind. If there is a something in human experience that corresponds to what these writers are trying to discuss—think they are discussing—when they inveigh for or against atomism, privatism, subjectivism, and unsituatedness, that something is outside of the realm of the meaningful and there can be no discussion concerning it.

IV

Does Wittgenstein advance positive or constructive generalizations parallel to those that make up the refuted object-word theory? Can the claim that meaning and language are situated in "mechanisms" and "practices" be elaborated in more specific, less metaphorical terms? If so, does the appropriate elaboration show that human actions are so impeded or constrained by the factors that actuate them that we should say they are unfree?

The answer to the first of these questions is primarily negative. Wittgenstein has no comparably systematic or comprehensive theory of language and meaning to put in place of the object-word account that he refutes. Unlike the proponents of that and analogous general theories, he thinks that the project of identifying the essential characteristics of language and meaning and providing an explanation for them is misbegotten. On the one hand, the languages we know display a "prodigious diversity" (*PI*, II, xi, 224) of characteristics and the idea of reducing these to an essence is a misunderstanding. On the other hand, we have no need, no use, for general "explanations" of language and meaning. The meaning of our language is in its use and our use is not only "in order as it is," "but open to view." Philosophical attempts to generalize and explain distort and confuse rather than clarify or illuminate. What is needed is not generalizations and explanations but descriptions of the specifics of our practice (*PI*, I, 109), descriptions that remind us of what we already know and thereby dispel the mists of misunderstanding rising from the misconceptions of philosophers. We can show that language does *not* have certain characteristics that have been attributed to it and offered as explanations for its meaning. As a part of showing this, certain positive generalizations emerge—such as that meaning is in language, that it is in "mechanisms" and "practices," that it is in the uses to which language is put. But these generalizations are crude and uninformative; they are of value primarily as antidotes to the equally crude but mistaken generalizations advanced by other philosophers.

Accordingly, Wittgenstein characterizes the results of his investigations as making up no more than an "album" consisting of "sketches" of our actual practices. But these brilliantly executed sketches can be read as elaborating somewhat on the extremely general propositions about mechanisms and practices and hence as giving an answer of sorts to my second question. To combine and follow out two of Wittgenstein's own figures, someone who peruses an album of family photographs is likely to come away with certain general impressions concerning that family. To peruse Wittgenstein's sketches of the family that is language and meaning is to learn that those whose activities make up the mechanisms and practices in which language and meaning are situated characteristically agree in many judgments, know about, accept, and generally follow a variety of rules, customs, and conventions, have been exposed to and have more or less assimilated certain kinds of training, and have mastered certain techniques of following rules and commands, of acting on advice and suggestion. This perusal, moreover, reminds us that there are certain very general facts of nature, facts to which attention is seldom given by participants in such practices, which must be more or less as they are if the mechanisms and practices are to remain more or less what they have become. We are also reminded that these circumstances do not always obtain; that human beings sometimes find one another and one another's activities alien, opaque, and incomprehensible.

I return to these notions—agreements, rules, training, and so forth—below. But we can see at once that none of them are at all technical. They recur in Wittgenstein's sketches because they are prominent in the activities and arrangements he is sketching. If they were not familiar, ordinary, and even homely notions they would not serve as "reminders" of what we already know and would not help to dispel the confusions created by philosophers. Arriving at and acting upon agreements, adopting and following rules, giving and receiving training and instruction, these are among our most familiar experiences. By invoking them in the course of his philosophical discussions, Wittgenstein gives a certain substantiality, a certain definiteness, to more abstract notions such as "mechanisms," "practices," and "language-games" and to the yet more general idea that meaning and meaningfulness are "situated" in character. At bottom, the situatedness of human affairs consists in such facts as that there are agreements and conventions, rules and directives, that people who share these thereby "know how to go on" in and with various activities, and so forth. As we might put it, when elaborated in these familiar terms the idea that meaning and meaningfulness are situated itself becomes a something, not an anything or a nothing.

What of the third question raised above? What bearing does this elaboration have on questions about human freedom and unfreedom? Of course it has the bearing already anticipated in my earlier discussions. Questions about freedom and unfreedom arise—as all questions do—only within the realm of the meaningful. We now see that this means that such questions arise only where human beings agree on certain judgments, only where some conventions and rules have gotten established and are generally respected, and so forth. And it might be thought that this shows that Wittgenstein's views, if correct, do much more than identify the conditions that must be satisified if questions about freedom are to arise and be discussed in a meaningful fashion. It might be thought that his views settle major questions about freedom. Notions like facts of nature, technique and training, custom and rule—even the notion of agreement in the Wittgensteinian sense of something about which a consensus exists despite not having been self-consciously and self-critically reached or adopted—these notions can easily be made to suggest limitation and constraint, restriction and obstacle. If the situatedness necessary to meaningfulness entails these elements, it might yet appear that human beings acquire the meaningfulness of their lives at the cost of their freedom.

The questions that present themselves in this regard concern such notions as obstacles and impediments, constraints, interferences, and restrictions. Are we to say that the features or conditions that Wittgenstein associates with meaningfulness are obstacles or interferences that render us unfree? At this stage my discussion will focus on the feature, namely, rules and rule-following, in respect to which an affirmative answer has at least initial plausibility. But I preface this discussion with some preliminary observations.

First, it is not to be thought that Wittgenstein himself has *any* questions about freedom—let alone the question whether the conditions of meaningfulness exclude or limit freedom—in mind. We can bring considerations from Wittgenstein's philosophy to bear on questions about freedom, but we cannot explicate "Wittgenstein's theory of freedom." Second, from a Wittgensteinian perspective the question I propose to address has more than a faint air of absurdity about it. Most generally, if there are meaningful questions about freedom and unfreedom, they quite obviously must arise under or within the conditions of meaningfulness. If the conditions of meaningfulness themselves categorically excluded freedom, there would seem to be no use for the concept "freedom" in meaningful discourse. This consideration suggests that my question will have sense, if at all, only if it is asked in much narrower terms, much more concretely. Did these rules, in this set of circumstances, interfere with or constrain these attempted actions to an extent that justifies us in saying that some person was made unfree? It is a delusion to think that there is a general analysis of the concepts "rule," "restraint," "freedom," and "unfreedom" which would allow us to conclude that rules as such exclude or impede, create or facilitate freedom or unfreedom.

But what is absurd in practice may seem plausible to the theorist. As we have seen, political theory is no stranger to the idea that society itself excludes or severely limits freedom. This notion is at work in various ways in state-of-nature and social-contract theories and something like it is not far beneath the surface in romantic individualisms and other theories that treat freedom as—in Charles Taylor's phrase— radical self-dependence. More pejoratively, the idea, though rejected, is taken seriously indeed in attacks on freedom as "license" or as "doing as one lists." Finally, what might be regarded as its opposite is frequently encountered in slogans such as "liberty is life under the rule of law."

We should also note that Wittgenstein himself gives many pages to refuting understandings of rules and rule-following according to which a sufficiently detailed and integrated set of rules would "determine everything in advance," would settle every question that could possibly arise in the activity governed by those rules. Wittgenstein's concern in these passages is not to defend the possibility of freedom. Philosophers have tried to find in strictly drawn rules the source, indeed the necessity and hence the guarantee, of a kind of certitude of meaning and of truth without which meaningfulness and knowledge seem to them to be in jeopardy. Wittgenstein thinks that as a practical matter we are sometimes certain about meaning (and about truth, validity, and many other things), sometimes much less than certain. He agrees that rules and rule-following are prominent in meaningful speech and action and he allows that some (but not all) of the areas of greatest practical certainty—such as doing logic and arithmetic and playing certain games—are characterized by quite closely drawn rules. But neither these nor any of our other activities or practices achieve or permit the kind of metaphysical or guaranteed certainty imagined by philosophers. This ideal of a certainty that derives from rules that form a "strict calculus" is not a result of investigations in logic, mathematics, or any other subject matter, it is a requirement imposed in advance on such investigations. Wittgenstein rejects it not because achieving it would threaten freedom but for the same reason that he rejects the object-word account of language, namely, that it prevents us from seeing our practice as it actually is.

The details of Wittgenstein's discussions of rules and rule-following are nevertheless pertinent to the questions now before us. Some rules do require and forbid, direct and deflect. If we do not understand that rules can be substantial impediments and inducements to action we have not grasped the notion of a rule. Moreover, "rules," "rule-governed conduct," "rule-following," and the like bulk very large in Wittgenstein's writings. There are a number of passages in which he makes rules necessary to meaning and hence to meaningful thought and action. Of "not," its negative force and such facts as that a double negative yields an affirmative, he observes that "There cannot be a question whether these or other rules are the correct ones for the use of 'not.' (I mean, whether they accord with its meaning.) For without these rules the word has as yet no meaning; and if we change the rules, it now has another meaning (or none), and in that case we may just as well change the word too" (*PI*, I, remark appended to pars. 548–51; cf. *PI*, I, 558, and *OC*, 62). At least in respect to the concepts under discussion in these passages, rules emerge as essential features of the "mechanisms" in which there can be a something as opposed to an anything or a nothing. Much more generally, Wittgenstein contends that all language "is founded on convention."[6] If we interpret "convention" to include prescriptive or normative rules, as opposed to regularities discerned by observers, this remark greatly extends the significance of the passages already cited.

We must also consider remarks that are yet more encompassing because they employ the concepts "normal" and "abnormal" as well as "rule" and "convention." "It is only in normal cases that the use of a word is clearly prescribed; we know, are in no doubt, what to say in this or that case. The more abnormal the case, the more doubtful it becomes what we are to say" (*PI*, I, 142). "Clearly prescribed," "we know," "are in no doubt," go together with numerous passages in which Wittgenstein writes as if prescriptive rules virtually settle what is thought, said, or otherwise done. For example, of someone who has learned how to pronounce the Cyrillic alphabet "we shall very likely say that he *derives* the sound of the word from the written pattern by the rule that we have given him" (*PI*, I, 162). Similarly, persons teaching algebra are likely to say to their pupils: "But surely you can see . . . ," which "is just the characteristic expression of someone who is under the compulsion of a rule" (*PI*, I, 240, 238). Again: "Disputes do not break out (among mathematicians, say) over the question whether a rule has been obeyed or not." And: having mastered the colour concepts "it is a matter of course for me to call this colour 'blue' " (*PI*, I, 240, 238). But these certitudes, these matter-of-course derivations and applications, these compulsions, are hostage to "normalities" which, while no doubt defined or delineated by prescriptive rules and perhaps partly created and maintained by allegiance to such rules, could be otherwise. Prescriptive rules and rule-following are interwoven with and vitally dependent upon "mere" regularities. Where rules in the latter sense do not exist, prescriptive rules and rule-followng lose their certainty and finally their sense. "And if things were quite different from what they actually are . . . ; if rule became exception and exception rule; or if both became phenomena of roughly equal frequency—this would make our normal language-games lose their point" (*PI*, I, 142; II, xi, 226).

If we translate these discussions into the language of freedom and unfreedom we might well infer that our freedom is the price we pay for the meaningfulness of our lives. We are under the compulsion of rules and those rules are, in turn, hostage to a nature that we did not choose and that we can alter little if at all. But are these the appropriate inferences? To pursue this question let us consider more closely the "things" that must be more or less as they are. Wittgenstein's immediate example is homely in the extreme: "if it frequently happened" that for no obvious reason lumps of cheese grew or shrank, "the procedure of putting . . . [them] on a balance and fixing the price by the turn of the scale would lose its point" (ibid.). In this same connection he observes that "What we have to mention in order to explain the significance . . . of a concept, are often extremely general facts of nature: such facts as are hardly ever mentioned because of their great generality" (*PI*, I, remark appended near pars. 142–43; cf. *OC*, 135, 338, 617). A certain constancy in the natural world is a background condition of rules and rule-governed activities and practices. But it would be wrong to think that these conditions themselves determine the content of the prescriptive rules—that they supply what moralists have called a Natural Law or a Natural Right that governs human affairs at least in the sense that in time a price will be exacted if the Law or Right is not heeded. Rather, they partly constitute the circumstances under which normative rules and rule-following—whatever their content—are a *possibility* for human beings.

This understanding is affirmed and deepened if we note that some of the general facts of nature that are in particular need of "mention" are facts about human beings themselves. All of Wittgenstein's examples of such "human" facts are mundane, but we may begin with an instance that is distinctive in being remarked with some frequency. For most human beings, use of color terms such as "blue," "red," and so forth is "matter of course." "There is," in other words, "in general complete agreement in the judgment of colours." But this agreement obtains only among "those who have been diagnosed normal." "There is such a thing as colour-blindness and there are ways of establishing it." These facts characterize "the concept of a judgment of colour" (*PI*, II, ix, 227). If these facts about human vision were otherwise, rules and rule-following—and hence the system of color concepts that we in fact have—would be impossible.

The case of colors stands out for remark because color blindness is fairly common and well understood. But capacities and characteristics akin to the ability to distinguish between colors are presupposed by all human activities and practices and hence by all rules and rule-following. Wittgenstein mentions various specifics in this regard. It is "natural" for human beings to know the position of their limbs even when they can't see them (*PI*, II, viii, 185–86), to see three-dimensionally (*PI*, II, xi, 198), to differentiate among the "aspects" of a drawing of figure (*PI*, II, xi, 213–14), to groan, grimace, or cry out when in pain (*PI*, I, 244), and to be sure how many toes they have despite wearing shoes (*PI*, I, 505; *OC*, 430). More generally, human beings characteristically respond in certain ways to teaching, training, and related experiences. Pupils grasp and accept what they are told or shown by their teachers. There is of course a sense in which it is *logically* necessary that for the most part they do so. I cannot doubt *this* without presupposing much else (*OC*, 115, 160). But Wittgenstein's point here is as much anthropological as it is a rejoinder to skepticism (or to the more grandiose delusions of those in quest of fully "critical," fully presuppositionless theories). Children who persistently doubted their teachers would be incapable of learning (*OC*, 283). Nor is the general point here limited to the young. "My *life* consists in my being content to accept many things" (*OC*, 344). There is an entire system of beliefs, indeed a "whole system of verification," that "a human being acquires by means of observation and instruction," one that provides a "picture of the world" that is the "background against which I distinguish between true and false" (*OC*, 279, 40). The "countless general empirical propositions" that make up this system, for example, that if someone's arm is cut off it will not grow again, if someone's head is cut off he is dead and will never live again, that cats do not grow on trees, that motor cars do not grow out of the earth (*OC*, 274; 282, 279), while not logically interdependent, "hang together" in our belief and thought. "We feel that if someone could believe the contrary he could believe *everything* that we say is untrue, could question everything that we hold to be sure" (*OC*, 279). "To have doubts about [these things] would seem to me madness"; if someone "were to pronounce the opposite of these propositions . . . we should not just not share his opinion: we should regard him as demented" (*OC*, 281, 155). "In order to make a mistake, a man must already judge in conformity with mankind" (*OC*, 156).

Elizabeth Anscombe has brought these Wittgensteinian thoughts directly to bear on prescriptive rules that enjoin and forbid. She writes: "These 'musts' and 'can'ts' are the most basic expression of such-and-such's being a rule; just as they are the most basic expression in learning the rules of a game, and as they are too in being taught rights and manners. . . . These 'musts' and 'can'ts' are understood by those of normal intelligence as they are trained in the practices of reason" (1978, 323). Prescriptive rules operate within the confines of the "natural" possibilities of human beings and their world. That is, it is characteristic for such rules to say that one must or must not act in a manner in which, as a matter of the Wittgensteinian facts I have been discussing, one plainly can act or can avoid acting. Thus such rules can be thought to narrow those natural confines, to place further limits upon us. Are they therefore impositions that are sources or causes of unfreedom? Let us follow Anscombe's discussion somewhat further. In some cases adults who are teaching prescriptive rules to children "will physically stop the child from doing what they say he 'can't' do. But gradually the child learns. With one set of circumstances this business is part of the build-up of the concept of a rule; with another, of a piece of etiquette; with another of a promise; in another, of an act of sacrilege or impiety; with another of a right" (1978, 321). The child may sometimes resist or resent the particulars of such teaching—perhaps rightly so. And it is worth remembering that on some views *all* such teaching runs counter to the child's "nature" in the sense not only of her original physical and psychological makeup but of tendencies and psychological dynamics that can be channeled and directed, perhaps repressed or sublimated, but never eliminated. On these views, the process of "being trained in the practices of reason" is one of losing natural freedom and may be regarded as a process of being denatured. Note, however, that Anscombe writes of the buildup of the *concept* of a rule, of a promise, of an impiety. A child who lacks those concepts, whatever her psycho-physical characteristics, can neither obey nor disobey rules, can be neither polite nor impolite, pious nor sacrilegious. Accordingly, the child who lacks these concepts could be neither free nor unfree to conform to or rebel against rules, to respect the rights of others or to violate those rights. True, the concept of a rule loses application if exception becomes as frequent as rule. In *this* sense, the child who learns these concepts thereby learns to obey or conform. But learning this general lesson is not to learn to obey *this* rule under *these* circumstances, to keep *this* promise made to *that* person. Rather, it is to learn to be a participant in the practices of rules and promising, practices that include disobedience and promise-breaking. Moreover, learning these general lessons is "natural" in the sense of Wittgenstein's "general facts of nature." In Anscombe's words, "It is part of human intelligence to be able to learn the responses to [musts and can'ts. If this weren't true, must and can'ts] . . . wouldn't exist as linguistic instruments, and these things: rules, etiquette, rights, infringements, promises, pieties and impieties [and much, much more] would not exist either" (1958, 321).

None of this is to deny that "linguistic instruments" and the rule-governed practices of which they are a part can be repressive or otherwise objectionable. Talk of "what the reasonable man accepts," of learning "the practices of human reason," and the like must not be construed as an endorsement of passivity, Panglossianism, or even the kind of conservatism that tends to find merit in the particulars of established social and political arrangements and to counsel acceptance and accommodation. Wittgenstein and Anscombe are discussing conditions that are equally necessary to conservatism and radicalism, conformism and antinomianism, fatalism and activism. Decisions to accept or reject an arrangement or practice, a norm or rule, an order or a piece of advice, presuppose the setting that they describe. It remains to be seen whether reflections of theirs have a more immediate bearing on such decisions. But before pursuing that question I pause to underline an implication contained in the foregoing discussion.

VI

The passages I have been considering deepen the senses in which rules and rule-governed conduct are "situated." Human and nonhuman nature provide the setting in which our conduct occurs, a setting that establishes conditions necessary to our conduct as we know it. If these general facts of nature were significantly different than we know and accept them to be, our concepts—and hence our activities and practices—would be impossible and/or quite different (*PI*, II, xii, 230). Taken at all literally, the notion of persons who are self-subsistent and whose conduct is sui generis is absurd because it denies or inadequately appreciates this fact. There are biologically human persons whose behavior departs strikingly from these regularities; noticing this may lend credibility to extreme versions of voluntarism, atomism, and "unsituatedness." The general facts of nature that Wittgenstein invokes are just that, that is, *general* facts; they are not necessary or even universal truths. But insofar as the behavior of a person or group is at variance with these general facts, to that extent the rest of us find it difficult to "find our feet with them" (*PI*, II, xi, 223; and see I, 206–7). Conduct that is mutually meaningful—and hence *possibly* freedom-evaluable—is conduct within these general facts as they are accepted by the "reasonable" participants in a form of life. These facts, and the limits they "impose" on our conduct, are for the most part beyond our powers to change. For example, no amount of training, no regimen, will enable any of us to jump, unaided, twenty-five feet straight up from the surface of the earth, to develop gills instead of or in addition to lungs, and so forth. But it is misleading to say either that these facts are imposed on us or to say that we choose to conduct ourselves within the limits they set. These facts and the broad patterns of our conduct within them are integral to, not alien from or chosen as part of, our lives. Few if any of us decide to stand upright, to walk by moving first one foot and then the other, or to see figures three-dimensionally (albeit physically normal children who are in rebellion against their parents or teachers may adopt bizarre postures and gaits, may refuse to see the dimensions of figures presented in a geometry lesson, and so on). These and innumerable other modes of acting are "natural" in the sense that from very early on they "come easily" to us and we become habituated to and comfortable with them. Departures and deviations from them may indeed occur and may meet with surprise, disapproval, and punishment. It is nevertheless rare for them to be viewed as chosen or freely done, as required or compelled. In respect to much of the "common behavior of mankind" most of us simply are "at home" in and with our world and ourselves. Our nature and our conventions are interwoven; descriptive regularity and prescriptive rule are largely continuous one with the other. In these deep respects our lives are—ineluctably—situated.

VII

The passages I have been examining might be viewed as an essential background to those of Wittgenstein's discussions that bear more directly on questions of freedom and unfreedom, background to his treatment of rules that are more explicitly adopted or promulgated and to rule-following that is more self-consciously obedient or disobedient. But there is no sharp distinction, no clear demarcation, between "background" and "foreground," between the conditions necessary to rule-following that is freedom-evaluable and such rule-following itself. The anthropology discussed thus far does not settle whether self-conscious rule-following and rule-breaking is done in freedom or unfreedom; it does place constraints upon any discussion of that question.

Most definitely and undeniably, from a Wittgensteinian point of view any thesis to the effect that rules and rule-following *as such* contribute to or detract from human freedom will be not so much true or false as absurd. Secondly, the elements and characteristics that make up the general anthropology enter into, are a part of, all human action. We should not think of them as merely a stage on which, or even a stage-setting in which, action occurs; rather, they should be regarded as characteristics of the participants in the human drama, characteristics that influence all of the events and actions that occur in all of the plays that are performed. These general characteristics are compatible with a prodigious diversity of practices and activities, of decisions and choices, interactions and outcomes. But for philosophical purposes (whether those purposes are understood as achieving a general understanding of the diverse array, or, more modestly, as dissolving puzzles and conundrums that develop concerning this or that activity or practice) we must attend to the general characteristics.

Thirdly and more specifically, in Wittgenstein's account rules and rule-following do not divide cleanly between, on the one hand, tacit, unstated and unself-consciously followed background agreements and norms and, on the other hand, explicit, codified, and deliberately obeyed or disobeyed rules or laws. Rather, all rules and rule-following present a complex combination or amalgam of these and other characteristics. Development of this third point should further clarify understanding of the relationship between situatedness and freedom.

Rules do not apply themselves. Whether as deeply settled, as matter of course, but as infrequently stated as the rules governing color concepts, or whether as clearly articulated but sharply controversial as the law that all eighteen-year-old males must register with the Selective Service system, rules must be applied by persons who are participants in or practitioners of the activity or practice of which the rules are part. To make such applications, to "know how to go on" with the activity, participants must know more than the formulation of the rules themselves and must have acquired qualities and abilities over and above the "background" characteristics discussed thus far. In some places Wittgenstein calls these further characteristics the "mastery of a technique" (*PI*, I, 199, 150). In another place he speaks of some of them as "knowing one's way about" in the activity in question (*PI*, II, xi, 203). "What tells us that someone is seeing the drawing three dimensionally is a certain kind of 'knowing one's way about'. Certain gestures, for instance, which indicate the three-dimensional relations: fine shades of behaviour" (*PI*, II, xi, p. 203)[7] These "techniques," this "knowing one's way about," are typically specific to an activity or perhaps to a family of related activities; experience with and training in that activity are virtually always necessary in order to acquire the techniques. Some learn more quickly and surely than others, and it is often difficult, or rather pointless, to set a minimum standard that must be satisfied in order to say that someone is "able to go on" (*PI*, I, p. 61). But in the circumstances in which questions of performance present themselves in practical form, this seeming indeterminancy does not prevent us from deciding who can go on and who cannot, who can go on fluently, easily, and sure-handedly, who is prone to mistake, to uncertainty, and to getting stuck.

There is nothing mysterious or even notably obscure in these notions. Consider activities involving, among other things, moderately complex or intricate physical skills and tasks. The rules for making omelettes and soufflés are readily available in any number of recipe books and cooking guides. If I wish, I can commit these rules to memory so that I can recite them flawlessly and in that sense teach them to others. Yet my omelettes and soufflés seldom come out well. Although I follow the rules closely, I am clumsy with the implements, my timing is poor, I do not adapt effectively to minor variations in ingredients and equipment. There is a technique that I have not mastered. Consider Wittgenstein's account of teaching concepts:

> How do I explain the meaning of "regular," "uniform," "same" to anyone? I shall explain these words to someone who, say, only speaks French by means of the corresponding French words. But if a person has not yet got the *concepts*, I shall teach him to use the words by means of *examples* and by practice.— And when I do this I do not communicate less to him than I know myself.
>
> In the course of this teaching I shall show him the same colours, the same lengths, the same shapes, I shall make him find them and produce them, and so on. I shall, for instance, get him to continue an ornamental pattern uniformly when told to do so.—And also to continue progressions. . . .
> I do it, he does it after me; and I influence him by expressions

of agreement, rejection, expectation, encouragement. I let him go his way, or hold him back; and so on.

Imagine witnessing such teaching. None of the words would be explained by means of itself; there would be no logical circle (*PI*, I, 208)

When the student can continue a variety of patterns, do various progressions, and the like, he "has got" the concepts, and the role of the teacher is at an end. When I can successfully make a variety of omelettes and soufflés, with various pans, in my own kitchen as well as in the one at the cooking school, I have mastered these culinary techniques.

Can I now, that is, with nothing more, follow the rules of soufflé-making? Is the kind of tuition Wittgenstein describes sufficient to allow his pupil to follow the rules governing "regular," "same," and "uniform"? Given the way the examples have been presented (and continuing to assume the more general conditions discussed earlier), the answer is almost certainly "yes." But that is because the presentations assume that the learners understand and accept what Wittgenstein calls the purposes of the activities and the ways in which the rules and techniques contribute to achieving them. Wittgenstein says: "The game, one would like to say, has not only rules but also a point" (*PI*, I, 564). If we do not see the reason for a rule, the way it connects to the "point" of the game, we are puzzled as to what to do with or in response to it, "as one wouldn't see the point . . . of a rule by which each piece had to be turned round three times before one moved it. If we found this rule in a board-game we should be surprised and should speculate about the purpose of the rule." (He imagines someone speculating, "Was this prescription meant to prevent one from moving without due consideration?") (*PI*, I, 567).

Wittgenstein is not advancing a fixed or a systematic teleology (any more than he is advancing a structuralism or a generalized *Rechtsstaat-philosophie*). If someone were to say "The purpose of language is to express thoughts," a proper rejoinder would be, "So presumably the purpose of every sentence is to express a thought. Then what thought is expressed, for example, by the sentence 'It's raining'?" (*PI*, I, 501). Purposiveness is a usual, an ordinary characteristic of human activities; it is sometimes helpful to remind ourselves of this fact. But there is no general purpose that is served by all of our activities, and there is no single, unvarying purpose or objective that is pursued in all instances of any kind, type, or class of activities. The purposes served by our rules and our rule-following are as diverse as our activities themselves. Any number of generalizations can be made. Capitalists seek to earn profits, coaches to win games, politicians to gain reelection. Someone who didn't understand these settled, ordinary purposes would have great difficulty in understanding the actions of capitalists, coaches, and politicians. For the same reason, capitalists or coaches who did not pursue these objectives would be eccentric and others would be at least initially puzzled and perhaps soon enough upset, offended, or even outraged by their actions. There are shared, established, ordinary purposes of activities and their rules and, pleonastically, the purposes of most participants coincide with them. But "subliming" or "hyposta-sizing" purpose is foolish; as foolish—and for the same reasons—as subliming "rule," "technique," or "fact of nature." Idiosyncratic, eccentric, and deviant purposes are not only possible but abound.[8] Indeed, "do I always talk with a very definite purpose?—And is what I say [or do] meaningless because I don't?" (*PI*, II, ix, 188).

The words "rules" and "rule-following," it emerges, refer to a large and diverse family of phenomena each member of which is itself a complex of elements or features. There are boundaries or limits to the family. For example, obeying a rule and acting on an inspiration "are surely not the same. In the case of inspiration I *await* direction. I shall not be able to teach anyone else my 'technique' of following the line. Unless, indeed, I teach him some way of hearkening, some kind of receptivity. But then, of course, I cannot require him to follow the line in the same way as I do" (*PI*, I, 232). For the same reasons, obeying a rule is not something that only one person could do, that a person could do only once, or that one could do "privately." "['O]beying a rule' is a practice," a "custom," a "use," an "institution" (*PI*, I, 197–202). Sometimes, in some classes of cases, such practices become "matter of course"; practitioners can engage in them as if "by the numbers." In other cases there is much deciding and choosing, inter-preting and adjusting, and hence there is likely to be disagreement and conflict. But in no case is this due to any magical properties of rules or any special illumination in the minds or distinctive foresight on the part of the rule-followers. Rather, it is because the several elements charac-teristic of rules and rule-following—the elements I have been discuss-ing—have or have not coalesced with firmness and in harmony. "Where is the connection effected between 'Let's play a game of chess' and all the rules of the game? Well, in the list of the rules of the game, in the teaching of it, in the day-to-day practice of playing" (*PI*, I, 197). Rules are not something apart from practice that can be invoked to explain the latter; they are part of practice, vary with variation in practices, and must be understood in or rather with them. (And doing so well takes practice.)

VIII

Let us now return to our starting point in the last section of this chapter. It emerges that such questions as "What is *the* relationship between rules and freedom?" and "Do rules and rule-following as such contribute to or detract from freedom?" betray misunderstandings at one or more levels. To summarize: First, rules and rule-following do not constitute a single, homogeneous phenomenon; hence they cannot stand in an invariant relationship to freedom (or to anything else). Second, in respect to many rules and much rule-following questions of freedom simply do not arise in a significant manner. Rules and rule-following are among the conditions that must be satisfied *in order that* questions of freedom can arise. Third, there are cases of rules and of rule-following that are freedom-evaluable in certain respects. But such evaluations turn not on features common to all rules and rule-following (there are no such features) but on features of the particular rules themselves and of the circumstances and activities in which they present themselves to be followed or not. All rule-following requires choices as to "how to go on," as to what the rule requires or allows, as to what will count as obeying or disobeying the rule. These choices may be made and implemented under circumstances that will warrant us in saying that they were made in freedom or in unfreedom. But because the rules and rule-following themselves, that is, the rules and rule-following understood as a complex of elements such as I have been discussing, do not themselves dictate or determine the decisions and choices, it cannot be said that the rules and rule-following eliminate or guarantee freedom. Of course such rules and such rule-following are "somethings," not "anythings" or "nothings." Accordingly, the choices of persons whose acting takes place in a practice or setting which involves rules will be circumscribed in various ways and to varying degrees. Thus a number of possibilities present themselves. Insofar as these circumscriptions are objectionable to those to whom the rules apply, we have elements relevant to (although rarely if ever conclusive concerning) a judgment on their part that the rules detract from their freedom. Insofar as the circumscriptions prevent or deter others from actions that would interfere with my conduct, or require of others conduct that enlarges my possibilities of action, we have elements relevant to a judgment on my part that the rules enhance my freedom. There are numerous other such possibilities, some of which I will consider in the next chapter. But at this juncture the further point to underline (that is, further to the point that rules do not apply themselves) is that rules and rule-following are integral to human thought and action. We can object to the content of this, that, or the next rule; but to object categorically to rules and rule-following is incoherent because the objections cannot be framed or stated without presupposing and following various rules. Equally, to object generally is to put oneself at war with a distinctive feature of human life and hence with oneself as a participant in human life.

The fourth point, although less explicit in Wittgenstein's discussions, is an inference warranted by those discussions (as well as a proposition one would be hard put to deny from any perspective). The fact that there are rules and a general practice or pattern of rule-following does not and cannot itself settle the question whether this or that agent will follow particular rules, will endeavor to act in a manner consonant with the rules that apply to her. We must remind ourselves once again that if exception and rule, if obedience and disobedience, became phenomena of roughly equal frequency, rules and rule-following would be at an end. But equally, the concepts "rule-following," "conformity," and "obedience" require such further concepts as "disobedience," "deviance," "rule-breaking," and even "indifference to rules." The possibility of nonconformity is conceptually necessary to the practice of rules and rule-following in every sense of "rule" other than mere observer-discerned regularity. Indeed, the fact that there is a rule requiring a mode of action is itself always eligible to be regarded as a reason for refusing to perform an action in that mode.

To these four points we can add a fifth which is also recognizably Wittgensteinian in character as well as familiar from our most basic experiences with rules and rule-following. Rules do not stand in isolation one from another. We encounter them in systems, in sets, in constellations or combinations. And it is not infrequently the case that the rules that make up a system or a set conflict with the rules that make up another or others. For these reasons, the most steadfast, even the most unthinking, of rule-followers, will from time to time find herself with no practical alternative to conduct that violates one or more rules. Consideration of such occurrences might tempt us to say not that obedience to rules is unfreedom but rather that we are, at least sometimes, unfree to obey rules. This temptation should of course be resisted; in its generic formulation the view it advances confuses impossibility, even logical impossibility, with unfreedom. But we know that rule-makers sometimes seek to prevent or diminish freedom by entrapping the law-abiding among their subjects in a web of conflicting rules. And we also know that moderately skillful rule-followers can enlarge their freedom of action by taking advantage of unintended and perhaps ineliminable conflicts within or among systems or sets of rules. In conjunction with the other considerations that have emerged from this examination of Wittgenstein, these commonplaces caution against generalizations concerning the relationship between rules and human freedom; they therefore also warn against the view that the situatedness of human activity tells for or against its (our) freedom.

6

Freedom and Modern Sociality

Reverting to MacCallum's analysis of "freedom" as involving agents, objectives, and obstacles, we can think of much of the previous chapter as examining whether situatedness as such is an obstacle that does or could prevent or significantly qualify human freedom. In this perspective, the outcome was that situatedness in the generic sense is a supposition of human freedom and hence cannot itself be an obstacle to it. Phenomena are of course bounded by their postulates but it is therefore absurd to think of the latter as apart from and hence as constituting obstacles or impediments to the former. Turning this outcome about, we can go further and say that, as Wittgenstein construes situatedness, freedom-evaluability is a supposition of it. That is, Wittgensteinian situatedness is an estate of creatures capable of and in fact more or less steadily conceiving of themselves as enjoying or being deprived of freedom$_2$. Freedom-evaluability is a supposition of situatedness because the latter is an estate of mutual or shared meaning-(fulness) possible only for creatures who form, hold, and alter beliefs, frame and attempt to act upon intentions, adopt and pursue goals and purposes. In conceptual terms, "situatedness" and "freedom-evaluability" stand in an internal relationship one to the other. "Situatedness" imports more than "freedom-evaluability" and "freedom-evaluability" more than "situatedness," but there cannot be the one without the other. Thus the notion that situatedness is an obstacle to or restriction upon freedom is incoherent.

This and my other previous conclusions are no more than bare beginnings concerning the concepts of obstacles and impediments, interferences and restrictions. Earlier I argued against the view that desires "enslave" on the ground that desires are integral to the actions and attempted actions in which they figure and hence cannot be obstacles to those actions. I have now made the analogous argument that situatedness cannot be conceived as an obstacle to freedom because it is itself a necessary condition of actions and attempted actions. If correct, these conclusions set limits to the cogent use of notions like obstacle and impediment, restriction and interference, and hence to the notion of unfreedom. But these limits are very broad. They are transgressed, and hence there is point in insisting on them, only in highly abstract discourse or, perhaps, in respect to views that are genuinely radical in their challenge to underlying assumptions and deeply established understandings and arrangements. The detailed work of clarifying the third of MacCallum's term variables, as they figure in discourse that is clearly within the limits I have thus far identified, remains to be done.

The present chapter attempts to take this matter somewhat further by examining the possibility that situatedness in the forms characteristic of modern Western societies constitutes an obstacle or impediment to the freedom of all or most of the members of those societies. To use the language of the previous chapter, I now move from a generic concept of situatedness to more specific and empirically instantiated conceptions. To use the language of the previous paragraph, I take up some arguments that are genuinely radical in their challenges to received assumptions and firmly established practices. To see wherein those challenges consist, and to appreciate the difficulties of assessing them, I need first to advance some claims of my own about the societies at issue.

I

I said that situatedness and freedom-evaluability suppose one another. Descending somewhat from these heights of abstraction, I now make the further suggestion that in the modern (again, post-Hobbes) societies of the Western tradition, the belief has become widely shared that freedom-evaluability is the proper state of affairs for human beings, the state of affairs that not only does obtain but that ought to be recognized and made a foundational element in thought and action. Human beings ought to be understood as agents, not merely as subjects, and their relations with one another ought to be regulated by this understanding. It is recognized and allowed that there are exceptions to this view. Some human beings (*Homo sapiens*) fail to develop, or lose, the characteristics that make for freedom-evaluability; others are obliged to recognize this fact and adjust their conduct to it. But claims

to this effect, claims that this or that human being lacks these characteristics, are suspect, and a heavy burden of proof falls on those who
advance them. More obviously, actions and policies that destroy or
diminish freedom-evaluability are deeply objectionable.

Freedom-evaluability is not to be confused with freedom itself; the
understanding just discussed does not settle whether any A or class of
A's are or should be free to do any X or class of X's. But the
understanding that human beings are and should be regarded as freedom-evaluable has a definite bearing on questions about freedom
versus unfreedom.

To subscribe to that understanding is to value manifestations,
embodiments, and exemplifications of the characteristics of which
freedom-evaluability consists. It is to value agency and action. And it
is therefore also to value the circumstances or conditions that are
conducive to agency and action. Among these conditions is freedom in
the negative sense, the condition of not being prevented from taking
the actions one has chosen to take. Freedom is of course not a necessary condition of agency or of freedom-evaluability. Freedom-
evaluability is manifested by, is embodied in, prevented attempts to
act as well as in acts that are successfully completed. For this reason
there is no formal contradiction involved in valuing agency, in conced-
ing that a person is an agent, but nevertheless regarding oneself as
justified in preventing many or even all of the acts which that person
attempts. On the face of it, however, such a combination of proposi-
tional attitudes would appear to be incoherent. To value a phenomenon is, other things being equal, to want it not only to obtain but
to flourish. The capacities necessary to freedom-evaluability might
sustain themselves in circumstances of persistent, widespread unfreedom; but because the objects and purposes of the agent would
seldom be achieved, it would be perverse to say that agency was
flourishing. As a matter of practical reasoning the understanding that
human beings should be regarded and treated as freedom-evaluable
creates a presumption that they should be free rather than unfree. Just
as the understanding places a burden of justification on those who
deny that some human beings are freedom-evaluable, so it puts such a
burden on those who propose to interfere with the freedom of agents.

The normative significance of the understanding can be further
elucidated by taking up means-ends relationships in more familiar
forms. Granting that freedom is strongly contributive to agency and its
flourishing, it does not follow that those who value the end of agency
are logically committed to promoting freedom. To want an end is not
in itself to want the means conducive (or even necessary) to it. Never-

theless, if Able professes to value an end but regularly or steadily refuses to support means conducive to it, doubt is cast on the clearheadedness or the sincerity of her commitment. Or rather, such doubt is created unless Able gives, case by case, cogent explanations as to why she stands against the means. Freedom being conducive to the flourishing of agency, those who claim to value the latter must either support the former or explain why they are not doing so. The understanding that human beings ought to be regarded and treated as agents creates a presumption in favor of freedom. As with the understanding itself, this presumption is rebuttable. If it can be shown that the freedom of action in question will not conduce to the flourishing of agency, that it will do so only minimally while adversely affecting other values or desiderata, and so forth, then the presumption will be rebutted for the case in question. Successful rebuttals of the presumption, moreover, have "accumulated" in the course of the continuing experience of the societies under discussion. It has become settled that certain kinds of actions will not be permitted; the presumption in favor of freedom has been reversed and the burden of justification has been shifted to those who propose to act in one of the proscribed ways. I suggest, however, that as a generalization concerning the societies in question, the presumption in favor of freedom is well established. Although limitations on and interferences with freedom are frequent and frequently thought justified, there is a relatively small class of cases in which the justificatory burden is clearly on those to whom the restrictions apply. (Examples of such cases would be murder and cruelty. If I demand a justification for being prevented from committing murder, those to whom I address the demand are likely to think that I am demented. Another, in principle, much larger class of cases, would be "actions" the point of which others simply cannot grasp.)[1]

In sum, I am positing that in the post-Hobbes societies of the Western tradition it is a widely shared understanding-cum-principle of thought and action that freedom-evaluability should be recognized and that the freedom of action of freedom-evaluable human beings should generally be respected. These understandings, values, and principles, I suggest, are among the deep conventions that make up (in Wittgenstein's terms) the language games and forms of life that partly constitute the situatedness of modern Western peoples.

II

These understandings were perhaps first articulated in what is to us an easily recognizable form by the Stoics of late antiquity, and the understandings (or ideas that prepared the way for wide acceptance of them in modernity) were given wide circulation and a greatly increased impetus by Christianity. The advent (or rebirth) of secularization in moral, social, and political thought required that these understandings be given justifications other than those provided by their alleged origin in divinely revealed truth, a task that continues to prove difficult because the understandings had an insecure position in pre-Christian (and at least in that sense secular) philosophical anthropologies and because the understandings are now so deeply established and pervasive that it is difficult to identify considerations independent of them (such as were provided by divinely revealed truths) in terms of which to argue for them. The attempt to meet this difficulty, in which major modern treatments of freedom and equality largely consist, has yielded and continues to motivate a large literature. There is no consensus on the argumentation that best supports the understandings, and for this and other reasons there is sharp disagreement as to when and why limitations and restrictions on freedom are justified. (The foregoing sketch is no more than one of numerous ways to formulate the understandings and is a defense of the formulation only in the weak sense that I have tried to make the sketch cogent.)[2] My suggestion, however, is that debate at both the foundational and the casuistic level is strongly conditioned by what I will call the "doubly normative" understandings I have tried to articulate, that is, the understandings that human beings both are and should be treated as freedom-evaluable (and that this creates a presumption that they should be free to act).

This suggestion is empirical in character; I am claiming that in fact the doubly normative understandings I have been discussing are deeply established in modern Western societies and that discussion of more particular questions about freedom typically takes place within the admittedly broad limits set by those understandings. I do not claim that in practice modern Western societies adequately live up to the ideals implicit in the understandings. The evidence for the claim I advance is provided by criticisms and attempted defenses of the all too numerous violations of the ideal as well as by its tacit invocations, by arguments for it, and by actions and policies chosen because they conform with it. Unfortunately, members of modern Western societies testify to their belief in freedom-evaluability and their commitment to freedom in considerable part by criticizing the failures of others to conform to it and by rationalizing their own failures to do so.

This important caveat brings me to the more radical challenges that I want to consider. Even as I have qualified it, my suggestion has been sharply challenged by a succession of intrepid modern Western think-ers. Some of these radical critics have denied that the understandings I have outlined are normative in modern Western societies. If the "evidence" that appears to support my claim does not demonstrate sheer hypocrisy, it is proof of a more or less encompassing false consciousness, one engendered and maintained by a dominant elite or class that rejects the understandings but fosters general belief in them for its own narrow purposes, or one that afflicts all of modern Western humankind—save of course the thinkers who have seen through it and have undertaken to disbuse the rest of us of it. Others have gone further; they have allowed my claim that the doubly normative under-standings prevail but lamented the fact and argued that those under-standings should be replaced by a radically different anthropology and morality. (To concretize just a bit, examples of the first of these tendencies are provided by Marx and some later Marxists, of the second by Michel Foucault, Jürgen Habermas, Alasdair MacIntyre, and Erving Goffman, and of the third by Friedrich Nietzsche.) These writers advance versions of the thesis that modern societies constitute obstacles to or restrictions upon freedom. Situatedness as we in fact experience it in modern societies is an enormous obstacle to freedom.

Marx's thought provides an accessible example of the first version of this thesis. In his view capitalist societies reduce the vast majority of their members to something very close to Aristotle's animate instru-ments; to creatures whose lives, in all but the narrowest respects, are in fact controlled by the dominant class and who can attain and assert their capacity for agency only by moving society to a further stage in its history. Foucault and Habermas modify this view by diminishing the distinctiveness and the significance of the dominant class and by mag-nifying, as compared with Marx, the cognitive component in the *praxis* that can liberate moderns from their thralldom. A pervasive false consciousness is at the root of the dehumanization of modern Western humankind and nothing less than a generalized true consciousness can remedy it. Although our false beliefs and distorted values are em-bodied in and reinforced by class structures and institutional arrange-ments, it is the beliefs and values themselves that deprive us of our freedom and all but fragments of our freedom-evaluability. In at least one respect communitarian antimodernists such as Charles Taylor, Robert Nisbet, and especially Alasdair MacIntyre echo this diagnosis. In their view, our thinking and our "practicing" has so deteriorated that in large and critical respects we have become unintelligible to one another. Of course the particulars of their proposed remedies differ sharply from the prescriptions of Foucault, Habermas, and Marx. But communitarians agree that radical changes in thought as well as in social organization must occur if we are to recover our humanity. Despite its apparent celebration of agency and of freedom, modernity itself is the great obstacle to them.

The reasons for Nietzsche's hostility to modernity are of course quite different. He would have no very serious quarrel with my sketch of the deep conventions of modern Western societies. The degradation of modern Western life results from the very fact that such hopelessly inappropriate beliefs and values were instilled in Western culture by Christianity and continue to inform and condition it. As manifested by the herd which constitutes the vast majority of any society, "agents" are slavish conformists to superstition and prejudice, and their freedom is little more than indulgence of the poverty that is their selves. The understandings I discussed should be reversed. Most human beings should be regarded as instruments at the disposal of the superior few; most human impulses and desires are vulgar and stupid, appropriately stilled, blunted, or deflected rather than encouraged or even condoned.

With something of an exception for Nietzsche, inspiration for these views might be taken from Hegel himself. Human life is variously but without exception deeply situated. Human beings are what they are and the actions they take have the character that they do because of the setting in which they occur. The succession of such settings that makes up human History is the march of Reason and Freedom. But this very fact indicates that, from the perspective of later moments, every stage in this progression—save the final, culminating stage—is a stage of unfreedom. From the Hebrews and Greeks forward, each historical era or epoch may have thought that it enthroned freedom. Moreover, when judged by the canons and criteria established in the several ages, these beliefs may have been warranted. Nevertheless, the same fate awaited each such set of beliefs; in the improved perspective of later epochs it would come to be seen that earlier societies had achieved no more than a poor approximation to freedom, no more than an anticipation of Freedom as it would finally be realized.

Hegel's critiques of the societies preceding his own were for the grand purposes of philosophical history and had "practical" significance only in that they put modernity in proper perspective. Certainly it was no part of his purpose to "unmask" or "discredit" earlier human experience. But later thinkers could and did find in Hegel's theory the idea that societies as such, despite the apparently well-founded beliefs of many or even all of their members to the contrary (and despite its being true that human freedom is possible only in societies), could be the source of a pervasive unfreedom. And some of these later thinkers, less cautious than Hegel himself, drew this conclusion about the societies of their own time and sought to discredit and radically to change those societies.

Karl Marx can stand for many of this persuasion. Marx accepted Hegel's view that human history is progressive and he believed that the capitalist societies of his own time were superior to all of those that had preceded them. Nor did he dismiss the bourgeois liberties. Properly understood and extended, those liberties should be preserved in the classless, history-terminating society that he hoped to assist in bringing into actuality. But he believed that the superior perspective afforded by his analysis showed that capitalism enslaved and dehumanized the bourgeoisie as well as the proletariat. The beliefs and values, practices and organization of capitalism excluded the possibility of genuine freedom. The beliefs of the bourgeoisie—and of at least some of the proletariat—to the contrary manifested their false consciousness and deepened the difficulties of effecting the necessary revolution. Thus the form or nature of situatedness represented by capitalist society had itself become the greatest obstacle to freedom.

Marx followed Hegel in trying to see forms or types of society whole and in trying to assess the significance of each form's distinctive, global characteristics for freedom. He radicalized the Hegelian enterprise by contending that critical aspects of the form of society dominant in his own time were antagonistic to human freedom. For all of his radicalism, however, Marx accepted many of the elements that Hegel had identified as distinctive of modernity. He proposed fundamental changes in the control of the forces of production and he believed that these changes would require (would bring with them) substantial changes in beliefs and attitudes and in the character of social relations. But he was as enthusiastic a modernist as Hegel in his appreciation of the possibilities opened up for agency and action by the complex, differentiated, subjectivity—ridden quality (in the sense in which Hegel said we must give subjectivity its due) of modern social life. We are not to abolish modernity, we are to correct its defects so as to extend its benefits and advantages to all. In this respect, later Marxists, as well as the socialists and liberals with whom they have been in political, moral, and philosophical contention, have followed his lead.

Is it open to us to consider a yet more radical possibility? Could it be that there are yet deeper respects in which distinctively modern forms of sociality doom us to unfreedom or even to nonfreedom-evaluability? Such a view seems to be adumbrated in more insistent communalist writers such as MacIntyre, in Habermas and perhaps

Foucault, and in the poststructuralist and postmodernist criticism of Jacques Derrida. It is strongly suggested that there is something illusory and at the same time insidiously harmful in modern life. The beliefs and values I sketched above, even if genuinely held by most of us, are somehow counterfeit. The individuality, agency, and action we celebrate are bogus, spurious; the freedom we think we have is a sham.

This is an elusive possibility, a thesis, even a question or concern, that resists attempts at clear expression or formulation. It is nevertheless a haunting concern, one that lends an unsettling quality to reflection about freedom. When we have dismissed state-of-nature thinking, when we have absorbed the teaching of Hegel or Bradley, of James or Mead or Wittgenstein, we may be left with a sense of dissatisfaction and of loss. Is there no core, no essence, no soul, in which personality or personhood and its dignity ultimately reside? Has the self no citadel, no inner fortress, secure against the intrusions of social or cultural forces? If not, what can be the source or spring of distinctiveness, of true individuality, of human actions and of the more or less patterned succession of actions that make up human lives? If not, how can there be, or why should it matter if there isn't, individual freedom? If not, isn't the set of beliefs and values discussed above an elaborate delusion? In the hope of considering these possibilities in something approaching a definite formulation, I examine the work of the sociologist Erving Goffman.

III

A word of explanation concerning my focus on Goffman rather than the other radical critics I mentioned. Moral and political theorists have not given close attention to Goffman's version of antimodernism. By comparison with Marx and later Marxist and neo-Hegelian critics, however, Goffman made a sustained and explicit attempt to show that modern sociality as such is incompatible with agency and action and hence not only with freedom but with freedom-evaluability. As I understand them, Marx and the Critical Theorists accept the modern ideal of freedom and believe that it could be realized in a fundamentally modernist society. They are radical in their estimates of how far modern societies in fact depart from that ideal and of the measures that must be taken in order to put that ideal into practice. By contrast, Goffman dismissed the ideal as delusory, as categorically incompatible with social life as we know it in modernity. Perhaps Foucault or Derrida share Goffman's unqualified and unremitting negativism in this regard. But Goffman is far less allusive and evasive than Foucault and Derrida, far more explicit and insistent about the implications of his analysis than these currently more fashionable writers. His works present the haunting but elusive thesis that I am trying to consider in the most definite form known to me.

(Of course my comments on Goffman must justify themselves by the light they shed and the critical purchase they provide on the issues that prompt me to offer them. If they illuminate and provide leverage on those issues, others can bring my results to the consideration of whatever other antimodernist formulations they judge most worthy of attention.)

We should note at the beginning that the extended series of splenetic "reports" that Goffman issued were understood by him to be restricted, for the most part, to modern Western societies. From *The Presentation of Self in Everyday Life* (1959) to *Frame Analysis* (1974) and the collection *Forms of Talk* (1981), his works are replete with phrases such as "in our Anglo-American society" (1959, 106, 109; 1961a, 177; 1967, 9), "throughout Western society" (1961a, 128, 244–47; 1961b, 4; 1971, xv), "in our middle-class society" (1963, 60, 140; 1971, 4) "our urban secular world" (1967, 47), and "in American society" (1963, 24, 131). In *Relations in Public* (1971) he defends his use of these "hedges" or "distribution qualifiers" (xv) and at various places he implicitly (and in *Frame Analysis* he explicitly and somewhat more philosophically) insists that universal propositions, for example propositions about "human nature," are empty, if not worse, and are typically discredited by "good ethnography" (1971, 93; 1967, 45; 1974). It is of course true that he generalizes freely within these broad limits and even permits himself entirely unqualified statements that are much more substantive than the essentially epistemological contentions he advances and in a manner of speaking defends in *Frame Analysis*.[3] For the most part, however, his intended argument is not that sociality or situatedness as such diminishes or excludes genuine agency and freedom, but that the form of sociality characteristic of modern Western societies does so.[4]

A second preliminary consideration appears to comport less comfortably with my objectives in examining Goffman's thought. There are dimensions or aspects of Goffman's work that suggest that his thought is ill-suited to the role in which I propose to cast it. Among these are his various discussions of "civil society" and the ways in which human interactions in this mode differ from those that occur in "situated activity systems" such as "groups," "gatherings," and especially "total institutions" such as asylums and prisons. The last of these contrasts, marking the distinction between "institutionalized" persons such as committed mental patients and incarcerated criminals on the one hand and persons not under such close physical restraint on the other, is the most usual in Goffman's writings. At times, however, he draws the former contrasts in a fashion that will have, at least initially, a familiar ring to students of modern political philosophy. Civil society is the realm of citizenship, a status that is a "generalized source" of rights that allow the individual to "distance" herself somewhat from the requirements and burdens of interactions in familial, occupational, and avocational groups and in the more transitory, episodic, but pervasive occasions that Goffman calls "gatherings" (1961a, 141). In groups and gatherings persons have roles to play and are subject to a variety of expectations as to how they may and must present and comport themselves. Civil society and its citizenship provides, at least in principle, something of a "refuge" (1961b) from these require-ments, allows a comparatively greater degree of "anonymity," and not only permits but requires mutual "civil inattentiveness" in passing encounters (1963, 83–87). In this usage, the norms and rules of civil society are the rules of "polite conduct" (ibid.) and concern not ends pursued or the means instrumental to achieving them but "proprieties and improprieties" of conduct irrespective of ends (1963, 7ff.). These discussions are at least reminiscent of Hegel, the notion of civil society containing elements of relations in the mode Hegel marked by that term itself as well as relations at the level or in the mode of the State. More particularly, they are at least analogous to Michael Oakeshott's concept of a civil society of *societas* as distinct from an "enterprise association" or *"universitas"* (Oakeshott 1975, esp. the second essay). Most important here, as with Hegel and (again, more particularly) Oakeshott (albeit for importantly different reasons), Goffman some-times contends that civil society and its citizenship is a realm and a mode in which individual freedom can flourish. The world of civil society, he goes so far as to say, is "incredibly thick with freedom and privileges" (1961b, 140).

Connected but further themes recur in Goffman's critique of role theory à la Ralph Linton and Robert Merton. The formulations of role theory that Goffman treats as standard in sociology are in his view overdrawn and reifying in their suggestion that role definitions can and do dictate, in fine detail, the conduct of individual role players. Roles and role playing are pervasive in our social life and Goffman gives qualified endorsement to the "model of man" that role theory pro-jects, namely as "a kind of holding company for a set of . . . roles" (1961a, 90). Typically, however, the several roles an individual plays "are not relevantly connected" (ibid.), that is, do not form a tightly integrated system such that their several requirements harmonize with or complement one another. Conflict among role requirements is commonplace and the individual is frequently confronted with choices as to which role to play in a given situation, choices that are not and could not be dictated by the role definitions themselves.[5] Moreover, the requirements of any single role are importantly indeterminate, leaving each role player scope for interpretation, judgment, and variation in conduct. Most important, while it is rarely possible for individuals entirely to reject roles and their requirements, they can and do "distance" themselves from their roles and particularly from the "images of self" that the roles project and appear to impose (1961a, 90, esp. 101ff.). From William (but not Henry) James to Robert Merton, role theorists have depicted the role player as marching "up and down like a wooden soldier, tightly rolled up in a particular role" (ibid., 143). But this is rarely the case. "Individuals are almost always free to modulate" what they are required to do and, as Henry James' novels teach us, it is better to think of roles as providing "the field an individual needs to cut a figure in—a figure that romps, sulks, glides, or is indifferent" (ibid., 151, 115).

In the discussions thus far considered, then, Goffman depicts persons who are clearly agents engaging in what must be regarded as action. In the terms I have been using, these persons are freedom-evaluable and they enjoy a substantial measure of freedom of action (freedom$_2$). Indeed many of his descriptions characterize those societies as valuing and respecting freedom of the latter kind. If we confined our attention to these passages we could hardly look to Goffman for an articulation of the idea that modern Western societies exclude or even notably diminish freedom and/or freedom-evaluability. (One can even imagine a reading of Goffman that aligns him with Hegel's view that modern Western societies embody the triumph of freedom. Such an account would stress the passages just reviewed and contrast the societies to which they refer with archaic, traditional communities—such as the community of the Shetland Islanders that Goffman studied—that survive on the margins or in the interstices of modernized societies.)

An exclusive or even a primary focus on these passages, however, would grossly distort Goffman's characterizations and unmasking critiques of modern societies. Just as Goffman insists that we can understand individuals and their activities only by situating them in their social contexts, so we can understand Goffman's remarks about civil society, about role playing, and about freedom only by placing them in the larger setting of his sociology. Behind a rather thin veil of disengaged social scientism, Goffman was a cynic, a moralist gone sour. At some level of his thought he may have valued the ideals implicit in his discussions of civil society, of individuality, and of freedom. The most spirited of his discussions of those themes are in his extended treatments of severely stigmatized persons, particularly those judged to be mentally ill and confined to institutions on the basis of that judgment. Many of the passages quoted above, particularly those concerning the freedom available in civil society, occur when he is expressing a kind of outrage concerning the plight of inmates of "total institutions" such as asylums and (less frequently and with less assurance) prisons. Arguing an interactionist and social functionalist version of the view of mental illness that we earlier encountered in Foucault, Laing, and Szasz, Goffman contends that the so-called mentally ill are capable of and in fact more or less continuously manifesting agency and action. The fact that they do so in the face of the pervasive, unrelenting tyranny of mental institutions makes them the closest thing to heroic figures that can be found in the "dubious" and "ludicrous" social life of modern societies (Goffman 1974, 2). And the fact that societies reduce these freedom-evaluable persons to radical unfreedom and subject them to mortifying indignities incited even in this self-styled "laconic" man (1971, xv) a kind of moral fury. In short, when examined in context, Goffman's apparently favorable remarks about civil society present themselves less as praise than as rhetorical devices for dramatizing the dismal circumstances of those who are most clearly victimized by modern societies.

This interpretation is reinforced and broadened if we follow out Goffman's admission that he himself can suggest no "better way of handling persons called mental patients. . . . If all the mental hospitals . . . were emptied and closed down today," tomorrow there would arise "a clamor for new ones" (1961b, 384). Why would this be? Not because the "insane" or "psychotic" are in fact "ill" and would actually benefit from the "treatment" mental institutions provide. Nor because the persons and groups ("relatives, police, and judges") who would actually raise the clamor *could* not cope with those they want put away. Goffman repeatedly emphasizes the absence of clear, medically defensible criteria of mental illness and the haphazard processes and procedures through which institutionalization is effected. Many persons whose conduct creates minor difficulties for those around them are committed, while persons who pose severe problems remain at liberty in civil society. Nor is Goffman a conspiracy theorist in the sense of someone who argues that some determinate elite or class sees to the hospitalization of those who threaten its position or its particular interests. Although it acts through assignable agents and agencies, society itself maintains the notion of mental illness and the terrifying apparatuses of "diagnosis," "hospitalization," and "treatment." This awesome machinery "functions . . . to protect the sanctity of the social occasion"; "psychiatry and mental hospitalization . . . serve as the therapy that our society gives to its threatened proprieties" (1963, 235, 239). "Just as we fill our jails with those who transgress the legal order, so we partly fill our asylums with those who act unsuitably—the first kind of institution being used to protect our lives and property; the second to protect our gatherings and occasions" (ibid., 248). It is these "sanctities," "proprieties," and "suitabilities," and their significance for agency, action, and freedom, that we must understand. In the perspective of his discussions of role theory we can say that Goffman takes modern individuals out of the frying pan of role only to cast them into the fire of a far more encompassing and constraining sociality.

We may begin by noting the opening sentences of the last of the passages quoted above. "More than to any family or club, more than to any class or sex, more than to any nation, the individual belongs to gatherings; and he had best show that he is a member in good standing. The ultimate penality for breaking the rules is harsh" (ibid.). Family, occupation, various organizational memberships, gender, class, the several levels of political association, each of these involvements confronts individuals with norms and rules, expectations and dissuasions, statuses and roles that influence, shape, direct, and limit their thought and action. Attached to each of these sets of prescriptions and prohibitions, moreover, are more or less definite, more or less severe, and more or less uniformly and insistently enforced systems of rewards and punishments. From the laws, police, and prisons of the civil society to the work rules, productivity norms, and promotion schemes of factories and corporate hierarchies, to the canons of good sportsmanship of the tennis club, individuals rarely if ever find themselves out of the ken of quite definite normative systems and their sanctions. In at least tacitly endorsing this familiar picture of life in complex modern societies, Goffman's sociology is unremarkable.

Nor is there anything especially novel or startling in his reflections about the significance or implications of this understanding for individuality, agency, or freedom. The individual and her repertoire of beliefs and values, interests and desires, objectives and purposes is in large measure a "product" (Goffman 1959, 252–53) of the social milieu in which she lives her life. There are biological and perhaps some psychological characteristics that are necessary conditions of any form of human life. But the only place in which Goffman attaches substantial significance to such factors is when he denies that the mentally ill are so distinct from other human beings in these respects that they are incapable of the usual interactions with the "normal" population.[6] It is for these reasons that "the individual is not the natural unit of our consideration," and that in the absence of a society replete with "ritual practices it would be very difficult to have a self" (1959, 149; 1967, 91). Yet the diverse, complex, ambiguous character of social norms, conventions, and rules leaves the individual "room for maneuver," allows her to disobey as well as to obey, to "distance" herself from, "break," and even "go out of" role, and in general permits not only "striving for" but a degree of success in achieving freedom (1971, 61 ff.; 102ff.; 1961a, 101–3, 108–20).

As already suggested, however, this sociologically quite conventional picture leaves out the distinctive and distinctively unsettling aspects of Goffman's analysis. Of deeper significance than the explicit, organized, perhaps codified norms of particular statuses and roles, groups and association, are the more general, the often unstated and implicit but ubiquitous and insidious conditions of "good standing" in "gatherings"; the requirements that every member of society must in some manner satisfy in order to maintain "face" on those countless occasions on which human beings come to one another's attention. Our lifelong and at best partially successful struggles to avoid being "discredited" and "stigmatized," and our incessant efforts to "remedy" the discredit and "manage" the stigma by which we are inevitably tainted, reveal the true character of life in modern Western societies.[7]

The "room for maneuver" that we enjoy because of the complexities and ambiguities of the most organized aspects of social life blinds us to more subtle and pervasive constraints (Goffman 1963, 7). Individuals may think of themselves as unique, as pursuing in a distinctive manner and style objectives that are their own. What they fail to realize is the deeper truth that a person's "most personal" characteristics, those that form "the center of his security and pleasure," are "only on loan to him from society" and "will be withdrawn unless he conducts himself in a manner society judges to be acceptable (1967, 10). "[E]very individual lives more or less in the mind of every other individual" (1963, 17n); the most vigorous efforts to achieve individuality and freedom of action unwittingly display and even deepen the control of social others. "While proclamations of alienation and gestures of situational contempt are certainly means by which the individual places some unapproved distance between himself and the establishment in which he finds himself, there is still the paradoxical fact that these acts may be symptomatic of deep concern about the establishment. For these are strategies by which the individual resolves the conflict between his presence in the gathering, and the reasons he has for showing alienation from it. . . . There is a sense, then, in which those who actively dispute the proprieties governing a gathering show the gathering (and hence the encompassing establishment) more respect than do those who give no attention to it at all" (ibid., 17n).[8]

The themes of this last passage require elaboration. Goffman is self-consciously in the Durkheimian tradition that understands society as a largely self-sustaining entity that cannot be reduced to or explained as an aggregate, sum, or product of the characteristics of its individual members (see, for example, 1963, 245). Accordingly, he places great emphasis on conventions, norms, rules, and expectations, on features of society that hold more or less constant despite continuous, large-scale changes in its stock of individual members and which form and shape the characteristics of those members. Yet Goffman's accounts of modern societies do not stress solidarity or uniformity; certainly they do not depict placid, tranquil, or harmonious relationships. Rather, he is fascinated by conflict and especially by deviance; by those at odds with, alienated from, disapproved, stigmatized, and punished by, the very societies that make them what they are.[9] This theme is so salient in Goffman's works that a kind of sociologized version of the theodicy problem presents itself to his reader. If all-embracing, all-pervasive, and all-powerful society shapes and controls its members, how and why does it happen that those members so frequently violate society's norms and proprieties? Although Goffman makes no reference to traditional formulations of this issue, there are places at which he in effect presents a variant of one of the familiar theological resolutions of it: Society permits, or rather arranges and induces, deviance for its own purposes. (The difference is that it is apparently both possible and proper for society's priests, that is, sociologists, to discern and announce the details of those purposes.) Society itself requires individual persons who *think of themselves* as free and autonomous agents; as persons who are not only self-activated in the sense of possessing *energeia* but *self*-determining in the reflexive sense of themselves determining the shape or character of the selves that then proceed to set themselves into action. Modern Western societies have seen to the availability of such individuals by constructing, inducing, and sustaining such self-conceptions on the part of its members. As early as *The Presentation of Self in Everyday Life* (in which there are passages which seem to credit the idea of a naturally given or at least partially self-constructed as opposed to an entirely socially constructed self), Goffman was writing that a "self is imputed" to the individual; rather than deriving "from its possessor" it "is a *product* of a scene that comes off, and is not a cause of it." The self "is not an organic thing that has a specific location, whose . . . fate is to be born, to mature, and to die; it is a dramatic effect arising diffusely from a scene that is presented, and the characteristic issue, the crucial concern, is whether it will be credited or discredited" (1959, 252–53). In the later works, when the dramaturgical perspective of *Presentation* and its emphasis on scenes, performers, and audiences has been largely replaced by a more holistic and structural-functionalist concern with society, the sense that the self is constructed and maintained by society for society's purposes is much more pronounced. Implicitly answering the potentially embarrassing question, "For whom or for what is it crucial whether the self is credited or discredited?" Goffman argues that the organization and functioning of modern societies requires individuals who attribute to themselves and to one another selves and self-determination. "[O]n the issue of will and self-determination turns the whole possibility of *using* territories of the self in a dual way, with comings-into-touch as a means of establishing regard. And on this duality rests the possibility of according meaning to territorial events and the possibility of so doing. It is no wonder that *felt* self-determination is crucial to one's sense of what it means to be a full-fledged person. Personal will or volition may be seen, then, not as something which territorial arrangements must come to terms with and make allowances for, but rather as a function which must be *inserted into* agents to make the dual role of preserves work"(1971, 60–61; emphasis added).[10] Society creates selves with these characteristics, invests them with a "ritually delicate," even a "sacred" character, and then arranges to provide them with the degree of "flexibility" in action required for them to perform their socially appointed tasks in a more or less effective manner (1967, 31, 95). Without such flexibility, without the possibilities of distancing, alienation, disobedience, and other apparent manifestations of individuality, "public life would become hopelessly clogged with the commission of minor territorial offenses and their adjudication—indeed, our present articulation of the territories of the self would become quite unworkable" (1971, 108). More generally, "Society" itself "might get hopelessly clogged without such deviation" (1963, 240).[11]

So understood, individuality, agency, and freedom of action are rather less grand than we might wish to think. Taken together, the views I have been considering amount to Goffman's characteristically jaundiced account of what, with a quite different implicit valorization,

I characterized as the doubly normative beliefs and values that are deep conventions in modern Western societies. The notions of the citadel self and of freedom of action are treated as illusory. The self is itself a creation of society and its sacred character is no more than a device or contrivance employed by society for its purposes. True, there is a kind of freedom of movement that is not available in total institutions. But when this freedom is examined by the laconic social scientist, several dispiriting features emerge. First, there is "incredibly little variation" in the tendency of individuals to maintain "an advocable relationship" to the norms and expectations of their society (1971, 184–86). Second, the variation in conduct that does occur is by the leave of society and is arranged by the latter for its own purposes. Finally, insofar as there is something resembling an autonomous self that enjoys a degree of freedom of action, the former is formed against the perceived requirements of society and the latter occurs primarily in such social "fissures" and "cracks" as the self can discover. In a passage reminiscent of one of the bleakest themes of Dostoevsky, Goffman writes: "It is . . . *against something* that the self can emerge . . . [O]ur sense of selfhood can arise through the little ways in which we resist the pull. Our status is backed by the solid buildings of the [social] world, while our sense of personal identity often resides in the cracks" (1961b, 320). Insofar as Goffman allows of a genuine and genuinely free self, it bears more resemblance to a cockroach than to the human persons celebrated in the modern thought and practice that claims to give individuality and freedom pride of place.

Few members of modern societies see through these illusions. Most people fail to appreciate the ways in which they are molded and directed by their societies. We might say that we moderns have achieved no better than what Hegel called a happy consciousness. Such a characterization would be appropriate in one respect, namely, that few of us have a critical perspective on the norms of the societies we inhabit. But this Hegelian concept is not sufficiently derisive for Goffman. Abandoning his usual pretense that he eschews personal judgments (1963, 5) in favor of "modest, naturalistic observations" (1971, 6) (and in the process invoking notions that would seem to be excluded by the deepest elements of his own position), Goffman turns to the post-Hegelian concept of false consciousness. "He who would combat false consciousness and awaken people to their true interests has much to do, because the sleep is very deep. And I do not intend here to provide a lullaby but merely to sneak in and watch the way people snore" (1974, 14). Uncritical acceptance of their societies makes "of every man his own jailer . . . even though each man may like his cell" (1967, 10). And when glimmers of the "poignant" (1959, 233), or rather the pathetic,[12] quality of our circumstances and our selves shine through the thick layers of our socialization, Goffman apparently thinks that we moderns are most likely to resent the thought that we might, and should, be other than we are. "It is strange, and more Durkheimian than it should be, that today, at a time when the individual can get almost everything else off his back, there remains the cross of personal character" (1971, 87).

On this reading, Goffman does serve the purposes that led me to consider his work. (A qualification of this statement will be entered below.) As he describes them, modern Western societies present no more than the appearance of agency, action, and freedom. The persons who regard themselves as agents engaging in (sometimes) free action are so stuffed with an infused and enforced sociality that they are little better than socially "serviceable objects" (1961b, 379). There is a certain amount of more or less unimpeded movement, but no agency and hence no freedom$_2$ and certainly no genuine individuality or autonomy and hence no freedom$_3$. And these characteristics, or this lack of character, is produced by the mode of society that has developed in the West in the modern period.[13]

IV

If we now have before us, in an at least apparently definite and coherent form, the idea that modern sociality is itself the great obstacle to freedom, what are we to make of it? Without attempting a detailed assessment of the verisimilitude of Goffman's "reports", I at least am not prepared to deny that he had an acute eye for baleful features of our social lives. "Face-work," "stigma-management," self-deception as the pervasive underside of attempts to deceive and manipulate others, all of these are surely part of our experience of ourselves. And while Goffman is perhaps distinctive in the single-minded, relentless quality of his insistence upon these features, their ubiquity in modern life is a recurrent theme in our fiction, our theater, and our fine arts as well as our social theory and criticism. Nor is Goffman alone in his contention that these characteristics give the lie to more celebratory formulations of the view that modernity is the epoch of freedom. From Tocqueville, Dostoevsky, and Mill to David Riesman, a succession of social and political critics have worried that an insidious, socially induced, self-destroying conformity was replacing political despotism as the great enemy of freedom. A theory of freedom in modernity must give these considerations their due.

Understood in the manner of my interpretation, however, Goffman's account cannot be credited. The decisive objections to it are not empirical, are not that Goffman failed to identify actual, real, and all too widely distributed characteristics of social life. The objections, rather, are conceptual and criteriological; they concern the understandings of what genuine identity, action, and freedom would be, understandings that are implicit in his discussion and that provide the tacit contrasts by which he denies the reality of individuality and liberty in the societies he studied.

We should first note two objections that are likely to be pressed but that do not go to the heart of the difficulties. The first of these is that Goffman committed, on a massive scale, what is sometimes called the fallacy of self-exception. How is it that he was able to exempt himself from the self-ravaging effects of modern social life so that he could unmask its pretensions and delusions? Goffman allows that each of us can achieve a certain distance from this or that role, from these or those situational constraints and obligations. His denial, which informs his entire discussion and is the primary source of its radically delegitimating and unsettling quality, is that any of us can distance ourselves from or gain critical perspective concerning the ensemble of social expectations and requirements that insinuate themselves into our thought and action. We are what we are (and are not what we significantly are not) by virtue of our place in that ensemble; accordingly, we can achieve neither intellectual nor any other kind of leverage on it. How then could Goffman, who lived his life in the societies he studied, attain such perspective, achieve the leverage he implicitly claims to have? In short, if we "do a Goffman" on Goffman do we not discredit his discreditings?

At one point Goffman seems to concede the force of this objection. "In countless ways and ceaselessly, social life takes up and freezes into itself the understandings we have of it. (And since my analysis . . . admittedly merges with the one that [its] subjects themselves employ, mine, in that degree, must function as another supportive fantasy)" (1974, 563).[14] At another, he appears to deny that the problem is genuine, offering what might be regarded as a Wittgensteinian view that the ordinary language of social life itself provides us "an adequate resource for discussing" that social life itself (ibid., 12ff.). Finally, his brief, in-passing remarks about non-Western societies might suggest the conviction that comparative study had provided him with an Archimedean platform from which to see modern Western societies whole—and hence to see through them.

Whatever the exact character or merits of Goffman's own thinking about this issue, the difficulty with pressing it against him (at least the difficulty of my pressing it against him at this juncture) is that the problem of reflexivity extends itself relentlessly to our own assessments of Goffman's assessments. If we reject (or for that matter endorse) the substance of Goffman's analysis of our society, we thereby tacitly claim to have attained a global perspective of our own. Alternatively, if we reject his analysis on the meta-level ground that such global analyses are impossible, we disqualify ourselves from discussing the question that led us to consider his work. In this circumstance we simply have to make the best arguments we can in support or in criticism of Goffman's formulations.[15]

The second objection is that the logic of Goffman's own position requires him to attribute a more substantial self, a self less entirely formed or constituted by society and hence more capable of agency and freedom, than his official account allows. Even in the Pirandello-like hall of mirrors that Goffman depicts, there must be reflections that are *of* something other than mirrors. The mirrors in a hall of nothing but mirrors would have images of nothing but mirrors. The "I" that lives in the reflections it sees of itself in others, and others who at once present "I" with those reflections and are themselves constituted by the reflections they see of themselves in "I," *must* have attributes over and above the properties of reflecting surfaces.

Another way to put this objection is to say that Goffman reifies or hypostasizes an abstract and empty entity that he calls "society." In order to unmask and discredit honorific conceptions of self and of individuality he "explains" individuals by explaining them away, by reducing them to somethings that are nothings in their own right. But this reduction is logically impossible. We of course want to recognize the manifold ways in which individuals are shaped and influenced by the others who are the parties to their social relationships. But we can do so only if we attribute to those parties characteristics that are sufficiently substantial and of enough duration to give a foothold to concepts such as "shaping" and "influencing," "being shaped" and "being influenced." The empty selves of Goffman's reports could not shape or influence anything or anyone else; and because they are without shape of their own there is no sense to the idea that their shape was, is, or could be reshaped by their society.

As with the objection that Goffman's argument logically falls victim to a vicious, reflexive regress, it is difficult to bring this second objection effectively to bear on Goffman's actual formulations. At various places he allows to the self something more than raw capacities plus the empty desire to maintain face ("empty" because what "face" is and what is necessary or appropriate to maintaining it are entirely given by the responses of others); it may be that his verbally most emphatic denials of self are no more than rhetorical gestures designed to weaken the hold of exaggerated notions of individuality. More important, Goffman displays relatively little interest in the kind of issue this objection (and the first one considered) raises. A quite definite and encompassing point of view emerges from his work. But that point of view is typically articulated against alternative sociological and socio-psychological theories—and against what he evidently regards as received ideologies—only occasionally in the context of meta-theoretical debates about the suppositions and requirements of inquiry and theorizing. Refined considerations about reification and reductionism are better pursued in response to writers more self-conscious about them. Having noted these possible objections, I propose to leave them in the background of the remainder of my discussion.

In the present context, Goffman's most important claim is that those who distance themselves from, who substantially reinterpret, or who refuse to comply with social requirements and expectations, thereby betray their deep indebtedness to those very requirements and expectations. It is tempting to render this claim through familiar metaphors such as the bird in the limed twigs or the person in a bog of quicksand; the more these unfortunates struggle, the more belimed, the more deeply mired, they become. But these figures underestimate Goffman's dismissal of individuality and action. There is no independent self whose struggles are defeated by superior external forces. Rather, the "struggling" itself is a manifestation of the socialized character of the self. "Struggle against," "unthinking acquiesence to," "enthusiastic acceptance of" are at bottom the same in the fundamental sense that they are all behaviors that occur because the individual is integrated into, is constituted by its place in, a pervasive network of social relations.

Recognizing this, we might ask the Popperian question whether this contention is in principle falsifiable and hence meaningful. Let us rather continue to treat Goffman as a moralist and social critic and ask what more positive ideal of individuality and action he might have in mind in advancing these views. By what standard, in contrast to what alternative conception, does Goffman judge these individuals to be *individus manqués,* their relations "ludicrous," and their lives "poignant"?

Perhaps he is implicitly endorsing a thoroughgoing Stoicism. If individuality cannot be achieved by standing for or against society, perhaps it could be attained by indifference, by "going with the flow" without stooping to judge or assess the content of the "flow." Is it possible that Goffman dismisses and derides the persons he encounters in modern Western society by implicit comparison with an ideal of detachment which allows of physical presence in and submission to society so long as one remains aloof from and indifferent to it?[16]

This possibility comes to mind because Stoicism has always represented a concern to sustain a core of individuality in the face of overweening sociality. Physical removal may be impossible and even undesirable—the Stoic is not a hermit or a recluse—but individuality can be sustained by a spiritual or psychological withdrawal into indifference.

Such a strategy would not avail against Goffmanesque discrediting. However resolute, or rather by virtue of her resolution, the Stoic defines herself by reference to society. Her studied indifference to the merits of her society's arrangements testifies to the hold society has upon her. It could even be argued that from Goffman's perspective the thorough-going Stoic is the ultimate heteronomic; the person whose stance toward her society is the *sole* defining principle of her self. It is because society has such a hold on her, or rather it is because she is what she is because of her sociality, that she goes to such lengths to "prove" that she is independent of it.

In a sense, then, the Popperian question-cum-objection is the right one. No evidence can be brought against Goffman's claims because all conceivable evidence counts for them. Accordingly, we can say that his claims are neither true nor false but empty and insignificant. But it is not enough to say this; to dismiss Goffman in this way is to forgo an opportunity to clarify our own thinking by responding to his sustained but failed attempt to think clearly about matters that are difficult and important.

The radical, apparently impregnable, but in fact unacceptable character of Goffman's position results from the uses he attempts to make of concepts such as self and individual, independence, autonomy, and freedom. For Goffman a self is genuine and independent and free only if or only to the extent that its characteristics owe nothing to its sociality. (Put the other way around, sociality would be consistent with selfhood and freedom only if it were nothing more than an emergent property of the aggregation of a number of entirely discrete individuals.) For the reasons considered in the previous chapter, this criterion is impossible to satisfy or even to formulate coherently. The thoughts, actions, and so forth that constitute and distinguish selves, whether free or unfree, independent or dependent, authentic or inauthentic by ordinary criteria, can only occur in a public language. They are "thoughts" and "actions" as opposed to something else or nothing, and they are *this* thought or *that* action as opposed to any other or none, by virtue of the language in which they occur. And to say this much is to say a good deal more about their social character. Languages are part of, presuppose and are enmeshed with, an array of more or less settled, established, and respected arrangements and practices, conventions and norms. If there were no such practices, conventions, and so forth, there could be no selves. For this reason, and because Goffman himself must use public language to formulate and to express his ideal of the self, his attempt to do so tacitly invokes the very features of sociality that his ideal seeks to eliminate. His attempt to radically discredit individuality as we know it in modern society defeats itself.

At a very general level, then, Goffman's failure is instructive in that it shows us the impossible lengths to which one is driven if one tries to set up a thoroughgoing opposition between sociality and freedom (to make an antinomy of that relationship). Bizarre as it may seem, this critic who claimed to be supersensitive to, superinsightful into and about sociality, failed to escape from naive forms of state-of-nature thinking. (This is the qualification I anticipated to the statement that Goffman presents a coherent formulation of the view that modern sociality is the great obstacle to freedom. In its most general formulation, Goffman's work attempts—and fails—to formulate an objection not to modern sociality but to sociality itself.)

But we can also garner instruction of more refined kinds from Goffman's sustained but failed attempt to grasp the scope and significance of modern sociality. In order to do so we must appreciate why the concepts he was trying to use—"self," "identity," "autonomy," "freedom"—are vulnerable to the kind of misuse he made of them. Much in modern life hinges upon and swirls around these concepts. It seems to follow that if these concepts are not exceptionally secure, are not firmly anchored, our deepest beliefs and values will be in jeopardy. It seems imperative that they have a superstrong grounding, a foundation secure against the very possibility of assault. Finding no such foundation for them, Goffman concludes that they are illusory. Another response, but one that evidences the same concern, is the frequent attempt by modern thinkers to provide such a foundation. For all of the differences among them, Descartes' rationally undeniable thinking being, Kant's superautonomous noumenal self, the naturally given atomic individuals of Hobbes's thought, the transcendental selves of Emerson and Whitman, Nietzsche's *Ubermensch* and its pale, democratized counterparts in existentialist doctrines, those bearers of inalienable rights that populate natural-rights theory from Locke to Gewirth and Nozick, all of these somewhat desperate entities and doctrines provide—or would do so if they were tenable notions—an unimpeachable foundation for the doubly normative beliefs that are deep in the fabric of modern moral and political life. These abstruse formulations of high philosophy, moreover, reflect features of more prosaic, more mundane thinking. In particular, they echo the sometimes categorical, either-or, character of these concepts as they are used in moral, political, and legal practice. Those to whom we owe duties and against whom we hold rights, for whom we vote and from whom we expect services, who are found guilty or innocent and put in jail or left at liberty, these creatures are not typically regarded as more or less separate and distinct one from the other, as more or less continuous, as more or less independent in their thought and action, as more or less responsible for what they do. Unequivocal identifiability, assignability, and responsibility might be regarded as axioms of much of our practice. If we cannot make these postulates good, if we cannot articulate and defend absolute notions of identity, agency, and responsibility, our practice is discredited. In this perspective, when Goffman invokes (however tacitly or unreflectively) ideas of this sort he displays his own (uncritical) indebtedness to ordinary thought and practice as well as a kind of native cunning. Like the confidence men he admires, he "sees" (a part of) and "sees through" his "mark," thereby enabling himself to exploit the mark's weakness for his cynical purposes.

The centrality of notions of self, identity, individuality, and the like is not in doubt. Nor is there any question that for many purposes and in numerous settings we deploy these notions with entire confidence. We often single out individuals, make attributions to them, comparisons among them, without a trace of hesitation or uncertainty. The person who reads the *Times* in my office each morning, who teaches my classes, comes home to dinner at my house most evenings, and to whom the traffic policeman gave a ticket yesterday is not, for these and a very large number of other purposes, more or less me, it is me. Neither I nor the news vendor, colleagues, students, family, or policewoman have any doubt of this.

Where Goffman goes wrong is in his implicit contention concerning the conditions that would have to be satisfied if, contrary to what he thinks is the fact, this certitude were to be warranted. If we infer these conditions from the discursive remarks through which he seeks to discredit our notions of self, identity, and individuality, something like the following list (not unfamiliar to anyone acquainted with other skeptics about identity and related notions) emerges. (1) There must be an unequivocal, invariant criterion or tightly integrated set of criteria by which to make such identifications. (2) "I" must invariably and unequivocally satisfy that test or those tests. (3) "I" must be the only creature who does, ever did, and ever will satisfy them.[17] These conditions are of course not satisfied in our practice. There is no reason to think that the policewoman, the news vendor, my colleagues, students, or family key on the same characteristics in identifying me. For the policewoman, I am me because I have certain cards in my billfold; for the news vendor because I typically arrive at a certain time, ask for a particular paper, display certain reactions if that paper isn't available. As things stand, the former wouldn't be able to identify me as me without the documents I carry and it is unlikely that the latter would recognize me if he encountered me in another setting. And for those who know me better, who have a longer, richer list of identifying characteristics for me, the idea that I change over time and have changed in quite decisive respects over stretches of time is perfectly intelligible. "REF isn't himself today" mutters a colleague as she leaves my office. "Let's be patient with Dad tonight, he's badly out of sorts." "REF is an entirely different person than when I knew him in graduate student days." In many cases, continuing association with a person over an extended period involves forming a sequence of changing and perhaps partly incongruent patterns of identification for that person. Nor is it especially rare for us to have trouble distinguishing between or among two or more persons. Even leaving aside identical twins, suspects in a police lineup, etc., there are any number of settings in which, or any number of purposes for which, distinguishing among persons is difficult (or immaterial or even inappropriate).

Of course the unavailability or unsatisfiability of more stringent criteria of identity and individuality is sometimes a source of practical as well as theoretical difficulties. When we try to decide whether Charles Colson and John Ehrlichman have truly been "born again," are truly different persons from those who were guilty of gross misconduct in the Watergate episode, the complex, diffuse, less than fully agreed character of our criteria of identification all but assures controversy. More generally, it is unlikely that we will readily achieve widespread agreement over such questions as whether our society allows and encourages an adequate diversity and individuality. Some say that it is fragmenting into idiosyncracy and self-indulgence; others that it is stifling its members into conformity and uniformity; perhaps a few believe that it is striking a nice balance between commonality and singularity. But we assess our efforts to cope with these difficulties not by the standard of notionally precise and authoritative criteria but by comparison with our practical successes and failures in more manageable cases such as those mentioned above. To paraphrase and run together several thoughts of Wittgenstein, if it were generally the case that we were unable to identify, distinguish, make generalizations about and comparisons among persons, if we were usually, standardly, at a loss in these regards, many if not all of the practices that make up our social relations, our morality, our law, and our politics, would be impossible. But just as we can do arithmetic despite not being able to reduce our knowing "how to go on" in calculating simple sums to a precise formula, so our social, moral, and legal practices neither include nor require superstrong, superclear, controversy-excluding criteria or standards.[18] If the assumptions on which Goffman's unmasking critique are tacitly premised were warranted, there would be nothing for him to unmask.

This discussion of identity and individuality is also pertinent to agency and autonomy—and through them to freedom. If we extend the foregoing remarks it may be possible to make some progress in respect to the latter notions. An identifiable, continuing self is a supposition of agency and autonomy. Insofar as Goffman's skepticism about identity is unwarranted, and insofar as it explains his at least equally dismissive stance toward agency and autonomy, that stance has little to recommend it. But both agency and autonomy require more than identity and individuality and we have to ask whether Goffman and like-minded critics have better grounds for generalized doubt concerning the reality of the former pair than the latter in modern Western societies.

Both agency and autonomy connect directly and necessarily to action and hence posit the physical and intentional qualities necessary to form and to pursue ends and purposes.[19] In most contexts, moreover, "autonomy" posits or requires more in this regard than agency. A person qualifies as an agent (although not necessarily as having exercised agency in a particular setting or sequence of events) even if her ends and purposes are habitual, imitative, poorly coordinated, and even if her attempts to act are frequently influenced, frustrated, and even prevented by the actions of other agents and agencies. By contrast, attributions of "autonomy" usually suggest that the agent's ends and purposes, and the courses of action taken to pursue them, are chosen reflectively, that they are her own at least in this sense and typically in the further sense that they are in some degree distinctive by comparison with the actions of others with whom she is involved. They also suggest efficacy in the sense that she is more or less regularly successful in carrying through on her intentions—successful even when confronted by the disapproval, resistance, opposition, and so forth, of others.[20]

In the next chapter I will attempt to refine the foregoing discussions by examining a variety of kinds of obstacles to, interferences with, and limitations upon agency and autonomy. Assuming that the foregoing provides an initially serviceable sketch of the distinction between them, is there reason to credit Goffman's view that in fact neither are in evidence in modern Western societies?

As regards agency the answer is clearly negative. The reasons for this conclusion are largely of the same kinds as those given above concerning identity and individuality. In terms of Goffman's own discussions we can make the relevant points by recalling his comparisons between civil society and total institutions and his criticisms of role theory. In making these comparisons and criticisms he concedes that most citizens of civil society are properly regarded as agents. By the ordinary, the generally employed, criteria they deserve this characterization and the presumption of liberty that goes with it. Nor does he question the established criteria. His insistence, rather, is that by those same criteria persons who are now incarcerated in total institutions are at least equally capable of agency and ought to enjoy the same liberties. When in other contexts he changes his stance and denies the reality of agency his denial depends on a shift to some more stringent criteria (to criteria more closely resembling the ordinary requirements for the attribution of autonomy). Familiar devices such as distancing, deviance, and disobedience open up, at most, a modicum of variability in behavioral patterns that are in fact produced by the one true agent in the modern Western world, namely, society itself. Because of this criteriological shift, his denial of agency as ordinarily understood is no more than verbal; it amounts to his refusal to use "agency" in the ordinary way. And when we ask why the rest of us should adopt the way he (sometimes) uses the terminology, we encounter the difficulties discussed at length above.

Goffman's sociology of modern Western societies, then, gives us no reason for *generalized* doubt about the reality of identity, individuality, or agency in those societies. Accordingly, if we are prepared to regard these characteristics as sufficient conditions of freedom-evaluability, the question whether or to what extent there is freedom in these societies cannot be settled at this global level. To settle it we have to examine more closely such questions as which members or classes of members achieve and maintain identity, individuality, and agency under what types of circumstances, and when, where, and why attempts at action are obstructed, interfered with, and prevented.If freedom-evaluability and freedom are understood in these ways, the argument that modern Western sociality excludes or prevents them fares no better than the argument that sociality as such does so.

What if we raise what professional poker players call the buy-in costs of playing the freedom game; what if we say that autonomy, not merely agency, is a condition of freedom-evaluability? Do our discussions in this and the previous chapter allow us to say something more about the up to now largely neglected distinction between freedom$_2$ and freedom$_3$ and the implications of preferring the one to the other as our account of freedom?

If we allow that somewhere in Goffman's soul there lurked at least a particle of the belief that autonomy would be a good and a possible thing, a measure of his disaffection from modern Western societies is provided by the fact that on his account autonomy is found (if at all) in those societies only among those who are driven from society or driven by society to isolate themselves psychologically from it. Goffman concedes that most of us display a kind of counterfeit agency. But the engulfing sociality that conditions our thought and action renders our pretensions to autonomy risible and pathetic. Thus if we accepted Goffman's sociology, the decision to prefer freedom$_3$ as our account of freedom would be tantamount to concluding that neither freedom-evaluability nor freedom itself have any genuine place in our societies.

Resting as it does on the cluster of exaggerations, confusions, and illicit inferences that I have been examining, this extreme conclusion would hardly be warranted. It is nevertheless in respect to autonomy (and to the stronger notions of individuality and authenticity mentioned above) that Goffman's observations are most troubling. He does repeatedly confront us with striking instances of subservience to social requirements and unwitting adaptation to social expectations. We will need a more refined analysis of the concept of autonomy before we can adequately assess the significance of these observations, but much of the behavior that Goffman reports is patently inconsistent with claims to or attributions of it. Even if such behavior is much less characteristic of our social life than Goffman contends, theorists of freedom in modern societies must come to terms with it.

The issue with which Goffman in fact confronts us, then, is not whether modern Western societies somehow categorically exclude or are incompatible with freedom as I have been construing that concept here. The impression he creates that this is the case depends on a tacit identification of freedom and autonomy, unfreedom and what is commonly called heteronomy. It depends, that is, on rejecting freedom$_2$ and insisting upon freedom$_3$ as our account of freedom and unfreedom. Accordingly, I conclude this chapter with an initial discussion of this distinction and of the merits of moving from freedom$_2$ to freedom$_3$.

If we credit Goffman's account, we certainly would want to say that the face-saving, stigma-managing persons he describes lack autonomy. And most of us would want to regret these among their characteristics. They (we) lack qualities that are prominent in the ideals of our culture and that are exemplified in the lives of admired people who keep our ideals before us. It would be impossible to give an exhaustive list of the qualities that make for autonomy, but prominent among them is a substantive rationality that enables continuing assessment of the ends and purposes one has thus far adopted or that have as it were been assigned to one by others. As Goffman describes us, we modern Westerners regularly display a quite impressive instrumental rationality. We are skillful, clever, even ingenious in our pursuit of the objectives we happen to have. But we have little capacity to assess the merits of those objectives and to alter them substantially if experience calls them into question. Related qualities are independence of mind, a certain equanimity in the face of disapproval, a willingness to try out novel ideas and to experiment with courses of action that are untried and perhaps risky. As Goffman describes them, modern Western societies feature a kind of grumbling, sulky dissatisfaction and discontent, considerable deviance and conflict. But there is little adventurousness or sense of adventure, service and certainly heroism are rare if not unknown, and there are few stimuli to significant change, little that is spirited or dynamic. Lacking these qualities, there are satisfactions that are unavailable to us, contributions that we cannot make.

It is worth noting that the excellences we are said to lack are distinguishable from (although the distinctions are not sharp) the communally established virtues that have pride of place in the theories of positive freedom that insist upon freedom$_4$ or freedom$_5$. For one thing, they are more in the nature of ideals than of obligations and requirements. Those who lack them break no rule, fail in no duty. Those who have them are admired because of the example they set, the contributions they distinctively make. For another, they are qualities of degree, qualities that one has, that one's thought and action manifests, more or less rather than entirely or not at all.

Because of these characteristics, difficulties that we encountered in respect to freedom$_4$ and freedom$_5$ either do not arise at all or present themselves in more tractable forms in respect to freedom$_3$. In Chapters 3 and 4 we noted that proponents of freedom$_4$ and freedom$_5$ either directly equate freedom with virtue and hence declare unvirtuous conduct to be unfree or argue that the unvirtuous are unfree because enslaved by passions. In both versions we are either virtuous and free or unvirtuous and enslaved. The less categorical character of the ideals and excellences we are now considering makes it difficult to formulate these stark, counterintuitive alternatives. If we understand autonomy as an array of valued qualities that obtain in various combinations and to greater or lesser degree, we can make a conceptual connection between it and freedom without incurring the more obvious difficulties of freedom$_4$ and freedom$_5$.

Are there more constructive reasons for making such a connection? An obvious answer is that those well supplied with the qualities that make up autonomy readily attain to a variety of achievements and satisfactions unavailable to those lacking in them. In shorthand, autonomy opens up possibilities, heteronomy closes or abridges them. Variously elaborated, this has been the view of modest and sensible proponents of that version of the positive theory of freedom that shows up in my schema as freedom$_3$.

From the freedom side of the freedom-unfreedom polarity, the chief objection to this line of thought is that it confuses freedom with abilities, capacities, powers, and the like. Understood as a cluster of qualities that enable effective thought and action, autonomy is undoubtedly a good that is strongly complementary to freedom. It is a good that someone who values freedom will also value. It is nevertheless one thing to have the capacity to do, to be, or to achieve X, another to be free to X. Consider an example. Andrei Sakharov is as unGoffmanesque a figure as one can imagine; substantively rational, independent of mind, prepared to stand up to disapproval and much more. Yet Sakharov is largely unfree. On the other hand, the most obsequious, sycophantic toady can be largely at liberty. Because the autonomous person can do much more with freedom than can the toady, freedom may be much more highly valued by the former than by the latter. But this is reason to keep the distinction clear, reason not to confuse the one with the other.

As often in the theory of freedom, however, clarity comes most easily by focusing on unfreedom. Is the toady *unfree*? Are the courtiers to Queen Society that Goffman makes us out to be *unfree*? Assuming that we have avoided an uncritical equation of unfreedom with diminished quality of life, the temptation to think so is created by the at least apparent fact that something prevents the toady from achieving a better life, something compels her to the lamentable life she in fact leads. Literal readings of the terms "autonomy" and "heteronomy" suggest this view. If autonomy is self-rule, if it is rule of one's own thought and action by oneself, it seems to follow that the absence of autonomy is its opposite, namely the rule of the self by someone or something apart from or other than the self. (Thus we have the standard, at least apparently straightforward, Kantian antinomy "autonomy-heteronomy.") Goffman's sociology sometimes employs this conceptualization and claims to provide an identification of the something—Society—that rules individual lives. Despite a certain show of recalcitrance and truculence, the members of society are reduced by It to chameleons. Thus it makes perfectly good sense to say that those who lack autonomy are unfree.

I have resisted this familiar but simplistic account of autonomy in part because it eliminates any significant distinction between unfreedom and lack of autonomy. If it is in fact true that a person's life pattern is brought about and maintained by force and coercion, then we will indeed want to say that she is unfree. If we find, for example, that black slaves in the United States tended to be irresolute, timorous, pliant, and even craven (at least in the presence of masters and overseers), and if we also find that the slightest show of independence of thought or action, indeed any hint of an attempt to raise the quality of their lives by any standard, was brutally repressed, then we should certainly say that those slaves were unfree. (Talk of autonomy in such a setting would badly underestimate the plight of the slaves.) The contrast with the toady or sycophant is sharp and important. The latter may indeed expect and fear disapproval, may indeed convince herself that she will suffer grievously if she essays the slightest departure from the expectations of those around her. Her disposition to curry favor may have become so settled that it would be inconceivable for her to do otherwise. This disposition, moreover, may have been inculcated and cultivated in various ways by her society generally, her parents, teachers, husband, and others. She is clearly not to be envied or emulated; her misfortune is surely not to be dismissed or minimized. Nor is it surprising that members of a culture that makes freedom one of its chief values will be tempted to describe her as unfree.

But whatever terminology we use, the toady's circumstances and plight are importantly different from the circumstances and the plight of the black slave, of Sakharov, of battered wives, of ghetto residents in respect to crime and police brutality, of civil-rights workers in the United States in the 1960s, of communists and communist sympathizers in the same country. Others may have played a nefarious part in making and keeping her the way she is; others may have a duty to help her change her character and her dispositions; it is she who acts on and from them. If she succeeds in changing them sufficiently to attempt acts of a different kind, others will not prevent the success of those attempts. If we mark this difference by saying that she is free but lacks autonomy, while the slaves, Sakharov, et al. are unfree even if in many respects autonomous, we are warranted by a persistent, well-articulated tradition of thought and practice. More important, marking the difference in this way identifies the locus of what is unsatisfactory in these several dismal states of affairs and helps us to be clear about the appropriate strategies, and their respective costs, of improving upon them. No one except racists or Soviet officials would say that Frederick Douglass or Andrei Sakharov lacked the qualities of character that make up autonomy; no one save the types just mentioned would propose to remedy their unfreedom by providing them with therapy, a program of behavior modification, or even friendly concern and advice. They are unfree because of the actions of others and it is to those others that their friends and the friends of freedom must address themselves. By contrast, the friends of the person lacking autonomy must address themselves to her. And if they are true friends of her and of freedom, it will be well for them to take care not to take away her freedom in the name of improving her character.[21]

To repeat, nothing in the foregoing discussion establishes that the beliefs and values sketched at the outset of this chapter are adequately respected in our social life. We can and must reject Goffman's discreditings without lurching to uncritical apologism or celebration. What the discussion shows is the failure of an attempted demonstration that those beliefs and values are and must be either delusional or a "fantasy" "supportive" of a quite different reality. The special pertinence of Goffman's formulations (special among more or less radical antimodernisms) resides in his claim to have understood and taken seriously the professions of modern Western societies to freedom and to have discredited those professions by "good ethnography"; to have laid bare what in fact is the profoundly antifreedom logic and dynamics of modern life. Having realized the extent to which his radically delegitimating conclusions are the result of conceptual and theoretical confusion, we are better positioned to put behind us the elusive concerns that motivated this and the previous chapter and to look more closely at the cluster of issues that surround concepts such as obstacles and impediments, interferences and restrictions. Thus far, our project of situating negative freedom remains viable.

7

Freedom, Rationality, and Coercion

A passage from Jon Elster's *Ulysses and the Sirens* provides perspective on the transition from Chapters 5 and 6 to the present chapter: "Any given piece of behavior may be seen as the end product of two successive filtering devices. The first is defined by the set of structural constraints which cuts down the set of abstractly possible courses of action and reduces it to the vastly smaller subset of feasible actions. The constraints are assumed to be given and not within the control of the agents; . . . the second filtering process is the mechanism that singles out which member of the feasible set should be realized. Rational-choice theories assert that this mechanism is the deliberate and intentional choice for the purpose of maximizing some objective function, be it a real one (like profit) or a purely notional one (like the utility function representing preferences)." Some theories of human conduct, which Elster calles "Structuralist," assign so much significance to the first "filter" as to reduce the second to insignificance. "In an extreme version, this would mean that the [structural] constraints jointly have the effect of cutting down the feasible set to a single point; in a weaker and more plausible version the constraints define a set which is so small that the formal freedom of choice within the set does not amount to much" (1979, 113).

Blinking for the moment obscurities in these remarks, let us rehearse briefly the discussion of the last two chapters in their terms. Generic situatedness in Rousseau and Wittgenstein establishes a "structure" which is a necessary condition of meaningful action and hence of a set of possible actions. Using "feasible" in a stronger sense than Elster intends, Rousseau and Wittgenstein identify conditions necessary to the feasibility of action. We can go on to say that, in any

actual, concrete instance, this structure, consisting as it does of substantive conventions, rules, shared understandings, beliefs, values,
and the like, narrows the feasible (in Elster's sense) set of actions open
to those whose lives occur within it. If (*per impossible*) we took an
inventory of all the actions possible in all the forms of life known to us,
we would find that some subset of that global set is or was excluded
from each of those forms of life at any moment of its history.[1] Whether
the subset that remains feasible is large or small, significant or insignificant, and hence whether "the formal freedom of choice" that
remains "amounts to much," can only be answered by studying the
form of life in its particularity.

Marx, Foucault, Goffman, and others claim to have made such
studies and to have demonstrated that the feasible subset and hence
the genuine or meaningful freedom of choice in modern Western
societies is insignificant in its proportions. Accordingly, these writers
tend to disdain as trivial or worse Elster's "second filter." The rationality, irrationality, or nonrationality of individual actors (and the ways in
which such individuals facilitate or impede one another's attempts to
act), pales into insignificance by comparison with the constraining and
otherwise harmful effects of social structure.

Elster believes that "as a general theory of action" structural
theories are "too obviously wrong to merit much discussion" (1979,
114). He allows the possibility that "At particular times and places the
constellations of [structural] constraints may have been such as to
exclude all but a very small subset of possible actions," but goes on to
insist that for this "to be generally true there would have to be a
mechanism to bring it about, and in the Structuralist literature I have
never come across any attempt to provide this." More concretely, his
sympathies with Marxism bring him to agree that "the ruling classes in
most societies have tried to consolidate their rule by reducing the set of
opportunities open to the oppressed classes"; here again, however,
"this very statement implies that the ruling classes themselves were
acting freely and rationally in their own interest" (ibid.). Accordingly,
the attention of students of society should be directed primarily to the
second filter. More specifically, he thinks that the theory of rational
choice, which has developed to understand and explain decisions
within the feasible set, "is by far the most important."

Although based on importantly different patterns of reasoning than
those employed here, Elster's conclusions about structuralism corre-
spond to the results of my examination of the significance, for freedom, of situatedness in general and of modes of situatedness said to be
characteristic of modern sociality. It would be foolish to deny that

social structures limit and otherwise influence conduct, but arguments that they eliminate freedom altogether or reduce it to insignificance are simply not convincing. Elster's filtering metaphor, although misleading in respects that will have to be discussed, conveys this combination of understandings.

Something akin to Elster's notion of the second filter has also played a role in our discussions to this point. We have thus far said little about *rational* choice, but we have posited and assigned a crucial place to agents who form, hold, and change beliefs and values, frame intentions, and act in the pursuit of ends and purposes. Little if anything is gained by thinking of this as a process of filtering out action bits from some medium in which they are suspended and which, like a stream, carries them preformed to waiting individual agents. But the more basic idea behind the metaphor, namely, that the actions which actually occur in a society are chosen by the individual agents it comprises, is essential to the theory of freedom.

The complex and problematic aspects of Elster's position concern the notion of *rational* choice and the implications of this qualifier for questions about freedom. To appreciate those complexities and move closer to the topic of obstacles and impediments, I will first extend Elster's scheme by positing a third filter. Situated in a society that at once creates and limits action possibilities, agents attempt to act upon their decisions and choices. These attempts constitute the "pieces of behavior" that emerge from the two-stage filtering process. But now the sometimes placid but usually tumbling stream of social life reaches a third stage. Insofar as they notice these attempts, other agents and agencies decide either (a) to act or (b) not to act in response to them. In the former case, some of their actions (a_1) have no effect on the attempts, some (a_2) facilitate the attempts, and some (a_3) impede or obstruct them. If the attempts go unnoticed or if (b), (a_1), or (a_2) prevail, the attempts succeed in the sense that the agent in fact performs the action she has chosen to take. On the analysis thus far, in these cases we may say (if there is any point in doing so) that the agent is free. If (a_3), the attempt succeeds only in part or fails and we may say—and there will usually be point in doing so—that the agent is partly or entirely unfree in respect to the action in question.

This schema supplements the notion "pieces of behavior" with the notion "pieces of free or unfree behavior" and treats interactions between and among agents as a third filter, the operation of which serves to explain the full array of pieces of behavior that actually occur in a society. The set of "abstractly possible courses of action" is first reduced by structural constraints, reduced further by the decisions and choices of individual agents, and reduced to its final, actual dimensions by the responses that other agents and agencies make to those decisions and choices.

Keeping in the back of our minds the difficulties with the metaphor, the addition of the third filter substantially improves the verisimilitude of the picture. Large numbers of action possibilities that make it through the first two filters fail to make it through the third one. An account of behavior that omits the third filter blinds us to this fact and hence to the phenomenon, crucial to the theory of freedom, of attempted but externally prevented acts.

With this extended (but of course inadequate) scheme before us, I turn to the question of rationality and its bearing on obstacles, impediments, and freedom. For the most part, I leave "rationality" in the conveniently vague condition in which we find this protean notion in nonspecialist discourse. If we do so, there will be little dissent from the proposition that rational and externally unhindered action is the standard case of freedom, the case from which instances involving admixtures of agential irrationality and effective extra-agential interference are departures into various degrees of unfreedom or nonfreedom-evaluability. However capable of rationality, a person whom others have locked in a tight-fitting mummy case is unfree. However physically unrestrained, the person in a catatonic trance is not freedom-evaluable. External interferences that fall short of the limiting case of the mummy box in the scope and effectiveness of the restraint constitute the usual subject matters of inquiries concerning MacCallum's third variable. In Elster's technical discussion, and no doubt in many nontechnical discussions, instances of nonrationality and irrationality less severe than the limiting case of catatonia are treated as instances of more or less entire unfreedom. The equation of direct and effective physical constraint and unfreedom is controversial only within the "forced to be free" tradition and only to the extent that it can be shown that physical constraint now or in this respect will enhance the likelihood that the agent subjected to it will act more rationally later or in another respect. In this dimension, controversy concerns not whether effective physical constraint is incompatible with freedom but whether various external intrusions and interferences short of direct physical constraint (intimidation, threats, other forms of coercion; incitement, temptation, seduction, deception, and other forms of manipulation) are sufficiently akin to direct constraint to produce unfreedom.

The equation between irrationality or imperfect rationality and unfreedom is more controversial. I argue against regarding the fact that an action or course of connected actions is imperfectly rational as reason for saying it is unfree. But a (weak) notion of rationality does and should play a role in our more global or all-in notion of agency (our notion of who counts as an agent at all). More particularly, we need a (weak) notion of rationality in order to analyze and assess the significance, for freedom, of external interferences short of direct physical constraint. Otherwise put, if we encounter persons who are externally unhindered in their attempts to act on imperfectly rational choices, and if in other settings those persons manifest sufficient rationality to count as agents, we should regard them as acting in freedom. But the rationality of such an agent's identification and assessment of the actually or potentially interfering actions of other agents or agencies has a bearing on whether or to what extent she is free or unfree. Of course this argument implies that we largely abandon the distinction between the second and third filters. Indeed it requires that we replace the whole notion of a sequence of distinct filtering processes with a conception of intentional and more or less intelligent action and interaction situated in a shifting field of possibilities and limitations.

Elster endorses the widely accepted working assumption that the second filter consists of a process of making rational choices among members of the feasible set (1979, 116–17, 154–56). But this working assumption (Donald Davidson's principle of charity) is more than that only in the sense that it forms a part of the concept that we use to distinguish agents from nonagents. An abundance of experience teaches that individuals sometimes act irrationally, and reason tells us that there are classes of cases for which it is impossible to identify a single, unequivocally rational choice and hence, to that extent, conceptually impossible to assign either rationality or irrationality to agents acting in such cases. Of course we can deal rationally with our own irrationality (as Ulysses did when he had himself bound to the mast) and we can act more or less rationally in circumstances that either theoretically or practically do not allow of an unequivocally rational choice (as when, in "Catch 22" situations we "keep our heads" so as not to do avoidable harm to ourselves and others) (ibid., 153ff.). In Elster's view, investigation of the qualifications to the working assumption is a primary task of social theory and social science. As he has pursued this task in his published works, investigation of the first type of qualification consists in examining phenomena such as inconstancy of preferences, weakness of will, wishful thinking, and "sour grapes" mentalities, that is, cases in which agents suffering no externally imposed constraint or compulsion nevertheless fail to make or act upon the rational choice among the members of the feasible set of actions. Investigation of the second qualification involves clarification of the notions "rational" and "rationality" and consideration of classes of cases in or to which these notions appear to have no clear application. Our concern here is with the bearing of these discussions on freedom. We will concentrate on the first type, but a consideration of the second will help to focus conceptual issues.

I

Elster's discussion of the theoretical limits of rationality is primarily concerned with "games" that formal analysis shows do not admit of an optimal, noncooperative solution, that is, cases in which it is impossible for an individual agent to determine by and for herself the course of action that it is, uniquely, rational for her to take. For our purposes, however, the relevant questions can be raised by considering the rather more widely familiar idea expressed by the slogan *de gustibus non disputandum est*. Construed by the philosophical doctrine of emotivism to hold for all but the instrumental or derivative issues of morals and politics, this is the notion that *a*, perhaps *the*, most blatant form of irrationality is to think that it is possible for us to make rational choices in these axiological and otherwise normative realms. Now if some version of this doctrine is true, and if we make rationality of choice a necessary condition of freedom, and irrationality or nonrationality of choice a sufficient condition of unfreedom, it follows that we cannot be free, are necessarily unfree, in respect to any but the derivative choices we make in these areas. As the thought has commonly been expressed at least since Hume, *given* that we have "plumped" for a particular food or drink, a certain mode of painting or sculpture, a more or less definite moral or political purpose or objective, we can make rational choices about how to satisfy or achieve our desire or purpose. But it is a straightforward mistake to think that there is one criterion or several by which to decide which "plumping" would be rational and hence (on the view I am considering) it is impossible that such "plumpings" could be free. Any very substantial step away from an account of the substance or content of our moral, political, and other practical preferences as possibly objective (or at least possibly intersubjectively valid) is a step toward the conclusion that our moral and political behaviors are unfree. Even moderately skeptical forms of value pluralism, voluntarism, or subjectivism, such as Isaiah Berlin's, seriously diminish the possibility of freedom. In terms of Elster's metaphor as I have extended it, the availability of a generous feasible set of alternatives, and the absence of effective external interferences, are by no means jointly sufficient to establish the possibility of freedom. To the extent that doctrines such as emotivism are true, or to the extent that Elster and others have demonstrated limits on the applicability of the notion of *the* rational alternative in various behavioral settings, we must either deny the connection between rational choice and freedom or we must resign ourselves to limitations on our freedom.

In the strong, categorical formulation just considered, the equation between freedom and substantive rationality (rationality about ends or values or preferences) must be rejected. There are various senses of "rational" and "irrational" in which it can sensibly be said that a person's preference for one flavor of ice cream or one's distaste for certain foods developed or was arrived at rationally or irrationally. But I at least do not know what to make of the idea that these tastes and distastes, as such, are either rational or irrational. It nevertheless seems to me to be undeniably true that one can be free or unfree to act on one's tastes and distastes.

Some will regard the idea of freedom to gratify one's tastes as trivial or even degenerate. I do not share this gloomy, self-indulgently ascetical view and I will be arguing against it at a later stage.[2] But there is nothing trivial or degenerate about freedom of religion and of partisan political affiliation. Moslems, Roman Catholics, Lutherans, and Methodists may well think that they have good reasons for holding their particular religious beliefs, and Democrats, Republicans, Socialists, and Christian Democrats may think the same about their choice of political party. But it is by now a deeply rooted tenet of modern Western thought and practice that it is impossible to demonstrate that any one of these beliefs or choices is somehow the uniquely rational one—whether for the individual who happens to have made it or more generally. Unless we are to say that expressions such as "religious freedom" and "freedom of political association" are confused or incoherent, we cannot endorse the unqualified view that substantive rationality of choice is a necessary condition of freedom.

Some of the considerations that support this conclusion should also give us pause about endorsing strong formulations of the view that procedural or instrumental rationality is a necessary condition of freedom. Let us say that Able (who in numerous other dimensions of her life conducts herself in a tolerably rational fashion) identifies herself as a Lutheran. Setting aside the Kierkegaardian view that such commitments, if they are genuine, have nothing whatever to do with reason or rationality, let us operate with the more usual view that there are better and worse grounds for such confessional choices, that some people are more rational than others in making their religious commitments. We further suppose, however, that Able has only the most rudimentary understanding of the doctrines of Lutheranism. She was confirmed in the church at the age of twelve, having paid scant attention in confirmation classes and has given little or no thought to such matters since. She is even more ignorant of the teachings of alternative denominations and faiths and hence is quite incapable of justifying or explaining why she sustains her identification with Lutheranism in particular. It is true that her family has been Lutheran for several generations and this fact may explain to our satisfaction her original association with that church. But as she grew older her ties with her family became tenuous and strained. She sees family members rarely, holds them and their views and life-styles in low esteem, quarrels with them when she does see them, and generally takes the fact that they hold a certain view to be reason for skepticism about it. The hypothesis that she remains a Lutheran to please or to avoid conflict with her family is disconfirmed. To round out the picture, we can add that Able shows little inclination to fellowship or association, her church membership being her only regular nonvocational involvement, and that the people with whom she works are of other faiths or of none.

In short, there is almost nothing that Able or anyone else could point to that would count as reasons for her continued affiliation and hence for the various actions that constitute that affiliation. Those actions are at best non- or extra-rational, and their lack of fit with her other actions and the beliefs and preferences that inform those other actions make it plausible to say that they are irrational. Certainly it would be difficult to regard Able's expenditure of large amounts of time, money, and effort in this involvement as rational.

Are we to say, then, that Able's churchgoing, money-giving, grace-saying, and the rest are unfree? There is at least one perspective from which we clearly do not want to say this. Despite the foregoing description of Able's religious commitment, or rather without reference to that or any comparable description, her attendance at services, her financial contributions to the church, her mealtime prayers, and so forth, are constitutionally protected. Within quite broad limits, engaging in these activities is her right. It is a right, moreover that is ordinarily denominated the right to the free exercise of religion. This right, and the substantial freedom of action it establishes, is not contingent upon Able's having arrived at, or sustaining, her religious convictions through a process of rational choice. True, public authorities are authorized to consider the character of her convictions for certain purposes and to forbid some classes of actions (polygamy, ritual infliction of pain or harm) that she might claim are required of her by her religious beliefs. They are also authorized to deny to her certain immunities (such as exemption from conscription and from some taxes) that may be granted to others out of regard for their religious beliefs if the authorities judge her convictions to be wanting by certain criteria. But these inquiries, and the judgments to which they may lead, are not inquiries into the rationality of the religious doctrines to which Able subscribes, nor (with an exception to be taken up below) into her rationality in adopting and continuing to accept these doctrines. In the first case, actions are forbidden on the ground that they violate rights of others or disserve some social or public interest or good. In the second, Able's petition for immunities may be denied on the ground that her beliefs are not genuinely religious in character, on the ground that her admittedly religious beliefs do not in fact forbid the performance of the duties from which she seeks exemption, or on the ground that she does not sincerely hold the beliefs that she professes. Rationality enters the picture, if at all, only indirectly or circuitously.

Insofar, then, as Able's constitutional rights are respected by her government and by other persons, there is an obvious and important sense in which her conduct is free in the realm of religious faith as she understands and practices it. This freedom is without regard, or virtually without regard, to the substantive or procedural rationality of her thought and conduct vis-à-vis her religion.

We might call the freedom just discussed religious freedom in the public law sense—or somewhat more grandly, the public or political sense of religious freedom.[3] In a study that is at least nominally focused on *political* freedom, freedom in this sense must be accorded great significance.

It might be argued, however, that this is both a deliberately and uniquely relaxed or latitudinarian conception of freedom. Finding it impossible to maintain anything approaching the uniformity in religious belief and practice that one would expect if belief and practice were substantially rational in character, modern Western states made the second-level rational decision to abandon the attempt for public and political purposes. As one might put it, confronted with a powerful and a burgeoning irrationality in respect to religion, these states decided, faute de mieux, to uncouple rationality and freedom in this one respect or this one realm of conduct. For purposes of maintaining social peace—and hence maximizing the possibility of effective freedom?—they decided not merely to permit irrational behavior (which they had of course been doing all along in many respects), but to christen that behavior with the honorific name of "freedom." The important point is that those who effected this decision knew full well that the public-law freedom they were establishing was inferior if not ersatz in character. Insofar as religious conduct and practice lacked rationality, it was free only in the deliberately weakened public-law sense. To return to that rather pathetic Lutheran of my earlier discussion, one could agree that she is and should be free in the public-law sense of religious freedom and yet insist that, by virtue of the nonrational or irrational character of her religiosity, she is unfree in every sense of the term not corrupted by regrettable political necessities. The statements "She is free" in the public-law sense and "She is unfree" in any other sense do not contradict each other. And the fact that they can be jointly true discloses the deplorable state of affairs of public life in modern Western societies.

I return below to the case that might be made for saying that my Lutheran is unfree in other than the public-law sense of freedom. But first we must examine somewhat more closely the conceptual dimensions of what I have provisionally called the public-law sense of freedom. On the account I gave, it is difficult for Able or anyone else to say *why* Able is a Lutheran. "Rational," "rationality," and their negative or privative counterparts are of course terms of assessment and evaluation. When we say that a person's commitments and choices are substantively and/or procedurally rational, we are usually (unless we are extreme romantics or 60s radicals opposed to "linearity") praising her and them; when we say they are nonrational and especially irrational, we are usually criticizing. But these terms, especially in their positive mode, are also terms of explanation and understanding (see Nagel 1970, chaps. 6, 7). Or rather they are place holders for kinds of explanation that we frequently give ourselves for human actions. Noticing that Able goes to church most Sundays, we ask why she does so. An explanation of sorts, which we can give even on the above account of Able's Lutheranism, is that she is a person of religious faith. In our cultural tradition (as in numerous others), it is not only common but commonly expected that people who are religious believers will regularly attend church services. (At least in this sense, Able's churchgoing is not an *acte gratuit*.) Indeed people who claim to be believers but who rarely attend such services often feel some need to explain why they don't. The association between religious belief and church attendance is strong enough that the claim to the first is put into doubt by the absence of the second. Whatever one's own views about religion and about the relationship between religion and church attendance, as an even moderately well-informed participant in the culture one accepts that there is a rational—or at least an intelligible—relationship between the belief and the action.

The rationality of that relationship, however, is not somehow inherent or self-evident. Except in the thinnest sense of rationality, we recognize and accept the relationship as rational because we are aware of a number of further, more specific doctrines and beliefs that connect the two. (Rational nonattendance consists, for example, in accepting some of the doctrines that make up a religious faith but rejecting on reasoned grounds the particular tenets that require or recommend church attendance.) This consideration focuses a possible difficulty about Able's Lutheranism and about the claim that the actions it involves are free. As described above, Able neither holds nor rejects any such further doctrines and beliefs. As a person of religious faith, she accepts that it is appropriate for her to attend church. But if we ask her why, if we ask for a more detailed and at least in that sense a more satisfying explanation for her more or less regular attendance at services, she can make no (further) response. Imagine that she is confronted by a fellow Lutheran who always plays golf on Sunday morning and who has a well-developed version of the argument (the rationalization, as the more orthodox will say) that there is no authority in scripture, in the writings of Luther or in those of other authoritative figures, for a duty of attendance, that she can better worship God among the beauties of God's nature than in a stuffy auditorium, that every believer is her own priest, and so forth. Having no response to these or any analogous arguments, Able has no reason grounded in the particulars of her professed faith to attend or not to attend church services. Her attendance is shown to be nonrational from the point of view of her faith as she professes it. And if we assume that she would enjoy playing golf on Sunday mornings, her church attendance is irrational and must be explained, if indeed it is not simply inexplicable, in terms of some other kind.

The question presents itself, then, whether the move that all but eliminates rationality from the public-law conception of freedom of religion leaves that conception unintelligible in respect to the very cases that motivate it. Insofar as religious conduct has a rational component, we can identify and understand instances of it and hence we can decide when the public-law doctrine applies and when not. By contrast, if confronted with behavior that is devoid of rationality, we have no way to decide whether it is religious conduct and hence whether the public-law protections properly apply to it. "Behavior" that is devoid of rationality is unintelligible. If there is to be a "public law" (or any other) conception of freedom, it can apply only to agents who are, and to conduct that is, in some degree rational.

Several observations are appropriate here. First, public law conceives of and concerns itself with religion as one of a number of dimensions or aspects of human conduct. The judgment that religious beliefs and actions are distinctive in various aspects could not be made if there were no commonalities and continuities between them and beliefs and actions of various other kinds. Persons who form and act upon religious beliefs also form and act upon an array of beliefs of other kinds and they must maintain some degree of consonance or at least coordination among the several kinds. If or to the extent that the working assumption of rationality is sustained in respect to the non- or extra-religious activities of a person and in respect to the coordination she maintains between her religious and her extra-religious activities, to that extent others can make sense of the latter by attending to the commonalities between religious and nonreligious conduct and by attending to the coordination among her several kinds of activity. If, *per impossible*, Able were nothing but a Lutheran, her Lutheranism might be unintelligible. Given that she is also a member of a family, a consumer, a citizen, a job-holder, and given that she is all of these things in a society and a culture, her Lutheranism is less intelligible than the more evidently rational of her activities, but it is not unintelligible.

Second, the public-law conception of religious freedom at least tacitly assumes a rational component in religious conduct itself. There may be no such component in certain aspects of religion—say those aspects, if any, that depend exclusively on revelation—but there can be rationality around or in connection with those aspects. My Lutheran is exceptional, even deviant, in this respect. We make such sense of her as we can by interpreting her behavior on the model provided by other religious people. She cannot articulate a connection between her faith and her churchgoing, but we are familiar with the idea that there is an intelligible connection between them because many people make it.

These first two observations are particular instances of a generalization that is commonplace in the literature concerning rationality. Judgments about the nonrationality and irrationality of human conduct are made against a background of and by comparison with the repeatedly justified assumption that human conduct is more or less rational. In this perspective, the public-law conception of religious freedom, as a conception generally understood and employed in our culture, is distinctive not in abandoning assumptions of rationality altogether but in knowingly and deliberately reducing the expectation and requirements of rationality in respect to particular aspects of religious thought and action.

It does not follow, however, and this is my third observation, that rationality in particular behaviors is a necessary condition of the intelligibility of those behaviors. It does not follow, that is, that the absence of rationality in a subset of the activities of a person requires us to remove those activities from the category of action and into the class of behaviors or movements to be explained (and in that sense understood) as brought about by the workings of a patterned set of causal forces over which the person in question has no control. Against the background of assumptions such as those just discussed, Elster is correct that "intentional analysis does not presuppose rational actors" (1979, 153). "Contradictory and paradoxical intentions may be intelligible in terms of a project even if that project is not rational." Recognition of this limits "the scope of rational-choice models" of human conduct, but it also opens up "the possibility of making sense of behaviour that would otherwise be thought of as pathological and as subject to causal analysis only" (ibid). When we observe Able taking herself off to church on Sunday morning we start with the assumption that she has a reason (however good or bad we may judge it to be) for doing so; she thinks doing so will help her to attain salvation, that it will firm her moral resolve in the coming week, please her intensely religious daughter, provide her with an excuse for not embarrassing herself on the golf course, or something of the sort. If this assumption is disconfirmed by the evidence, if there is no evidence for it independent of the theory or assumption of rational choice with which we began, we give it up (ibid., 156). Unlike the practitioners of what Elster rightly calls a "shallow kind of social science," we do not rush to the assumption that Able is in the grip of some biological, neurophysiological, or psychopathological force. In the setting of a culture with traditions, conventions, established practices, shared understandings, and the like, we can make sense of what Able is doing. She is intentionally doing one of the things that people who conceive of themselves as religious do. We can classify her action as of a familiar kind, we can sketch the relationship between that action and a variety of related actions, we can trace out the implications and consequences of that action for a variety of arrangements and practices and for other actors and their actions.

We are, however, sometimes obliged to give up the assumption of intentionality as well as of rationality. Imagine that Able regularly attends church and at least appears to do so intentionally, willingly, even enthusiastically. Others notice, however, that on occasions when she is prevented from going by the flu or a cold she displays apprehension, can't sleep Sunday night, is depressed for much of the ensuing week, and so on. Inquiry into her past reveals that as a child she had repeatedly been badly frightened by a hell-and-damnation preacher. She doesn't mention this experience, but family and friends suspect that both her depression and her usual churchgoing are best explained by it.

There are intricate conceptual questions about how such information should be interpreted. Suppose that between Monday and Saturday Able makes clear her intention to attend church on the coming Sunday. She says she intends to do so, rejects proposals for alternative Sunday morning activities for this reason, and so forth. If we adopt John Searle's distinction between (prior) intentions and intentions in action it seems clear that Able has the prior intention to go to church (Searle 1983, esp. chap. 3). But the facts that Able intends to go to church, and in fact goes, are not sufficient to show that her going to church is an intentional act.

To take clearer cases first, if on awakening on Sunday Able changed her mind, decided to play golf, but went to church at the point of a gun wielded by the neighborhood religious fanatic, her *churchgoing* would be a movement of hers caused by the actions of the fanatic. (Of course she acted intentionally, out of fear, to save her life.) If in the more difficult case first imagined we also deny that the usual churchgoing is the intentional act it appeared to be we may be (1) positing a conscious but concealed intention to act so as to avoid anxiety and depression, we may be (2) attributing an unconscious intention directed to the same objective, or we may be (3) asserting that Able is in the grip or under the control of internal psychological forces and is not acting at all.

In the first case, Able's "churchgoing" has turned out to be intentional but less religious and more rational than we allowed in our initial discussion. In the second, we can also say that, objectively, Able's action is rational. The question whether Able is *acting* rationally will turn on exactly what is involved in our saying that her intention is unconscious. My driving to work is consciously intentional. In the course of carrying out that action I perform many "subsidiary" actions—shifting gears, changing lanes, maintaining a certain distance from the car in front of me—that are intentional but not done within conscious awareness of them (Searle 1983, 2). Suppose having a passenger who is learning to drive makes me conscious of these actions. If

I can give reasons for them, state how and why they contribute to my driving, I am, and all along was, acting rationally in performing them. By contrast, if Able's unconscious intention is to stave off anxiety and depression, but she has no concept of *why* churchgoing has that effect, only *that* it does, then her action stands in a rational relationship to the intention with which and the purpose for which she takes it, but *she* gets no very high marks for rationality.

The third case is difficult to establish conclusively. If in general Able seems a tolerably ordinary sort of agent, then philosophy of inquiry and explanation as well as elementary civility counsel against rushing to embrace the notion of controlling psychological forces. How exactly should we formulate the *explanans* and the *explanandum*? Does Able go into depression if she misses Sunday services when she is on vacation? If she fails to make the Sunday evening sing? Wednesday church dart-ball? Does everyone who was subjected to fire-and-brimstone preaching as a child have this problem? Everyone who was subjected between age four and eight? Between four and eight plus having one older brother, two younger sisters, and a father with a drinking problem? Does church attendance stave off the depression for everyone liable to it? For some specifiable subclass of those who are? The substantial complications created by giving up the assumption of Able's rationality are modest by comparison with those resulting from the denial of her intentionality. Nevertheless, there are cases in which we must accept and confront these complications. For the limited purposes of the present discussion we can do so by employing again the formula used in earlier chapters. If Able's "churchgoing" genuinely is unintentional, then Able is not an agent engaged in action, she is not freedom-evaluable, and her behavior raises questions about the public-law conception of freedom only in the sense that those who are close to Able might properly attempt to assist Able in extending her freedom-evaluability to those areas of her life that involve religion.[4]

The "public law" law conception of religious freedom is neither incoherent nor trivial. It makes a quite standard presumption of intentional agents engaged in intentional action in a cultural setting and it assigns to all such agents a right to a wide variety of such actions, a right that is as highly valued as it is socially, morally, and politically consequential. It makes a working assumption that these agents are more or less rational in various aspects of their religious conduct, but neither the possession nor (with few and conceptually ambiguous exceptions) the exercise of the right it establishes are conditional upon satisfaction of that assumption by any particular action or by the actions of any particular agent. It would be wrong to say that the public-law conception uncouples rationality and freedom. It would certainly be wrong to say that it abandons, dismisses, or even derogates rationality. But it is true and important that this salient feature of modern Western thinking concerning freedom, a feature which to my knowledge distinguishes Western modernity from all other cultural traditions, makes decidedly modest demands upon the rationality of those who participate in its freedom.

II

So far as the role of rationality in religious freedom is concerned, there remains the question of the basis of the agent's assessment of attempted interferences with her religious conduct. Constitutional and/or legal rights and the understandings that underlie and inform them reduce but manifestly do not eliminate attempts at coercion and compulsion in the religious realm. If the agent misassesses these attempts, allowing herself to be unnecessarily deterred from courses of actions she would prefer to take, the resulting loss of freedom is arguably a consequence, or in part a consequence, of a failure of rationality on her part.

This question, however, is entirely general. There may be forms or methods of coercion, deception, manipulation, and the like that are distinctive to or distinctively prevalent in the religious dimensions of life, but in one mode or another they are encountered throughout human affairs, and freedoms of all kind depend to some extent on the ability to cope with them. To the extent that this ability involves rationality, as a practical matter rationality will be (instrumentally) necessary to freedom in all cases save those in which agents are protected by good fortune, by societal arrangements, or by other agents, from external interferences with their actions. Accordingly, I will consider the question in general terms. This consideration will be facilitated by some final remarks about the public-law conception of religious freedom.

"Until the wars of religion in the sixteenth and seventeenth centuries . . . social cooperation on the basis of mutual respect was regarded as impossible with those of a different faith; . . . As a philosophical doctrine, liberalism has its origins . . . with the development of the various arguments for religious toleration. . . . A crucial assumption of liberalism is that equal citizens have different and indeed incommensurable and irreconcilable conceptions of the good. In a modern democratic society the existence of such diverse ways of life is seen as a normal condition which can only be removed by the autocratic use of state power" (Rawls 1982b, 17–18). On the view Rawls here states, as a historical matter modern Western thought about freedom evolved through the spread (the generalization), to much of moral, political, and legal life of conclusions first reached about freedom of religion. In theoretical terms, the public-law conception of religious freedom, so far from being limited or even special to religion, embodies the fundamental elements of the dominant modern philosophy of freedom.[5] It is assumed that individual agents will be more or less rational in the formulation and pursuit of their personal ends and purposes (of their conceptions of their own good, as Rawls says); but across the entire range of personal ends and goods society as an organized system of cooperation disavows authoritative criteria of substantive rationality. The individual's standing as a member of society deserving respect— and hence as a holder of the rights society creates—is independent of the rationality of her ends. If her ends or her ways of pursuing them violate the rights of other members or otherwise contravene the basic terms of association (the principles of justice in Rawls's system), they will be disallowed. But this is because they are unjust and unreasonable, not because they are irrational. The rationality of ends is a matter for interaction below the level of the state or public association; in numerous respects in addition to that of religion, the state will intervene to protect freedom of action—including actions of the most doubtful rationality—against interference from a variety of sources. Of course many people think this practice ill-conceived, if not degraded. But the fervor with which they press their objections may testify to the basic verisimilitude of Rawls's account. At the level of public life (and hence of private life insofar as it is regulated by the norms of public life), the public-law conception of religious freedom will serve as well as the public conception of the relation between rationality and freedom.

This understanding is of material significance for the question of the rationality requisite and/or desirable in coping with threatened interferences with attempts to act. Insofar as the public conception of freedom is in fact implemented, what historically have been major grounds or justifications for such interference are delegitimated or disqualified.

Modern Western societies have pursued a delegitimating and deflecting strategy through a variety of more or less organized and formalized devices. Legal systems adopted and enforced by government consist in important part of prohibitions against interferences with freedom of action; these prohibitions are enlarged and extended by established rights that have constitutional or other specially privileged standing. True, these arrangements generally suppose agents who are familiar with and able to assert and defend their legal and constitutional rights. But government is assigned a variety of affirmative responsibilities in this regard, responsibilities that range from maintaining armies and police, prosecutors, courts, and prisons, to what by now is a vast administrative apparatus devoted to, among other things, reducing the extent to which individuals must fend for themselves in maintaining their own freedom of action.

Governments are the clearest example of what we might think of as a developed system of specialization of the function of protecting freedom. The task of determining the scope of legitimate and illegitimate freedom of action is assigned, first and foremost, to them. Of course the entire population may, and to varying extents does, participate in this process, and it is clearly a generalized assumption of modern Western societies that the preponderance of its members are able and to some extent at least willing to do so. But an elaborate system of representative institutions, invested with the exclusive authority to make and administer many such decisions, creates and sustains a quite clearly defined division of labor in this regard. Most members of modern societies do their thinking and acting within a structure or system that is maintained primarily by a small fraction of the population.

Nor does this "specialization of function" stop with government and governmental institutions invested with formal authority. Most members of modern societies are also members of subsocietal groups that have representative organizations of their own. Unions, professional and trade associations, churches and interdenominational organizations, all of these are charged with protecting and advancing rights and interests—including the right to, and the interest in, various freedoms of action—of their members. In addition, there are organizations such as political parties and "cause" and "public interest" groups that act on behalf of otherwise less well organized constituencies. Finally, individuals who may have few if any doubts about their ends and purposes but are uncertain as to their ability to hold off intrusions and interferences have available to them a variety of hired hands—most obviously lawyers—who claim to be skilled at just this task.

Let us treat this elaborate array of specialized functionaries as part of the structure of modern Western societies. To do so yields a perspective on social structure quite different from those we encountered in Elster, in Goffman, and in Foucault and Marx. Although the last three of these writers would reject Elster's filtering metaphor as anodyne, they all regard social structure as eliminating action possibilities and hence as constricting freedom. Of course this is necessarily the correct view if one begins with an obscure notion such as Elster's "abstractly possible" array of actions, and it is no doubt morally and politically an at least partially correct view in the sense that all such structures exclude action possibilities that are concretely available and quite eligible by normative standards. But it is also possible to think—as Rawls and a long line of predecessors have done—of political and social structures as protecting individual freedoms from intrusions and interferences that would otherwise beset them. More specifically, we can think of such structures (especially to the degree that they are Reasonable in something like Rawls's sense) as reducing the extent to which an individual's freedom depends upon her own capacity to assess and form effective responses to threatened interferences. By virtue of the fact that an individual lives her life in a society with the kind of organized division of labor I have been discussing, she is at least partly relieved of the necessity of taking her own measures to sustain her freedom. Society assumes but does not require that she is rational in forming her own ends and purposes and it organizes itself to provide and maintain the freedom necessary for her to pursue those ends and purposes.[6]

It would be utopian to think that such collective arrangements could entirely eliminate the need for rationality on the part of private individuals. All political and social structures interfere with justifiable individual freedoms to some extent; in numerous societies coping with such structures and their functionaries is itself much the most difficult task confronting individuals attempting to maintain their freedoms. Moreover, while just or "reasonable" political and social structures diminish the, as it were, day-by-day need for defensive rationality, societies with such structures require a considerable number of more, rather than less, rational agents to perform specialized functions; moreover, they are advantaged by the presence of a large number of citizens who participate rationally in public life.[7]

Most important, it is central to what I am calling the public-law doctrine of freedom that there be large areas of activity that are ordinarily of public concern only in the sense that the public authorities will (should) protect certain fundamental rights of those involved in them. The religious activities that gave the doctrine its initial impetus provide a leading example. "Free exercise of religion" is construed to mean that individuals and groups may practice the religion of their choice without interference from public authorities. But within faiths, denominations, sects, and cults, individuals subject one another to a barrage of influences and pressures. Indeed in a society in which religious activities abound, it is sometimes difficult to shield oneself from importunate demands for and against various religious commitments and involvements. Another example is family life. An entrenched aversion to public interference in family affairs is characteristic of modern Western societies. Within very broad limits, individuals must fend for themselves in sustaining their freedom of action against what not infrequently are the very difficult to resist interferences of other family members. In varying degrees the same is true of the workplace, the marketplace, the school, and indeed of all of the settings in which members of society encounter one another. As critics of what Rawls calls liberalism have long objected, societies that adopt what I have called the public conception of freedom typically also adopt the Hobbesian view that individuals "worthy" of freedom can and should sustain it for themselves in most of their activities. As the same critics have pointed out, the conjunction of these commitments is no accident. If value-pluralism is as central to the public conception of freedom as Oakeshott, Berlin, Rawls, and others argue, a society that adopts the one will be hard-pressed to avoid the other.

It is not as though the public conception of freedom bears upon private activities and interactions exclusively in the ways discussed thus far. If we look behind or beneath the conception, we find what I earlier called the doubly normative beliefs and values about freedom and equality. (On this view the public conception of freedom is in effect one of several specifications and elaborations of those beliefs and values, others being libertarianism and democratic participationism.) Widespread acceptance of these beliefs and values informs and sustains the public conception. It also influences thought and action in the family, the marketplace, the church, and so forth. The members of a population that acculturates, socializes, and educates itself within these assumptions will be less disposed to interfere coercively with one another's activities, more disposed to disapprove of such interferences when they occur. It was Hobbes's mistake to think that a satisfactory freedom (indeed that a Sovereign devoted to protecting freedom) could be sustained in the absence of such dispositions, and it was Goffman's mistake to deny that such dispositions exist and influence conduct in "gatherings" and other informal interaction settings. By reducing the incidence of attempts at coercive interference, informal social processes diminish the need for individuals to assess and respond effectively to such attempts.[8]

III

Our discussion to this point has proceeded on the assumption that concepts like "interference," "obstacle," "coercion," and "constraint" are nontechnical notions that are regularly and successfully used without special explanation. We know what counts as an interference with freedom, we can distinguish between successful and unsuccessful attempts at such interferences, and so forth. In one respect this assumption is clearly warranted. When we use and encounter these concepts we do not have to consult dictionaries or experts; the claims and assertions we advance are rarely corrected in the sense in which parents and teachers correct the diction of their charges.

At the same time, disputes about such claims and assertions are frequent and difficult to resolve. I know what my daughter means when she objects that my questions and comments intrude and interfere, but I deny that they restrict her freedom. My Dean understands my claim that her memorandum about declining enrollments in certain seminars impinges upon my freedom to teach the courses I prefer, but she denies that this characterization is appropriate. Officers of the United States government realize that allied nations, state governments, universities, and other recipients of aid with strings attached regard such offers of assistance as coercive, but they insist that acceptance of the aid is voluntary and that although the "strings" may influence they neither do nor could coerce. Advocates of prayer in public schools deny that the practice menaces the freedom of nonparticipating students. They look to students who are nonreligious or who for other reasons choose not to participate to stand firm against whatever pressures they may experience. Advertisers claim they are providing information valuable to the consumer; the charge that they victimize their audience is insistently denied. Religious cults claim that their followers are disciples, not zealots, and that their proselytizing practices are no more than evangelical. Anarchists argue that law and formal authority are incompatible with freedom, libertarians contend that taxation is forced labor and conscription slavery. Contractarians rejoin that all these institutions and practices might well be based on freedom-preserving consent, while liberals and socialists contend that they are essential to and may enhance freedom.

Because we the parties to these controversies command the language in which they are conducted (and share in the form of life in which that language has meaning), the disputes are genuine, i.e., mutually intelligible, (sometimes) intelligently conducted, and not infrequently resolved for longer or shorter periods among larger or smaller numbers of people. We are not typically talking past one another, and the considerations we advance are not necessarily rationalizations of or masks for interests independent of the considerations we advance. As the examples indicate, however, the controversies recur and persist. Neither our culture and its language nor the efforts of jurists, theorists, and other persona of our high culture provide decision procedures or criteria fine enough of mesh or grain to banish or to still them.

This defect—if that is what it is—is not likely to be remedied. For reasons that will emerge in the following discussion, it is most unlikely that we can extract or construct a calculus that could, even in principle, settle all questions of the form "Was some A made unfree by some B to do some X?" It does not follow that general discussion of these matters is without profit. An abundant recent literature on the subject shows that much can be done to assemble and to sort the kinds of considerations pertinent to answering such questions. Such efforts are of practical value in that they identify confusions and inappropriate argumentative strategies. More important here, they help us to see the significance of questions (and the manner of their resolution) about interference, constraint, and coercion for the larger theory of freedom.

To get our bearings let us recur to the distinction between freedom$_1$ and freedom$_2$. Theorists of Pure Negative Freedom restrict freedom to the former and claim as a major advantage of doing so that questions about obstacles, impediments, and interferences thereby become straightforward and manageable. Given that A is capable of self-movement and here and now is moving in direction and fashion X, B interferes with A's freedom insofar as she makes A's movement impossible. Granting that such cases are more manageable than questions about coercion, duress, intimidation, and the like, numerous complications nevertheless arise. We must satisfy ourselves that A is moving herself as opposed to being moved by some other agent or agency. Again, if A is already under some restraint, we must have means to discover that she is disposed or trying to move. If A is, in her own right as it were, inert, we can say that B makes it impossible for her to move, perhaps that A is in fact unfree to move because of B, but we cannot say that B is interfering with A's freedom of movement. The notion of self-movement is simpler than the notion of action, but it involves more than the mere fact of A's body crossing or failing to cross spatial coordinates.

There will also be questions about the potency of B's interference. B is herself in A's path or has placed or left obstacles in that path. But could A push B or the obstacles aside? Easily, or only with vigorous, perhaps painful, or otherwise costly effort? If we view A as a physical entity, there are some obstacles that she simply cannot overcome, some forces that are quite irresistible for her. But within the limits of her physical constitution, A generates sometimes more sometimes less force depending on her emotional state, her sense of what is at stake, her relationship with B, and many other factors. If A could overcome B's interference but uses the fact that B is in her path as an excuse for moving in another direction or not at all, B has not made A unfree.

Many further complications present themselves concerning B. One sure way to prevent A from moving is to kill her; a sure way to prevent a wide range of movements is to cripple her. But to do these things is not to make A unfree, it is to destroy what on the Pure Negative Freedom conception are the necessary and sufficient conditions of her freedom-evaluability. B's interference must remediably or "undo-ably" prevent A's movement. Accordingly, in many cases the question of whether B has interfered with A's freedom will turn on judgments about what B intended to do. Further, we want to distinguish between intentional inference and unintentional or even unavoidable obstruc-tion. If B has been tethered by C to a location through which A's movement is to pass, B's body blocks A's movement; but if anyone has interfered with A's freedom, it is C. We can take a heroic version of the behavioral line and restrict "unfreedom" to the "fact" that A's move-ment is blocked; but then we will have to devise some different language to deal with the further questions just mentioned, questions that as a matter of unheroic course are dealt with in the language of freedom. Even if we were able to do without agency and action concepts in respect to A, we would need them in respect to B.

None of this is to deny that physical constraint of bodily movement is the type case of unfreedom. But this is because most human *actions* necessarily involve such movements and hence are prevented by physical constraints. The closer and more effective the constraints, the greater the array of otherwise possible actions that are prevented by them. Accordingly, cases of such constraint are prominent in discus-sions of *the value of* freedom, of the reasons for protecting, enhancing, or diminishing it. We can easily agree about the objectionable charac-ter of bondage and imprisonment because we can do so without having to agree about—or even to identify—the value or justifiability of any particular action or array of actions. Contrary to Berlin, this is not because imprisonment is objectionable without reference to interests or desires, ends or purposes, but because imprisonment prevents the pursuit of a vast array of the ends and purposes that human beings are known to adopt and pursue (cf. Berlin 1969, xliiin).

It is for reasons related to the points thus far discussed, however, that cases of direct physical constraint and compulsion figure mainly as distant benchmarks in discussions of *what counts as* unfreedom. In this context the interesting and the disputed cases are those in which B acts on or against A not by directly controlling the movements of A's body, but rather, as we might put it, through the medium of A's beliefs and desires, hopes and fears, thoughts and judgments. B makes A unfree not by literally preventing or compelling the movements of A's body, but (roughly) by inducing A to forgo or to take actions that, in the absence of B's intervention, A would not take or not forgo.

We already have reason to appreciate the recalcitrant and at least apparently paradoxical character of these issues. It is the burden of Chapters 5 and 6 that there are no human actions or attempted actions that are uninfluenced by other persons. If such influence is pervasive, how are we to distinguish those influences that make A unfree from those that leave her in freedom or even contribute to her freedom? In a more paradoxical formulation, how can we say that an event is at once an action taken or forgone by A *and* an event brought about or prevented by B?

If we abstract from a valuable but convoluted literature on this topic, the first point to recognize here is that our statements about freedom and unfreedom are not merely descriptive but normative. Consider examples that are, descriptively, relatively straightforward because they involve effective physical compulsion or prevention. Descriptively, it is true that pulling guards interfere with the freedom of linebackers to tackle halfbacks; it is equally true that the fact that Baker has occupied a parking place prevents Able from taking it. It would nevertheless be surprising, inappropriate, and even false for a linebacker or for Able to complain about interference with their freedom. Given the rules and conventions of (American) football and of the parking game, these do not count as instances of being made unfree.[9]

The point is of course conceptual: it is about the circumstances or setting in which judgments about constraint and compulsion, coercion and intimidation are made, not about the moral or other merits of any particular set of norms. And as is suggested by Benn and Weinstein's phrase "the normal conditions of action," these circumstances include many kinds of features in addition to such explicit, codified norms as the laws of labor-management relations, the rules regarding interference in football, and the customs concerning competition for parking spaces. There is a set of beliefs about normal as opposed to defective human capacities, about what is intelligible as a human end, and about the comparative importance of various recurrent ends, about the temptations and inducements, the costs and frustrations, with which human beings can be expected to cope or to bear without giving up their own ends and purposes, about the obligations and responsibilities that we owe to one another and the communities we form. These general beliefs, values, norms are supplemented by local, temporally delimited understandings concerning, in Robert Nozick's phrase, "the normal or expected course of events" in various activities and interaction settings (1969, 447ff.).

Among the most general of these beliefs and norms is what Benn terms the principle of noninterference, "the minimal or formal principle that no one may legitimately frustrate a person's acting without some reason" (1975–76, 109). The interpretation and application of this principle occurs in the setting of the wider array of beliefs and norms to which I have been referring. "Person" refers to human beings with something like the normal physical and mental characteristics; "acting" to the intentional, purposive pursuit of ends intelligible to others; "frustrate" to forces too powerful, obstacles too high, burdens, costs, and temptations too great, for human beings to bear and still continue with their course of action; "legitimately" and "reason" to authorizing, licensing, or justifying considerations such as rules or norms against what A is doing, understandings according to which B is entitled to compete with A in the activity in question, obligations or responsibilities that B has to intervene in A's affairs for A's benefit, and value rankings according to which the ends B is pursuing are more worthy or more pressing than A's and should take precedence when as a practical matter there is a conflict between them.

In the absence of some such array of beliefs and values, the principle of noninterference would be empty in a stronger sense than that in which Hegelians say Kantian principles are empty. The concepts of which the principle consists would apply to anything and hence to nothing. On the other hand, with such an array as the setting in which the principle is invoked, it is possible to generalize concerning what counts as an instance of B's illegitimately "frustrating" A's attempt to act. Thus we have instructive discussions distinguishing compulsions from pressures and influences, threats from warnings and advice, bribes from offers, provocations from invitations, intimidation from persuasion, propaganda from education.[10] Despite the considerable complexity of the best of these accounts, their authors recognize that the formulas they present take life from the illustrations through which they are developed, and that the formulas capture no more than the "central cases" of the phenomenon with which they are concerned

(Nozick 1979, 445 and passim). This is both what one would expect and a point of theoretical and practical importance. Shackles that will hold most of us will not contain Harry Houdini; blocking patterns that will handle the average linebacker will not do for Bronko Nagurski; "your money or your life" may not work with the mother taking her savings to pay for a vital operation for her child; fines and jail sentences quiet many impulses and deflect many inclinations but do not deter the hardened criminal and may be an incentive to disobedience for the civil-rights worker; propaganda that sways a mob and advertising that proves irresistible to millions of consumers may be laughable to those who are well-informed or disciplined in critical thinking. We cannot make a beginning concerning unfreedom without generalizations about human beings, but neither can we resolve concrete questions about it on the basis of such generalizations. The question whether an assignable B made an assignable A unfree in respect to a particular X is a matter for practical deliberation, not for discourse at the theoretical level.

IV

The position I have just taken provides a background for discussing the topics I want to consider anew by way of concluding this chapter, namely, the relationship between freedom and rationality and the distinction between freedom of agency (freedom$_2$) and autonomy (freedom$_3$).

Many will find unwelcome the conclusion that there is no set of generalizations, and no calculus or decision procedure, that will assure correct judgments as to whether an assignable B compelled, coerced, intimidated, or otherwise deprived an assignable A of her freedom. The conclusion appears to leave such judgments—and the many further matters that depend on such judgments—subjective and indeterminate, thereby promising unresolvable dispute and making conflict all too likely. If disputes are resolved and conflicts avoided, this is a matter of chance or luck, not something brought about by deliberate, purposive efforts.

The concepts "reason" and "reasonable," "rational" and "rationality," are the notions we most commonly use in talking about reducing subjectivity and indeterminacy, arriving at conclusions that are correct for anyone, reducing disagreement and conflict. "Let us reason together" is a summons to employ shared human capacities in assessing and disciplining the subjective, idiosyncratic characteristics and concerns that divide us and bring us into conflict. Insofar as we are rational in our thought and action, we can resolve questions about freedom and unfreedom to our mutual satisfaction. Insofar as we are irrational or nonrational, we have little prospect for doing so. In this perspective it is hardly surprising that theorists have sought to establish a strong connection between freedom and rationality.

The matter of autonomy is more complex, partly because the range of disagreement about the concept itself is wide. On many construals, however, the autonomous person is someone who is rational in a distinctively strong sense. In particular, autonomy involves making and acting on rational assessments of more than one's own ends and choices of means and more than the actions of others with whom one is directly involved. Those who have attained to autonomy employ their powers of rationality concerning the traditions and institutions, the conventions and rules, that provide the setting in which day-to-day activities occur. Such persons are better able to protect and to profit from their individual freedom, and they make a unique contribution to their societies.

There are at least two respects in which the views just sketched command assent. The first is that freedom in modern Western societies presupposes persons who are rational in the sense of having the faculty of reason and in the sense of conducting themselves more or less rationally in many aspects of their activities. An indeterminate but substantial element of rationality in these senses forms a salient part of the notion of "normal" persons that we have encountered and invoked in several contexts; various defects of rationality largely define abnormality.[11]

The second is that rationality contributes to achieving and enhancing freedom in the sense that it is instrumentally valuable to those who seek freedom. Other things being equal, persons who are steadily and comprehensively rational are better placed to achieve and enhance their own freedom and the freedom of others than persons who are inconstantly and meagerly so. This is true because our rationality allows us to understand, influence, and adapt effectively to the world in which we act, and because it clarifies and sometimes helps us to resolve freedom-threatening differences and conflicts. Writers who set up an antinomy between freedom and reason misconstrue both.

But these remarks, which might be thought platitudinous were they not sharply contested in influential quarters, leave the hard questions about rationality and freedom untouched. We have discussed respects in which the *requirement* of rationality has been deliberately abandoned or severely qualified in modern thinking about freedom. The considerations that led to this policy, and the fact that the policy is widely regarded as responsible for the great modern successes in regard to stability, harmony, and human well-being as well as freedom, are reasons to hesitate before endorsing strong connections between freedom and rationality. With this in mind, along with the others cautionary notes that have already been struck, I consider an articulate version of the argument that there is a conceptual—and in that sense a necessary—connection between freedom and rationality in respect to what (direct physical compulsion aside) is arguably the most important source of unfreedom, namely, coercion.

Bernard Gert analyzes the concept of unfreedom that is brought about by coercion through the notion of an "unreasonable incentive," that is, an incentive "that it would be unreasonable for any rational man not to act on" (1972, 34).[12] "Incentive" combines "reason" in the sense of warranted or grounded beliefs about good and evil and "motive" in the sense of beliefs that are actually held by A and that explain her actions. Thus B coerces A to do or omit doing X (coerces her to X) only if B provides A with beliefs that actually move her to X and make it rational for anyone in the situation to X. It follows that coercion can occur only if: (1) there are standards of rational action that hold for anyone who is rational; (2) there are persons who know and correctly apply those standards; (3) A is such a person and is acting as such a person in the situation in question; (4) applying the standards of rationality shows that B provided A with unreasonable incentives to X.[13]

Taken as generalizations about ordinary discourse concerning freedom and coercion, this list of conditions seems to me unobjectionable and informative. Are they necessary conditions or even invariable features of that discourse? Should they be? In answering these questions it is important to emphasize restrictions that Gert places on his thesis. First, he distinguishes between coercion and enticement. If B entices A to X by offering A some good, Y, B has not coerced A. This is not because "good" is a subjective, voluntaristic, or otherwise agent-variable notion. There is an exhaustive list of goods, namely, "abilities, freedom and opportunity, and pleasure" (Gert 1972, 33) that are universal in the sense that they are, in fact, good for all rational persons. No rational person will avoid these goods unless she has a reason for doing so. But rational persons "need no reasons for not seeking goods, they need reasons only for avoiding goods or not avoiding evils" (ibid.). It follows that "consequences which involve the gaining of a good only generally, but not always, provide motives to rational men" (ibid, 34). A's claim to have been coerced to X by B's offer, bribe, or other enticement Y is invalid because A might rationally have chosen not to seek Y. On Gert's view, rationality is importantly contributive to the freedom to pursue one's good because it is rationality that tells one what the goods are and hence the range within which one's good in a particular situation must fall. But it is not dispositive concerning action to achieve good in any particular case, and hence is not necessary to the freedom to so act, because one needs no reason not to pursue the goods available in a situation. At least in this respect Gert's rationalist account of freedom makes concessions to pluralist, voluntarist, and extrarationalist theories. And because he treats persons pursuing their choices of good as agents engaged in action, he incorporates freedom of agency or freedom$_2$ into his account.

Gert argues that rationality is yet more decisive as regards evils and their avoidance. As with goods, he begins with an allegedly exhaustive list of the things that are evil for all rational persons. "The evils are death, pain, disability, loss of freedom or opportunity,. and loss of pleasure. Anything else that is . . . an evil is so because it involves one of these" (1972, 33). But there is no analogue to the option to decide not to seek a good and yet give no reason for one's decision. "Consequences which involve the avoiding of an evil always provide motives to all rational men, for all rational men must seek to avoid any evil—unless they have a reason" (ibid., 34). The thesis I am considering is nevertheless importantly qualified, this time by a distinction between significant and minor evils coupled with a notion that rational action requires a balancing of evils and goods. It is further qualified by recognition of the rationally underdetermined character of at least some decisions about evils and hence of a degree of justified variability in the conduct of rational agents: "Of course, not all consequences that involve the avoiding of an evil will be unreasonable incentives. The evils must be significant; usually only death, severe and prolonged pain, serious disability, and extensive loss of freedom will be unreasonable incentives. Only serious evils such as these provide motives that make it unreasonable to expect any rational man not to act on [sic]" (ibid., 34–35). As to balancing evil and good: "Unless we know what act he was supposed to perform, we cannot determine whether an incentive was such that it was unreasonable to expect any rational man not to act on it. A threat that provides an unreasonable incentive for telling a trivial lie will usually not provide an unreasonable incentive for killing a person. In determining whether one is in a coercive situation when being threatened with some evil if one does not do X, the relevant factors are the amount of evil that will result from doing

X, the amount of evil that will result from not doing X, and whether doing X involves violating a moral rule" (ibid., 42–43).

Sensibly, Gert recognizes that people disagree about these often intricate judgments. Having essayed a couple of judgments of his own concerning something approaching concrete issues, he immediately enters the following disavowal: "I do not claim that everyone must adopt the same . . . standards that I have adopted in making my judgments in the previous examples" (1972, 43). Much more generally (and perhaps inconsistently), he allows that "What is an incentive for one man is not always an incentive for another. For though consequences provide reasons independently of anyone's attitude toward them, whether they provide a motive depends upon the agent's attitude toward them. If he does not regard the consequences as part of an acceptable explanation for his doing X, then they do not provide a motive for him and so they are not incentives for him" (ibid., 34). If the "he" referred to in this passage is acting rationally, the statement is inconsistent with Gert's definition of an incentive but it is further evidence (further in relation to the evidence provided in the previously quoted passage) of Gert's recognition that there is warranted variability in judgments about evil and hence coercion. (If A is not acting rationally, the statement is consistent with the rest of the discussion but it is also a recognition of imperfect rationality in Elster's sense and hence of the need for persons other than A to discount if not dismiss A's judgments as to whether A was coerced. I return to this point below.)

When we take account of these circumscriptions and qualifications, the bite of the thesis that agential rationality is a necessary condition of unfreedom due to coercion is weakened. If we focus on the last passages I have quoted, the claim that the conditions I numbered (1) to (4) are necessary conditions of unfreedom might amount to little more than the obvious fact that persons other than A must sometimes judge whether A was in fact coerced by B, together with the standard view that it is our rationality that (sometimes) allows us to elevate such judgments above the merely idiosyncratic or capricious. In the absence of rationality, concepts such as "evil," "threat," "coercion," and "unfreedom" would be unusable. Gert's interconnected formulas do no more than systematize, at the conceptual level, conditions of our practice that have to be recognized by any account of it.

This interpretation is supported by further consideration of the passage about variability of judgment together with a distinction not yet mentioned between acting in freedom and acting freely. Let us assume that those not motivated by threats of what in fact are significant evils are acting nonrationally or irrationally. A refuses to X; she goes ahead with the course of action chosen prior to or independently of B's threat. This is of course a familiar phenomenon, indeed a salient instance of the very phenomenon that led me to moderately skeptical conclusions about the possibilities of generalizing over interferences with freedom. In dealing with it, Gert sticks to his conceptual guns and insists that A is unfree. "To be deprived of freedom it is sufficient that one be threatened with unreasonable incentives" (1972, 39). The fact that B's threat fails to bring about the intended alteration in A's conduct is neither here nor there as regards A's freedom and unfreedom. But Gert allows that A does "act freely." "A man can . . . act freely when he is not free to act, but is being coerced. This can be seen easily enough when he is being coerced to do X but does not do it, in spite of the coercing. Being coerced, though it deprives one of freedom, does not necessarily prevent one from acting freely" (ibid., 40). As in the case of nonrational and irrational decisions not to seek this or that good, Gert here uses "act" and a variant of the notion of freedom to characterize irrational or nonrational performances. In respect to a phenomenon widespread in human affairs, he amends his thesis that rationality is a necessary condition of freedom. In response we might adjust the foregoing characterization of his views along the following lines. In the entire absence of rationality, concepts such as "good" and "enticement," "evil" and "threat," would be unavailable to us. The availability of these concepts, the extent to which we can use them with mutual understanding and in the hope of settling rather than stirring up issues, resolving rather than engendering or exacerbating disagreement, increases in proportion to improvement in the rationality of our thought and action.

We might also describe Gert's argument as allowing proponents of freedom of agency (freedom$_2$) most of what they want to say about freedom, rationality, and coercion but at the same time insisting that more can and must be said about the relationships among these concepts. There are uses of "freedom" and "freely," "coercion" and "coercive" that presuppose rationality only in the weak, generalized sense in which they are supposed by the notions of agency and action. But there are also more closely disciplined senses of those concepts, senses that require a stricter, more universalistic, more conclusive or dispositive rationality. At least in respect to unfreedom due to coercion, the latter senses are primary; they provide a firm intersubjective anchoring for discourse and judgment about coercion: the rationally indisputable instances of coercion that they identify serve as proximate benchmarks in dealing with more or less powerful enticements and inducements, with threats of inconvenience, added costs, comparatively minor harms and injuries, and the like. The *standard* case of coercion is the one involving unreasonable incentives and hence the four conditions I identified at the outset of my discussion of Gert. More disputable cases are properly judged by the extent to which they depart from that standard, can only be judged because we have that standard available to us.

So construed, what might at first have appeared to be an excessively abstract, schematic, and rigidly rationalistic argument takes on a more plausible character. Certainly we require some basis for interpersonal assessments of coercion and allegations of coercion; certainly rationality must play an important role in providing that basis.

In its strongest and most distinctive claims, Gert's argument is nevertheless unacceptable. Even with the qualifications just discussed, his proposed connection between rationality and unfreedom due to coercion is stronger than actually obtains in our ordinary practice and would eliminate or adversely affect valued and valuable features of that practice.

The deepest objection to Gert's view, which I will mention but not pursue, is that it depends upon an untenable metaethics. There could in principle be wide, even universal, agreement that death, or pain, or unfreedom are evils that every rational person must avoid, and there could therefore also be agreement that certain"incentives" are "unreasonable" in Gert's strong sense. Even if that were so, and even if rationality were prominent in the processes through which agreement was reached, this would be no more than a fact about what people have come to believe. The idea that there is some method or procedure by which such beliefs could be conclusively or incontestably warranted is a familiar confusion, one that has been thoroughly exposed by modern philosophy.

Gert is of course aware of this objection and has defended his views against it (most systematically in his book *The Moral Rules* [1970]). The issues are pertinent because most versions of the view that rationality is necessary to freedom invoke some species of rationalist or objectivist or naturalistic ethic. By comparison, the best-known arguments for a less than necessary connection between freedom and rationality are recognizably antinaturalist, pluralist, voluntarist, or subjectivist in their metaethics. Fortunately, however, there are decisive objections to Gert's argument that are yet more proximate to present concerns. For this reason I propose to bracket the metaethical issues for the remainder of my discussion of freedom and rationality, returning to them only as necessary in later chapters.

An objection already familiar from our previous discussions might be termed a historical-sociological version of the argument that a universally correct, rationally indisputable account of good and evil is not available to us. Whatever reasoning might in principle achieve or establish, in fact diversity and disagreement are prevalent in these regards. Moreover, it has come to be widely and deeply believed that this circumstance will continue to obtain. Even if philosophically unwarranted, the consensus on this point engenders skepticism about and antagonism toward claims to have arrived at universal truths about good and evil. Such claims are associated with dogmatism, intolerance, and fanaticism and hence with conflicts that are destructive of freedom. This is not to deny that there are points of wide and rationally well-supported agreement concerning morals, politics, and related matters. Such agreement may extend to beliefs about evils that no one else can reasonably expect a person to endure. But it is both profoundly misleading and dangerous to treat these areas of agreement as "standard" in the sense discussed above. In stable societies agreement may be standard in the statistical sense of frequent, ordinary, even typical. In addition to the fact that such agreement is regarded as far from guaranteed, in other, at least equally important, senses agreement is atypical, not to be expected. What is to be expected in morals, politics, religion, and related realms of life is that reasonable people will arrive at and seek to act upon a variety of divergent and very likely incompatible beliefs.

From this perspective Gert's proposal to treat rational agreement as the standard by which other cases should be judged diminishes or demeans some or all of the beliefs that are held and expressed and patterns of action that actually occur. If rationality and reason are universal, then diversity and plurality, and the partial, the particular, the idiosyncratic, the deviant, that make up the diversity, are nonrational or irrational. We may have to put up with irrationality, but we certainly should not celebrate it, certainly should not treat it as somehow essential to or even a main repository of our freedom. More particularly, what Gert calls "acting freely" in the face of "unreasonable incentives," which might be thought an exemplary assertion and defense of freedom, is nonrational, irrational, and hence reckless. It may even confute our standards of judgment, thereby making difficult the resolution of other cases involving coercion or allegations of coercion. Or to take an example with a different tendency, imagine that A submits "too readily" to B's threats; she regards herself as coerced by threatened consequences that have no place in the rationally warranted inventory of significant evils. She genuinely feels coerced, genuinely believes that she cannot endure the evil that B threatens. Perhaps B is A's priest, Puritan divine, or imam and threatens A with eternal damnation unless she X's. On Gert's view, the rest of us may sympathize with A's irrationality and resultant weakness; we may regard her weakness as a mitigating factor if she commits an evil or shameful act. But we cannot credit, cannot even entertain, the possibility that coercion has actually taken place and that A is unfree. These possibilities are conceptually excluded by Gert's thesis.

To repeat, it is true that the rest of us often must assess A's performances, including her claims and laments about coercion. It is also true that we cannot do so without employing some standard of judgment. The initial plausibility of Gert's position resides in these facts together with three further facts, namely, that standards are by definition general, that they ought to be defensible, and that "reasonable" and "rational" are the concepts we ordinarily employ in determining whether standards are general and defensible. But general is not universal, and there are any number of general standards that are themselves rationally defensible but that do not require rationality of the agents and actions they are used to assess.

In general, human beings are coerced if threatened with death, severe pain, bondage, and so forth. It is therefore rational to employ such threats when trying to coerce someone and reasonable to treat such threats as excusing the performances of those subjected to them. But some people are indifferent to or welcome death; pain thresholds and the capacity to tolerate pain vary; prison has been said to be the just person's proper place in an unjust regime; on a cold night jail may be the preferred abode of derelicts. There are good reasons for supporting the public-law conception of religious freedom and of political association. But the question whether any particular A was coercively prevented from exercising such freedoms does not turn on whether A's religious or political beliefs are substantively rational or whether she was procedurally rational in arriving at them.

What I have called the historical-sociological objection to Gert's thesis provides elements that can be reformulated into conceptual and normative arguments against it. Gert makes it a condition of unfreedom due to coercion that A's beliefs about the significance of the evils with which she is threatened by B are rationally justified in the strong sense that they are beliefs that every rational person in the situation must adopt and act upon. If (by this exacting standard) A underestimates an evil she may think that she acts in freedom but in fact she only "acts freely." If A overestimates the significance of an evil she may think she is coerced, but in fact she acts in freedom. This condition is too strong. There are essentially three reasons for this conclusion, two or which are primarily conceptual in character, the third of which is more insistently normative.

The first reason is that Gert's strong condition precludes our talking about coercion in kinds of cases in which the stringent concept of rational justification has no application. But as we have seen in our discussion of religious examples, talk about coercion in respect to such cases is meaningful and important to us.

The second reason is that Gert's requirement excessively diminishes that significance, for freedom and unfreedom, of *the fact that* A forms and attempts to act upon beliefs about the evil threatened by B. If A believes that Y is an evil she must avoid, she is coerced by B. There are conditions that must be satisfied for this rough formula to be applicable and true. A must be an agent capable of belief and of acting in a manner influenced by her beliefs. For reasons already discussed, the formula is not applicable if, for example, A is suffering from paranoia in the strong sense of a form of psychosis. Assuming this first condition is satisfied, A's belief about Y must be sincerely held, not feigned. As a practical matter this will sometimes be difficult to determine. But Gert's requirement is of no use in making this determination because a merely pretended belief might satisfy that requirement. There must be some intelligible basis or explanation for A's belief, some ground on which A accepts it, some connection with A's other beliefs. But this is only to say that the belief is a belief held by A; it is not to say that the belief is true, or well grounded, or strongly justified. It is certainly not to say that the belief passes Gert's test. If we could be coerced only insofar as we held and acted upon beliefs that must be held and acted upon by all rational persons, coercion would be a much smaller problem among us than in fact it is.

The normative objection can be stated as follows. Much of the savor of freedom comes from actions that are nonrational or irrational by Gert's standard. B threatens A with an evil that is, objectively as it were, significant in Gert's sense. A "underestimates" that evil but nevertheless succeeds in taking her preferred course of action. A's sense of herself and her freedom, her estimate of what matters most about herself and her freedom, may reside importantly in her conviction that actions which many would regard as recklessly irrational are possible for her.[14] On the other hand, much of the sorrow of unfreedom consists in finding oneself constrained and prevented when others are not. A regularly overestimates the significance of evils threatened by others, regularly desists or draws back from her preferred courses of action because of such threats. She is easily victimized. To try to convince her that she overestimates threats, to reason with her and counsel with her, may be a kindness. But to tell her in so many words that she is in fact free is insensitive to the point of being a form of cruelty.

Freedom and unfreedom are properties of the actions of human agents, of this, that, and the next human agent, with the beliefs, desires, and other characteristics that distinguish them from one another. Because human beings differ importantly, the conditions under which they are severally able to attain and sustain freedom differ as well. It serves neither our understanding of freedom nor our freedom itself to blanket this diversity under a spurious conceptual uniformity. Questions about moral and political freedom can be raised only about human beings who are more or less rational in the loose, generalized sense in which we say of ourselves that we are the only creatures on this earth who are rational. There is no stronger sense in which rationality is or should be a necessary condition of our freedom or unfreedom.

V

None of the foregoing discussion and argumentation is antirational, irrationalist, or even subjectivistic in any nontrivial sense. I have denied that rationality in Gert's strong sense is a necessary condition of freedom, and I have at least tacitly expressed doubts about the availability of norms of good and evil that are rationally compelling for all rational persons. But there is a great distance between these denials and doubts and extreme antirational positions found in the traditionalism of de Bonald or Illych, the romanticism of Schlegel or Hesse, the existentialism of Sartre's *L'être et le néant*, or the emotivism of Ayer and Carnap. To disallow Gert's stringent standard in respect to many judgments about good, evil, and coercion is far from denying that some judgments about these matters are more defensible than others. To reject a conceptually necessary connection between freedom and rationality is by no means to deny that rationality contributes to achieving and maintaining freedom. The point is to recognize the diversity and complexity of reason and rationality and let them work with and for the diversity and complexity of freedoms; the point is to avoid hammering that diversity and complexity down to a weapon against freedom as it occurs among and matters to human beings.

It will be easier to maintain this intellectual (and no doubt emotional) stance if we have a clearer account of the distinctions between freedom and autonomy, unfreedom and heteronomy. On the one hand, these concepts are closely related and often are used more or less interchangeably. On the other, there is a tradition in which they are quite sharply distinguished, with one of the salient differences being that autonomy requires rationality in a stronger sense than freedom. If someone learns to use "autonomy" in the stronger sense (perhaps by reading Kant or by exposure to moral philosophy influenced by Kant) but also participates in the tendency to assimilate autonomy and freedom, the likelihood is that freedom will take on the more boldly rationalistic coloration of autonomy. Motivated in part by this speculation, I conclude this chapter by drawing on helpful recent discussions to extend the remarks about autonomy presented at the end of Chapter 6.

A number of recent writers on freedom, notably Stanley I. Benn and John Gray, have developed distinctions between autarchy and its opposite, heterarchy, and autonomy and its opposite, heteronomy. As construed by these writers, autarchy is closely akin to what I am calling freedom of agency or freedom$_2$. In respect to the qualities of agency that it assumes, autarchy, in Benn's words, "is normal, both in the statistical sense and in the sense that human beings who fail to qualify [as manifesting it] are held to be in some measure defective as persons" (1975–76, 123–24). Benn sets out, in quite general terms, some of the positive attributes of the autarchical person (recognizes canons of evidence and inference, is able to decide between alternatives, adjusts decisions to changes of belief), but the bulk of his discussion is in terms of the "defects" that render a person "inner impelled" and hence heterarchic. These defects are roughly the same as those marking the first two or three stages of the continuum I set out in Chapter 4; psychoses, compulsions, more or less severe neuroses, and the like, that is, the disabilities that prevent, wholly or partly, freedom-evaluability (see ibid., 112–17). Gray's view is closely analogous. He argues that in thinking about freedom we should adopt a "conception of rational choice that is . . . minimalist and meagre . . . stipulating only that an agent *have a reason* for what he does. What such a requirement disqualifies as rational conduct is only . . . behavior . . . where no goal or end may be imputed . . . which renders intelligible what he does" (1980a, 530). Accordingly, "autarchic agency denotes the freedom of action of an agent who . . . exercises unimpaired all the normal capacities and powers of a rational chooser" (Gray 1983, 74).

So far as their abilities and dispositions are concerned, the autar-

chical have the characteristics that we routinely (and of course sometimes mistakenly) attribute to the run-of-the-mill people we encounter
in everyday life. Such people (ourselves) draw upon these characteristics in coping, with various degrees of success, with the interferences
and obstacles that confront them in the course of their activities. But
this loosely defined, variously combined set of qualities is not sufficient
for autonomy. "To be a chooser is not enough for autonomy, for a
competent chooser may still be . . . choosing by standards he has
accepted quite uncritically from his milieu. He assesses situations,
adapts means to ends, and so on, but always by norms . . . absorbed
unreflectively from parents, teachers, or workmates. It is not that he is
incapacitated from making independent judgments like the heterarchic man; it is only that he has little inclination for making them and
rarely does so. Such a person . . . governs himself, but by a *nomos* or
set of standards taken over from others" (Benn 1975–76, 123–24). In
addition to the characteristics of an autarchic agent, "an autonomous
agent must also have distanced himself in some measure from the
conventions of his social environment and from the influence of the
persons surrounding him. His actions express principles and policies
which he has himself ratified by a process of critical reflection" (Gray
1983, 74).

Neither Benn nor Gray is implying that autonomous persons
"get it right" in the sense of arriving at undeniably true or indisput-
ably warranted judgments about the issues they confront and consider.
They are not even implying that the notion of "getting it right" has any
unequivocal application to those issues. Nor is autonomy a transcen-
dent good, a good that necessarily or invariably takes precedence over
all others. As Benn insists, his account of autonomy concentrates "on
process and modes of consciousness" and leaves "out of account the
content of the autonomous man's principles and ideals. There is no
reason why an autonomous man should not be deeply concerned about
social justice and community—but I have said nothing to suggest he
will be." Injecting a more ominous note, he adds, "If Cesare Borgia
turned out to have been no less autonomous than Socrates, one would
still be hard put to it to share Machiavelli's unqualified admiration"
(Benn 1975–76, 129–30).[15] The account is Kantian in inspiration but
manifests loss of whatever faith Kant had that the procedural requirements of an enhanced, stringent rationality would yield rationally
indisputable but substantive moral and political principles.

Autonomy is nevertheless an "ideal" as opposed to a "characteristic of normal choosers" (Benn 1975–76, 123), an "achievement"
rather than . . . a natural human endowment or original inheritance"

(Gray 1983, 75).[16] *Given* the minimal rationality and negative freedom of autarchy, autonomy presents itself as a further, more elevated possibility to which we can and should aspire. It is not an ideal that can be fully or permanently realized, but we approach it in part by extending the ambit and heightening the intensity of our rationality. And while doing so *guarantees* neither improvement in the substantive quality of our decisions and actions nor greater agreement among us, it is an assumption, hard to reject if only because of the very meaning of "rationality," that it will tend to produce both.

It is easy to understand the resonance of the ideal of autonomy. If we follow Benn and Gray in viewing it as an enhancement and intensification of freedom and rationality, it gives focused expression to values central to our culture. If we set aside elitist and irrationalist views, the reservations one encounters concerning it are most frequently of the kind briefly adumbrated by Benn, namely, that it is an excessively egoistic ideal that undercuts communal values such as social justice and willingness to subordinate oneself to the common good. But this kind of objection is easily parried. One pursues autonomy not by extracting oneself from society and culture but by relating to them in a critically rational manner. To be reflective about norms and rules I must know their content and must understand how and why they are interpreted and applied (Gray 1980a, 95–96; Feinberg 1980, 19–21). Moreover, the norms to which I relate autonomously can be as individualistic or egoistic, as collectivist or altruistic as you like; my critical assessment of them can as well lead to hearty endorsement as to doubt or disaffection. The ideal of autonomy leaves these questions open.

But there are genuine and genuinely difficult questions about autonomy. They are not about the ideal taken abstractly and alone, but about how efforts to pursue and cultivate it should be adjusted to other purposes and ideals. In the present context the most pressing of these questions concern the relation between autarchy or freedom of agency and autonomy. The fact that autonomy requires a more extended and intensive rationality than does freedom entails the possibility that A can be free but heteronomous. It also follows that decisions and actions, policies and arrangements that respect freedom might disserve autonomy, and that efforts to pursue and to cultivate autonomy might infringe upon freedom. I argued that the Lutheran of my earlier example, although approaching the limits of the meager rationality necessary to agency, enjoys freedom in her religious practice. But she hardly exhibits autonomy in that aspect of her life. Imagine that the council of the congregation to which she belongs, distressed by doctrinal ignorance and indifference among its parishioners, institutes a Reconfirmation Program that requires all those twenty years or more past their original confirmation date to appear before the congregation to answer questions about Lutheran dogma. Classes are offered for those interested, and if Able takes them, thinks critically about the materials presented, looks into the alternative doctrines of other denominations, and so forth, she may become a more autonomous person in her religious beliefs and practices. But if she is terrified by the prospect of appearing before the congregation and drops her church membership, the attempt to enhance her autonomy will have eliminated a freedom she once enjoyed. This may benefit the congregation, in some longer or shorter run it may be good for Able herself, and for these and other reasons the policy may be justified. If so, it is justified despite its adverse effects on Able's freedom.

It is not hard to think of real and important cases in which the pursuit of autonomy, and especially the cultivation of autonomy by and through public and other more or less authoritative policies, results in more or less extensive, more or less lasting conflicts with freedom. Child-rearing and compulsory educational schemes would have to be regarded in this way (and justified in this light) except that children and adolescents have not been regarded as having fully attained to the standing of agents in this respect. Societies that have extended compulsory school-attendance into early adulthood have strained this understanding. As a consequence, many parents, teachers, and school officials have had intensely practical experience in justifying palpable interferences with present freedom in the name of future autonomy.

If we generalize from this already large and salient class of cases, we can see that more than a little of the untidiness that I earlier remarked in modern liberalism results from its inherently problematic attempt to respect and protect freedom at the same time that it seeks to foster and cultivate autonomy. Whereas the thinly varnished perfectionism and moralism characteristic of modern versions of freedom$_4$ and freedom$_5$ can readily be shown to conflict with the modern Western commitment to freedom and equality, the cultivation of autonomy seems consistent with if not in fact required by those very commitments. Others interfere with Able's thought and action not to make her virtuous (or secure, or happy) by standards of someone other than Able, but to enhance Able's capacity for thought and action genuinely her own. If educational programs in the narrow sense of formal schooling are the clearest instance of efforts of this kind, a considerable variety of programs, ranging from the straight-out compulsory (such as prohibitions on the use of drugs, gambling, or prostitution) through the more or less coercive and enticive (heavy taxes on alcohol and tobacco, an array of tax credits and deductions), to the hortatory and merely informative, have been adopted and implemented in whole or in part on this rationale.

Liberals are torn between two inveterately conflicting impulses: to celebrate the freedom of human beings to be what they are and to do what (being what they are) they are disposed to do, and the desire to see human beings become more self-conscious and self-critical about what they are and do. Acting on the former impulse frequently involves acceptance not only of dispiriting, unseemly, and vulgar conduct, but of conduct that is undoubtedly harmful to those who engage in it. Acting effectively on the latter impulse frequently involves interferences with other people that offend against values concerning human beings without which liberalism would be unrecognizable. The concept of autonomy, close kin both to freedom and to more tangibly perfectionist notions, appears to allow a resolution of this dilemma.

But this appearance, while less manifestly deceptive than the positive-freedom formulas considered earlier, is nevertheless illusory. Freedom and autonomy are different; respecting freedom and cultivating autonomy can and often do conflict. Intellectual strategies for avoiding, minimizing, and coping with such conflicts will be considered in the following chapters. The sine qua non of all such strategies is recognition that the conflicts are genuine and difficult to resolve.

Part Three
Evaluating Freedom

8

Freedom and Good, or the Human Good of Freedom

The chief task that remains is to assess arguments for and against freedom as a high-order moral and political good and for and against certain freedoms that are especially prominent in modern Western societies. These assessments are not settled by the foregoing discussions, but the task of making them is shaped and disciplined by the main conclusions arrived at in those discussions. Chief among those conclusions is that the subject of the normative theorizing to follow must be freedom of agency, or freedom$_2$. Freedom$_1$ (and the yet less complex notions exemplified by waving tree branches and cloudless skies) is genuinely a kind or sense of freedom, but it is of interest to the moral and political theory of freedom only insofar as it is an element in freedom of agency. By contrast, autonomous conduct, conduct that is virtuous by the standards of established communal norms, and conduct that is virtuous by standards that transcend communal norms (freedoms$_{3-5}$), should not be regarded as kinds of freedom. Conduct with these characteristics may be free or unfree, but this is to be decided by the criteria of freedom and unfreedom of agency. In giving arguments for or against the value of freedom as such, for and against freedom as a distinct human good, we argue for or against freedom of agency. In considering particular liberties such as those of speech and association, of emigrating from one's country, of acquiring, using, and alienating property, we consider the scope and consequences of these subclasses of action and we assess arguments for and against the freedom to perform them under various circumstances of conduct.

Autonomy and virtue are nevertheless salient topics in normative theorizing about freedom. They are salient not as kinds of freedom but as distinct, prominent, and often highly regarded features of the moral and political practices of which freedom is also a part. Along with a considerable array of other considerations and desiderata (for example, security, justice, rights, and welfare), the pursuit and cultivation of autonomy and virtue sometimes complements, and sometimes competes and conflicts with freedom. To the extent that such high-order considerations complement or harmonize, the task of justifying any one among them is eased. To the extent that they compete or conflict, justifications for any one of them must meet arguments grounded in the value of the others. We distinguish freedom from other values with which it has been conflated and confused not to banish or diminish those other values but to clarify the questions that normative theorizing must address.

Shaping of a somewhat more determinative character results from the conclusions reached above concerning issues disputed within the tradition that identifies moral and political freedom as freedom of agency. Recall the discussion in Chapter 2 of the shift that occurs in Isaiah Berlin's account of freedom. Beginning with the essentially Hobbesian view that freedom of agency is the condition or circumstance of being unprevented by others from acting to satisfy one's interests and desires, Berlin changed to an "open door" or "open options" view according to which A's freedom is a function of the number of action options in fact open to her. The question whether A's occurrent interests and desires incline her to take those options is relevant to whether A feels free or regards herself as free, but not to the extent to which in fact she is free.

Berlin gave up the Hobbesian position because it allows of saying unqualifiedly that A is free despite some B or B's having intervened—presumably in unjustifiable ways—in A's life so as to reduce or otherwise alter the array of interests and desires that A has. In the somewhat broader terms in which Elster and others have elaborated this same concern, in assessing A's freedom we have to look not merely at the interests and desires that A now has and attempts to act upon but at the history of how A came to have that particular set of interests and desires, came not to have some larger or otherwise different set. If examination of that history reveals that A has been intimidated, manipulated, or the like by some B or B's then—notwithstanding A's success in acting on the interests she in fact has—we must say that A is unfree or importantly unfree.[1] The open-options account of freedom of agency is preferable because it allows us to say this.

Anyone disposed to deny that there are genuine phenomena here, or to deny that they pose important questions, need only read *1984*, *Brave New World*, or *Walden Two*. I have contended against the positive freedom view that A is unfree because of limitations, or failures, or defects that are as it were personal to her. In keeping with the Hobbesian tradition I have argued that for purposes of thinking about freedom we should take A as we find her—that is as she discloses herself to us through her thought and action—and to treat her freedom as a feature of her interactions with others. Nothing in this stance denies that what A is and does now is in part a result of her past interactions. (Rather, the argument that freedom is situated is a way of insisting on this point.) More important here, nothing in this stance justifies blinking the fact that some of these interactions are deeply objectionable from the standpoint of freedom and have enduring consequences that are objectionable from that same stand-point. The anti-utopias depicted (intentionally or unwittingly) in the fictional works I mentioned dramatize but do not invent realities that require qualification of the "take agents as we find them" version of freedom as freedom of agency.

The open-options formulation, however, is not an acceptable response to the realities in question. Saying why it is not acceptable will launch our consideration of freedom as a distinctive human good. On the one hand, Berlin's argument for the open-options view underestimates the extent to which the Hobbesian view can deal with the difficulties that led Berlin to question and reject that view. If B employs compulsion, coercion, intimidation and the like to alter A's interests and desires, B's actions are obviously objectionable from the Hobbesian as well as from the open-options point of view. It may be true that Hobbes tended to underestimate the prolonged or permanent effects of such interventions. Although I think it is false to say that he failed to anticipate phenomena now called "brain-washing," "mind control," and the like (he was, after all, intimately familiar with religious movements that produced highly skilled practitioners of these black arts), he perhaps overestimated the resilience of people who had been subjected to them. However this may be, a theory that objects to compulsion and coercion on the grounds of freedom is well placed to object to the results, including the long-lasting results, of compulsion and coercion. For one thing, if B has demonstrated her willingness and capacity to use compulsion and coercion against A, and if B continues to be a part of the environment in which A acts, the constraining effects of B's actions are likely to expand or extend outward and into the future. Having a bully in the neighborhood is objectionable, from the standpoint of freedom, even during the stretches of time that the bully is occupied with some other unfortunate. For another, although freedom of agency focuses on actions and attempted actions, it does not deny that those actions form sequences and patterns featuring continuities of various kinds.

It is, however, worth reiterating in this context two distinctions that have concerned us several times. First, if B's interventions genuinely *disable* A, genuinely *destroy* A's capacity for action, then we should say that A is no longer freedom-evaluable (in the respects in question), not that she is unfree. Putting the matter in this way worsens the charge against B at the same time that it instructs the rest of us as to how we should, and should not, think about and relate to A. Second, we should maintain the distinction between A's freedom and A's autonomy. To recur to an earlier example, many black slaves in the United States lived in constant terror of the most serious harms and deprivations. Some of them were no doubt importantly disabled by this experience, and those who were not were certainly rendered continuously unfree to perform a wide array of actions that they would otherwise have taken. Their case should not be assimilated to cases such as ghetto residents, children of overbearing parents, women in societies that are at once liberal in certain respects and deeply sexist, and the like, that is, with cases of persons who by every manner of discouragement, dissuasion, and frustration short of compulsion and coercion are conditioned to accept narrow limitations on their life possibilities. Anyone who celebrates human agency will lament and oppose all of these evils; no one who is clear-headed will deny the differences among them. Recognizing that we must sometimes take account of the history of a person's interests and desires is a first step in correcting the not infrequently insensitive judgments of theorists of negative freedom; learning to take that history into account in a discerning fashion is a further and equally valuable step.

On the other hand, if taken at all literally, the notion of "open options" is uncomfortably reminiscent of Elster's notion of the "abstractly possible set of feasible actions" and makes all too credible Charles Taylor's objection that the theory of freedom of agency is informed by a notion of entirely unsituated human life. As I think William James says somewhere, the options that are open to A must be "live," must be options that A could conceivably choose (as she is or as she might plausibly or by intelligibly connected steps become). It is abstractly possible for me to become chairman of the Politburo of the Communist party of the Soviet Union or to succeed the present Dalai Lama and lead the Tibetan people to freedom from the Chinese yoke. But neither these nor an indefinitely large number of other abstractly possible "options" have any place in my life or any bearing on my freedom. Berlin assaults the Hobbesian view through a *reductio* that posits A achieving freedom by giving up all of her desires or tailoring her desires to the demands and expectations of those around her. There is a corresponding but more telling objection against the open-options theory; although admittedly prevented from the actions she most ardently desires to take, A is said to be free because she has at her disposal a very large number of "options" that mean nothing to her.[2] Avoiding this absurdity does not mean tailoring A's options closely to her present inventory of interests and desires narrowly described or understood.[3] As a desiring, interest-seeking, objective-pursuing person, A has a "second-order" interest in being able to satisfy her desires, pursue her interests, and so forth. As a "normal" human being, A knows that the content or substance of her interests and desires (her occurrent, "first-order" interests and desires) regularly do (or at least manifestly can) change more or less rapidly. Accordingly, she has a "second-order" interest in a realm of freedom or a range of freedoms that will accommodate diversity and fluctuation in her "first-order" interests and desires. Avoiding the absurdity does require insisting that freedom is an attribute of the actions of and interactions among actual, situated, human beings, not of ghostly abstractions conceived as nothing more than choosers.

The second of the foregoing pair of arguments against the open-option account of freedom of agency will have to be adjusted somewhat when we reach the question of which freedoms should be protected by public law and other authoritative procedures. (The necessary adjustments will consist primarily of enlarging upon and generalizing from the remarks about the diverse and changeable character of human interests and desires and the consequent "second-order" human interest in a capacious realm of freedom of action.) Before reaching that question, however, we must gather the elements of the discussion into a more positive (as opposed to critical or polemical) and more explicitly normative argument. And we must consider objections to that argument.

I

Among other things that they are, human beings are desiring, interest-pursuing, end-seeking, purposive creatures. Partly because of the character of their interests and desires, ends and purposes, and partly because of characteristics of the environment in which they live, in most cases they must take action to achieve their ends. Given these characteristics of human beings and their environment, freedom of action is a high-order human good, a condition or state of affairs on which human beings will, and in reason should, place high value. The value of freedom is not tied to a particular inventory of interests and desires, ends and purposes. The content or substance of human interests and desires varies from one person to the next and often changes substantially during the life history of a single person. Freedom is a good of great general value because it is necessary to the pursuit and satisfaction of a great many interests and desires, the achievement of many ends and purposes, and contributive to the satisfaction and achievement of yet many more. Unfreedom is a serious evil because it prevents or inhibits achievements and satisfactions and produces frustrations, distress, and harm.

There is a certain commonsensical quality to the foregoing remarks. If or insofar as we understand human beings in the ways I have employed, it seems obvious that a substantial freedom, a generous area of discretionary action, will be something valued by them and valuable to them. On the face of things, it is not easy to see how it could be denied that human beings have these characteristics or that, having them, freedom will be valuable to them.

In fact, however, there is nothing necessary, nothing rationally undeniable or indisputable about this reasoning or its conclusions. Empirically, we know people who have very few desires, purposes, and the like, and others who, owing to the combination of the character of their desires and the fact that their circumstances are especially favorable or unfavorable to satisfying them, have been understandably (if shortsightedly) indifferent to freedom. We are also familiar with thought experiments that imagine changes in human beings and their environment that would, if implemented, require us to qualify or abandon this reasoning. Finally, human beings and the human environment have features other than or additional to those on which my reasoning relies. Readers who have persisted to this point do not need to be told again of the many attempts to ground normative thinking about freedom in considerations quite different from those I have summoned.

It will emerge that the most important type of objection is the last one mentioned. But the more (or at least initially more) empirical objections require consideration in their own right, and examination will show that they merge into the difficulty last mentioned.

My initial response to the objection that the above reasoning misrepresents the facts on which it relies is as follows: Perhaps the project of developing a general argument for freedom as opposed to particular freedoms is misbegotten. Perhaps such arguments will either be so abstract as to be vacuous or so hedged with qualifications as to be useless. But if there are to be such arguments, and if such arguments are to be based in part on facts about human beings, they will have to rest upon generalizations, not upon universal truths. The significant question about the reasoning I sketched is not whether we can identify exceptions to the generalizations I advanced about human beings and their circumstances; rather the question is whether exceptions occur so frequently as to make it clumsy and distracting to rely upon the generalizations in forming a general orientation toward or perspective concerning freedom. If we accept the reasoning I sketched, we will approach concrete issues concerning freedom with a certain set of expectations and with concepts and principles in which and with which to assess what we actually encounter. If our expectations are confuted, if our talk of the importance of freedom to pursuing and satisfying desires and interests, achieving ends and purposes, regularly elicits incomprehension or hostility, what was intended to be a simplifying and facilitating move will complicate and divert our reasoning and our judging. Rather than being able to subsume particulars under agreed categories and principles we will have to defend the generalizations on which our categories and principles depend. But if this happens only rarely or exceptionally we will (so far as the objection I am considering is concerned) be justified in taking our bearings from those generalizations so long as we remain alert to the possibility of exceptions to them.

There is every reason to believe that the reasoning I sketched would be irrelevant or distracting in numerous societies and cultures. Implicit in that reasoning is an understanding that I have elsewhere called the liberal principle (hereafter LP), namely that it is, prima facie, a good thing for individuals to form, to act upon, and more or less regularly to satisfy their interests and desires, their ends and purposes (Flathman 1976, 7–8, 44–47, 167–81).[4] But this idea has or has had little or no acceptance, little or no standing, in numerous cultures and societies. Some cultures have regarded desires and interests, particularly desires and interests of individual persons, as prima facie or even categorically bad or wrong (cf. Hirschman 1977). The first, perhaps even the exclusive, concern of members of these cultures has been to abide by the divine laws and commands, to discharge duties assigned by the collectivity, to pursue the common good, advance the mission of the church, the class, or the party. Individual interests were or are to be subordinated if not rooted out. If individual freedom has been valued at all in such societies (and characteristically such societies prize the authority of the collectivity over its individual members, the freedom of the collectivity vis-à-vis other collectivities) it has not been for the reasons I sketched above but because individual freedom (or the freedom of certain select types of individuals) enhances extra- or supra-individual goods and ideals. If one argued for individual freedom on the grounds I sketched, one would be arguing against, not from, the prevailing conceptions of, the prevailing beliefs about and values concerning human beings.

These remarks underscore the underdefended character of the reasoning I presented for the value of freedom. The factual generalizations I advanced may be true of only some cultures and societies. But even if they are quite generally true, they will be accepted as elements in an argument for freedom only in societies in which they are positively valorized. A premise in my reasoning is axiological in character and attributes positive value to the states of affairs described by the empirical generalizations I advanced about human beings and their circumstances. LP is one possible formulation of such an axiological premise or principle; human beings do, or should, not only recognize but accept that they are desiring, interest-seeking, end-pursuing, purposive creatures whose well-being consists in important part in being able to pursue and satisfy their individual interests and desires, ends and purposes, and whose well-being is therefore enhanced by circumstances that are conducive to their doing so.

It is clear that premises of this character have been entirely rejected (or never considered) in some human societies and have been accepted only with severe qualification in numerous others. But it seems equally clear that such premises have been promoted to the standing of principles by persons influential in the shaping of modern Western societies and are in fact widely influential among the members of those societies. The fact that my sketch, abbreviated as it is, is intelligible and even commonsensical can perhaps be taken to testify to the correctness of these assumptions. The sketch is intelligible because it proceeds from, is a modest elaboration upon, thinking that is widely received in modern Western societies.

My sketch is nevertheless eminently disputable, disputable from within the confines of thinking widely received in the societies in question here. It can be controverted without adopting ascetical, perfectionist, or collectivist views more radical than those influential in the societies in question.

One way to dispute this sketch is to argue that it provides too weak an argument for freedom. By making the value of freedom instrumental to the goods which are the pursuit and satisfaction of interests and desires, ends and purposes, it leaves freedom's value hostage to psychological and cultural contingencies. The value of freedom may be augmented by considerations such as those I have adduced, but its deeper grounding is more secure, or should be made so. Freedom is an inherent or intrinsic, not an instrumental, good. Or at least its value in human life is due to features of human beings that are less variable, less culture-specific or culture-dependent (and more noble, elevated, or at least dignified?) than "interestedness," "desirousness," and purposiveness.

"Intrinsic,"inherent," and related terms are sometimes used as epistemological concepts signaling a direct or unmediated intuition or other apprehension of truths about which evidence or argumentation other than the experience of the intuition itself are impossible or irrelevant. The deepest difficulties with this notion need not be rehearsed here. It suffices to say that as a moral and political matter this view engenders dogmatism and helps not at all in resolving questions about conflicts among freedoms and between freedom and various other goods.

There are, however, more plausible versions of the idea that freedom is an intrinsic good. Some of these are at no great distance from the argument sketched here, others form parts of the deeper challenges to that argument. Considering a number of them will help in developing and defending the view set out above.

An important version is the idea, argued for by Kant and adopted in less metaphysical formulations by, among others, Berlin and Oakeshott, that freedom as distinct from or contrasted with thoroughgoing or "hard" versions of determinism is intrinsic not so much in the sense of intrinsically good but in being a supposition of the moral and political practices which involve judgments about good. Demonstrating the incompatibility between our practices and the theses of hard determinism does not establish that such determinism is false. All it shows is that we cannot consistently embrace determinism and continue with practices such as holding one another responsible for actions, distinguishing between proper and improper conduct, assigning blame and praise for conduct, and the like.[5] Insofar as we continue to engage in such practices we suppose that we are free as opposed to determined. (And insofar as we value those practices we at least tacitly suppose the value of our freedom in this sense.)[6]

A second version of the idea that freedom is an intrinsic good can be regarded as intermediate between the idea of freedom as opposed to determinism and the argument that freedom of action is an instrumental good for human beings understood as interest-pursuing, end-seeking creatures. A primarily descriptive version of the idea is familiar to us from the theory of Pure Negative Freedom. Given the ordinary human capacities for self-movement, it is all but impossible for one human being entirely to eliminate the freedom of movement of another human being. A person locked in a prison cell can move in thousands of ways; even a person in a tight-fitting straitjacket or mummy case may be able to wiggle her toes, blink her eyelids, flex certain of her other muscles, and so forth. Attending to these primitive considerations leads to the wider reflection that as a practical matter not more than a small percentage of any population can in fact be held in any very close physical constraint. Thus freedom in the sense of a substantial latitude for physical movement is probably an ineliminable feature of human life. Nor is it necessary to add much to these descriptions in order to give a normative coloration to this view. Given the human capacity for self-movement, we have to go to great lengths to imagine human beings who will not be disposed to move, who will not "prefer"—in at least this behavioral sense of the term—freedom of movement to unfreedom of movement and prefer more to less freedom of movement.[7] It is plausible to treat freedom in this sense (freedom$_1$) as intrinsic to human life and not implausible to treat it as an intrinsic good for human beings as we know them.

For reasons already considered in other contexts, neither of the two foregoing versions of the idea that freedom is an intrinsic feature of human life takes us very far in thinking about freedom as a moral and political good. If either version helps our thinking at all in this regard it is by suggesting that the question that matters is not whether or why we should value freedom as such but why we should prefer this as opposed to that array or constellation of freedoms. It will nevertheless repay us to consider one further version of the idea that freedom—but now freedom in the normatively more pertinent sense of freedom of action—is an intrinsic not merely an instrumental, good.

The argument in question is that both the fact of and a high regard for freedom of action is one of the deepest conventions of, and (in that Wittgensteinian sense) a starting point for thought and action in our culture. It is intrinsic to our moral and political practice in the normative sense that any practice which is deeply incompatible with or generally destructive of freedom of action is therefore, that is, without the need of further evidence or argumentation, deemed unacceptable. We do not argue for the value of freedom, our moral and political argumentation starts from, is premised on, its value. This view is consistent with dispute as to what counts as freedom and unfreedom, as to whether this or that arrangement or action serves or disserves freedom, and whether freedom in this or that respect should properly be subordinated or sacrificed, here and now, to some other value or good. But arguments against freedom as such, and hence arguments for policies and practices that are categorically or even generally antifreedom, are not countenanced.

Something like this sense of freedom as an intrinsic good is involved in Stanley Benn's discussion of the principle of noninterference (PNI) (1975–76). Insofar as we have made it a *principle* that the burden of justification falls on anyone who proposes to interfere in or with the actions of other persons, our day-to-day reasoning *begins with* the idea or belief that freedom is a high-order good. Interferences with freedom must be justified in the face of or despite the fact that they contravene or diminish that good. The fact that we entertain and accept such justifications shows that freedom is not an absolute in the sense of a good that takes precedence whenever it is involved or at issue. But it is an intrinsic good in the sense that it is a feature of our practices that must be understood in order to comprehend those practices and one that must be accepted in order to participate intelligently and defensibly in them. An observer who did not grasp what might be called the constitutive character of the good would fail to understand much of what goes on among us; the actions and arguments of participants who did not grasp the standing of that good would almost certainly—that is, apart from quite remarkable coincidences—meet with antagonism or incomprehension from other participants.

Unlike the first construal of "intrinsic" considered, this one does not exclude the *possibility* of arguments for the value of freedom. Of course the claim that the good of freedom is intrinsic in this sense suggests that such arguments will rarely be encountered in explicit form: for the most part arguments for the good will be unnecessary in the sense that they will be redundant. Moreover, for reasons noted in Chapter 6, it may be difficult for participants to think of considerations, independent of the good, in terms of which to argue for its standing as such. But this difficulty is social-psychological, not logical or epistemological, in character and there are reasons for thinking that we should do what we can to overcome it.

Leaving aside reasons that hold for all of our beliefs and values (for example Socrates' view that the unexamined life is not worth living, J. S. Mill's view that people who do not know, or who have lost sight of, the reasons for their beliefs and values do not fully know *what* they believe and value), two such reasons are especially pertinent. The first is grounded in the fact that freedom of action as a high-order value is rejected in many cultures and societies. If it is true that the value is deeply embedded in modern Western societies, it is important that those who reject or challenge it understand that this is the case, and why. True, it is a kind of response to such challenges to say, "This is what we think; this is how we do things hereabouts." As with differences of religious belief, disagreements about the value of freedom of action might prove to run so deep that mutual understanding and accommodation is the best that or even more than can be hoped. But even this endeavor is facilitated if the parties to the disagreement can articulate for themselves and to others the grounds on which their views rest. And we should not rush to the conclusion that differences are irreducible.[8]

The second reason is grounded in two facts. The first of these is that we experience freedom and its value and disvalue by exercising various freedoms and that these freedoms sometimes conflict with one another and with other of our values. Conflicts among freedoms obviously cannot be resolved by appeal to the value of freedom per se, and such an appeal would resolve conflicts with all other values only if we elevated freedom to the top of a strictly hierarchical value structure (to the first position on a lexically ordered list of values), that is, only if we made freedom an absolute as well as an intrinsic value. As we see in the sequel, having more rather than less clearly delineated general reasons for valuing freedom of action will not settle, certainly it will not still, all questions about the comparative importance of freedom or of various freedoms. But it would be irrationalist or antirationalist to assume that no such reasons are available or that having such reasons will be of no use in resolving such issues (or at least in remaining civil with one another as we attempt such resolutions and as we live with our no more than partial successes). The second of these facts is that there is lively controversy in the literature of moral and political philosophy concerning why freedom should be valued and how its value should be compared with a variety of other desiderata. In addition to being intellectually engaging in its own right, this controversy reflects—no doubt imperfectly—issues, positions, and arguments that are prominent outside of philosophical books and journals.

To summarize the last stretch of discussion, it is plausible to treat freedom of agency as an intrinsic good in our moral and political practices in the sense that its being a good is a datum in or of those practices. If so, the fact that it is no less than a datum is vital to understanding and to participation in those practices. The fact that it is, qua *intrinsic* good, no more than a datum means that the question why freedom of agency should be valued (and hence, finally, whether and how much it should be valued) invites our reflection. Because the last version of the idea that freedom is an intrinsic good is the only one that is both plausible and pertinent to our present concerns, I can summarize the discussion of that beguiling idea by restating my original contention: freedom of agency is a contingent and an instrumental good, albeit one that is contingent upon factual generalizations about human beings that are difficult to dispute and instrumental to values that are widely shared and deeply established in modern Western societies. The further, more refined questions concern just which factual generalizations this good is instrumental to.

II

I henceforth refer to the belief-cum-principle that freedom is a high-order good as the General Presumption in Favor of Freedom or GPF. On the reasoning I have thus far given (as distinct from my claim that something like this belief-cum-principle is a datum of our culture), GPF is an inference from (not an entailment of) the evaluations expressed by principles such as PNI or LP. If we accept these evaluations we will have reasons to endorse and to act upon GPF. The questions then become whether we can further strengthen the case for GPF as a general presumption or principle of thought and action and whether we can elaborate it and refine it so that it will assist us in choosing among conflicting freedoms and between freedoms and other high-order values with which freedoms may conflict. The latter questions will be primarily taken up in Chapters 9 and 10, the former in the remainder of this chapter. But of course the questions are too closely connected to allow strict separation.

Disposed as I am to defend GPF, I will treat the first questions as how best to argue for it. But in pursuing this objective I must identify and assess the merits of arguments against the principle.

Continuing to work with the sketch I first set out, I have as my chief task the further defense of LP or some principle analogous to it. I say this because the other main elements in the argument, generalizations about human beings and their circumstances and about features of our culture, are less likely to be disputed. Of course there is no shortage of objections to self-interest and its pursuit or to desires and desirousness (although arguments against end-seeking and purposiveness are rare, a point to which I return below). But most such objections, certainly within our culture, are to the effect that human beings *should not* do these things or *should* subordinate the doing of these things to other of their activities, other of their characteristics.[9] People who advance such arguments typically allow that the generalizations are all too accurate concerning human beings as we in fact encounter them in our culture. Their contention is that these characteristics are unfortunate and that the freedom to indulge them is anything but a good thing.

The first task, accordingly, is to defend the idea that it is good for human beings to form, to act upon, and to satisfy interests and desires. If this idea can be defended, the further ideas that freedom of action is a high-order human good and that a heavy burden of justification should fall on those who propose to limit, qualify, or interfere with it, will be easier to defend.

The most uncompromising opposition to LP comes from proponents of various forms of asceticism or self-denial. In considering this source of objections we should first note that at least some of their force is blunted by the results of our earlier investigations and by the formulation of LP itself.

Asceticism is at its apparently most potent (at least in its secularized forms) when it objects to desires and desire-satisfaction, particularly when it interprets desires as passions that "well up in," "take over," and otherwise supplant or obliterate the more rational, the more disciplined, the higher human faculties. Surrendering to these passions, "wallowing in them" in the sense of letting them and their satisfaction become the sole or primary raison d'être of one's existence, is "de-grading"; instead of living up to one's "grade," one's capacities or potential as given by God, or nature, or the culture into which one is born, the desirous, sensual, hedonistic person sinks to or below the level of nonhuman animals. Insofar as the sensualist can be said to have an aim or project, that project is self-defeating. Desires beget desires in a "bad infinite" that may spiral down to "polymorphous perversity" and that in any case excludes the possibility of more than ephemeral, more than unsatisfying satisfactions.

This picture is implausible if desires and action on desires are understood as analyzed in Chapter 2. Beliefs that are subject to correction and that if corrected will alter the desire, identification of objects that will satisfy the desire, choice of courses of action likely to attain those objects, all of these are features of desires and of actions to satisfy them. None of this prevents desires from being unseemly, debased, or repugnant to others, and it certainly does not guarantee that the actions taken to achieve them will be acceptable to others. But the idea that forming and acting to satisfy desires is itself an abandonment of the true or higher human qualities is largely a misunderstanding. The unqualified, necessarily debased sensuality attacked by asceticisms from fourth-century anchorites to Schopenauer is in the realm of behavior, not of desires and action on desires. There may be a case for freedom of such behavior (for freedom$_1$), but it is not the same case as for freedom of action. (Insofar as the theory of Pure Negative Freedom is normative, it advances such a case.)

The second element in LP, namely, interests and attempts to pursue and to serve them, is most commonly attacked not on the ascetical ground that it is degenerate but rather that it is narrowly calculating, egoistic, and socially divisive. The "interested" person uses her capacities for discernment, judgment, and evaluation, but she does so with no more than instrumental regard for others and hence, on some formulations of anti-interest argumentation, shortsightedly from the standpoint of her own larger or longer-term interests. As the last clause reminds us, however, the objection that actions motivated by interests are selfish in antisocial or immoral ways, or even imprudent, is contingent upon the character of certain interests and certain strategies for satisfying them. Notions such as Tocqueville's "enlightened self-interest" and J. S. Mill's "permanent interests of man as a progressive being" (and of course even wider uses of the concept such as in the philosophies of Ralph Barton Perry and Jürgen Habermas) make it clear that these objections have no application against much thought and action standardly characterized as "self-interested."

It is no part of my intention to deny that much that occurs in human affairs in the name of desires, interests, and their pursuit and satisfaction is objectionable and—although this is a further point—justifiably prevented. But recognizing this provides no reason for objecting to LP. LP says that it is, prima facie, a good thing for human beings to have, to act upon, and to satisfy desires and interests. If categorical objections to desires and interests (or "desirous" and "interested" conduct) are without merit, it remains open to us to adopt LP and the presumption it establishes in favor of human desires and interests and then to consider arguments that this or that desire or interest, as pursued in these or those circumstances, is nevertheless objectionable.[10] Nor does this stance or strategy debar the conclusion that certain subclasses of desires and interests are generally objectionable and to be discouraged. If we are committed to LP, we will of course view such reversals of the burden of proof with suspicion; but the logic of the principle itself, featuring as it does both "prima facie" and the comparative notion of "good," requires that we remain open to the possibility that they will sometimes be justified.

Aside from the last comments about LP, my remarks thus far are modest elaborations of the point that the concepts "desire" and "interest"are situated in the Wittgensteinian sense that they are part of a conceptual system governed by widely accepted conventions and rules. Although capacious in that they accommodate a wide range of beliefs and objects, they are concepts, not mere words or markers; "somethings," not "anythings." The desires and interests that we can form and pursue are restricted in ways either misunderstood or ignored by ascetical critics.

The conventions and rules that govern "desire" and "interests" are of course open-textured and subject to change. They are part of language games and forms of life that are internally complex and changeable and that are influenced by activities and developments more or less independent from them. I am not suggesting that there is a fixed inventory of possible interests and desires or that either the fear of declension or the hope of an ascension in their usual or predominant character are *necessarily* misplaced or misbegotten. But attention to secular tendencies in the language games of desire and interest will further disqualify the more fervid concerns that they sometimes arouse.

According to Albert Hirschman, the concepts of interest and self-interest came into prominence in Western thought in contrast with and as means of controlling the very notions, that is, "passions," to which ascetical and anti-interest writers are prone to assimilate them. To further abbreviate a complex story that Hirschman himself has severely compressed, as confidence declined that reason (and, one should add, faith and its discipline) could control the violent and destructive passions, the idea developed that interests could help to tame them, to domesticate them sufficiently to make peaceful social life possible. Denoting "an element of reflection and calculation with respect to the manner in which . . . [human] aspirations were to be pursued" (Hirschman 1977, 32), interests came to be regarded as more potent sources of motivation than abstract reason and yet less divisive and destructive than passions. "Once passion was deemed destructive and reason ineffectual, the view that human action could be exhaustively described [in their terms] meant an exceedingly somber outlook for humanity. A message of hope was . . . conveyed by the wedging of interest in between the two traditional categories. . . . Interest was seen to partake in effect of the better nature of each, as the passion of self-love upgraded and contained by reason, and as reason given direction and force by passion" (ibid., 43).

On the view of interests Hirschman describes, severely ascetical forms of anti-interest argumentation are not only archaic but self-defeating in that they demean and condemn the forms of motivation-cum-reason for action most likely to prevent degeneration to the unbridled and destructive sensuality that those who advance such arguments fear and despise. Strikingly, the "element of reflection and calculation" of which Hirschman writes corresponds closely to features still "denoted" by "desire" as well as by "interest."

In an analysis that endorses but extends Hirschman's, Stephen Holmes develops further themes pertinent here. Focusing primarily on seventeenth-and-eighteenth-century materials, Holmes argues that interests were distinguished from and preferred to notions of privilege and paternalism. The allegedly more elevated character of the latter bases for and motivations to action came to be viewed as devices for giving a spurious legitimacy to social and political arrangements that were oppressive insofar as they were effective and increasingly ineffective in maintaining peace and order. "Liberals turned a friendly eye toward self-interest to discredit the degrading ranks of prestige and chains of dependency characterizing the old regime." Again, "By focussing on [desires and] interests, and by attributing paramount importance to self-preservation, Hobbes strove to put an end to the English Civil Wars. His aim was not to promote the interests of the merchant class, though that may have been a side-effect of what he did. By discrediting [for political purposes] the ideals of glory and salvation, he hoped to encourage peace" (Holmes 1984, 253).

Holmes's remark about the merchant class alludes to objections to interests and interest-oriented conduct that became familiar after the period he is discussing and that will require our attention in the next chapter. The arresting feature of the contrasts he is most concerned to draw is that they are between, on the one hand, the desires and interests promoted by liberals and by Hobbes and, on the other, forms of thought and action that *in fact* are self-indulgent and self-defeating in just the ways *attributed to* desires and interests by severe critics of the latter. Holmes's liberals distinguish claims based on shareable and in principle mutually reconcilable desires and interests from entitlements of place and privilege that their holders and defenders insist are incommensurable with such desires and interests. Because the entitlements are regarded by their claimants as intrinsically superior, they can be accommodated to or harmonized with the ordinary run of desires and interests only in the weak sense that the latter might be given consideration after the superior entitlements have been fully honored. Holmes's Hobbes distinguishes desires and interests that can be pursued and satisfied by all members of a society from ideals of character and conduct that their partisans insist are categorically superior to desires and interests and that their partisans at least tacitly concede to be unshareable or at least undistributable. In fact, however, the privileges the liberals attacked are self-, class-, or caste-indulgent in at least two senses: (1) they are *excessive* in demanding a gross superfluity or wealth and power; (2) they are unjustifiably *exclusive* in that they are restricted to a small and assignable number of persons or to specific classes or castes with fixed memberships. Because of these characteristics, claims to the privileges are self-defeating: if satisfied, they corrupt their beneficiaries at the same time that they harm those from whom the benefits are extracted; the corruption of the former and the oppression of the latter delegitimate the claims to them so that the claims must either be abandoned or enforced by tyrannical means that are costly in themselves and that sooner or later incite revolts that destroy the system of privileges. The ideals of character that Hobbes attacks are (again from a political standpoint) self-indulgent in the sense of having an exclusivity closely analogous to that already discussed (they are aristocratic ideals) and self-defeating because conduct in pursuit of them is incompatible with a society stable enough to allow such conduct to flourish. By comparison with both the privileges and the ideals, the *allegedly* self-indulgent and self-destructive desires and interests are shareable and are supportive of a peaceful and stable social and political order.

The particular passions, privileges, and ideals at issue in the controversies Hirschman and Holmes report play a smaller part in the debates of our own time. But in form these early defenses of desires and interests are responsive to any attempt to discredit the latter as self-indulgent or self-defeating. Because such attempts remain common in our time, the defenses are pertinent to present concerns.[11] The timeliness of yet wider moral and political views that were part of the thinking Holmes discusses is evident from a further passage from his work. When asserted against views such as Maistre's that "human individuality" is a "nullity" from God's point of view, "Self-interest was a dimension of self-affirmation." Yet more broadly, it was important to the thinking of Constant and others of his time that interests "are distributed without regard to birth: they are just as independent of the social status of your family as they are of your religious beliefs. To act upon interest is to claim the status of an equal—of a masterless man." Here we have much more than a defense of desires and interests against various traditional charges; much more than a claim that interests and desires do not have various unacceptable characteristics and consequences. In these formulations, developing, pursuing, and satisfying interests and desires are positive goods, are characteristics that deserve to be valued, protected, and promoted. They are made central to conceptions of individuality, of equality, and of freedom and hence fundamental to a society suitable to human beings as liberals had come to conceive of them. We are not to apologize for our "desirousness" and "interestedness," we are to insist upon them.

These last views are in effect arguments for LP (or at least PNI) and GPF. They say that human beings have certain pronounced characteristics and they make connections between those characteristics and values that should be central to their society. If analysis of "desires" and "interests" helps to defend these notions against certain persistent forms of attack, the linkage between them and equality and freedom not only legitimates but positively promotes them. Combining Hirschman and Holmes, we can say that the thinkers Holmes discusses were doing two things at once. They were promoting equality among, and the freedom of, individuals in a society that had begun to accept these values but in which opposition to the values remained strong. In order to do so, they drew upon the emerging legitimacy of desires and interests to affirm a notion of the individual for whom equality and freedom were appropriate. By tying the two sets of notions together, they gave support to both. And the resulting combination constitutes an argument for LP and GPF.

Of course this combination and hence this argument for LP and GPF can be and has been resisted. If Rawls is correct that an at least implicit commitment to freedom and equality is the distinctive feature of moral and political thought and practice in modern Western societies, then one of the pairs that form the combination has been generally accepted. And while it can hardly be denied that desires and interests are widely regarded as *legitimate*, and are viewed yet more positively than this term suggests by many people in these societies, more or less vehement anti-desire and anti-interest views remain familiar among us. Perhaps some who hold such views are also opposed to freedom and equality, but it is implausible to think that this is always or even commonly the case. As we have seen in discussing theorists of positive freedom, thinkers who are firmly committed to some version of freedom and equality have at most a qualified enthusiasm for desires and interests; they rely primarily upon other characteristics of human beings in formulating and defending their views about freedom and equality. We cannot assume that arguments for LP and GPF that depend upon the combination just discussed will be generally convincing.

Let us *reculer pour mieux sauter*. Let us assume that Hirschman is correct in his claim that desires and interests have been recognized as prominent characteristics of the members of our societies and that these characteristics have been legitimated to the extent that general-ized stigma no longer attaches to them. Forming, pursuing, and satis-fying desires and interests may not have attained to the standing of prima facie goods, but they have shed the disrepute that once attached to them. (Or at least let us assume that the arguments supporting generalized hostility to desires and interests have been shown to be without merit and hence that in reason generalized stigma ought not to attach to them.)

On these assumptions, a number of further arguments can be made for LP and GPF as normative principles. These arguments can be introduced by making a comparison. Consider the phenomenon of children, wives, employees, soldiers, and others who are told to "think for themselves," "take initiatives," "be independent," but whose every thought and initiative is disapproved and rejected. Such people quickly learn either to dismiss as insincere the advice and await the forthcoming directives (perhaps simulating thought, initiative, and independence) or to rebel against the disapprovals and rejections and pursue their chosen courses as best they can. Either way, the practical incompatibilities among the demands made upon them are a source of severe and often damaging confusion and frustration.

There is a strong and positive analogy between this phenomenon and the situation that would obtain in a society that legitimated the formation and pursuit of desires and interests but that rejected LP (or at least PNI) and GPF. Encouraging an employee to think for herself and to take initiatives does not commit superiors to agree with her every thought or to applaud the particulars of all the initiatives she takes. But good-faith encouragement creates, or rather carries with it, several presumptions. The most obvious of these are the presumptions that the superior believes that the employee is in fact capable of the kind of conduct in question (at least latently so) and that the superior genuinely encourages or perhaps authorizes her to engage in it. Taken together, these two presumptions carry a third, a guarded formulation of which (akin to PNI) is that if the superior disapproves or rejects the employee's thoughts and initiatives she must justify the disapproval in terms responsive to the particulars of the employee's thoughts and initiatives. We might say that the superior must present such justifica-tions in order to avoid engendering dissonance, exasperation, and the like in the employee. But since it is only very likely and not certain that these consequences will be produced, we should first say that in practical reasoning anyone who understands the first two presump-tions will also accept the third.

The parallel between the first two presumptions and my Hirsch-manesque assumptions about the recognition and legitimacy of desires and interests is clear enough (a possible difference being that "legitimacy" may be a weaker term than "encourages" or even "authorizes" in the second presumption). In the guarded form in which I state the third presumption, something like Benn's PNI is more closely parallel to it than is LP. This is because neither PNI nor the third presumption as stated imply or even suggest a disposition positively to approve, or even an expectation that one very likely will approve, the content of the thoughts and initiatives. The idea is more formalistic; having licensed or authorized the thinking or the initiative-taking, the superior is obliged to justify disapprovals and rejections of their content; having recognized and legitimated a tendency to form and pursue desires and interests, society is obliged to justify interferences with manifestations of that tendency.

The less-guarded formulation of the third presumption parallels the more positive idea expressed by LP that forming, pursuing, and satisfying desires and interests is, prima facie, a good. Having judged the employee capable of thinking for herself and of taking initiatives, and genuinely approving of her doing so, the superior is disposed to approve her thoughts and her initiatives or at least maintains a grounded expectation that she will approve of them. Rather than a mere, perhaps even a somewhat grudging, formal authorization, the superior has wholeheartedly and out of genuine conviction encouraged the thinking and the initiating. (The more positive formulation of the third presumption goes better with "genuinely approved" than with "legitimated" in the second presumption.) Her reasons for having done so create and support a disposition or expectation to approve the actual content of the thinking or of the initiatives. Society's reasons for recognizing and genuinely approving the formation, pursuit, and satisfaction of desires and interests carry over to and inform its response to the desires and interests actually formed and pursued. "Prima facie" does not mean "initially and formally but readily subject to justified exception," it means "for good general reasons that are expected to hold in most cases albeit subject to the possibility of justified exceptions."

My claim, then, is that the legitimation of desires and interests charted by Hirschman and Holmes itself supports an argument that goes beyond legitimation. In the weaker forms that stop at rebutting generalized objections to desires and interests, the legitimation of the latter supports PNI and GPF. It does so in the internalist sense that those who understand and accept the legitimation and the reasons for it will understand and accept PNI-GPF and also in the consequentialist sense that accepting legitimation but rejecting PNI-GPF will very likely create confusion, frustration, and conflict. In the stronger formulations involving genuine approval of desirousness and interestedness (for example, those formulations that link desires and interests closely to freedom and equality), legitimation itself supports LP in both the internalist and the consequentialist renderings of "supports." In short, to reject PNI-GPF or LP-GPF entirely, one would have to adopt some version of the views that come to be rejected in the period studied by Hirschman and Holmes and that comport very badly with the present logic of "desires" and "interests." At a minimum we are entitled to conclude that generalized anti-interest and anti-desire arguments are either confused or deeply radical in the sense of rejecting an interwoven and mutually reinforcing set of beliefs and values that are very firmly established in modern Western societies.

It seems doubtful that there are entirely general grounds for preferring the stronger LP to the weaker PNI or vice versa, that is, grounds for saying that we should adopt the one or the other in our thinking about the entire range of desires and interests that we develop and encounter. Responding to categorical objections to desires and interests, I have tried to identify considerations of equally general applicability. In the next chapter I take up views (especially Rawls's views) that endorse LP (or at least PNI) and GPF but go on to argue that certain subclasses of desires and interests (and objectives and purposes) are especially important and ought to have further and stronger protections. But even if we reject proposals for established, settled rankings of interests and desires, we have to acknowledge distinctions among various realms or arenas of thought and action involving interests and desires. It may be, for example, that the weaker PNI is more appropriate for those in various tutelary roles or in roles with the special responsibilities that attach to positions of formal authority in organizations. The fact that a teacher has authorized (or even instructed) her students to propose paper topics obliges her to give reasons if she rejects topics that students desire or have an interest in pursuing. But it is too strong to say that the authorization does or should dispose the teacher to approve the topics as proposed or even to expect generally to do so. Rather, it is her responsibility to examine the proposals in a critical, even a skeptical, spirit. Many would say the same about parental relations with young children, about commanding officers in armies, about executives and managers in corporations and bureaucracies. To generalize somewhat crudely, where there is wide agreement about objectives and concomitant agreement about the distribution of expertise to achieve them and about responsibility for doing so, PNI may be the most that is justified. (On the other hand, if there genuinely is agreement about objectives, then thinking, initiative-taking, and proposing will themselves be influenced and constrained by it. Teachers occasionally receive proposals for papers that are so manifestly inappropriate to the subject matter of the course in question that they are appropriately rejected out of hand. But because most students understand and accept the objectives of the courses in which they are enrolled, the teacher's usual role is not to "accept or reject" but to suggest modifications intended to make the topic more manageable, fruitful, and the like. The specifically situated character of these activities is a part of the first two presumptions and carries over to the third.) By contrast, in politics and general morality, where there is less agreement about objectives and where "experts" play peripheral roles or none at all, the stronger presumption expressed by LP is the appropriate stance. (Of course neither LP nor PNI would be so much as possible, perhaps not so much as an intelligible, stance in a society in which there was little or no agreement on moral and political questions. In contemporary Lebanon, PNI and LP operate, if at all, only within the warring factions).

We might say that LP is the appropriate stance except in circumstances in which the weaker PNI is justified (for some agents) by an at least tacit understanding about objectives and how best to pursue them. From quite early in their years in school, students come to expect teachers to approach their proposals in a critical spirit; people who take jobs in large corporations expect analogous responses from their superiors. But it is characteristic of modern democratic societies that no such detailed, content-specific, understandings or agreements inform relations and interactions among citizens or moral agents simply as such. It is expected that desires and interests will differ, and this is regarded as a good thing *at least* in the sense that it is better that it should be so than that social life be conducted in the manner of a school, corporation, or army or that we relate to one another in a mutually censorious fashion. In a society that recognizes and has legitimated desires and interests, LP is appropriate *at least* as a principle of mutual toleration or a weak principle of equality. In a society which genuinely respects individuality and diversity, certainly in one with a genuine enthusiasm for them, LP recommends itself much more strongly. If desires and interests are in fact among our salient characteristics, and if we genuinely accept and value this fact about ourselves, we will accord one another's desires and interests the presumptions expressed in and required by LP.

III

If it is easy to list moralists who object to desires and interests, it is difficult to identify any who object to "end-seekingness" and purposiveness. Neither "end" nor "purpose" has been associated with passions, impulses, and other subjectivist or even "animal" notions that are prominent features of the literature concerning desires and interests. It is true that virtue-, duty-, and rights-oriented theorists argue that the pursuit of the ends and purposes we form should be disciplined by principles and rules of conduct that are in some sense independent of those ends and purposes. It is also true that teleological and consequentialist theories that reject or seem unable to accommodate such disciplining principles and rules have been much criticized. But virtue-theorists identify the virtues they promote as qualities of character that are necessary or strongly conducive to the achievement of certain end-states judged to be suitable to human beings at their best; most deontologists have allowed that the constraints of duties and of rights, even if in some sense self-justifying, are constraints upon end-seeking, purposive activities and would have no application to creatures who do not engage in such activities (see esp. Rawls 1982b, 49; 1980, 530).

The fact that LP includes ends and purposes among the prima facie goods means that, formally or conceptually, it has room for, it can accommodate the as it were positive concerns or objectives just mentioned. When combined with the foregoing arguments about desires and interests, this suggests that, formally, LP should prompt few if any objections. Indeed, in respect to the more individualist of the rights-oriented deontological theories we can make the stronger claim that something akin to LP is presupposed by them. Rights are discretionary, not mandatory; they typically leave it to the right-bearer to determine whether to take the class of action that the right protects. At a minimum, this allows that agents may make these determinations on the basis of their ends and purposes as they see them. If end-seeking, purposive conduct were not at least a prima facie good, it is difficult to see how such discretion could be justified. In this perspective, decisions to establish rights are based on judgments that certain classes of ends and purposes are especially important and deserve not merely the protection afforded by LP and GPF (the protection afforded by a right in the sense of a "liberty" in Hohfeld's schema [1919]) but the further protection afforded by a right (a "claim-right" or "right in the strict sense" in the Hohfeldian vocabulary).

Of course proponents of some of the doctrines just mentioned argue not for end-seeking or purposiveness as such, but for particular, more or less definite ends or purposes that they regard as embodying the ideals or excellences of human life. In the moderately technical language now current, proponents of these doctrines are advocates of perfectionism.[12] Accordingly, the fact that LP includes an endorsement of "ends" and "purposes" in abstract, generic terms is not likely appreciably to heighten their enthusiasm for it. Perfectionists cannot deny that LP as an axiological principle formally *encompasses* the ends and purposes they favor. Nor can they deny that an argument for freedom of action grounded in LP will provide support for freedom to pursue those ends and purposes. But they will surely object that the support it offers for those freedoms is much too weak and they surely will also object that it offers at least initial support for freedoms that are insupportable. The axiological principles of society should *coincide with* the inventory of substantive ends and purposes that perfectionists favor (or at least the axiological principles should exclude all ends, purposes, and other reasons for action that conflict with pursuit of the ends and purposes perfectionists favor).

It will be helpful for us in assessing these objections to consider again the case of freedom of religious belief and practice. For people who are indifferent about religion the public law conception and practices discussed in Chapter 7 might well be a good in the sense used in LP. The religious desires and interests, ends and purposes that people in fact have and pursue are as eligible for the standing of prime facie goods as any other. Moreover, according a wide freedom for religious practice diminishes conflicts that might prevent or inhibit other activities supported by LP.

But what about people who are convinced that their beliefs, whether pro- or anti-religion, are true not merely in the sense that they themselves hold them but simply or unqualifiedly. Consider the atheist who is satisfied that she has conclusive arguments against the existence of a divine being and who is also convinced that all forms of religious belief are worse than vulgar superstition. Or consider the believer who is "morally certain" of the truth of her specifically religious beliefs and who is equally convinced that irreligion and religious diversity make so much as decency impossible in human society. For such people the public-law doctrine of religious freedom will seem much worse than a poor thing. How can it be, even prima facie, a good thing to maintain practices that are false and harmful? How can society allow, let alone endorse as a good, ends and purposes that lead to actions destructive of human well-being?

Of course atheists and believers can accept the public-law practice of religious freedom as a lesser evil. If it has proven to be genuinely impossible to win general acceptance of the beliefs and practices that are true and good, we retreat to that arrangement to protect such truth and goodness as obtain among us and we regretfully pay the price of tolerating beliefs and practices known by us to be false and harmful. But we do not pretend that what we know to be false is prima facie true or that what we know to be harmful is prima facie good. Indeed we do not pretend that the arrangement which protects the false and the harmful is anything better than an unfortunate necessity, an evil that we accept because it is least among the evils with which we are confronted. (Somewhat more positively, the arrangement might be defended as a way of buying time. By protecting the good practices that exist among us, we preserve the possibility that example and argument will win converts enough to permit us to advance to something better.)

Perfectionist positions in respect to moral and political questions are analogous to (but not necessarily fully parallel with) the position of the atheist and believer as just discussed. There are ends and purposes that are good simply or all things considered, not merely prima facie. There are others that are clearly wrong or harmful or evil. In the latter cases the burden of justification falls on anyone who proposes to pursue those ends and purposes, not on those who object to them. How we should go about promoting good ends and purposes, and how dispositions and attempts to pursue bad or evil ones should be discouraged or prevented, are of course further questions. There will be questions about the efficiency and efficacy of various means of achieving any particular good end; there may be a number of good ends and purposes, and efforts to achieve them will have to be harmonized. Some means of preventing the pursuit of evil ends and purposes will be ineffective and others may themselves be wrong or evil. But actions and arrangements that are means to achieving good ends take at least initial justification from that fact about them, and actions and arrangements that are means of preventing the pursuit or achievement of evil ends take initial justification from that fact about them. Insofar as perfectionists have concerned themselves with freedom, freedom to pursue good ends is easily justified; certainly freedom to pursue evil ends is objectionable and restrictions on such freedom are easily justified.

As with strongly convinced atheists and with religious believers in respect to freedom of religious, convinced moral and political perfectionists might accept or accommodate themselves to the public-law conception of freedom that maintains wide latitude in the pursuit of individual ends and purposes. They could accept a public practice of moral and political toleration as a lesser evil or as a temporizing device. Society averts its glance, at least its organized, collective glance, from much that is undoubtedly objectionable and even harmful, reserving its collective notice and its collective, authoritative action to the most directly and seriously harmful activities of its members. Nevertheless, within the compass of their perfectionism, that is in respect to the ends and purposes that they judge to be undeniably evil or harmful, moral and political perfectionists must regard such arrangements as arrangements of toleration. They can no more cherish or delight in such arrangements and the freedoms of action they establish than the deeply committed atheist or believer can cherish or delight in freedom of religious belief and practice.

IV

The preceding discussion of ends and purposes is overly schematic in several respects that must be recognized and at least partially remedied. One such respect is that there are numerous versions of perfectionism, and it would be wrong to suggest that they all involve the same stance toward or the same implications concerning LP and freedom. To mention just one version that deviates importantly from the pattern I have outlined, Nietzsche can be regarded as a perfectionist at least in the sense that he drew a sharp contrast between the ways human beings are and the ways they could and should be and he hesitated not at all in his condemnations of the former and his celebrations of the latter. The moderate skepticism, the somewhat diffident latitudinarianism, of LP has no place in his thought. But the idea that there is one set of ends or purposes that is proper to all or even to any number of human beings, the idea that all human beings should submit their conduct to the discipline of a single moral ideal, was intolerable to Nietzsche. The excellence he celebrated was self-assertion of heroic proportions: the pursuit of the "overman's" own desires and interests, ends and purposes untrammeled by the concerns of others. Although he would find the terminology "liberal principle" repugnant and would disdain the idea that his ideals are appropriate for more than a few, the agonistic individualism that makes up his perfectionism shows that the latter doctrine shares features of the basic ideas behind LP.

Another such respect is that there are positions that oppose both LP and perfectionism. In my judgment the most challenging of these is the "Kantian constructivism" of John Rawls. Because he develops a complex and powerful alternative to the argument advanced here, I consider Rawls's views in detail in the next chapter. But we should also consider two lines of antiperfectionist and at least apparently profreedom argument against which Rawls's theory is in important part a reaction and that share at least some features of the position advanced here. Of a number of such possibilities that might be taken up I comment briefly on Bentham and J. S. Mill.

Bentham's classical utilitarianism begins with an all but unqualified endorsement of the development and expression of individual interests and desires, ends and purposes. He shows little or no disposition to inquire into the history, the content, or the merits of these, and he is strongly hostile to asceticism and to the natural law, natural right, natural rights, and moral-sense versions of perfectionism that claim to be able to distinguish between worthy and unworthy desires, interests, and so forth. In these respects Bentham appears to be a strong supporter of LP and GPF. But this appearance is quickly destroyed. Actually pursuing and satisfying this or that desire or end counts as good only if a further, highly demanding condition is met, namely, that doing so contributes to the sum or aggregate that is the greatest happiness of the greater number. If the pursuit or the satisfaction of an interest detracts from or conflicts with the general happiness then they (either or both) can and should be prevented. It is no doubt in part for this reason that Bentham had a low estimate of the value of individual freedom of action; it is for the same reason that a theory that seems individualistic and liberal in its starting point ends with strongly antiindividualist and illiberal conclusions.

It would, however, be wrong to treat Bentham as a perfectionist in thin disguise. The good, that is, the greatest happiness, has no fixed or definite content that can be known in advance of or apart from the development of individual desires and interests, ends and purposes. Being a sum or aggregate of those interests, it takes its content from them and cannot be determined—or rather has no reality—independent of those interests. Put in slightly different terms, in Bentham's doctrine it is impossible to find any single interest, or the entire array of occurrent interests, unworthy as such or in its own right. "Perfectionism" is less than a closely defined concept, but such criteria as have developed concerning its use exclude its application to such a doctrine.

These remarks also indicate that Bentham's doctrine is individualist and egalitarian in the weak sense that it requires *consideration* of each individual's interests and desires. The doctrine also favors liberty in the more substantial but nevertheless inadequate sense of supporting the freedom to form desires and interests and to make them known to others. But freedom of *action* is a good only if satisfaction of the desire or interest contributes to the greatest happiness of the greatest number. Of course we cannot make it a condition of the liberalism of a doctrine that the doctrine makes freedom of action to pursue interests and desires, ends and purposes, an on-balance or all things considered good. Nor can we exclude the possibility that conflict between an individual's freedom to act in a particular way and the general happiness (assuming the latter to be a tenable concept) will sometimes be a sufficient reason to restrict that freedom. Bentham's doctrine is anti-freedom and illiberal because it makes it a logical or conceptual impossibility for individual freedom of action to be justified if it is in conflict with the general happiness. There are, surely, many cases in which there is a genuine conflict between individual freedom of action and the general happiness, common good, or public interest. There are surely cases in which such conflicts are properly resolved against individual freedom of action. But no one who genuinely values freedom of action can follow Bentham in eliminating the very possibility of the opposite resolution of such conflicts.[13]

By contrast, persuasive recent interpretations of the utilitarian doctrine of John Stuart Mill suggest that he was less willing than Bentham to subordinate the individual to the aggregate or collectivity. But they equally suggest that he was much more willing to make qualitative distinctions among the interests and desires, ends and purposes, that individuals actually develop and pursue. Of course Mill is famous for a vigorous defense of freedom of belief and action. But there is reason to think that he valued freedom more for its contribution to autonomy or the realization of the higher potential of the individual than for the reasons suggested by LP. Although hostile to perfectionism in the sense of the doctrine that there is a set of substantive goods or excellences to which all of humankind should aspire, he thought moralists—and in limited respects legislators and jurists—should help their follow human beings realize their higher selves. Given his estimate of the character of the preponderance of his fellow citizens (to say nothing of "barbarians"), Mill was apparently reluctant to accept, even for the limited purposes of a theory of freedom, the notion that we should take human beings as we find them. This view requires close consideration. Rawls's treatment, no doubt in part because he has benefited from Mill's reflections, is more systematic than Mill's and will be my primary focus.[14]

9

Freedom, Justice, and Rights

It is impossible to deny that freedoms to pursue interests and desires, ends and purposes, must be limited in various ways. The most obvious reason for this conclusion is that freedoms of action sometimes conflict with one another so that as a practical matter either there will be some sort of standoff or one freedom must take precedence over another or others. Further, because freedom and its value will be on both or all sides of such conflicts, if the conflicts are to be resolved the resolution must be in part in terms of considerations other than freedom itself. In this and many other ways, beliefs and values not reducible to beliefs and values about freedom necessarily enter into interactions involving freedom.

The recurrence of distinctions such as that between freedom and license is powerful evidence that further limitations are required. In barest principle it is not impossible that "license" could be restricted to cases in which one or more sets of freedoms are in conflict. In fact, this and related notions have regularly been invoked in the name of numerous beliefs and values other than freedom. The warm disagreement over what should be regarded as license in no way diminishes the significance of this feature of our practice.

Of course the arguments for LP and GPF are compatible with the view that freedoms of action must be limited. Because LP announces no more than a prima facie good and GPF no more than a general presumption, they are explicitly open to the possibility that claims based on them can be overridden—possibly in a wide variety of ways. Nor would there be any contradiction in the view that, all things considered, judgments about such claims should be made circumstantially rather than systematically; should be made by assessing such claims and the considerations that compete with them as they present themselves in day-to-day interactions rather than on the basis of a theory or schema adopted in advance. True, general concepts are presupposed when we identify "considerations"; true, judgments about the classes of considerations relevant to a choice or decision will necessarily reflect more than circumstantial rankings or orderings. But from these undeniable facts it does not follow that the array of considerations regarded as relevant must be fixed or closed, and it certainly does not follow that the items making up that array must be permanently ranked—or even given a ranking that is to hold unless and until it is explicitly altered through some designated procedure. However impracticable it might be to let the needed limitations on freedom emerge out of a fluid process structured only by weak principles such as LP and GPF, in thought this is a perfectly eligible possibility.

I say a bit more about specifically political versions of this antinomian alternative in a moment and I argue for a qualified version of it as I proceed. But it is obvious that our moral and especially our political traditions, despite their generalized bias toward freedom, have not been receptive to it. Of course no society or culture could settle all questions about limitations on freedom of action systematically and in advance. Indeed no society or culture could settle all such questions by specified, deliberately adopted, authoritative procedures. (A literal-minded interpretation of the notion of totalitarianism might suggest that certain modern societies have at least aspired to such an arrangement, but we know that in actuality the societies we call totalitarian leave—and must leave—many such questions to be resolved locally and circumstantially. The distinctive characteristic of totalitarianism, rather, seems to be that local and circumstantial resolutions of issues about limitations on freedom are subject to ex post facto rejection by "authorities" that operate arbitrarily in respect both to their choice of occasions for intervention and to the limitations they impose on freedom.) Nevertheless, there has been a powerful disposition to settle, in advance and in a fashion that is systematic at least in the sense of being somehow principled, the most salient questions about the limitations on freedom. The assumption has been that circumstantial resolutions of such issues will be merely "intuitive," will exacerbate conflict or lead to an uncritical endorsement of inherited arrangements and practices that do not merit endorsement, and hence will leave the most important values and objectives at unacceptable risk. In particular, there is no adequate reason to expect that such a practice will protect the most important freedoms of action. The political, legal, and other institutions and procedures that have been adopted for these purposes have varied widely, as have the modes of reasoning that have supported them and that have informed and justified the limitations on freedom they have adopted.

It is arguable that the appropriate response to these features of our moral and political life is to deny their propriety. Should we blithely accept practices which presume not only that restrictions on freedom are necessary but that at least some of the restrictions should be determined and imposed by collectivities invested with authority to enforce their freedom-restricting judgments and decisions? These assumptions, and particularly the assumption that individual freedoms can properly be restricted by politically organized societies, can be and have been challenged. Radical antinomians and their anarchist descendants have challenged them explicitly and directly, and a variety of self-styled liberation movements seem implicitly if not always ingenuously to reject them. To be sure, individuals and groups must adjust and accommodate their actions one to the other, and doing so will often involve both self-imposed restrictions and restrictions adopted by families, communities, and other social groups. But these restrictions should develop and change consensually, by unforced agreement; they should not be imposed by authority.

Perhaps more pertinent here, a number of influential modern political theorists have written as if the assumptions I am considering might be indefensible and as if they are providing a needed defense for them. These latter theorists (Hobbes and Locke, Rousseau and Kant, are salient examples) have defended the assumptions by articulating what they have believed to be persuasive conceptions of freedom-restricting moral and political arrangements. In this tradition the refutation of radical forms of antinomianism and (later) of anarchism has proceeded by a kind of circumlocution rather than by direct confrontation of the arguments for the latter views; it has attempted to provide convincing reasons (convincing to persons who believe they are "by nature" free) for accepting politically imposed restrictions on freedom of action.

Among the modern political theorists to whom I have just referred, and in the political thinking and practice partly shaped by their influence, the classes of considerations most commonly and potently invoked to justify restrictions on freedom are justice and rights. If an action is unjust, or if taking that action violates the rights of others, there should be no freedom to take it and there are at least the fundaments of a justification for authoritative collective measures to prevent the taking of the action. Or—if this is too strong—at least the person who proposes to take such an action must present a justification for doing so that meets the objections grounded in justice or in rights. In respect to such actions, the burden of justification shifts from those proposing to restrict freedom to those proposing to exercise it. On this view, which (with at least residual feelings of regret that may intrude themselves) informs the following discussion, in their most pressing forms the questions before us are how a theory of freedom of action that begins with LP and GPF can accommodate the requirements of justice and of rights. Of course these are by no means the only sources or types of restrictions that are widely thought to be justified. Societies that give great prominence to justice and rights also endorse freedom-restricting duties and proprieties (for example, duties to help others in distress, various virtues and civilities) that are not part of justice and that do not involve rights; and of course many contemporary societies justify extensive restrictions on freedoms without invoking—except perhaps ceremonially or propagandistically—justice and rights at all. Nevertheless, the centrality of justice and rights in modern Western theory and practice warrants making them the focus of attention.

I

There are a great variety of theories of justice and of rights, and sharp disagreements as to the bearing of these notions on freedom. Utilitarians begin their thinking about them with desires and interests and with the idea that liberty is more or less valuable to the satisfaction of both of them. They then construe justice and rights as among a number of constraints on liberty, constraints that are justified if they are necessary to maximize the aggregate or average satisfaction of desires and interests. Some utilitarians, most notably J. S. Mill, allow that in moral, legal, and political practice justice and rights are widely regarded as considerations superior to interests and to the liberty to pursue the satisfaction of interests (Mill 1951, chap. 5). They insist, however, that justice and rights are properly derivative of and at least in that sense subsidiary to interests and desires and are to be given content by determining what is necessary to maximize the satisfaction of the latter. Principles of justice and specifications of rights that do not serve this purpose are indefensible.

The polar opposite of the utilitarian view is provided by theories of divine, natural, or rationally necessary justice and rights that assign these entities (often as a more or less highly ranked element in divine or natural law or right) superior philosophical standing. The supreme position of considerations of justice and of rights is a priori in the sense that it follows from their superior philosophical justification, not from merely instrumental and hence contingent considerations. On these views, we are to determine what is just and unjust, what rights people have and do not have, and we are to entertain desires, interests, and the liberty to pursue them only insofar as the latter are consonant with the requirements of the former. In the wide sense of the term that I have adopted from Rawls, theories that treat justice in this way are typically perfectionist in character, while such theories of rights are strictly deontological.

It is now widely thought that utilitarianism fails to provide an adequately secure place for justice and for rights; fails to accommodate what I will call the independence and stringency that justice and rights do and properly should have in moral and political practice. By making the delineation and enforcement of justice and rights dependent upon interests and desires and what will best serve them, utilitarians leave justice and rights vulnerable to contingencies in much the same way that, as we have seen, they leave liberty itself at risk. At the same time, theories of natural or rationally necessary justice and rights strike many as dogmatic and rigid. If more than formalistic, these theories fail to provide a satisfactory account of and justification for the content of justice and of rights, an account that is convincing among the (in this respect skeptical) members of the secular and pluralistic societies of modernity. Moreover, they call for an inflexible implementation of the rights and the principles of justice that they promote. If utilitarianism fails to secure justice and rights against the ravages of the licentious, perfectionist and deontological theories excessively constrain the pursuit of interests and desires.

II

The intense interest in the work of John Rawls is no doubt importantly due to his incisive identification of these weaknesses in utilitarianism and perfectionism (readers familiar with Rawls's work will recognize his influence in the previous paragraph) and his at least partly successful attempt to harmonize freedom with justice and rights. Sharing this widely received judgment, I now take up Rawls's theory, commenting on it as a means of extending the argument of Chapter 8.

The strategy of the following discussion is chosen to serve this constructive (as opposed to exegetical) purpose. There are dimensions of Rawls's thought that are compatible with but go beyond LP and GPF. I draw on these to enlarge the above discussion of freedom of action in order to encompass considerations of justice and of rights. At the same time, I attempt to strengthen my previous arguments by defending them against objections, based on considerations of justice and of rights, that Rawls in effect brings against them.

These purposes will be served by an expository procedure that is also recommended by the history of Rawls's theorizing. Although his thought is no doubt most widely known through *A Theory of Justice*, in later essays Rawls has arrived at a view concerning the enterprise of theorizing about justice that may or may not have been at work in his book (I follow Rawls himself in leaving this question open [Rawls 1985, 1]) but that in any case is importantly complementary to the stance I took in Chapter 8 and previously. From at least the third of his Dewey Lectures (1980) forward, and most emphatically in "Justice as Fairness: Political Not Metaphysical" (1985), Rawls has insisted that his purpose in theorizing about justice is restricted to an attempt to resolve or to reduce a dilemma—very roughly the dilemma of how to harmonize liberty and equality—that is salient in political life in the constitutional democracies of the modern period. This understanding of his enterprise has led Rawls to employ the "method of avoidance" (1985, 231). "Whenever possible," he tries "to avoid disputed philosophical, as well as disputed moral and religious, questions." His theory of justice "deliberately stays on the surface, philosophically speaking," leaving as far aside as possible such controversies as "between realism and subjectivism about the status of . . . values," "questions of philosophical psychology or a metaphysical doctrine of the nature of the self" (ibid., 230), and "the search for truth about [a] . . . metaphysical and moral order" independent of the constitutional and democratic societies of our actual political experience (ibid.). It is not that "these questions are unimportant or regarded with indifference" (ibid.). They are to be avoided, rather, because "No political view that depends on these deep and unresolved matters can serve as a public conception of justice in a constitutional democratic state" (ibid., 231).[1]

The question of how far Rawls is in fact successful in avoiding questions such as those just mentioned will arise as we proceed. But we should first note some of the more positive aspects of his method and the similarities and differences between them and positions I have thus far taken. His purpose is to articulate a conception of justice that would provide a fair basis for social cooperation in the constitutional democracies of modernity. Such a conception must be public, not esoteric, and it must be one that could be adopted by uncoerced and unmanipulated members of the society in which the conception is to operate. It is neither enough nor essential that the conception be true in the sense of based on certifiably correct premises or even that it be developed by "valid argument from listed premises" (Rawls 1985, 229). Rather, "it must always proceed from some consensus, that is, from premises that we and others publicly . . . recognize as acceptable to us for the purpose of establishing a working agreement on the fundamental questions of political justice" (ibid.). Such a conception "need not be an original creation but may only articulate familiar intuitive ideas and principles so that they can be recognized as fitting together in a somewhat different way than before" (ibid.). In order to develop such a conception we "collect . . . settled convictions [such as the belief in religious toleration and the rejection of slavery] and try to organize the basic ideas and principles implicit in" them (ibid., 228). "These convictions we can regard as provisional fixed points which any conception of justice must account for if it is to be reasonable for us. We look, then, to our public culture itself, including its main institutions and the historical traditions of their interpretation, as the shared fund of implicitly recognized basic ideas and principles. The hope is that these ideas and principles can be formulated clearly enough to be combined into a conception of political justice congenial to our most firmly held convictions" (ibid.).

The settled convictions and shared basic ideas and principles from which Rawls works are data of our public culture in much the same sense as I claimed that LP and GPF are deeply established assumptions in our culture. But we must note important differences between the uses to which Rawls puts such data and the stance I have taken toward them. Rawls is surely correct that political philosophers must work with the established features of the culture or cultures they address. The issues of political philosophy take their shape and character from those features; argumentation that is uninformed about them or that ignores them (assuming that such argumentation is in fact possible) would have no bearing on the issues of political life. I further agree that political philosophy must attempt to achieve a critical stance concerning the conventions of the culture it addresses. But it is in this regard that there is a difference between us. Whereas I want to ask whether LP and GPF deserve acceptance, and want to advance arguments for accepting them, it is part of Rawls's method of avoidance that he restricts himself more narrowly. He avoids either endorsing or criticizing the basic ideas of the public culture of constitutional democracies, deliberately limiting himself to the attempt to think out the implications and consequences of accepting those ideas. He does not attempt to say, in his own name as it were, whether or why we should, for example, reject slavery and embrace a wide religious toleration. *Given* these and certain other more or less settled beliefs (and assuming a commitment to achieving a fair basis for social cooperation), he asks how the basic institutions and practices of political society (the "basic structure" of such societies) should be arranged and conducted in order to achieve fair social cooperation. He criticizes various familiar ways of construing, combining, and deploying the settled beliefs and commitments of constitutional democracies (for example, utilitarianism, perfectionism, and intuitionism), but he leaves aside the question whether the settled beliefs and commitments should themselves be sustained. His reasoning about justice and rights and their bearing on freedom of action is not in his own name, it is in the name of "representative persons" who are assumed to be heirs of and participants in the culture of constitutional democracies. (To keep this feature of Rawls's theorizing in mind, in phrases such as "Rawls argues" and "Rawls's argument is," I from time to time put his name and pronouns replacing it in quotation marks.)

Here again there is a question whether Rawls succeeds in conducting his enterprise in the manner he claims;[2] whether his proposed resolution of central conflicts and dilemmas in our public culture does not depend on beliefs of his that are not, or are not merely, beliefs about what others believe. More important, there is the issue whether his proposed resolution of dilemmas in our culture deserves acceptance in the sense that it is grounded in beliefs and values (or rather construals of beliefs and values that are hardly univocal) that ought to have the standing that Rawls claims they have in our culture and that ought to play the role that Rawls's construal proposes for them in our public life. In particular, there is the issue whether Rawls's construal gives freedom of action its due.

III

A conception of persons as at once free and equal is a "basic intuitive idea" that is "implicit in the public culture of a democratic society" (Rawls 1985, 234, 231). Accordingly, a theory of justice that is political in the sense discussed must work within such a conception. A theory that entertained, say, the view that slavery is justified or that society is "a fixed natural order or . . . an institutional hierarchy justified by religious or aristocratic values" (ibid., 231), would disqualify itself for a role that is political in Rawls's sense. It would be so sharply at variance with the culture to which it is addressed that its contentions, whatever their merits by the standards of other cultures or by notionally transcendental philosophical standards, would either be ignored or would deepen and exacerbate rather than resolve or diminish disagreement and conflict.

Because it forms part of the "shared fund of implicitly recognized basic ideas and principles (ibid., 228), the conception of persons as free and equal opens up the possibility that we can reason from it to achieve agreement on disputed questions. At the same time, disagreement "as to how the values of liberty and equality" are to be understood and "best realized" is the source of "sharp and divisive" political disagreement and hence sets philosophizing that is political in Rawls's sense its "first task" (ibid., 226). "The course of democratic thought over the past two centuries or so makes plain that there is no agreement on the way basic institutions of a constitutional democracy should be arranged if they are to specify and secure the basic rights and liberties of citizens and answer to the claims of democratic equality" (ibid.). In admittedly "stylized" terms familiar to political theorists, this disagreement is exemplified by the conflict between Locke and Rousseau and between Benjamin Constant's "liberties of the moderns" and "liberties of the ancients" (ibid., 227). In the more widely familiar terms of ideologies or "isms," it is at the center "of the liberal critique of aristocracy, of the socialist critique of liberal constitutional democracy, and of the conflict between liberals and conservatives . . . over the claims of private property and the legitimacy (as opposed to the effectiveness) of social policies associated with the so-called welfare state" (ibid., 234). Faced with this long-standing and divisive disagreement, "political philosophy in a democratic society is . . . to examine whether some underlying basis of agreement can be uncovered and a mutually acceptable way of resolving those questions publicly established." Or if this proves to be impossible ("as may well be the case"), perhaps political philosophy can help to narrow the divergence of opinion sufficiently "so that political cooperation on a basis of mutual respect can still be maintained" (ibid., 226). (If this conception strikes some as a coming down from the aspirations traditional or proper to political philosophy, it is not notably modest. "Until we bring ourselves to conceive how this could happen, it can't happen" [ibid., 231].)

Given the combination of agreement and disagreement (including disagreements that cannot be sidestepped by the method of avoidance) that marks the culture he is addressing, Rawls believes that he requires a mode of reasoning that incorporates the main points of implicit consensus and yet gains improved leverage on disputed issues.

The much-discussed original position and veil of ignorance are intended to meet this need. In the recent essay to which I have been responding, he characterizes these as forming a "device of representation" that "models" "what we regard as fair conditions" (ibid., 236–37) under which to specify "the most appropriate principles for realizing liberty and equality once society is viewed as a system of cooperation between free and equal persons" (ibid., 234–35). The terms "representation" and "models" are not free of obscurity, but the following ideas seem to be prominent in Rawls's use of them. The original position "represents" fair conditions of choice in two ways. On the one hand, it *includes* those features which members of the culture implicitly agree are necessary components of fair social cooperation. The "parties" to the original position are to view one another as free, as equal, and as committed to achieving a system of mutually advantageous cooperation. This means that they credit one another with two "powers of moral personality" requisite to participation in such a system, namely, a capacity for a sense of justice and for a conception of the good (together with "the powers of reason, thought, and judgment connected with those powers") (ibid., 227, 233). On the other, the "device" *excludes* types of considerations or of reasons which, Rawls assumes, are regarded as incompatible with fairness. It "abstracts from" all "contingencies of the social world" that give some members "bargaining advantages" over others, advantages that take them out of the "symmetrically situated" circumstance that "is required if they are to be seen as representatives of free and equal citizens" (ibid., 236–37). Somewhat more specifically, "one of our considered convictions, I assume, is this: the fact that we occupy a particular social position is not a good reason for us to accept, or to expect others to accept, a conception of justice that favors those in this position" (ibid.).

The device, then, "represents" in the sense of "re-presenting" (albeit in more orderly and definite formulations) what Rawls takes to be settled beliefs of the members of the cultures he is addressing. In so doing it also "models" fair conditions of choice in that it abstracts from and simplifies a complex reality; it abstracts from the details of the circumstances under which political choices are actually made. The veil of ignorance enables us to achieve not only an unprejudiced but a "clear and uncluttered view of what justice requires" (ibid., 238).

The device of the original position, then, is a "means of public reflection and self-clarification" that we can use "to help us work out what we now think." It is neither historical in the sense of a notion of a past moment in human affairs nor purely hypothetical in the sense of imagining persons or societies other than those familiar to us. "We can, as it were, enter this position any time simply by reasoning for principles of justice in accordance with the enumerated restrictions" that make up the device, restrictions that represent and model beliefs we already hold. Thus "the conception of justice the parties would adopt identifies the conception we regard—*here and now*—as fair and supported by the best reasons" (ibid., 238–39).

"Rawls's" reasoning from the postulates of freedom and equality to the conception of justice favored by the parties proceeds as follows: corresponding to the two "moral powers" (capacities for an effective sense of justice and to form, revise, and act upon a conception of good) through which Rawls partly construes freedom and equality, are two "highest-order" interests, namely, to realize and exercise the two powers (1980, 525). Given the *highest*-order interest in forming and pursuing their conception of the good, the parties would not accept conceptions of justice which put that interest in jeopardy. When supplemented by a generalization that I mention just below, this consideration disqualifies all those conceptions of justice that accept the idea, "dominant" in moral and political philosophy "since classical times," that "there is but one conception of the good which is to be recognized by all persons, so far as they are fully rational" (1985, 21). This idea could be accepted only if it could be known with certainty that there is a single conception of the good that encompasses all of the permissible conceptions of good that the parties or the citizens they represent might adopt. (Very roughly, "permissible" means con-sonant with the other highest-order interest and with both moral powers.) But there is no prospect of satisfying this condition. Of course the veil of ignorance prevents the parties from knowing what their conception of the good will be. But this feature of the "choice situation" is adopted because it represents the belief that the members of society (at least those living under reasonably favorable conditions) form and pursue a great diversity of conceptions of the good. Just as it is widely accepted that no single religious doctrine will encompass the religious beliefs of all of the members of a modern democratic society, so no single moral or political ideal will accommodate the diversity of defensible conceptions of the good.

Accordingly, the conception of social justice favored by reasoning from the original position must allow "for a plurality of opposing and even incommensurable conceptions of the good." The "question that the dominant tradition has tried to answer . . . has no answer suitable for a political conception of justice for a democratic society. . . . [P]ublic agreement on the requisite conception of the good cannot be obtained" and must not be sought (1985, 21). Doctrines (such as perfectionism) that advance an answer to this question may or may not be acceptable as individual life-ideals or as a basis for fair cooperation in substate voluntary associations, but they are to be rejected by political society and hence by political philosophy.

There are extensive similarities between this reasoning and its implications for freedom, and the reasoning for LP and GPF. Conceptions of the good as Rawls discusses them may not be equivalent to an array of interests and desires, ends and purposes, but on Rawls's essentially Sidgwickian understanding interests, desires, and so forth certainly figure importantly in conceptions of the good. Again, both treat freedom of action as an instrumental, not an intrinsic, good, arguing that freedom so conceived is vital to the members of modern societies because it is essential to forming and pursuing a conception of the good or a set of interests and desires. Finally, by reasoning from these claims, both attempt to rebut or disqualify justifications for restrictions upon freedom that have been potent in our tradition.

IV

In the respects discussed thus far, then, Rawls's contractarian liberalism is at no great distance from the form of liberalism I have been advancing here, and the complementarities between the two lines of argument may diminish resistance to one or to both. In addressing the further questions specifically before us in this chapter, however, Rawls advances views that should be rejected.

"To be sure," Rawls allows, there is "a general presumption against imposing legal and other restrictions on conduct without sufficient reason." But this—in itself less than ringing—endorsement of GPF is immediately and sharply qualified. We are not to think that "priority is assigned to liberty as such, as if the exercise of something called 'liberty' has a preeminent value and is the main if not the sole end of political and social justice" (1982b, 5–6).[3]

According to Rawls there are two (related and already familiar) problems with the idea that protecting "liberty" is the main purpose of justice in a well-ordered society. First, freedoms of action conflict with one another. GPF provides no way of resolving such conflicts and hence to give it priority would leave us to cope with them through circumstantial and uncertain balancing of our intuitions (our circumstantial intuitions as distinct from the deeper variety on which the theory relies). Rather, Rawls claims, the parties will judge some liberties to be vastly more important than others. Instead of adopting

GPF as a fundamental political principle, they will identify the liberties that matter most and give "priority" to them. In this regard Rawls claims that we should think not in terms of an undifferentiated notion of "liberty" or "freedom" but of "liberties" and "freedoms."[4] Thinking from the perspective of the parties, he proposes a list of "basic" liberties to which the stronger protections of justice-based rights will be accorded, and he advances the (further) idea that these rights can be sacrificed or subordinated only to one another, *never* to any other consideration or set of considerations. That is, he argues that fair social cooperation in a modern democratic society requires justice to have "absolute weight" against all other considerations and that the first of the "lexically ordered" principles of justice must be the following: "Each person has an equal right to a fully adequate scheme of equal basic rights and liberties, which scheme is compatible with a similar scheme for all" (1985, 227). It follows that the pursuit of interests, desires, and so forth which conflict with this principle and these rights, so far from being a prima facie good as with LP, is not a good at all and is impermissible. It also follows, contrary to GPF, that there is no presumption in favor of freedoms to act on such interests and desires. Rather, there is an unqualified prohibition upon or against such actions.

The second problem is that some freedoms of action conflict with desiderata other than the basic liberties, including some which the parties will judge necessary to fair social cooperation and hence among the requirements of justice. These further concerns involve inequalities in the distribution of "primary" goods other than the basic liberties. A system of fair cooperation, the parties will conclude, requires that all such inequalities satisfy the following two conditions: "first, they must be attached to offices and positions open to all under conditions of fair equality of opportunity; and second, they must be to the greatest benefit of the least advantaged members of society" (1985, 227). These conditions form the (bipartite) second principle of justice. Because the two principles of justice are lexically ordered, the "basic liberties" (rights) established and protected by the first principle cannot be sacrificed in order to meet the requirements of the second principle. But all other freedoms of action must be compatible with those requirements. Interests, desires, and so forth, and freedoms to act on them (other than the basic liberties) which conflict with the requirements of the second principle, are unjust and hence forbidden.[5] LP, GPF, and hence the less differentiated notions of good and of freedom that they employ, are systematically subordinated to the second principle. When we have determined that an action conflicts with the second principle, we are not to weigh, circumstantially as it were, the value of that action or the freedom to take it against the values embodied in the second principle. Rather, we are to act on that principle and eschew all actions it forbids. (It is important to note, however, that Rawls defends the second principle in part on the ground that it helps to assure what he calls the "equal worth" of the basic liberties and the "fair value" of those basic liberties that he regards as most explicitly and importantly political in character. In part for this reason, hereafter I focus on the first principle and the rights grounded in it and established by it.)

These are substantial qualifications of LP and GPF. Indeed, it is tempting to say that they amount to a rejection of those principles and the reasoning that supports them. In what follows I argue that "Rawls" gives *too strong* a standing to the basic liberties and that his case for the second principle as a source of categorical restrictions on "something called 'liberty'" is unconvincing. But it would be wrong to say that he rejects LP and/or GPF; seeing why is important in assessing the qualifications he enters to those principles. To do so we must note the carefully prescribed limitations on the realm of activity in which his two principles of justice apply. This requires attention to his notion of the "basic structure" of society.

Throughout his work Rawls insists on the limits within which his theory of justice is confined. It is a theory of *social* justice when the qualifier is meant to single out the justice or injustice of the institutions and arrangements of societies as politically organized and largely self-sufficient entities that are voluntary only in the sense that if they are "well-ordered" there will be good reasons for accepting the restrictions they place upon our freedoms. Most important, Rawls's theory is all but exclusively concerned with the institutional arrangements and the distribution of rights and duties that make up what he considers the fundamental features of politically organized societies. The subject matter of his theory is the "basic structure" of society, that is, "the way in which the major social institutions distribute fundamental rights and duties and determine the division of advantages from social cooperation. By major institutions I understand the political constitution and the principal economic and social arrangements" (1971, 7).

There are two contrasts or differentiations here. The first is with justice as a virtue of individual persons or a merit of individual actions. Rawls does not deny that these are among the subjects of which justice and injustice are properly predicated. Indeed he anticipates that justice as a virtue of persons and their actions will flourish in a society with a just basic structure. But this is not the focus of his theory.

The second contrast is with justice and injustice as characteristics of distributions, made by a politically organized society, of *particular goods* to *assignable individuals and groups*. As to the first of these, justice as fairness is concerned exclusively with "primary goods," that is, goods that all rational persons will want regardless of the particulars of their conceptions of their good. (In "broad categories," the primary goods are rights and liberties, opportunities and powers, income and wealth, and "a sense of one's own worth" [1971, 92].) These are "social" goods in the same sense that justice as fairness is a theory of social justice, namely, "in view of their connection with the basic structure; liberties and powers are defined by the rules of major institutions and the distribution of income and wealth is regulated by [those institutions]" (ibid.). As to the second, "No attempt is made to define the just distribution of goods or services on the basis of information about the preferences and claims of particular individuals. This sort of knowledge is regarded as irrelevant from a suitably general point of view; and in any case, it introduces complexities that cannot be handled by principles of tolerable simplicity to which men might reasonably be expected to agree" (ibid., 304; see also Rawls 1978; Mapel 1983). Instead, justice as fairness works with the notion of "representative persons holding the various social positions, or offices, . . . established by the basic structure. . . . I assume that it is possible to assign an expectation of well-being to representative individuals holding these positions. This expectation indicates their life prospects as viewed from their social station. In general, the expectations of representative persons depend upon the distribution of rights and duties throughout the basic structure" (1971, 64). It is this distribution of primary goods that is the exclusive concern of "Rawls's" theory of social justice.

These restrictions are motivated by the desire to achieve a general theory of justice and of rights without adopting the politically unworkable notion already discussed, namely, that there is a single conception of the good that all rational persons must accept and that society ought to maximize. Rejecting that notion, the parties achieve the generality necessary to a theory of social justice by working with the idea of primary goods distributed among representative positions. Society distributes liberties, opportunities, wealth, and so forth, among representative positions, and it refuses to "look behind the use which [assignable] persons make of" them. "Once the . . . [basic structure] is set up and going no questions are asked about the totals of satisfaction and perfection" (1971, 94; see also ibid., 280). From this "suitably general point of view" we are to take people's conceptions of their good as we find them.

It is therefore wrong to say that "Rawls" rejects LP and GPF. Although *insufficient* as a basis for a just basic structure, LP and GPF are among the starting points for thinking about such a structure and the rights to and restrictions upon freedom that it establishes. Rawls does not reject the presumption in favor of freedom of action. Rather, for the circumscribed purposes of a political conception of social justice, he offers refinements and extensions of thinking that begins from that presumption.

These considerations suggest that LP and GPF should play a major role in thought and action outside of the basic structure. It is not that the principles of justice are the only justifiable restrictions on freedom of action. The original position is only the first of a four-stage sequence (in the scheme of *A Theory of Justice* and later, the constitutional, legislative, and judicial stages follow it) (ibid., sec. 31) in which freedom-restricting and -protecting rules may be adopted. Nor is there an abundance of statements arguing explicitly that we should assign heavy weight to the presumption outside of the basic structure. But this is at least in part for the same reasons that LP identifies a prima facie good and GPF a general presumption, not a categorical imperative. Decisions about further restrictions require circumstantial information inappropriate to a general theory, and in any case there is no reason to think that there will be one best answer to such questions.[6]

But "Rawls" does endorse a principle closely akin to GPF: "legal and other restrictions on conduct" should not be imposed "without sufficient reason." We have also seen that he disqualifies a generous selection of the kinds of reasons commonly advanced in favor of such restrictions. The notions of excellence promoted by perfectionist theories cannot be admitted for this purpose. These are "imprecise as political principles and their application is bound to be unsettled and idiosyncratic, however reasonably they may be invoked and accepted within narrower traditions and communities of thought" (1971, 330–31). Similarly, utilitarian arguments that liberty should be restricted in order to maximize the general happiness, common good, or "shared highest-order preference function" also fail to pass these tests and are equally to be rejected (see esp. 1982a, secs. VI-VII).[7] Social justice "is not to be mistaken for an ideal of personal life (for example an ideal of friendship) or an ideal for members of some association, much less as the Stoic ideal of a wise man" (1982b, 28). There are many such ideals; in principle there might be as many as there are persons and groups that form conceptions of their good. From various perspectives and for purposes of life in a family, in a religious, avocational, or entrepreneurial association there are better and worse ideals and better and worse ways of arriving at and pursuing them. But from the perspective of a "political" theory of justice persons who do not meet these standards "are not to be criticized." "[I]n the liberal view there is no political or social evaluation of conceptions of the good within the limits permitted by justice" (ibid., 83).

This view extends to the basic liberties themselves. These liberties are guaranteed by the political association. They cannot be infringed by that association itself and it is the responsibility of that association to protect them against infringement by agents and agencies other than itself. Nevertheless, "even in a well-ordered society some citizens may want to circumscribe or alienate one or more of their basic liberties." In pursuing their good as they see it they may make promises and contracts, pledge their faith, surrender their judgment, and so forth. "Relationships of this kind are obviously neither forbidden nor in general improper." Due to its overriding commitment to justice and hence to basic liberties, the political society must not itself "enforce undertakings which waive or limit the basic liberties." Whatever promises, contracts, or subscriptions they may have made, citizens qua citizens "are always at liberty [for example] to vote as they wish and to change their religious affiliations" if they become so disposed. The political association intervenes exclusively to maintain these liberties against infringement by parties other than the persons whose liberties they are.

Once again, "The essential point here is that the conception of citizens as free and equal persons is not required in a well-ordered society as a personal or associational or moral ideal. . . . Rather it is a political conception of justice." Effectively establishing such a conception "of course" protects the liberty of citizens "to do things which they regard, or which they may come to regard, as wrong and which indeed may be wrong. (Thus, they are at liberty to break promises to vote in a certain way, or to apostasize.) This is not a contradiction but simply a consequence of the role of the basic liberties in the political conception of justice."[8]

Taken together, these passages amount to considerably more than a mere acknowledgment of a presumption in favor of freedom. The argument for the value of the basic liberties to the citizen is strong enough to justify the traditional view that they are "beyond all price" (1982b, 183). Yet individual citizens are not to be criticized for, are to be protected in their liberty to, restrict, qualify, and even to alienate their own basic liberties.

A just basic structure is essential to human well-being. But this judgment disagrees with LP and GPF mainly in that it assigns yet greater significance to characteristics LP and GPF single out. The argument for the basic liberties and their priority depends directly on the view that forming and pursuing a conception of the good is not only a prima facie good but one of two highest-order interests that cannot be compromised. In this perspective, "Rawls's" argument deepens as well as extends the case for liberty. And his extensions of it, his arguments for justice-based rights to the basic liberties, are motivated not by a belief that liberty must be accommodated to or harmonized with other high-order values but by the fact that liberties conflict with one another. Rawls seeks an ordered scheme of liberties primarily in order to protect liberty from the diminutions that might occur in the absence of such a scheme. With a scheme in place, the presumption in favor of less basic liberties that do not conflict with the basic ones is very powerful.

V

Many would argue for political protections for and restrictions upon freedoms (including protections and restrictions that are established, fixed, permanent) well beyond those Rawls proposes and condones, but it is not easy to think of conceptions that give a plausible account of justice and rights and yet involve fewer or less substantial qualifications of LP and GPF. Rawls is certainly justified in viewing his argument as within the liberal tradition. It may well be that liberals must either endorse something close to his view or heroically adopt an antinomian or anarchist position that rejects politically established principles of justice and rights which rank and restrict freedoms of action. (This thought is perhaps given plausibility by the fact that libertarian doctrines, such as Robert Nozick's, empty justice of all content except freedoms of action protected by so-called natural rights—and are no more than dogmatic concerning the rights they assert.)

I want to defend a liberal, democratic, and constitutionalist view, not an antinomian or anarchist one. And I want to defend such a view in a form that gives rights, as they figure in our moral, political, and legal practice, a secure place as protections for and limitations upon freedoms of action. In doing so I continue to treat the "Rawlsian" views I have been discussing both as a source of supporting arguments and as an opposing view that should be rejected in the name or on behalf of freedom of action.

Some headway can be made by noting a perspective on Rawls from which I at least could readily endorse most of what he says about protections for and restrictions upon freedom. If we view Rawls as a participant in practical political and constitutional discussion in the United States, he articulates positions which are reasonable (in the ordinary sense rather than in the sense of his stipulated notion of the Reasonable) in themselves and in the manner of their presentation. Among these positions are his notion that there are certain basic liberties that should be given special standing in constitutional arrangements, his view that freedom of political expression should exclude the crime of seditious libel (ibid., sec. X), his treatment of subversive advocacy (ibid., secs. X-XI), his argument about the "fair-value" of the political liberties and the steps appropriate to securing it, and his view that in other respects a rough equality of the "worth" of the liberties is all that should be collectively attempted and that the material conditions necessary to it should be sustained indirectly and by ordinary legislation subject to amendment by the ordinary political and legal processes (ibid., sec. VII). Rawls is certainly entitled to his claim that these positions form a coherent and otherwise eligible articulation of the beliefs and values from and with which he is working. Of course a variety of the details of Rawls's scheme can be disputed. But such disputes could be set aside if we keep in mind that he aims to delineate no more than "the general form and content" that the basic liberties (ibid., 7) should have under "reasonably favorable conditions" (ibid., 11), and indeed only the "central range of application" (ibid., 9) that those liberties should have under such conditions.

Some of the following remarks will be from this circumscribed perspective. But Rawls himself emphasizes that his discussion "is not intended to advance any of the problems that actually face constitutional jurists." His conception of justice "is not to be regarded as a method of answering jurists' questions, but as a guiding framework, which if jurists find it convincing, may orient their reflections, complement their knowledge, and assist their judgment" (ibid., 84). Although this conception is perhaps unassuming ("We should not ask too much of a philosophical view" [ibid.]) when compared with the ambitions and claims of certain "praxis" theorists, it would be no small thing to construct a "framework of deliberation" that identified the form, content, and central range of application of the basic liberties and thereby enabled "conscientious persons" in a political society to achieve "effective and fair cooperation" (ibid.) As we have already seen, Rawls thinks that these objectives have eluded theorists for several centuries and cannot be achieved unless we find a "new way of organizing" our deepest beliefs and values, one that ranks those beliefs and values, now and into the indefinite future, in lexical order such that in public life some among them will invariably have "absolute weight" against all of the others.

Rawls says that the test of his proposals is practical-political, not philosophical. The appropriate test is whether they will, or would, be acceptable to members of modern democratic societies as a basis for fair cooperation. It is out of the question that we conduct this "test" in any literal sense. We cannot induce whole populations to adopt the standpoint of the original position and then conduct a referendum pitting justice as fairness against utilitarianism, perfectionism, and intuitionism. "Political" has to mean that theorists show themselves to be responsive to the beliefs and values most influential in the societies they address.

Rawls claims that his conception meets this requirement and I have assented to this claim in a number of respects. There is, however, at least one important respect in which Rawls's theory is at odds with the political cultures and traditions that most concern him (and is very likely to be at odds with any pluralistic and democratic culture). The modern democracies that Rawls has in mind do treat certain liberties as "basic." They accord the exercise of these liberties the special protection of rights, and in a number of societies these rights have distinctive, usually constitutional, standing. Moreover, Rawls's list of the basic liberties will be familiar to anyone who is knowledgeable about these constitutional democracies. But it is a large further step to the contention that these liberties are or should be "basic" in the sense that their "priority," their "absolute weight" against all other considerations, is or should be viewed as a requirement of justice and hence fair social cooperation.

Leaving aside the question whether Rawls's theory of the basic liberties is a theory of *justice* as that concept is ordinarily used, an at least apparent conflict between his theory and actual practice concerns his view that there are certain liberties that *must* be basic, that could be subordinated to other considerations, if at all, only under less than "reasonably favorable conditions." Treated as a doctrine concerning constitutional and democratic practice, one of the practical implications of this view is that procedures for change, including amendment procedures, could operate concerning the basic liberties only if the circumstances of the society in question deteriorated below the (not very high) level of reasonably favorable conditions.

Rawls is not the first theorist to argue that there is a pre- or extra-constitutional position in which we are to reach conclusions binding upon the constitution and the constitutional processes themselves. This idea is a familiar feature of theories of natural right and rights, and something like it can be found in numerous other theories that advance strongly objectivist doctrines of good, of right, of justice, and so forth. Nor is there any doubt that these doctrines have influenced constitutional and democratic practice; they have been the more or less proximate sources of ideas as to what rights (and/or other provisions) ought to be constitutionally established and they have promoted the thought that some of those rights should be regarded as sacrosanct. Nevertheless, it is no part of any known constitutional arrangements that there are pre- or extra-constitutional conclusions that are binding upon the constitution. Conclusions such as Rawls urges may be part of what I have elsewhere called the *authoritative*, the array of beliefs and values that forms the setting within which constitutional practice occurs, but they become constitutional, are invested with *authority*, only when they are adopted as part of the constitution itself. In the practices of the modern constitutional democracies Rawls is addressing, the "basic" law *is* the constitution and the "basic" liberties *are* the liberties established by the constitution (Flathman 1980).

As these last comments may suggest, it might be argued that this conflict between Rawls's theory and received practice may be no more than apparent, even no more than terminological. Rawls's concern is not with constitutional or legal procedure as such, it is with the judgments and conclusions that in reason we ought to accept. We can sustain the understanding that formally there is no authority superior to the constitution and the constitutionally established procedures and yet commit ourselves unqualifiedly to a substantive conception of justice that features Rawls's list of basic liberties and his second principle of justice. Rawls is not proposing a change in constitutionalism or democracy as forms or methods of governance, he is advocating a conception of justice that is to give political and moral content to those forms.

If my first formulation of the conflict between Rawls and received practice made too much of formal constitutional procedure and doctrine, my reformulation makes too little of them. We must ask *why* the modern constitutional democracies that Rawls is addressing have developed and sustained the distinction between authority and the authoritative, have maintained the understanding that the constitution gives the basic content of authority, the arrangement that all constitutional provisions are subject to change through procedures that the constitution itself establishes for constitutional change. Returning to the comparison drawn above, we must ask why modern constitutional democracies have been influenced by but have not adopted natural law, right, and rights doctrines which, as with Rawls's doctrine concerning the basic liberties and their priority, would permanently fix parts of the constitution on the basis of preconstitutional considerations and reflections.

It would not be easy to improve upon Rawls's own answer to these questions. Such doctrines involve theological and philosophical assumptions that are inveterately controversial; they advance and seek to privilege conceptions of the good and the right that cannot be known to be compatible with the interests and desires of the members of the societies to whom they are proposed; they can be effectively implemented and enforced only by a degree of reliance on state power incompatible with freedom and equality. Of course every society must choose among liberties and hence must establish protections for and restrictions upon them. All politically organized societies do so in part through binding legislation, and numerous societies have taken the further step of giving some protections and restrictions special constitutional standing. But whether for the Rawlsian reasons just rehearsed or some other (for example, Jeffersonian arguments that no generation can properly bind its successors, Millian arguments about fallibility), they have rejected the notion that some protections and restrictions can justifiably be made permanent. All legislation is subject to revision and repeal, all court decisions to reinterpretation, qualification, and reversal, all constitutional provisions to amendment. The view that has prevailed is the liberal doctrine previously discussed; we must reach and act upon conclusions about political and moral questions and—at least often—we can do so on reasoned grounds, but all such conclusions must be regarded as subject to reconsideration, revision, and rejection.[9]

In this perspective, Rawls's argument for the unqualified and permanent priority of a list of basic liberties is sharply at odds not only with formal constitutional doctrine and actual constitutional and political practice but with beliefs and values that—by his own account—are deeply established in modern constitutional democracies. By the criteria he himself says his theory must meet it seems clear that in the respects under consideration his theory fails.

This conclusion might nevertheless be unwarranted. If there are deep conflicts and dilemmas in our public culture, we cannot expect to achieve a theory that is consonant with all of the salient features of that culture. Perhaps fair social cooperation will become possible only if we qualify the constitutionalist and meta-ethical views and practices I have been discussing so as to eliminate or at least substantially to diminish reliance upon implicit views and the conflict that such reliance makes continuously possible. Perhaps Rawls is also correct that his proposals comport well—comport better than the practices and beliefs they qualify—with the culturally fundamental ideas that we are and should be free and equal.

We might view the issue here as a version of the question whether rational persons thinking within the constraints of the original position would opt for the two principles of justice in lexical order and would decide to give those principles absolute weight. Numerous critics have argued that Rawls's choice situation is less determinate than he claims in this respect. Depending on assumptions further to those Rawls specifies, the parties to the original position could rationally adopt different principles and/or a different ordering of Rawls's principles than Rawls proposes.[10] My own inclination has been to the stronger objection that *no* principles of justice could be chosen in the original position because the veil of ignorance screens out considerations necessary to the cogent use of the concepts in which thinking about such principles occurs (Flathman 1972, 386-87). A very general formulation of this objection would be as follows: "Justice," "interests," "rights," "rational," and the other concepts that figure in such thinking have their meaning in the language games of actual moral and political life; Rawls abstracts severely from those language games and hence deprives the concepts he is trying to use of the situatedness necessary to their meaning. More concretely, Rawls insists that principles of justice must be acceptable to rationally self-interested persons, but "the parties" to the original position cannot know what their interests in any usual sense are or will be. Rather, they are obliged to make their calculations in terms of the primary goods together with certain other very general propositions about human nature and society. Of course these calculations are exclusively for the purpose of settling the basic structure. But this is no small thing. The basic structure defines "men's rights and duties and influence[s] their life-prospects, what they can expect to be and how well they can hope to do" (Rawls 1971, 7). It "shapes the wants and aspirations that . . . citizens come to have. It determines in part the sort of persons they want to be as well as the sort of persons they are" (ibid., 259). It is less than clear that thinking about judgments with consequences such as these, thinking that takes place under the restrictions of the original position, can properly be called thinking about one's interests.

This objection can be formulated in yet another way. Beliefs about freedom and equality are at once widely distributed in modern Western societies and the focus of long-standing and sharp disagreement among the members of those societies. For limited but vitally important purposes, Rawls attempts to reduce the multivocality of these concepts and diminish the disagreement that surrounds them. To do so he suppresses many of the concerns and considerations that inform and give content to political debates and he formulates principles that are henceforth to regulate such debate. Granting that theorizing of any sort involves collecting particulars in general categories and subsuming them under general principles, a theory of freedom and equality which excludes particulars that are recurrently salient in the practices it theorizes will speak to those practices only by a kind of inadvertence, only to the extent that it in fact fails in its attempt to exclude particulars.

In response to those objections we might move to the kind of argument developed by T. M. Scanlon. Rights "place limits on what individuals or the state may do, and the sacrifices they [the rights] entail are in some cases significant" (1979, 519). These limitations and sacrifices need to be justified, "and how other than by appeal to the human interests their recognition promotes and protects?" (1978, 93). In an established system of rights the work of justification can sometimes be done "simply by consulting our conception of what" particular rights entail, and there is often "a wide range of cases in which we all seem to arrive at the same answer" (1979, 519). But even in such cases, and more urgently in the many instances of disagreement, we must probe beneath questions of "policy" and of the content of particular rights to what Scanlon calls the "foundational level," a level "concerned with identifying the ultimate sources of justification relevant to the subject at hand" (ibid., 535). Our reflections at this level will bear some resemblance to the reasonings of Rawls's "parties"; we will seek to identify interests important enough to justify the sacrifice of lesser concerns. But despite his use of the unfashionable language of foundationalism and ultimate justification, Scanlon thinks of these reflections as fully situated and as subject to adjustment and amendment in the light of changes in our circumstances. His argument concerning the right to freedom of expression is abstract in that it is in terms of the interests of "participants," "audiences," and "bystanders" and of "categories" of expression such as political, religious, commercial, and pornographic. But these classifications are used to organize information about more particular interests and forms of expression, not to exclude such information from consideration. "To claim that something is a right . . . is to claim that some limit or requirement on policy decisions is *necessary* if unacceptable results are to be avoided, and that this particular limit or requirement is a *feasible* one, that is that its acceptance provides adequate protection against such results and does so at tolerable cost to other interests." Accordingly, what "rights there are in a given social setting at a given time depends on which judgments of necessity and feasibility are true at that place and time. This will depend on the nature of the main threats to the interests in question, on the presence or absence of factors tending to promote unequal distribution of the means to their satisfaction, and particularly on the characteristics of the agents . . . who make the relevant policy decisions: what power do they have, and how are they likely to use this power in the absence of constraints" (ibid., 535-36).

The kinds of considerations Scanlon mentions are of course unavailable in the original position. The parties must decide the scope of the right to the free exercise of religion without knowing the range and distribution of religious doctrines in their society; without knowing, for example, whether the members of their society are fervently religious or only mildly or blandly so, whether there are sects that are militant in their belief that other religious doctrines are false or pernicious, whether prevalent religious doctrines include socially divisive beliefs about education, politics, the family, gender, and race. They must settle the "general form and content" of the freedoms of speech, press, and association without reference to the technologies of communication and travel that are available, without knowing whether their society will have peaceful relations with other nations or will be under siege by them, and entirely without regard to the degree of consensus or dissensus concerning beliefs and values beyond the purview of the basic structure. They must conclude not only that the two moral powers and the corresponding highest-order interests are of paramount importance, but that certain rights are necessary and feasible means of protecting those interests—that the interests will of certainty be disserved in the absence of those rights and that those rights can be effectively implemented and enforced at acceptable cost to other values. And because the decisions made in the original position are to be binding into the indefinite future, they must conclude that all of these propositions will be acceptable regardless of changes in the society and its circumstances save those that reduce it below the level of "reasonably favorable conditions." If any one of these conclusions is unwarranted or ceases to be warranted in respect to any of the basic liberties, the exercise and enforcement of the rights to those liberties will constitute unjustified interference in the freedom of action of members of the society.

It is of course impossible for me to demonstrate that these among Rawls's claims will cease to be warranted. I have allowed that at least some among them are reasonable here and now; that is, I have opined that his list of basic liberties comports well with the constitutional practices of at least one modern democratic society and I have endorsed his construals of the general form and content of the basic rights he has proposed. These (casual, badly underdefended) judgments are of course influenced by my own perceptions and assessments of circumstances that obtain in the society in question. If I were to argue that Rawls's claims are not reasonable concerning other present-day societies or would not have been reasonable concerning this society at some earlier time, I would be at least tacitly claiming to have the requisite comparative or historical information. Most important, if I were to argue that these among Rawls's claims will certainly or even probably cease to be reasonable in the future, I would be making the very mistake I am attributing to Rawls. In the absence of powers of prognostication that none of us have, the question whether Rawls's claims will continue to deserve acceptance must await events. What we can say now—which is all that needs to be said—is that justifying rights requires information not available at all in the original position and subject to change as principles adopted in that position are implemented. If Rawls's list of the basic liberties and his construal of the rights to them is now reasonable it is because *he* has information that his "parties" could not have. If those judgments continue to be reasonable into the future—a judgment that will have to be made in the future—that will be owing to the contingent fact that the society has remained the same in the relevant respects. The most powerful of Rawls's claims, namely, that his basic rights should, now and into the indefinite future, have absolute weight against all other considerations, must be rejected.

Rawls might respond by underlining the several qualifications on his argument: it purports to be no better than the presently best available construal of freedom and equality; it holds only for the basic structure and only under reasonably favorable conditions; it gives no more than the general form and content of the rights and allows that (owing to conflicts among them) those rights must be "regulated" with outcomes that cannot be fully determined in advance. Such a response is available to Rawls in the sense that the qualifications just rehearsed are all present in his argument, and of course I am suggesting that his theory would be strengthened if he gave these features greater prominence and put increased emphasis on them. To do so, however, would cause a major change in the theory, a change that would alter its distinctive claim that we can achieve fair social cooperation only by adopting a basic structure under the constraints imposed by the original position. The idea that a structure based on reasoning under such constraints will hold constant into the future is fundamental to the calculations of the parties and to Rawls's theory of the just society.

VI

There is, moreover, a more pertinent rejoinder that might be made to my objections. The most general version of this rejoinder is the one just mentioned, namely, that views such as Scanlon's would make fair cooperation impossible in the societies in question. Either we establish basic rights and duties on the basis of unbiased and uncluttered reasoning or we continue to face disagreements and conflicts that are resolved, if at all, by more or less arbitrary and more or less strongly resented impositions. Perhaps the more adaptive, information-sensitive procedures and processes that Scanlon discusses would be workable in a society with a deeper and more encompassing consensus on beliefs and values;[11] in the pluralistic, divided democracies that we have, we must choose between such procedures and a just society, between a perhaps more finely tuned attention to consequences and terms of cooperation that are not manifestly unfair to any class or group of citizens. More refined concerns such as those urged by Scanlon may be attended to, but only outside of the realm of the basic structure.

By stipulating that fair terms of cooperation consist of his two principles in lexical order, Rawls takes the position just stated. But there is another version of the rejoinder in question that does not presuppose—as does Rawls's stipulation—the very features of Rawls's theory I have been controverting. According to influential theorists of rights and of constitutionalism (and influential critics of utilitarianism and consequentialism), considerations such as Scanlon mentions— certainly yet more circumstantial considerations such as I have invoked—are categorically excluded or at least narrowly circumscribed by rights of all sorts and most emphatically so by moral rights and by legal rights with constitutional rather than merely legislative standing. It is part of the very meaning of rights (or the meaning of "taking them seriously") that they "trump" (Dworkin 1978) or are "inviolable side-constraints" (Nozick 1974, pt. 1) upon all other considerations. On natural or rationally necessary versions of this view of rights, rights exclude appeal to considerations of consequences from beginning to end; such considerations are to play no role in identifying and adopting, exercising and respecting, enforcing, interpreting and revising rights. On conventionalist, constructivist, and related views, consequences, interests, and the like may be consulted in establishing and amending rights, perhaps in formally or officially construing their scope as controversies arise about them; but once adopted and once construed, rights trump all such considerations. To suggest that claims based on rights may be overridden by appeal to consequences, or even that they may be adjusted or modified (except through formally designated procedures) in the light of expected consequences or "mere considerations of social utility" (Scanlon 1978, 93) is to fail to understand them or to fail to take them seriously. Whatever we may think of Rawls's list of basic rights or of the details of his reasoning in support of those rights, his view that basic rights have "absolute weight" against all competing considerations is simply a correct account of rights as they figure in our moral, legal, and political practice. We might adopt rights under circumstances of fuller information than Rawls specifies, but from then on we either accord them absolute weight or do without them. Since it is my purpose to accommodate rights and constitutionalism within my theory of freedom of action, this rejoinder requires attention.

It will be a useful first step to broaden the discussion by recalling what might be regarded as the opposite number of the view of rights just sketched. From Bentham to the Legal Realists and beyond, skeptics about rights have denied that they do or could play anything remotely approaching the role of trumps or side-constraints. Whether because of the de facto dominance of interests, the ineliminable ambiguity of the language in which they must be conceived and stated, or a combination of these and other factors, rights neither do nor could determine what is or is not, ought or ought not to be done. Extended to all general and prospective rules and principles of conduct by some of the jurisprudential radicals in the school of Critical Legal Theory and to all language by uncompromising deconstructionists, this view says that it is no better—and often much worse—than an illusion to think that the "central range of application" of notions such as freedom of religion, expression, and association could be settled in advance of particular cases and apart from the interests and objectives that motivate the parties to those cases. Resounding statements to the effect that certain rights have or could and should have absolute weight in our deliberations and our conduct are no more than well- or ill-intentioned gestures.

I advert to these unmasking and delegitimating views not to endorse them but because they mirror the deficiences and the at least apparent strengths of the doctrines against which they are largely a reaction. Echoing the early natural-rights theorists to whom Bentham was reacting, such theorists as Rawls, Dworkin, and Nozick advance unrealistic claims and hold out unrealistic expectations concerning the actual, possible, and desirable independence and stringency of rights; rights skeptics reduce rights and rights claims to something else (for example, nodes or clusters of individual, group, or class interests) and attribute any practical significance rights might appear to have to the power or influence or manipulative skills of those who effectively assert them. Rights theorists are correct in claiming that rights are distinct and distinctively valuable features of moral, political, and legal life in a number of modern societies; skeptics are correct that rights cannot be understood or assessed apart from interests and desires, beliefs and values, and they are correct in saying that in fact the distribution of effective enforcement of rights commonly reflects the distribution of power, privilege, and wealth.

The question of the efficacy of rights and rights claims in this or that time or place can be answered only by empirical investigation. But neither celebratory nor dismissive theories of rights rest on such investigations. They depend, rather, on remarkably similar and implausible a priori claims about what must be the case in order that rights can be distinct and distinctively important notions and devices. Rawls insists that if rights are not entirely independent of considerations other than the basic powers and highest-order interests in which they are grounded (an independence signaled by the fact that the basic rights are adopted and affirmed under the constraints of the original position), and if they are not invariably accorded absolute weight against all other interests and powers, then a just and well-ordered society is impossible. Dworkin and Nozick insist that if the fundamental or natural rights are left hostage to utilitarian or other calculating processes, or if they are adopted or construed to serve the patterning requirements of notions of distributive justice, then they are not taken seriously or they themselves become engines of injustice. Since it is easy enough for skeptics to show that these demanding requirements are not in fact met, it is not difficult for them to make their own case that rights are illusory entities—and often enough "entities" deployed by moral and political illusionists.

In its most general character this is of course a familiar story. Of all concepts whatsoever either we can state the necessary conditions of their proper application or we abandon them as meaningless; of concepts which purport to have empirical referents either those conditions are or could in principle be instantiated or we abandon the concepts as figments; of concepts which purport to have moral or political import either those conditions are or could by practicable steps be satisfied or we abandon the concepts as utopian.

Salutary as this tale may sometimes have been as an impetus to disciplined thinking, the ideal that informs it is not creditable.[12] But this conclusion leaves us to formulate an account of rights that both accommodates their independence, stringency, and distinctive importance (that is, that avoids the a priori reductions of the various "realisms") and has room for the kinds of considerations that theorists such as Rawls, Dworkin, and Nozick exclude from thought and action about basic or natural rights. Scanlon's papers will be of further assistance in this regard, but before returning to them I consider anew an analysis by G.E.M. Anscombe (1978) that is strongly continuous with the Wittgensteinian views already invoked.[13]

Anscombe's discussion of the "stringency" of rights begins with a puzzle that arises about them as well as about a number of related practices and institutions. How can it be that the fact that you have a right (or that I have made a promise to you, or that there is a prescriptive rule) creates an obligation for me; that owing to your right I *must* act in a certain manner or *can't* take certain actions? If these "musts" and "can'ts" are philosophically puzzling (of course they are rarely *puzzling* to us as participants in the practice of rights), it is at least in part because they are typically invoked when it is obvious that in fact I *can* do or refuse to do the prohibited or required action. Their puzzling character is deepened by the fact that the necessity or impossibility seems to derive from nothing more than a certain combination of words. "But how on earth can it be the meaning of a sign that by giving it one purports to create a necessity of doing something—a necessity whose source is the sign itself, and whose nature depends on the sign?" (Anscombe 1978, 320-21).

In attempting to resolve these philosophical puzzles, Anscombe takes up and endorses Hume's view that the necessities that go with promises and rights are "naturally unintelligible" and arise only as part of a system of human conventions. For Hume, this means at least two things: first, the words "promise," "right," and "obligation" stand for no perceived object or event; second, even if there were such an object or event our perception of it could not of itself give rise to that "inclination to perform," the conviction that one must perform, which is a salient feature of promises and acknowledged right claims. Both the promise or right and the sense that there are duties connected with them are artifacts of decision and agreement.

In respect to Hume's first point Anscombe follows Wittgenstein in extending Hume's argument to all "words and their relation to their meanings." All uses of language involve rules and rule-following; the meaning of language is inseparable from the rules that govern its use. Now the "musts" and "can'ts,"the duties and obligations, attendant upon valid promises and rights are part of the meaning of those concepts; anyone who undertstands the concepts knows that to make a valid promise is to undertake an obligation and knows that to acknowledge a right (in most of the Hohfeldian senses [Hohfeld 1919]) is to recognize the duties that correlate with it. It follows that the words themselves, the bare marks or symbols, cannot be the basis of the duties and obligations. Quite apart from psychological considerations such as Hume adduced, we can make sense of the duties and obligations only by reference to the rules according to which duties and obligations are created by, or are a feature of, valid promises and rights.

Viewing rights in this way makes their stringency less puzzling, more ordinary or familiar, than they are made to appear by rights theorists. There are a very large number of practices that involve "musts" and "can'ts" which are like rights in that they have little or nothing to do with physical or other natural limitations and necessities. At least in the sense that there are ways in which we must and can't use the elements of language, such modal pairs are a feature of every activity that involves language. And many of these requirements and limitations are more than "merely" linguistic, are features of activities in which we engage in part by using language. For example, the correct and incorrect ways of using the language of etiquette largely coincide with the proprieties and improprieties of polite conduct. We learn what etiquette requires and the language of etiquette together. For the most part this learning is unproblematic. "It is part of human intelligence to be able to learn" the proper response to such imperatives. Without such intelligence "they wouldn't exist as linguistic instruments" and without such instruments "these things: rules, etiquette, rights, infringements, promises and impieties would not exist either" (Anscombe 1978, 321). The instruments and the activities in which they figure "are understood by those of normal intelligence as they are trained in the practices of reason (ibid., 323). If they are puzzling—or rather mysterious—it is in the deep sense in which we might find human intelligence and the practices of reason mysterious.

Anscombe's analysis of modals is also helpful in understanding the sense in which rights are and are not independent of consideration of interests, desires, and the like. The "musts" and "can'ts" we are considering are often "accompanied by what sounds like a reason" for them (1978, 323). "You can't take that seat, it's N's." "You must pay Able $50.00, the terms of your contract require you to do so." The second clause in these statements is a reason for the requirement announced by the first clause. But it is a reason of a special kind, "a 'reason' in the sense of a *logos*, a thought. . . . [I]f we ask what the thought is, and for what it is a reason, we'll find that we can't explain the 'You can't' on its own; in any independent sense it is simply not true that he can't. . . . But neither does 'It's N's' . . . have its peculiar sense independent of the relation to 'You can't'" (ibid., 322). The "can't" and its *logos* are interdependent or interwoven. "If you say 'You can't move your king, he'd be in check', 'He'd be in check' gives the special *logos* falling under the general *logos* type: a rule of a game." If one of her superiors says to a police officer, "You must permit Able to speak, it is her right under the First Amendment," "it is her right . . ." gives the special *logos* of a constitutional right falling under the more general *logos* type "a right." Anyone who knows chess will understand why the king cannot be moved. Anyone familiar with rights and with constitutional practice in the United States will understand why the officer must permit Able to speak. People unfamiliar with these activities and practices are unlikely to understand either the imperatives or the reasons for them.

Anscombe's account is a description of rights, not a derivation, explanation, or justification of or for any particular right or set of rights. She attempts to diminish philosophical puzzlement about the stringency and independence of rights by reminding us of the features in which their stringency and independence are embodied or through which they are manifested. It emerges from her discussion that these two characteristics are intimately connected and mutually reinforcing. On the one hand, it just is part of the concept of a right, a feature of the concept understood by anyone who commands it, that valid rights involve requirements and prohibitions. In this respect the philosophical task is to remind us that the imperatives rights involve are conventional, not natural, and to situate them in the larger array of convention- or rule-governed practices and activities that likewise involve "musts" and "can'ts." On the other, the stringency of rights is enhanced by their independence; by the fact that the reasons for—or better, the reasons of—the imperatives they involve are internal to them. In *understanding* those imperatives we do not look outside of or beyond the rights themselves to reasons such as the interests that are served by them or the good that is done by exercising, respecting, and enforcing them. Because they are self-contained in the further sense of having a *logos* (further to the sense that they just do involve imperatives), their stringency is not directly subject to diminution by such contingent facts as that interests which the rights might be thought to serve are not in fact served in particular cases or that the good which their exercise might be thought to bring about is not in fact done in those cases. Whatever might be the case as regards such external considerations, for persons practiced concerning them, rights are *intelligible* as nonarbitrary bases of thought and action.

It might be thought that Anscombe's analysis supports the very view of rights I am disputing. By detailing the ways in which rights are stringent and independent, she in effect shows that explicitly prescriptive arguments such as Rawls's and Dworkin's are consonant with the concept and practice of rights. She does not advance or endorse normative arguments for particular rights, but she provides criteria that all such arguments must satisfy and she in effect establishes that the arguments I am presently considering, whatever their other merits, satisfy those criteria.

It is true that Anscombe provides criteria that a theory must satisfy if it is to be a theory of *rights* as we in fact know and practice them. Because I think her account is essentially correct concerning the points she takes up (albeit it would have to be further elaborated in order to encompass differences among the Hohfeldian types of rights), my own theory of rights as protections for and restrictions upon freedoms of action must accommodate their stringency and independence as she analyzes those characteristics.

It is not true, however, that her account supports the view that rights as such, or the members of some subclass of rights as such, have absolute weight or are trumps or inviolable side-constraints. Rather, her account calls such views into serious question.

Anscombe's analysis is of promises and prescriptive rules as well as of rights. If we were to attribute absolute weight to rights on the basis of her analysis, we would thereby be attributing the same standing to all valid promises, all of the established rules of morals, law, and etiquette, and presumably all of the rules adopted by churches, corporations, unions, universities, and so on through a long list. But while Anscombe's analysis seems to me to be essentially correct concerning promises and prescriptive rules, few subscribe to Kantian rigorism concerning promises and certain other moral rules or to so-called legal absolutism concerning law, and fewer still to parallel views concerning the vast further array of prescriptive rules that confront us in various dimensions of life. Certainly the strong rights theorists I am discussing reject—must reject—such views. It is one thing to say that all promises and prescriptive rules involve "musts" and "can'ts" which stand in an internal relation to a *logos*, quite another to assign absolute weight to this otherwise multifarious array of entities. If rights or some subclass of rights have or ought to have this quite special standing, it is due not to formal characteristics they share with the entire array of phenomena that Anscombe has analyzed but to the normative arguments that are made in support of them.

Anscombe provides an analysis of rights that accounts for their independence and stringency without according them, as a conceptual matter, absolute weight or the standing of trumps. She thereby opens up the possibility of a theory that genuinely accommodates rights as we know them but that allows a place for considerations such as Scanlon emphasizes. Returning to our starting point in this section, she disqualifies the possibility that Rawls's argument for the absolute weight of rights to the basic liberties is supported (even if Rawls himself does not adduce such support for it) by the very concepts in which he presents that argument. Rawls's claim that his basic rights ought to have this extraordinary standing must be supported by a kind of argument we have already concluded he fails to give, namely, a convincing normative argument.

VII

By further subverting rigorist views of rights, Anscombe's account of stringency and independence also enhances the plausibility of theories such as Scanlon's. We will assume that participants in Scanlon's three levels of argumentation understand the concept of rights. They know that rights involve requirements and prohibitions which are nonarbitrary at least in the sense that there is a *logos* for them. In a relatively stable practice of rights, most of the thought and action that involves rights occurs at the "intermediate level" at which there is often general agreement about the content of the established rights. When participants exercise rights they expect others to discharge the duties that correlate with them; when someone else exercises a right they recognize that they have duties in respect to it and that they are liable to disapproval and perhaps other sanctions if they fail to discharge those duties. They understand the "musts" and "can'ts" of rights to mean that there is an established, a widely agreed, presumption in favor of freedom to take actions protected by rights, a presumption that is stronger than the one given by GPF. If they consider interfering with such an action they know that they will have to justify that interference with arguments responsive not only to GPF and the reasoning that supports it but to the reasoning that supports the particular right and the further reasoning that supports the practice of singling out particular types of action for the special protection of rights. Because they know these things they know that what otherwise might be cogent and convincing arguments in justification of an interference will not as a practical matter, or rather will not as an immediate practical matter, avail. If for example they show no more than that their interests in the issue at hand are more important than the interests of the right-holder in that issue, they will not have justified interfering with the exercise of the right. Making such a case might begin or continue a process of reconsidering the right in question, a process that might lead to reinterpretations of the right and might culminate in amendment or repeal of it. But until such processes have been concluded, other participants will properly judge the proffered justifications inadequate and will hold those who offer them to the performance of their duties.

Before taking up Scanlon's "foundational level" of argumentation, however, it is important to distinguish between justifications (type 1) intended to show that one's conduct is consistent with the norms of the practice of rights and attempts (type 2) to show that the conduct is justified despite its admitted contravention of those norms. This distinction (as with Scanlon's distinctions among "policy," "the level of rights," and the "foundational level") is often difficult to apply, but neglecting it in theorizing about rights gives unwarranted credibility to rigorist views of rights (and, as usual, also to deeply skeptical views of them). As already suggested, the first type divides into two subclasses. The first of these (1a) encompasses attempts to show that conduct alleged to be a violation of an established right is not in fact so or is consonant with a more fundamental right (for example one with constitutional standing) that in the circumstances in question is in conflict with the less fundamental right that is—or would otherwise be—violated by the action in question. The second (1b) consists of efforts to show that the right in question, although admittedly established in the form and with the content alleged by its claimant, ought to be adjusted or amended to permit of an action now proscribed by it. Arguments of type 1a, which will presumably be the most common in stable practices of rights, have the characteristics discussed just above.

If they are unsuccessful in the sense of failing to convince those to whom they are addressed, those who advance them (and who understand and accept rights) will forgo the proscribed action or, at a minimum, will accept that they are properly liable to disapproval or other sanctions if they persist in the action. In cases falling under 1b, the arguer understands and accepts the practice and therefore either discharges the established duties or accepts as proper the imposition of sanctions for not doing so. But she uses the conflict between herself and the right-holder as an occasion to promote changes in the formulation of the right. To do this she will often, even typically, have to challenge the reasons that are taken to support the right, and hence justifications of this type tend toward argumentation at the foundational level.

Justification of actions that admittedly violate unchallenged basic rights (type 2) would be impossible on Rawls's theory. To attempt such a justification would amount to a proposal to return to the original position and reconsider the entire basic structure of society. In this regard, however, Rawls's theory is at some distance from concepts, beliefs, and patterns of activity salient in the societies he is addressing. Potent as it is, the valid claim that one is exercising a well-established basic right does not obviate the cogent expression of opposition, distress, and outrage. The concept and practice of rights coexists and sometimes conflicts with a variety of other normative concepts and practices. That I have a clearly established right to do X does not itself establish that it is seemly or decent, good or right, for me to do X. Others, including others who have no doubt that I do and should have a right to X, are not lacking in conceptual and ratiocinative resources in which to argue for the view that it is wrong for me to exercise my right and right for them to prevent me from doing so. Not all of the citizens of Iowa who have opposed foreclosures on farm mortgages, who may have felt justified in taking vigorous measures to prevent the implementation of such foreclosures, are opponents of the rights of contract or even proponents of changes in the definition of those rights. Not all of the citizens of Skokie who opposed and attempted to prevent the march of the American Nazi party are against the First Amendment or in favor of changes in the authoritative interpretations of that amendment according to which the Nazis had a right to their proposed activities. Just as civil disobedients can and do present cogent justifications for the violation of laws they do not want changed, laws promulgated by governments whose authority they do not question, so people who understand and support rights and the practice of rights present cogent justifications for circumstantial refusals to respect particular attempts to exercise those rights. And just as so-called legal absolutists assert that the doctrine of civil disobedience is incoherent (or that civil disobedients are insincere in their professed commitments to the governments and laws they disobey), so some theorists of rights allege that justifiable "civil encroachment" on rights is a conceptual and theoretical impossibility. Neither of these rigorist assertions accords with the practices it claims to be about.[14]

On these understandings, the protections for and limitations upon freedoms of action that rights provide can be as firm, as reliable, as one could wish. Insofar as and for as long as there is consensus about the rights and the duties that go with them, the rights will govern both individual and group conduct and the policy-making processes of politically organized society. Of course this does not mean that there will be no disagreement or no conflict; nor does it mean that it will be unnecessary to enforce respect for rights by the use of sanctions of various kinds. An effective practice of rights presupposes a quite general, a quite encompassing consensus about the content and signifi-cance of the rights that make it up. But if that consensus were entire and entirely reliable as a basis of conduct in the society, the rights would be superfluous in that society. Along with agreement that the actions which the rights protect and restrict are important enough, consequential enough, to be protected and restricted, there is the expectation that individuals, groups, agencies of government, and so forth will continue to be tempted, even continue to have strong inclina-tions, to interfere with the protected actions and to attempt to exercise the restricted freedoms. If rights are to be effective, much of the restraint and discipline that counters such temptations and inclinations will have to be self-restraint and self-discipline; participants will have to forgo the pursuit of interests and desires, objectives and purposes, out of the conviction that, despite the importance of those interests to them, the rights that conflict with them ought to be respected.

Of course individuals and groups do not form, sustain, or act upon such convictions in isolation from their society. A rights-oriented society is one in which upbringing, education, and law, and the more diffuse processes of approval and disapproval, encouragement and preferment, promote and reinforce the conviction that rights should be respected. Such societies seem also to promote attitudes that are testing, competitive, and adversarial so that relations in terms of rights are often litigious and otherwise tense and conflictful rather than irenic or even mutually accommodating. But for the practice to work as a practice of rights (as distinct from the practices of power, domination, and manipulation that skeptics say all purported practices of rights actually amount to), a preponderance of participants must recognize that there are valid rights claims and that they must be respected.[15] If or insofar as Anscombe's analysis of rights is correct, it is correct because there have been and are practices with a preponderance of such participants.

Although nowhere fully effective (taking this to mean not that all of the duties specifically correlating with all attempted exercises of valid rights are in fact discharged, but rather that all participants understand and accept rights, generally discharge their duties in respect to them, and attempt to meet the appropriate burdens of justification when they decide not to do so), practices that have these characteristics are now prevalent in the Western world. But they are a relatively recent development, they differ importantly from one another, and they do not lack critics. If they change substantially or disappear, Anscombe's analysis will continue to be correct concerning something that once was a part of some societies, but a new analysis will be needed of the practices—whatever participants may call them—that then obtain.

VIII

I began this chapter by acknowledging that freedoms of action must be ranked, that some of them must be specially protected and restricted, and that in modern democratic societies rights have been among the favored devices through which to do these things. Our issue, accordingly, became whether rights could be harmonized with the theory of freedom of action proceeding from LP and GPF. Prominent theories of rights suggest that such a harmonization is possible only in the weak sense that our theory of freedom might be satisfactory outside of the realm of activity governed by basic rights. Within that realm, basic rights and the reasoning that supports them supplant, even exclude, reasoning about freedom based in LP and GPF. What ought and ought not to be done, what we are free and unfree to do, is to be determined by consulting the basic rights.

Examining these theories, however, led to the conclusion that rights partly substitute for but do not supplant or exclude LP and GPF. Once rights have been established, and for as long as they are generally accepted, much moral, political, and legal thought and action does go on in terms of them, in terms of the actions they protect and the duties they create. But participants who understand and accept the established rights can and do consult and invoke other concepts and considerations (for example, LP, GPF, and the reasoning that supports them) in identifying and attempting to resolve issues that arise in rights relationships. While a thoroughgoing antinomian might nevertheless object to the rule structure that the practice of rights involves, on the conclusions reached here the theory of rights and the present theory of freedom are not only compatible in the sense of coexisting in distinct realms of activity but complementary within the realm of rights itself.

Of course the character of the relationship between rights and the theory of freedom of action depends importantly on the understandings and modes of argumentation that inform the selection of rights. If rights are adopted for perfectionist or classical utilitarian reasons, the beliefs and values that characterize those ideals or theories will presumably be the primary and perhaps the sole considerations invoked in interpreting and amending rights and in justifying refusals to perform duties created by them. As we have seen, on most versions of perfectionism, certainly on Bentham's version of classical utilitarianism, the considerations promoted by LP and particularly by GPF would have no more than an indirect and subsidiary role in such a practice of rights.

It is in this regard and for this reason that Rawls's "foundational" reasoning for basic rights, and the rejection of perfectionism and classical utilitarianism that it carries with it, serves to reinforce and extend the arguments for LP and GPF presented in Chapter 8. That reasoning is in terms of interests, goods, and an associated "purpose" (the highest-order interests, the primary goods, and the "purpose" of achieving fair social cooperation); the basic rights are chosen to provide further protections (protections further to those provided, for example, by LP and GPF) for those interests and goods which due reflection shows to be fundamental to all persons who conceive of themselves as free and equal. Because those interests and goods (and hence fair cooperation) are put in avoidable jeopardy (or cannot be known to be adequately protected) by perfectionisms and classical utilitarianism, those ideals or theories must be rejected as the foundation for the basic structure of a democratic society.

Despite these advantages, Rawls's foundational reasoning for basic rights is objectionable on the two related grounds discussed above. Although he reasons in terms of the types or classes of considerations promoted by LP (and qualifiedly endorses GPF because it serves those considerations), he severely confines the instances or examples of those classes admissible for purposes of foundational reasoning. As a consequence, his reasoning is at best distant from the concerns of the members of the societies he is addressing. This severe narrowing of, or extreme abstraction from, the interests, goods, and purposes in fact familiar and valuable to us is specifically for the purpose of establishing basic rights that are to have, into the indefinite future, absolute weight against all of the considerations excluded from the foundational reasoning. Once again, in these respects his theory is sharply at odds with salient features of the practices it addresses (and hence with Rawls's own criteria of political theory), features that are strongly recommended by LP and GPF and indeed by Rawls's own view that the conceptions of the good on which people in fact act are various and changeable.

Of course something *akin* to Rawls's foundational reasoning is unavoidable if there are to be rights at all. Rights are rule- or convention- governed; qua established, recognized rights that are the basis of claims and corresponding duties the rules are not only general but prospective. Forming such rules requires abstraction from the particulars of interests and purposes; it requires generalization, classification on the basis of generalization, and a continuing process of subsuming new particulars under the generalizations and classifications previously arrived at. In the case of legal rights these processes are explicit, formal, and readily observed. With rights that are "merely" conventional, the generalizations and classifications develop in the course of diffuse reflections and discussions that are not invested with formal authority and that eventuate in assertible rights only when a quite encompassing consensus has developed. But the latter process is influenced by the legal rights already established, while the formal procedures of the legal system typically depend upon generalizations that have been formed and widely agreed to in less formal ways. For present purposes the important point is that by virtue of their rule-governed character all rights presuppose thinking and judging that abstracts from and generalizes over immediate, narrowly personal, or group interests and objectives. Such thinking and judging is not and almost certainly could not be done under the severe constraints of the original position, but neither is it nor could it be done in the highly particularistic fashion by contrast with which the notion of the original position is formulated and urged upon us.

In this perspective, Scanlon's account of foundational reasoning, both in its general formulation (1978) and as detailed and amended in his discussions of the right to freedom of expression (1971 and 1979), has much to recommend it. He says that, instead of attempting a radically unsituated form of reasoning, we do, and should, consult the interests we in fact have and attempt to find commonalities among them that will be a sufficient basis for acceptable classifications and enforceable rules.[16] In respect to freedom of expression, for example, we distinguish among the "interests we have in being able to speak, those . . . we have in being exposed to what others have to say, and those we have as bystanders who are affected by expression in other ways" (Scanlon 1979, 520). Along with identifying these "participant," "audience,"and "bystander" interests, we seek to classify recurrent types of expression such as political, commercial, pornographic, and so forth and we ask whether the interests we have as participants, as members of audiences, and as bystanders vary from category to category in ways relevant to the formulation of acceptable, enforceable rights. We go on to consult and generalize over our experience with the recurring sources of interference and we ask ourselves whether there are rules that would counter those threats effectively and at acceptable cost. In conducting these inquiries and reflections we bear in mind that the rights we are adopting are chosen in the light of our circumstances as we perceive and assess them and that we should therefore be attentive to changes in those circumstances as we exercise, interpret, and enforce the rights.

This more situated, more empirical (but not empiricist) process or procedure of reasoning about the foundations of rights is "intuitive" or "intuitionist" in the sense in which Rawls insistently is, and the sense in which he is insistently not, an intuitionist in his methods. (It is important to remember that neither of these senses posits any special faculty of cognition or apprehension.) As with Rawls's reasoning, it at least tacitly begins with beliefs and values that are widely shared among the members of the society, beliefs such as that discussion contributes to knowledge and mutual understanding, values such as that knowledge and mutual understanding are good things. In the absence of a quite encompassing consensus on such beliefs and values, the types of interests Scanlon identifies in respect to expression would not be formed, and questions about rights to protect and restrict those interests either would not arise or would have a quite different character. It is not that any subset of beliefs and values is immune to reconsideration or alteration or that the process of thinking about the rights we should have might not lead to changes in them. But any process of reasoning must begin somewhere, and as Rawls rightly insists there are compelling reasons to think that political argumentation should take its bearings from beliefs and values that are already widely shared in the societies to which the argumentation is addressed. In this respect Scanlon's foundational reasoning is intuitionist in a sense that is not only unobjectionable but to which there may be no practicable alternative.

Scanlon's procedure is also intuitionist in the sense that Rawls claims defeats the purposes of political philosophy. By proceeding in terms of interests that are more particularistic and circumstantial than those that "the parties" to the original position can form, he threatens his procedure with, or rather subjects his procedure to, bias and clutters it with a welter of distracting and conflicting claims and considerations which can be sorted out and reconciled, if at all, only by an uncertain process of balancing the intuitions of the participants. Given that there is an ineliminable plurality of conceptions of the good, that there are deep-seated advantages and disadvantages in existing life-circumstances, and hence that there is disagreement and conflict in the society in which the procedure is conducted, Rawls claims that there is little prospect that general agreement will be reached concerning basic rights and no prospect that such limited, temporary agreements as might be arrived at will be fair to all citizens.

Rawls's parties cannot know their particular interests or the historically specific circumstances of their society, whereas Scanlon's foundational reasoners know and are instructed to consult these considerations. We are therefore compelled to agree that Scanlon's procedure is vulnerable to difficulties and failures that could not beset Rawls's parties. Of course this conclusion credits the possibility of radically unsituated reasoning, of reasoning that is genuinely behind the veil of ignorance in that it is not in fact influenced by factors supposedly screened out by the veil. As indicated, I share the widely expressed skepticism in this regard. From the broadly Wittgensteinian standpoint I have adopted throughout, the idea that there could be such reasoning, or at least that it could be reasoning about interests, rights, purposes, duties, fairness, and so on as those concepts matter to us in moral and political life, is deeply suspect. But this is not the objection I now want to emphasize. Rather, I want to argue that the intuitionist method is superior to the Rawlsian one.

Despite Rawls's claim that bias, disagreement, and conflict cannot be avoided by intuitionist methods, foundational reasoning of Scanlon's type is more likely to lead to rights that are actually effective. Of course there will be disagreement at the foundational level and it will carry over to and be exacerbated at the levels of rights and of policy. As we have seen, however, disagreement and even conflict are a part of the practice of rights and their presence does not itself make the rights ineffective. In a procedure such as Scanlon's, the interests and concerns that the participants actually have and that motivate their actions will—or at least might—be expressed and considered in the deliberations about rights. Some of the proposals based on those interests will be accepted, some rejected, but in any case the connection between the rights and duties and the activities of the participants will be manifest and substantial, not distant and abstract. Also, as Scanlon emphasizes, the rights will from the beginning be adapted—or again at least might be adapted—to the actual circumstances of their exercise, particularly to the main sources and kinds of interference and the main resources available to cope with those interferences. Participants will not adopt a list of putatively absolute rights in studied disregard of the circumstances of their society and then be required to adjust themselves and their society to those rights. If we accept that theorizing about rights should be political in Rawls's sense, these are clear advantages of the intuitionist procedure.[17]

Thus far, then, intuitionist procedures are to be preferred because they are more likely to produce rights that actually protect the interests they are intended to serve. This thought can be extended in the following ways: If we think that the formation, pursuit, and satisfaction of interests and desires, objectives and purposes are, prima facie, good things, and if we regard freedom of action as a high-order instrumental good, then we will (should) be cautious in imposing restrictions upon them and flexible or adaptable in implementing those restrictions. Such a cautious, adaptive, approach is facilitated by Scanlon's procedure in ways already discussed (roughly, because of its empirical character) but also in the practical political sense that the participants in the procedure are positioned to argue for their interests. Proposals that would restrict freedoms have to be defended concretely and in response to those to whom the freedoms matter. Moreover, because the various rights that have been adopted at any time are not regarded as having absolute weight into the indefinite future, citizens whose freedoms are restricted by them can continue to advance such arguments without reopening the entire question of the basic structure.[18] It is of course not impossible for such procedures to eventuate in an unseemly melee among selfish interests, even a continuing and destructive succession of such melees. Confident predictions of such outcomes may betray perfectionist sympathies or perhaps a distrust of citizenries so unqualified as to suggest the impossibility of effective systems of rights or anything approaching well-ordered societies. But we should remember that participants are disciplined by the fact that they are debating rights (that is, a species of general and prospective rules) and, again, that a populace intent on unremittingly selfish behavior is not likely to be deterred from it by any procedures of foundational reasoning. Such a populace would never enter into the perspective of the original position and would reject the decisions of any "representatives" (who of course would not be representative persons in Rawls's sense) who did adopt a set of basic rights under the constraints of that perspective.

The argument just advanced tacitly invokes the meta-ethical voluntarism or qualified skepticism that lies behind LP. We can and do argue about normative matters in ways that are mutually intelligible and sometimes mutually convincing. The positive case for LP and GPF presented in Chapter 8 is an attempt at such argumentation, as is the present discussion of alternative procedures of foundational reasoning, and as are instances of such reasoning such as Scanlon's and Rawls's discussions of freedom of expression. If we denied this possibility altogether, political and moral philosophy would consist exclusively of meta-level argumentation in support of that denial. But LP is also partly supported by doubts concerning the possibility of conclusive, undeniable arguments for preferring this good to that, this array of goods over those. We adopt the latitudinarian principle LP in part on the basis of certain beliefs about the usual characteristics of human beings and their circumstances and certain attendant evaluations of what, given those characteristics, will be conducive to human well-being. But we also adopt it on the ground that arrangements based on and informed by it make fewer and less exacting demands on our limited abilities to convince one another of our moral and political views.

Decisions to establish rights are among the most forceful, the least tentative and qualified, of the moral and political decisions that we make. It is for this reason that forms of antinomianism grounded in meta-ethical skepticism are distrustful of if not antagonistic toward rights. It is also importantly for this reason that circumspection is appropriate in respect to rights. Rawls affirms voluntarist views and relies in important part on what might be called a sociologized and "politicalized" version of them (the claim that there is in fact an ineliminable diversity of conceptions of the good) in rejecting perfectionism and utilitarianism. Moreover, his foundational reasoning for rights is circumspect in the important respect that it is restricted to the basic structure. Within that restriction, however, he claims to have arrived at conclusions that in reason ought to be accepted into the indefinite future by all members of all modern democratic societies that enjoy reasonably favorable circumstances. Moderate skeptics who are prepared to entertain rights at all should be open to the possibility that the arguments for these seemingly immoderate conclusions are good enough to justify accepting them; but they will also view their immoderate character as itself a reason against accepting them and and against procedures designed to produce them. A major advantage of the alternative procedures of reasoning I have been discussing is that they carry caution and circumspection to the very foundations of rights.

IX

Thus far I have tried to show that the theory of freedom of action proceeding from LP and GPF is compatible with the practice of rights, and I have argued that there is a type of procedure for adopting and altering rights that is consonant with the practice and recommended by the theory. This procedure, along with the understanding of rights that goes with it, provides a means of justifying special protections for certain freedoms of action, protections stronger than are afforded by LP and GPF. Those arguments do not themselves justify or disjustify any specific right or set of rights. I have expressed the view that Rawls's proposed basic rights could readily be justified, but on the position I have taken adequate support for that view would require evidence and argumentation of kinds that I have not presented.

Rather than attempt such argumentation I conclude this chapter by returning to the relationship between freedom and autonomy. My chief purpose in doing so is to further strengthen the foregoing views about freedoms and rights by indicating some ways in which freedom and autonomy, despite the differences between them, can complement and enhance one another. If my view about the relation between freedom and rights can be shown to facilitate such complementarity, those who place a high value on autonomy may therefore find that view attractive. In this respect this concluding section is continuous with the rest of the chapter. But of course the freedom-autonomy relationship is of great importance in its own right and I have yet to deliver on my promise to do more about it than was done in Chapters 6 and 7.

It is not plausible to think that there could be a right to autonomy. If we continue to take autonomy to require freedom of action but to involve more than such freedom, rights that protect freedoms will contribute to the possibility of autonomy but will not themselves assure it. Of course there are various types of action and states of affairs that contribute directly and specifically to achieving autonomy, and rights to take or enjoy them will be especially valuable to those cultivating or promoting it. Rights to freedom of expression are a leading example, and the rights of participants, audiences, and even bystanders are often defended (for example, by J. S. Mill and in respect to political expression by Meiklejohn) on this ground. Again, education is commonly regarded as a strongly contributive if not a necessary condition of the capacity for critical thinking that is part of autonomy, and perhaps rights to education could be justified in this way. Yet, again, there is a familiar line of thought according to which autonomy is impossible apart from rights to private property. But a person could enjoy all of these rights and more and yet fail to become autonomous. We might say that autonomy is an ideal of character, not a mode of action or a distributable good, and that there cannot be rights to such ideals. It would perhaps be better to say that autonomy is an individual achievement; other persons and society generally can encourage and facilitate it in various ways, but because only individuals can actually achieve it, there cannot be a right to it.

But since freedoms, rights, and various other social arrangements and policies manifestly can contribute to or obstruct the development of autonomy, the question arises how they can best be made to assist such development and how doing so should be compared and coordinated with the pursuit of other objectives. In my earlier discussions I emphasized that attempts to foster autonomy can and not infrequently do restrict freedoms of action. I do not think that there is any general formula that would properly determine how to proceed in all cases of such conflicts, but I suggest that there should be a bias or disposition to prefer freedoms of action over the promotion of autonomy. This is partly because freedoms of action are necessary to the pursuit of virtually all human interests and objectives, whereas autonomy is an ideal that some pursue avidly but that is little understood by or of little concern to many. Another way of putting this is that there is a very direct, all but unqualified, relationship between freedom of action and a part of the good identified by LP. If pursuing interests and objectives is a good, and if freedom of action is necessary to their pursuit, then freedoms of action will serve the good that justifies it even if the interest is not satisfied or the objective not attained. (This does not affect the view that freedom is an instrumental, not an intrinsic, good. If there were no interests and objectives, or if they could be pursued without freedom, then freedom would either not be a good or its standing as such would have to be defended in some other way. It is because there may be interests and objectives that can be served without action and hence without freedom that I said that there is an "all but" unqualified relationship between LP and GPF.) With autonomy, by contrast, the freedoms, rights, or policies serve the purpose that justifies them—as distinct from the purpose of allowing freedom to pursue objectives (including the objective of achieving autonomy) identified by LP—only if autonomy is actually achieved. And since that result cannot be guaranteed by the rights or policies, the case for the rights or policies is less strong. Nevertheless, there will certainly be cases when we will be justified in promoting autonomy at the expense of freedoms of action. Some interests and objectives and freedoms to pursue them are of comparatively little importance and others are harmful and properly restricted. Where such interests and freedoms conflict with policies to promote autonomy, the latter should be adopted. To repeat, it is implausible to think that there is a formula that would cover all cases.

In the present context, however, our interest is primarily in cases in which freedom of action and the pursuit of autonomy are compatible and complementary. Because autonomy is itself an objective, and because freedom of action is a component of it when it is achieved (although not a necessary feature of policies or arrangements that promote or contribute to it), there must be many such cases. Specifically, there must be many cases in which rights serve both freedom of action and the development of autonomy. Thus the question of how best to adopt, exercise, and enforce rights can be considered from the standpoint of how best to foster autonomy. A society strongly committed to autonomy will want to consider the question in part in this way.

I suggest that this perspective enhances the attractiveness of the view of rights and freedom that I have been urging. I said that autonomy is an achievement, an ideal of character to which individuals aspire and that they sometimes achieve in one degree or another. But of course one does not attain it once and for all in the way that one learns to do simple arithmetic or to ride a bicycle. Autonomy does involve capacities such as for critical thinking which, once developed, one may lose entirely only through mental or physical incapacitation. But it also involves effective dispositions to use those capacities. The autonomous person steadily thinks and acts autonomously in the important dimensions or aspects of her life. If this disposition weakens or disappears, autonomy diminishes or disappears with it. Thus it is not enough to acquire the capacities necessary to autonomous action, one must also maintain and use those capacities in thought and action. The degree to which one maintains autonomy depends on the extent to which one does so.

If we accept anything approaching Rawls's view that politically organized societies have a basic structure that importantly determines the life possibilities of its members, then it will be first and foremost in respect to the liberties and rights, institutions and arrangements that make up that structure that we will most want to encourage and promote autonomy. If autonomy consists in important part in critical thought and action concerning the basic norms of one's society, a society that values it highly will promote full and *continuing* critical assessment of those norms. The idea that the basic rights and duties should be arrived at by a highly specialized and confined mode of reasoning and thereafter treated as sacrosanct will be rejected as incompatible with the commitment to autonomy. The fact that intuitionism specifically invites and relies upon informed and critical reflection in respect to basic freedoms and rights is not the most important argument for it, but it is a potent addition to the other arguments previously given.

This discussion of autonomy prompts final remarks of a yet wider character. Literally construed, autonomy would mean self-rule and would be incompatible with life in political society. (Recall that it is a literal construal of autonomy and related notions that leads Goffman to the conclusion that autonomy is incompatible with social life.) Somewhat more plausibly interpreted, it means something like self-justifying: the autonomous person makes her own critical assessments of the norms and rules of her society and is first and foremost concerned to justify her conduct to herself, to see to it that her conduct satisfies standards that she believes appropriate. In actuality, of course, self-justification and hence autonomy must mean a more than usual regularity, persistence, and vigor in employing and satisfying the criteria of rational or critical assessment that are generally accepted in the person's society, traditions, and culture. The view I have advanced concerning freedom and rights is conducive to autonomy because it discountenances authoritative barriers to and restrictions upon such self-justification, and promotes continuous efforts to satisfy the best criteria of justification available in the culture.

Widening this theme by responding to a valuable paper by James Fishkin (1984), we can say that the view of freedom and rights I have advanced promotes not merely self-justifying individuals but what Fishkin calls a self-justifying society; a society in which the citizenry is steadily concerned to justify to itself what it collectively and collectedly does. The norms and conventions, the rules and rights, and the structures of authority that adopt and enforce rules and rights, are questioned and assessed by the best criteria of rational justification available. This is not an anarchist, antinomian, or anti-rights position. As we have seen, it can accommodate authority, rules, and rights as they are practiced in the closest things to self-justifying political societies that we know. But it is a position that is explicitly and steadily concerned with what Fishkin appropriately calls legitimacy, with knowing that and why the authority-structures, the rules, and the rights are justified.

Fishkin recognizes that the criteria of justification and legitimacy vary from society to society and particularly that what I have referred to as the best available criteria in liberal constitutional democracies differ importantly from those with comparable standing in other types of societies. In particular he recognizes the distinctive, one might even say the idiosyncratic, character of the notion that authority, rules, and rights must be justified *to* all those required to obey and respect them. (His argument is self-consciously "internalist" or "intuitionist" in that it attempts to identify the criteria of justification that are in fact widely accepted as appropriate in the societies he is discussing and to argue from and in the terms of those criteria.) *Given* that notion, however, he argues that liberal societies can achieve and maintain legitimacy only if they protect and otherwise promote continuing and widespread critical assessment of the requirements and prohibitions that they adopt and enforce. Obstacles to and restrictions upon such assessment delegitimate the very institutions and arrangements they may be alleged to protect.

Fishkin's notion of a self-reflective and self-justifying political society is very much in the spirit of the argument I have developed here. It might, moreover, be thought to provide a rejoinder to the objection that the present argument evades the question of which freedoms should be protected and restricted by rights and hence lacks definite political significance. Fishkin claims that arguments such as his and mine are sufficient to justify certain political liberties, that is liberties of political expression, belief, and association. If these liberties are not protected and otherwise promoted, neither individual nor collective processes of self-reflection and self-justification are possible and legitimacy cannot be sustained. It is not that these liberties are goods in themselves, it is because they are necessary conditions of a self-justifying and legitimate political society. Once this is realized, "the requirements for liberty take on a special status—one that insulates them from further criticism that they may be unnecessary or should be abandoned" (Fishkin 1984, 21). Thus by enlarging the argument to include not only individual autonomy but the kind of collective autonomy expressed by the concept of a self-justifying society, we move from a position that is committed to LP and GPF and open to the possibility of special protections for certain liberties to a definite, all-things-considered justification for certain liberties, a justification that is circumstantial only in the sense that it presumes a liberal culture operating under reasonably favorable conditions.

I agree that it is difficult to conceive of a convincing justification for denying or narrowly restricting the liberties Fishkin singles out.[19] In the terms used here, we might say that these liberties are required by, come along with, LP and GPF themselves. If departures from these principles are to be justified, it seems that there must be discussion and debate concerning the proposed qualifications and this in turn requires liberties of expression, belief, and association.[20] Indeed we might go further and say that these liberties are required *for* LP and GPF. If the standing of these principles is itself to be justified (as opposed to simply being accepted as starting points of moral and political reflection), the conditions necessary to such discussion must be satisfied. Taken with full seriousness, the notion of a self-justifying society goes all the way down in that it requires liberty of discussion of all normative questions.

We should note that Fishkin does not use the language of rights in discussing the necessary liberties, that he does not attempt to define those liberties with great exactitude, and that he allows that they must be "regulated" in Rawls's sense of that term (1984, 10, 17). It is clear, then, from my remarks in the previous paragraph and earlier that there is no great distance between Fishkin's argument and my own. At a minimum, his argument draws highly reasonable practical inferences from the more general argument we have both developed.

It is nevertheless too strong to say that those political liberties are necessary to the legitimacy of a self-justifying society, too strong to say that within such a society they are "insulated" "from further criticism." There is a paradox lurking here that can be put in the form of a question: how can a society committed unqualifiedly to freedom of political discussion exclude any remotely political belief or arrangement from such discussion, let alone what on Fishkin's account is its most fundamental political arrangement? Fishkin's liberties are among the basic institutions or arrangements of the society; as such his own argument would seem to forbid (on pain of loss of legitimacy) regarding them as beyond criticism.

Of course every theory has to start somewhere and we might treat Fishkin's argument as identifying the most appropriate starting point for political theory in or about liberal society. Even if we took this view, we would want to ask why we could not entertain, later on as it were, criticisms of the liberties. We might start with or from them, reason to other conclusions, and with those other conclusions in hand double back to examine our starting point. Put phenomenologically rather than ratiocinatively, discussion of liberties obviously requires liberty of discussion among the disussants, but such discussion might lead to the conclusion that thereafter liberty of discussion should be abolished or curtailed. Indeed this is precisely what Fishkin is proposing in one important respect. In arguing for certain liberties as necessary conditions of legitimacy in a liberal society, he is entertaining the question whether there should be such liberties. Having reached the conclusion that such liberties are essential, he proposes that discussion cease concerning the question he has entertained.

We do better to distinguish between liberties of expression for which there are very strong justifications in a liberal society and beliefs, values, and principles that we reason from in justifying liberties. Fishkin's argument for liberties would get no hearing in a society whose members rejected the view that discussion and debate contribute to knowledge and understanding or who placed no value on justifying norms and rules to those expected to obey them. The belief just mentioned in turn presupposes an array of further beliefs about human beings and their capacities and characteristic dispositions, and the value attached to justification would be incomprehensible apart from other values such as freedom and equality and those expressed by LP. Given an array of such beliefs and values, we can formulate strong arguments for certain liberties. But no such arguments would be convincing to persons who rejected the beliefs and values altogether, and the particular version of such arguments that is found convincing depends upon which of the many versions in which the beliefs and values are accepted by those to whom the arguments are addressed.

We should embrace the conception of liberal societies as self-justifying (as aspiring to the ideal of self-justification) because that conception conveys with admiral concision beliefs, values, and other characteristics prominent in liberal thought. Doing so has at least two further advantages. The first is that the conception is of material assistance in seeing that, and why, rights to political expression are so strongly justified in liberal societies. The second is that it helps us to understand but also to appreciate the instability and vulnerability of such societies. The beliefs and values that are characteristic of liberalism and that support and sustain its distinctive mode of legitimation have not been widely accepted in human experience and are various and changeable where they are accepted. But there is no way permanently or finally to alter this circumstance; and if there were, liberals would be obliged to reject it.

10

The Conditions of Freedom
Freedom as Elemental

Rawls and Fishkin claim that there are certain conditions necessary to a political society if it is to be acceptable by liberal standards (or to persons who conceive of themselves as free and equal). For Fishkin, these conditions consist of the availability of certain liberties; the claim that these liberties are necessary is an inference from other features of liberal thought, particularly its notions of justification and legitimacy. Rawls's list of necessary conditions partly overlaps with Fishkin's but includes further items; his reasoning for the list, while in part internal to liberalism, also appeals to generalizations about human beings and what are goods for them, generalizations whose standing do not depend upon an acceptance of liberalism.

Analogous to these views about conditions that are normatively necessary are various claims about conditions that are empirically (causally) necessary if an acceptable society is to develop and sustain itself. Rawls and Fishkin include such empirical conditions only in the weak sense that they assume "reasonably favorable conditions." But other writers, including some who leave their normative prescriptions less closely specified than do Rawls and Fishkin, present quite detailed accounts of the empirical conditions they judge essential to achieving and maintaining an acceptable society. If freedom is a feature of a good society, we must identify and see to maintaining the conditions of freedom. On this view of the matter, a major task, perhaps the single most imporant task in the theory of freedom, remains before us.

Assessing this view about the theory of freedom is important in itself and will help us to draw together several of the lines of argument developed in the foregoing chapters.

I

It is easy to think of claims of the kind in question. An example is the widely held view that an acceptable and acceptably distributed array of secure freedoms can be sustained only in a political democracy. Quite apart from any intrinsic value democratic arrangements may be thought to have, undemocratic societies confine important freedoms to a ruling elite and leave others vulnerable to invasion by the elite. Some form of political democracy is the only effective means of controlling those with authority and power, particularly of controlling the tendency of the powerful to destroy the liberties of the weak. Some views of this sort go further and specify that some more particular form of democracy (for example, representative or participatory) is necessary to freedom. Again, it is widely thought that democracy must be "social" in extending beyond government and politics to the school, the workplace, the church, and perhaps to assuring various further conditions (income, employment, medical care) regarded as essential to effective participation in democratic processes. In the absence of these conditions, freedoms are not only vulnerable to invasion but likely to be "merely formal." In the name of the conditions necessary to freedom we get encompassing and detailed political, social, and economic prescriptions. There is sharply drawn disagreement over these prescriptions, but a remarkably wide range of features have been elevated to the standing of necessary conditions of freedom.

Proponents of such views sometimes make (wittingly or otherwise) conceptual moves of kinds that we must continue to keep distinct. Rather than treating, say, welfare-state liberalism or socialism or capitalism as empirically necessary to freedom, "freedom" is so defined that, conceptually, it is possible only under welfare-state liberalism or socialism, conceptually impossible apart from them. A society that is undemocratic, or capitalist, or communist is *therefore* not a free society. If such moves are made, judgments about freedom and unfreedom require empirical investigation only to the extent necessary to determine whether a society is democratic, capitalist, socialist, and so forth. Conjunctions such as "undemocratic but free," "socialist and unfree," become contradictory, while phrases such as "free, socialist society" involve redundancies.[1] Arguments of this sort may take impetus or support from the observation that there is a strong correlation between, say, socialism and freedom. Moreover, if such correlations are widely observed, a conceptual connection between socialism and freedom might become generally established. On the broadly Wittgensteinian view I have adopted throughout, the possibility of such conceptual developments cannot be excluded. Concepts have more or less settled uses, and the criteria governing them can be stated. As of now, democracy, socialism, capitalism, and the like are not among the established criteria of "freedom." People who claim that such concepts have this standing are advancing a stipulation or a so-called persuasive definition. Perhaps they will persuade us; perhaps they will succeed in effecting the conceptual connection they are promoting. Until they do, we should interpret them as claiming that socialism (or democracy, or capitalism) is empirically necessary to freedom, and we should ask whether that claim is supported by the relevant bodies of evidence and argumentation.

There is, however, a tradition of thought that respects the distinction between criteria and conditions of freedom and seriously claims to have identified empirically necessary conditions of freedom. Proponents of liberal as distinct from participatory democracy such as Tocqueville and J. S. Mill are in this tradition. For these writers, freedom is not only distinct from democracy but of greater value than it. If there were an unresolvable conflict between freedom and democracy, freedom would properly take precedence. Empirically, however, such a conflict, at least in modernized societies and at least as regards liberal democracy, is an impossibility. Both Tocqueville and Mill saw democracy as a means to the end of (among other things) freedom, and both rejected certain conceptions of democracy on the ground that they threaten freedom. But both believed (for somewhat different reasons) that democracy had become a necessary condition of a secure freedom. A yet clearer source of examples is provided by thinking about the rule of law. Although some writers (Montesquieu at times [1977, bks. x–xi]) have equated freedom and life under the rule of law, there is a vigorous tradition, forcefully represented in our time by Friedrich von Hayek (1960, pt. II; 1982, vol. 1, chaps. 4–6) and Michael Oakeshott (1983, fourth essay), which insists that the two are conceptually distinct and that the rule of law is a necessary condition of a satisfactory moral and political freedom.

If arguments of this kind can be sustained, the distinction between the conditions and the criteria of freedom—on which, in various vocabularies, I have relied heavily throughout—would lose the significance I have attached to it. If as a practical matter freedom is impossible apart from democracy, or socialism, or the rule of law (or of virtuous or responsible selves, communal solidarity, and so forth), then the distinction between freedom and these other phenomena, while perhaps logically or technically viable, will seem insignificant and even puerile. Insisting upon it, giving it a central place in the theory of freedom, will present itself as scholasticism in the pejorative sense. Anyone who values freedom and who is clear-headed about it will insist upon democracy, socialism, virtue, or whatever else is empirically necessary to freedom. The old song about love and marriage will express the proper understanding; freedom and its conditions will be seen to "go together" such that "you can't have one without the other."

It is impossible to examine in detail the large and diverse array of claims concerning empirically necessary conditions of freedom. I proceed, rather, by discussing a well-developed and accessible claim of this sort. My aim in doing so is to call attention to difficulties that arise in any theory that includes such claims, difficulties that are hard to resolve.

II

A major line of thought about the conditions of freedom descends from "classical republicanism" (Pocock 1975). It is found in its clearest form in Machiavelli and Harrington, elements of it are retained by Montesquieu and Rousseau, and echoes of it are heard in some of the American Founders. Nineteenth- and twentieth-century theorists of democracy may in fact be influenced by it, but few among them tout this item from their intellectual pedigree. The view in question is especially pertinent to political theory because the conditions it claims are necessary to freedom are of a kind which, on any plausible construal of the protean term "political," are emphatically political in character.[2]

A forceful version of such a theory is available to us in Machiavelli's thought as interpreted by Quentin Skinner and other scholars.[3] Machiavelli's concept of freedom was freedom of action (albeit it sometimes shades toward what I have here called autonomy) and he shared the view that freedom is an instrumental good, one that is valuable because it contributes vitally to achieving the ends and purposes that human beings adopt and pursue. As he sees it, most people have quite modest objectives, wanting to live quiet lives in a degree of comfort and dignity. A smaller number are far more ambitious. They seek wealth, not merely comfort, glory, not merely dignity; and power over others, not merely security against others. Accordingly, the particular freedoms these two (somewhat loosely identified and differentiated) classes of people value, the actions they respectively want to be free to take, differ in various ways.

Despite these differences, or rather along with and in part because of them, in Machiavelli's view there are freedoms that are "basic" in a sense very close to the one we encountered in Rawls, namely, essential to the well-being of everyone. Most important here, there is also a certain set of political conditions that must be maintained if the essential freedoms are to be secure.

The essential freedoms are those of republican citizenship; the freedoms to participate in the institutions, practices, and political affairs of the society of which one is a member. The set of conditions jointly necessary to these freedoms are a politically organized society that is (1) independent of all others and strong enough to assure its continued independence; (2) organized to allow the full political participation of its citizens; and in which (3) the citizenry in fact engages in political participation with a view to the common good of the society.

The critical edge of Machiavelli's argument is in the claim (the one claim on this list that Rawls rejects) that every citizen's well-being requires the active participation of all citizens in public life. Human beings, Machiavelli contends, tend to be self-serving. Among the ambitious few, this tendency expresses itself in persistent attempts to dominate and exploit others. They seek to conquer and to keep control of societies other than their own, and they tyrannize over their fellow citizens when they can. These *attempts* are not harmful in themselves. Machiavelli is far from an ascetical or anti-interest writer. Without ambition and the striving for greatness that goes with it, a political society amounts to little in its own right and is easy prey to societies that do pursue greatness.

The real problem, the reason the ambitious few often destroy the liberty of others and finally of themselves, is that the more modest and retiring many tend to be shortsighted and otherwise imprudent in their pursuit of their interests and objectives. For example, while few among them welcome domination by foreign powers, they fail to realize that this fate can be held off only if the entire citizenry takes an active part in public life. In Machiavelli's view, political involvement generates and directs the energies and resolve necessary to keep foreign powers at bay and to constrain those nationals who hope to advantage themselves by intriguing with foreigners. The many, however, are attracted by the idea of leaving public affairs to those who have a taste for them. They tend to see political activity as time-consuming and otherwise disagreeable. A "division of labor" that accords with differences of inclination, preference, and talent recommends itself to even the more thoughtful among them, while others simply succumb to the temptations of (what is now called) free riding.[4]

These tendencies, this imprudence, are destructive of the essential liberties and hence of the possibility of achieving the ends and purposes that the many pursue. Either the political society will be conquered by a foreign power or the ambitious among its own members will take control of its affairs and rule it in their own interests. In the first case the entire population will be reduced to a slavish dependence on the whims of the conquerors; in the second, the bulk of the population will be subjected to the despotism of the ambitious few. These dismal outcomes take a sometimes longer, sometimes shorter time to assert themselves, but in Machiavelli's view they do so implacably and inevitably.

Machiavelli drew quite definite practical conclusions from this analysis. Because a generous array of freedoms of action is essential to human well-being, those freedoms must be protected. The immediate threats to those freedoms, that is, the ambitions of the few, are necessary to greatness, to independence, and hence to freedom itself. To stifle those ambitions would be disastrous. Rather, the unambitious many must be made to act prudently and effectively in their own interests, to act to protect their own freedoms from the ambitious. They can do this only through the same institutions and arrangements that will otherwise be used to oppress them, the institutions of political rule. They must participate actively in the ruling of their society. If education, persuasion, encouragement, and like devices do not convince them of this, they must be required by law to do so. They cannot be forced to be free in the Rousseauean sense, but they can and should be required to conduct themselves in the ways in fact necessary to the preservation of their freedom. Those who understand these truths but draw back from the necessary measures do not show regard for freedom, they demonstrate their indifference to it. They also put their own freedom at risk.

It is important to underline two features of Machiavelli's argument as, following Skinner, I have construed it. First, freedom is not *defined as* participation in a certain kind of political order; rather, participation in a certain kind of political order is a necessary causal condition of maintaining freedom defined as freedom of action. Second, freedom is an instrumental, not an intrinsic, good. A free people is not morally or otherwise better than an unfree one. A people can remain free only if they maintain the much-discussed *virtú* (which for present purposes can be rendered as the qualities of acting effectively to achieve and maintain essential freedoms), and doing so requires virtues such as courage, prudence, and a commitment to the common good. But these qualities are valuable because they are instrumental to the desires and interests, ends and purposes that people as we find them in fact have.[5]

Machiavelli was more than familiar with free peoples who go on acting in ways atrocious by moral standards. But he did not give way to the temptation to make "freedom" into an omnibus term for the good, the true, and the beautiful.

III

Given that Machiavelli resisted the temptation to make a vigorous republican politics a criterion of freedom (as all but hopeless romantics resist making love a criterion of marriage), should theorists of freedom as freedom of action incorporate his (or some analogous) claims into their theory? Are the claims distinctive of his argument properly a part of a general theory of freedom? There are three kinds of reasons for answering this question in the negative. The first concerns the empirical character of the generalizations on which the claims depend, the second (which we have already considered in other settings) the difficulties of identifying the essential freedoms that a republican politics is to secure, and the third the details of Machiavelli's argument that a vigorous republican politics is necessary to securing the essential freedoms.

Depending as it does on empirical generalizations, Machiavelli's argument is subject to qualification and disconfirmation by the continuing flow of the kinds of experience and hence of evidence on which such generalizations rest. Even if he were warranted in his claim that his generalizations held for all of human experience to the date of his writing, human beings might since have changed or might yet change. His theory must be subjected to the usual tests of theory formulation and confirmation. Are the categories clearly enough defined and consistently enough deployed so that the theory is in fact testable? Were the plausible rival hypotheses considered and have they been disconfirmed? In short, in this regard does Machiavelli deserve the reputation he has in some quarters as a scientific political scientist who put his conclusions on firm empirical foundations?

It is hard to avoid the suspicion that the theory would stand up poorly to the kind of testing that its claims invite. Perhaps it is a brilliant systematization of the evidence provided by Livy and the other Roman sources on whom Machiavelli relied. Maybe it fares well in the rough-and-tumble world of the Italian city-states of Machiavelli's time. We may be able to extend it to other times and places featuring arrays of states relatively small in size, roughly equal in resources, and characterized by domestic politics without rigid hierarchies legitimated by status- or ascriptive-oriented traditions.[6] Does it explain the emergence of an unprecedented religious liberty in Northern Europe and North America in the seventeenth and eighteenth centuries? Were the entrepreneurial freedoms of eighteenth- and nineteenth-century capitalists established by republican politics of a Machiavellian cast? Did France, England, Germany, the United States, and the Soviet Union successively achieve "greatness" and such independence of action as that greatness has from time to time afforded them because of Machiavellian politics? To what extent does the Machiavellian analysis explain the unfreedom of freedom-seeking citizens of present-day China or Iran, Finland or Poland, South Africa or Chile? Most generally, is it plausible to think that one analysis and one set of prescriptions hold and will continue to hold concerning the essential freedoms of all of the diverse populations of the human experience?

With the exception of the last, these questions require detailed studies in comparative social and political history. Machiavelli and theorists influenced by him such as Harrington and Montesquieu, Rousseau, Madison, and Vico, were modern pioneers in studies of this kind; their imaginative classifications, bold generalizations, and confident prescriptions deserve the close attention of their successors in history and the social sciences. The skepticism I am expressing about the strongest of Machiavelli's claims (or the strongest of the claims attributed to Machiavelli) does not extend to the enterprise of generalizing concerning the conditions contributive to freedom. My own qualified endorsement in Chapter 9 of a version of the Rawlsian system of liberty (which as we have seen is in the Machiavellian tradition in the sense that it attempts to identify essential liberties and the conditions—that is, the normative commitments and the basic institutional arrangements and practices—necessary to assuring them) is itself in recognition of the need for generalizations about the conditions of liberty. But generalizations are one thing, necessary or even universal truths quite another.

In shifting to the second kind of difficulty, we return to issues discussed in the previous chapter. Let us assume that Machiavelli's psychological and political generalizations hold for the circumstances that are our practical concern. Even so, there remains the question of which freedoms are essential to the well-being that he and—I will assume—we aim to promote and protect.

There is no such thing as freedom as such, freedom *sans phrase*. There are a host of actions that can be done in freedom or prevented so as to make the agents who attempt them unfree in that respect. We generalize over these instances of freedom and unfreedom when we speak of types of freedoms such as of expression and association, persons who are free and unfree, free societies, the free world, and the like. A person who is free in these generalized senses is someone who regularly, reliably, and in respect to the actions that matter most to her is not prevented from acting as she attempts to do. A free society is (roughly) one in which this is true of the preponderance of persons who are freedom-evaluable. (Or it is one which, as a collective agent— an agent that acts through some established procedure or authorized representative—regularly, reliably, and in respect to the actions that matter most to those who make up or act for the collectivity, is not prevented by other societies from acting as it attempts to do.)

Some of these freedoms are compatible with one another in the practical sense that Able's exercise of freedom X does not prevent or limit her exercise of freedom Y and does not prevent or limit Baker's exercise of freedoms X or Y. For example, within broad limits Able can practice the religion of her choice without interfering with Baker's freedom to do the same. In respect to such compatible (compossible) freedoms it is possible that we could identify a set of conditions invariably necessary to their reliable availability. Modern theories of religious liberty can be viewed as offering identifications of these conditions and modern practices of religious liberty are attempts to institutionalize and hence to assure the satisfaction of those conditions.

Even in this comparatively well-settled area, however, there is controversy about and substantial variation in the arrangements deemed necessary to freedom of religion. Many would say that it is a condition of religious freedom that the public law itself not restrict confessional choice and practice and that public authority protect both from private interference. But this formula, while by no means empty or insignificant, leaves open vital questions about just what will be protected and how those protections will be afforded. Should property owned by religious organizations be exempt from taxation? Should churches be permitted to offer accredited education in nonreligious subjects? Many view the resolution of such issues about church-state relations as determinative of the very possibility of religious freedom. They argue that it is a condition of religious freedom worthy of the name that there be parochial schools, that time be set aside for prayer and other religious observances in public schools, legislatures, and the like, that religious organizations be accorded special immunities, and so forth. Without such accommodations, freedom of religion is a mere formalism. Others insist that these very arrangements directly violate the most important religious freedoms and endanger religion itself by making it dependent upon the actions of secular authorities. Partly because of such controversy, societies that share a commitment to freedom of religion feature quite different arrangements and practices in these regards. Every society that is committed to freedom of religion must resolve these questions, but the general commitment does not itself imply a particular resolution of them. Those who insist that there is a single set of arrangements that is a necessary condition of religious freedom in all societies are dogmatic about the freedoms that matter as well as headstrong in their instrumental judgments. (Two recent headlines: "Prayer In [U.S.] Public Schools Condemned As Threat To Freedom Of Religion"; "Poles Demand Crucifixes In Schools: Prohibitions Called Hostile To Religious Freedom.")

These observations hold concerning other classes of freedoms about which there is broad consensus at a general level. Freedom of expression and freedom of association are fundamental features of virtually all modern Western democracies, but the laws and conventions that delineate their scope and regulate their exercise have changed substantially through the recent histories of these societies and vary significantly among them. Similarly, those freedoms commonly called rights of the accused and of the suspected—habeas corpus, trial by jury, immunity from double jeopardy and compulsory self-incrimination, though found throughout democratic modernity, differ importantly from one legal system to the next. And if we turn to the questions Machiavelli addressed most directly, questions about republican-cum-democratic politics and their relation to freedom, we find a startling variety of electoral and party systems, of legislative, executive, and judicial structures, of centralization and decentralization of government authority, and of encouragements to and dissuasions from citizen participation. General claims such as Machiavelli's, while important in some contexts or perspectives (for example, those involving comparisons between the "free world" and those "worlds" with which it is commonly contrasted), leave unanswered vital questions about the particular freedoms that matter and hence about the conditions necessary or even contributive to them. The fact that large numbers of political societies have arrived at more or less definite and workable answers to these questions is reason enough to deny that the questions are unanswerable. The fact that societies which share a commitment to freedom live comfortably with notably different answers is good reason to doubt that there is a single overriding or even a single best answer to them. It is a good reason to rein in the ambitions of that immodest figure, the theorist (or theoretician as Michael

Oakeshott would call her) who essays a general theory of the *essential* freedoms and their *necessary* conditions.

Strongly cautionary notes are also in order in respect to Machiavelli's argument for vigorous citizen involvement in politics. The argument that such involvement is *supportive* of freedom might win wide assent among those likely to read these pages. But agreement on this very general claim (a claim that was sharply controversial in the societies Machiavelli himself addressed most directly) is at some distance from contemporary controversies.

Machiavelli presumes not only the reality but the desirability of ambitious and self-serving conduct and of the competition and conflict that they engender. He favored a vigorous republican politics not as a means of transforming the *esprits forts* of a society into altruistic, self-sacrificing, or otherwise conventionally virtuous types, but to channel their energies and activities so as to bring about strength and greatness at the same time that they contribute to their own distinctive and conflicting interests and objectives. This strongly mechanistic view has not disappeared, and Machiavelli's version has the signal advantage of recognizing that it requires not merely mechanisms but commitment and sacrifice and hence agency and action rather than behaviors produced by psychological or neurophysiological stimuli. But (leaving aside the contentious issue of the proper criteria of citizenship) many heirs of this tradition would deny Machiavelli's claim that active involvement of all citizens is *necessary* to a free society and hence would reject his justification for compulsory participation. Perhaps in some sufficiently long run these rejoinders always prove wrong in the sense that acting on them proves to be destructive of freedom. Without rehearsing objections to this believer's (and Whig?) view about history and what is now called social science, such a demonstration would be dispositive for agents who are "interested" in a recognizably Machiavellian sense only if they also accepted further and sharply controverted views that Skinner's Machiavelli seems to take for granted (for example, views about later versus present selves, the claims of later versus those of present generations, and generally the significance of time and its passage for prudential, moral, and political reasoning).

Again, one could endorse the idea that conflicts among actively expressed interests are freedom-preserving and otherwise fruitful and nevertheless think it essential that (or better if) the full diversity of citizen interests undergo some degree of distillation, consolidation, or a least aggregation before engaging one another at the level of institutions and decision procedures of the politically organized society. Machiavelli gives us reasons additional to those discussed in Chapter 8 for encouraging the expression of desires and the assertion of interests in political life. Welcoming such expressions is recommended by understandings of how a diverse array of self-interested individuals can maintain the freedoms essential to satisfying their various interests. Nor was Machiavelli a stranger to the dangers of fragmenting factionalism and destructive conflict. He is eloquent in his appeals for concern for the public good and insistent on the need for leadership devoted to that good. Yet theorists of representative as distinct from direct democracy (however circumscribed in terms of criteria of citizenship), including some who have accepted those of Machiavelli's views I am discussing, have insisted that the more mechanical (even if dramatic to the point of being politically explosive) procedures of balancing and accommodation must be proceeded and accompanied by processes that refine or at least reduce the array of contending interests. It is not only the Burkeans and the Madisonians who have favored a variety of representative institutions.

There is a yet deeper conflict between Machiavelli's views and those of numerous later proponents of vigorously participatory politics. From Rousseau forward, many advocates of such a politics have despised the selfish, contentious scuffling that Machiavelli thought a necessary condition of a free society. They have promoted participatory democracy as a means, perhaps the only effective means in a society that had already legitimated desire and interest, to commonality of beliefs and values and subordination of personal and class interests to shared goals such as social justice. From this point of view (and even without redefining freedom to *mean* commonality, or communal solidarity, or virtue) Machiavellian politics, so far from being necessary to a free society, are destructive of it.

In the perspective of these controversies, Machiavelli's claims to have identified conditions necessary to a free society present themselves not so much as false as minimally helpful by the criteria he himself aims to satisfy. If we agreed with the propositions he advances in these regards we would still face the major issues that divide us concerning how to establish and maintain a free society. My argument is of course that the same would be true of any attempt to identify the necessary conditions of freedom. As with the analysis of the "structural" and "determining" features of a society, as with the analysis of coercion, and as with the identification, interpretation, and implementation of preferred freedoms, determining the conditions of freedom requires reasoning informed about and responsive to circumstantial considerations that could be encompassed within a general theory only by quite extraordinary coincidence.

IV

My conclusions about the conditions necessary to freedom, and the continuities between those conclusions and the conclusions I have reached concerning other sweeping claims advanced by theorists of freedom, are in part a product of the assumptions about inquiry stated at the outset. Along with these and other moderately skeptical positions I have taken, however, I have myself advanced a number of quite general, much less qualified claims about freedom. Along with objecting to the craving for generality of other theorists, I have myself succumbed to such a craving in a number of respects. I end by attempting to explain and justify this apparently ill-assorted combination of positions. I do so not in metatheoretical terms but by reference to freedom itelf.

Freedom is an *elemental* feature of our morals and our politics. This is the case, first, in that the conceptual conditions of freedom-evaluability are the capacities for agency and the exercise of those capacities in action (including attempted but prevented action). These are elements of all conduct and hence of all conduct that has a moral or political character. Whereas more differentiated or particularized categories or classes of action require further, more specific characteristics or qualities (such as particular desires, intentions, or dispositions), freedom-evaluability obtains in respect to agency and action as such. (Thus a large part of my argumentation has been against attempts to make further, more particular qualities or characteristics of agents and actions, such as strong forms of rationality, various virtues, particularly esteemed patterns of personal identity, and the like, necessary to freedom.)

The claim that moral and political freedom is elemental in this way is akin to but distinguishable from claims about metaphysical freedom or freedom of the will as opposed to determinism. If the latter claims are argued in fully metaphysical and hence culture-invariant form, a difference between the two notions is that freedom-evaluability as I am using it is a situated concept; it recognizes that the scope actually assigned to agency and action is influenced by beliefs held in cultures and societies. Cultures that accept and employ notions of agency (some do not do so) may also hold beliefs about divinities and their interventions in human affairs, about fate and fortune, about incapacitating mental illnesses without a known neurophysiological or biological basis, and so on. These beliefs confine, conceptually, the possibilities allowed to agency and action and hence of freedom-evaluability in the cultures in which they are held. Of course such beliefs might be false, whether by culturally accepted but misapplied criteria or by some others. Proponents of the metaphysical theory of freedom of the will assess such beliefs and assert the possibility of agency and action against them if they find the beliefs wanting. They accept that people who hold such beliefs might thereby be prevented from acting in certain ways, but they hold that this fact about them is contingent on their beliefs and can in principle be remedied by convincing them that their beliefs are mistaken. If the beliefs do change, the scope of freedom-evaluability, as it is understood in the society, will change as well, and theorists of freedom-evaluability, whose concern is with that scope as it is understood in the cultures they address, will take note of the fact.

A second difference of focus and emphasis concerns the point that freedom-evaluability specifically encompasses unfreedom in the moral and political sense. Agents capable of agency and action and in fact attempting to act may be prevented from acting by other agents or agencies. Unfreedom in this sense is compatible with freedom of will or metaphysical freedom, but theories of the latter are not concerned with it. Freedom-evaluability is a concept in moral and political philosophy, one that partly overlaps with a concept in metaphysical philosophy.

Freedom (as opposed to unfreedom) of action is elemental in the further sense that it is an element in a very wide range of actions that are also and more typically described in other, more differentiating ways. Freedom of action is not necessary to the formation of desires and interests, ends and purposes (albeit pervasive, persistent unfreedom may in fact stifle their formation), but it is necessary to the pursuit of most of those that are formed in our culture. It is therefore necessary or strongly contributive to the satisfaction or achievement of most desires and objectives. For these reasons, it is also normatively elemental in that everyone who understands and endorses these facts about themselves and their circumstances will value it highly. Thus freedom as opposed to unfreedom of action is an element in virtually all of the conceptions of human well-being that are seriously entertained in our culture.

By elemental, then, I mean two things. First, freedom-evaluability and freedom of action are in fact elements in a very great many of the activities that take place in modern Western societies. Second, in much thought and action in those societies freedom is elemental in that it is elementary—assumed, not explicitly attended to or controverted, below the surface of self-conscious acting and interacting. Attention focuses on other, more particular, features of the actions and interactions. Agency and action, and hence freedom-evaluability, are presumed or assumed, and GPF operates to forestall criticism and interferences with the acting as such; judgment and evaluation are directed to the more differentiating characteristics of this, that, and the next action. One attends to the prudence, the elegance or awkwardness, the sensitivity or callousness, of agents and their actions without opening the question whether the actions were freely taken or whether the agents should be free to take them. Indeed, as J. L. Austin reminded us, there are numerous occasions on which questions about freedom are simply out of place (Austin 1979, 180–82). This is of course not to deny that there are numerous, vigorous, and dramatic disputes in which freedom is explicitly and centrally at issue. But such disputes make up a small fraction of the exchanges and interactions that actually occur.

Of course these interactions and exchanges take place within the confines of social convention, morality, law, and other sources of prohibitions and requirements. If one thought in terms of Elster's notional "maximum feasible set of action possibilities," or Berlin's "open options" view of freedom, or Goffman's hyper-romantic notion of a self that could and should be sui generis and self-subsistent, freedom would almost certainly be continuously at issue in such settings and the issue would persistently if not invariably be settled against freedom. Much more plausibly, for those who are more or less thoroughly disaffected from these societies, for those who reject many of the beliefs and values, institutions and arrangements that set the confines of action, the claim that freedom is often, indeed most often, not at issue will be mistaken and indeed offensive.

We have seen the difficulties with the notions of Elster, Berlin, and Goffman, but the incidence of dissatisfaction, disaffection, and a consequent sense of more or less pervasive unfreedom are undeniable. It is not implausible to think that such attitudes are more widespread in contemporary Western societies than in any other human societies known to us. If it is true that these societies have at least tacitly adopted principles and presumptions such as LP, PNI, and GPF, if these or analogous principles are elemental in the ways I am suggesting, then pervasive disaffection is, distinctively, a possibility in them. Brought up to conceive of themselves and of their interactions with others in the manner that these principles endorse, each person has as it were a standing invitation to assess the justifiability of rules and laws, conventions and norms. It was Goffman's mistake to think that this could be done wholesale, that the entire ensemble of rules, conventions, and so forth could (and should) be judged to contravene individuality and freedom. But the absurdity of this view (why shouldn't the disaffection extend—as it does for communitarian critics of these societies—to LP and GPF themselves) in no way disqualifies the possibility that a large number of norms may be found objectionable and that this assessment may be generalized to form a strongly negative assessment of the society. By at least tacitly encouraging a generalized expectation of freedom, modern Western societies give potency to judgments that this expectation is generally and wrongly disappointed.

My claim, then, that freedom is elemental in modern Western societies is empirical in two intimately connected senses: first, it is a claim about the beliefs and values, norms and principles, that are widely if often tacitly endorsed in these societies; second, it is a claim, virtually pleonastic to the first on the Wittgensteinian view about rule and exception,[7] that in fact questions about freedom are well into the background of much thought and action in these societies. The incidence of certain modes of disaffection may actually support the first claim; freedom is expected, the reality of unfreedom resented, by the norms and principles endorsed by the society. Equally, a certain incidence of such disaffection does not contradict the second claim. The second claim would be contradicted, and the truth of the first claim progressively undermined, if it came to be generally believed that questions about freedom are usually in the foreground and usually settled against freedom, if it came to be the exception that such questions are below the surface and "settled" in favor of freedom. Put another way, writers such as Herbert Marcuse, various neo-Marxists, and Michel Foucault could be correct that (a) the conventions and rules of the societies they discuss are, objectively, unjustifiable because contrary to freedom and it could nevertheless be true that (b) freedom is "elemental" in those societies. Arguably, the practical political dilemma of radical writers such as Marcuse and Foucault consists in the fact that they believe that proposition (a) in the previous sentence is true but are obliged to recognize that (b) is also true.

It is because freedom is elemental in these ways that it has been possible for me to advance a number of largely unqualified generalizations about it. I have been able to generalize about freedom in respect to modern Western societies because these societies have adopted conceptions of agency and of interactions among agents in which freedom is elemental in these ways. It is tempting to generalize further and say that freedom is elemental in the same ways in all human societies. But the beliefs and values, norms and principles that give freedom of action (as opposed to metaphysical freedom) its elemental standing in modern Western societies seem to have been, and to be, little accepted or even little considered in many human societies. Of course one might argue that freedom of action *ought* everywhere to have the standing I claim it has in modern Western societies. For example, one might argue that it ought to have such standing everywhere because all human beings have those characteristics and are found in those circumstances that are central to the reasoning for LP and GPF. But to make such an argument one would have to give reasons for changing the beliefs and values that go with and support the various alternative understandings and arrangements that give freedom of action very different standing or none. A conception of freedom and its value is part of a larger system of beliefs and values; changes in conceptions of freedom both require and help to effect changes in that larger system. Thus the generalizations I have ventured are culture-specific, not universal. And because the culture over which those generalizations range is itself internally diverse (no doubt more diverse than I have allowed in succumbing to the theorist's craving for generality), they are no more than generalizations. Freedom of action is elemental in and to modern Western societies, but thought and action concerning it is not "of a piece" in those societies.

My remarks thus far are, as it were, on the one hand. One the other, the elemental quality of freedom of action explains and goes far to justify the skepticism I have expressed concerning various more ambitious tendencies prominent in the literature about freedom.

The clearest case in this regard is the tendency of theorists of positive freedom to conflate the concept of freedom with beliefs, values, and principles that are sharply controverted in the societies they address. The value of freedom of action can be widely accepted and yet be in the background in part because accepting and respecting it leaves room for disagreement over the value of this, that, or the next desire or interest, end or purpose, of actions to satisfy desires, and of the characteristics and dispositions that give impetus and content to such actions. But when freedom is conceptually attached to particular purposes or characteristics, it itself is thereafter directly at issue in all of the interactions involving and affecting the purposes and characteristics to which it has been attached. Apart from their normatively objectionable implications, such moves yield false generalizations about freedom and unfreedom.

The much greater plausibility of the views of Rawls, Fishkin, and

Machiavelli is due to the substantial consonance between them and the elemental character of freedom. These theorists accept that a wide diversity of desires and interests, patterns of character and action, are regarded, at the least, as legitimate in the societies they are addressing, and they recognize that freedom of action is an element in most or all of these. Moreover, the understandings and arrangements that they single out as normatively and/or empirically necessary are broadly conceived in their own right and chosen largely because they are instrumental to the pursuit and satisfaction of a generous array of desires and interests by persons with a wide diversity of characteristics and dispositions.

We might say, in addition, that both Rawls and Fishkin want to keep freedom in the "background" of moral and political life in an even stronger sense than that in which I am using that notion. Certain fundmental freedoms are to be so deeply established that their exercise can no longer be properly controverted. Because the freedoms that they want to promote to this standing are in fact widely and highly valued in modern Western societies, implementing their prescriptions would effect adjustments or modifications in established practices, not radical and deeply controverted departures from them. (It would be misleading to include Machiavelli in these last remarks because, on Skinner's interpretation of him, he was arguing *for* understandings and arrangements that Rawls and Fishkin argue *from*.)

There is a difference, however, between elemental as I am using that notion and fundamental in the sense of normatively or empirically necessary and hence incontrovertible. If Rawls et al. were successful in promoting certain freedoms of action to the yet stronger standing they propose, then those freedoms would be both elemental and fundamental. As matters stand, however (that the freedoms are now no more than elemental is perhaps sufficiently evidenced by the fact that the theorists in question recognize the need to present elaborate arguments for making them fundamental), arguments for the further privileging of certain freedoms are at odds with the very understandings and beliefs that account for the elemental character of freedom. It is not that there are no rankings, no more or less settled convictions, preferences, and the like. Rather, it is that there is a settled conviction that convictions and preferences can and do change and that we ought to be open and alert to the possibility that we should change them. And there is the further conviction that freedom of action is and will remain instrumentally important regardless of the content of other convictions, of dispositions, of purposes, and so on. These convictions are of course compatible with a variety of shared, settled, even unquestioned conventions and norms. Or rather, they presuppose the diverse array of settled conventions and norms without which consciously held convictions and preferences could not be formed or changed. They are also compatible (perhaps uneasily so, at least from the theorist's perspective) with deliberately adopted and enforced constitutional principles, legislative and other rules, and the like. But arrangements, principles, and rules fundamental in the superstrong sense promoted by the theorists in question are incompatible with understandings that are integral to the standing of freedom as elemental. Those understandings insistently hold open possibilities that would be foreclosed by "fundamental" principles and rules. Whether out of skepticism about the very idea of judgments that are as firmly (and permanently) grounded as such principles and rules suppose, out of doubt about the possibility of achieving and maintaining uncoerced agreement concerning such judgments, out of conviction that such judgments or agreement to them, even if correct, would be somehow diminishing, or (perhaps most usually) out of some less than articulate and possibly less than fully coherent amalgam of such views, a society that regards freedom as elemental has no "fundamental" arrangements, principles, or rules.[8] I claim that modern Western societies regard freedom in this way. If they don't, they should.

Appendix

Kinds of Freedom Distinguishable in the Philosophical Literature

Freedom$_1$ and Unfreedom$_1$ or Freedom and Unfreedom of Movement
   Self-activated movement plus the possibility of impediments to the movement in question.

Freedom$_2$ and Unfreedom$_2$ or Freedom and Unfreedom of Action
   Action attempted by an agent plus the possibility of impediments to that action placed or left by another agent or other agents acting with the intention of placing or leaving those impediments.

Freedom$_3$ and Unfreedom$_3$ or Autonomy and Heteronomy
   Action attempted by an agent in the pursuit of a self-critically chosen plan or project that the agent has reason to believe is consonant with defensible norms or principles, plus the possibility of impediments to that action placed or left by another agent or other agents acting with the intention of placing or leaving those impediments.

Freedom$_4$ and Unfreedom$_4$ or Communal Freedom and Unfreedom
   Action attempted by an agent in pursuit of a plan or project chosen to satisfy, and in fact satisfying, norms or principles that are authoritative in the agent's community, plus the possibility of impediments to that action placed or left by another agent or other agents acting with the intention of placing or leaving those impediments.

Freedom$_5$ and Unfreedom$_5$ or Fully Virtuous Freedom and Unfreedom
   Action attempted by an agent in the pursuit of a plan or project self-critically chosen to satisfy, and in fact satisfying, certifiably worthy norms or principles, plus the possibility of impediments to that action placed or left by another agent or other agents acting with the intention of placing or leaving those impediments.

Notes

Introduction

1. Attempts to formulate thesis (b) typically employ at least an implicit comparison between modernity and actual, pre-, or possible postmodernist societies that were, are, or would be superior to the former, but because these comparisons are rarely worked out in detail the formulations tend toward attempts to articulate the yet more sweeping thesis (a). Radical forms of deconstructionism and of Critical Theory—sometimes combined in so-called Critical Legal Studies—seem to me to exemplify this tendency, as does the work of Erving Goffman that I examine in detail in Chapter 6.

2. In previous studies of authority, rights, and obligation, I have used the notion of a practice as an organizing concept. I have written of the practice of authority, the practice of rights, and so on. (See Flathman 1980, 1976, 1972.) My claim that freedom is elemental in modern Western societies abbreviates my reasons for not using that concept in the same way in this study. Freedom is an element in practices; there is no practice of freedom.

Chapter One

1. It may prove necessary to recognize a variant of freedom$_2$ (and the other freedoms and unfreedoms to follow) in which the obstacles are not deliberately placed or left. According to most versions of Marxism, for example, the most important obstacles to freedom are not intentionally placed or left, if we take those expressions to mean placed or left by individuals or groups of individuals acting with the conscious intention of creating or maintaining the obstacles. On this and numerous related theories we can describe the most important obstacles as intentionally created only if we are prepared to talk about unconscious intentions or to attribute intentionality to impersonal agencies such as history, classes and class structures, forces and relations of production, and the like.

As John Gray has pointed out to me (personal communication), we might view social arrangements as impediments to liberty if they are alterable or remediable by human agency. If A is prevented from doing X by the class structure of A's society, and if that structure could in principle be altered by human decision and action, we can say that A is made unfree to X without imputing intentional or purposive interference to any assignable agent or agencies and without attributing unconscious intentions to a social class. By contrast, if A were prevented from doing X by an unalterable natural condition or circumstance, we would say that A was unable to X not that A was unfree to X.

The value of this suggestion can be seen by noting that conceptions of what is alterable and what is given and must be accepted themselves undergo change and that such changes are reflected in talk about freedom. When it came to be thought that full employment was an achieveable social goal, the unemployed could cogently complain of their unfreedom without identifying the particular culprits who were keeping them out of work. As the possibility of full employment has again been called into question, we see renewed need to single out responsible parties.

It remains the case, however, that claims of unfreedom are typically accusatory; they charge some party or parties with responsibility for deliberate interference, not merely with causal influence. In part for this reason, we should endorse David Miller's further suggestion that claims and attributions of unfreedom require that some agent or agency is morally (as opposed to merely causally) responsible for the obstacle or impediment to A's action. I disagree, however, with Miller's argument that for this purpose "morally responsible" should be limited to cases in which B has a moral *obligation* not to place or leave the obstacle or impediment that prevents or restricts A's action. Unless we inflate "obligation" unduly, this restriction excludes cases in which A and others will properly say that B (perhaps along with others) is morally responsible for A's unfreedom (see Miller 1983). I am indebted to conversations with Miller on this and related questions.

2. My scare-quotes around "enslaved" are in effect my first comment on this controversy. Talk of being enslaved is question-begging because to say that someone is enslaved has come to be equivalent to saying that she is unfree. Thus to say that passions and desires render a person unfree by enslaving her is to put the *explanandum* into the *explanans*.

I should add a further comment concerning the above remarks. The distinction I have thus far drawn between negative and positive theories is nonstandard. The more usual distinction, familiar from the exchanges between Isaiah Berlin and Gerald MacCallum, turns on whether the agent must be free *to* achieve some objective or purpose, *to* serve some interest or satisfy some desire, as opposed to merely free *from* restraints and limitations. My larger purpose in drawing the distinction as I have done is to make conceptual connections between human freedom and human action and human unfreedom and attempted but prevented human action. Because all human action is intentional and purposive, human freedom must be freedom *to* as well as freedom *from*. In this respect I agree with MacCallum (1967). But this move does not itself establish the superiority of theories of positive freedom. The more controversial thesis of such theories is that the agent's purpose must be chosen to satisfy and must in fact satisfy some normative criterion, and, in some versions of the theory, that the criterion itself must be worthy. The mere fact that an agent has adopted and is engaged in the unhindered pursuit of an objective or purpose is not sufficient to warrant saying that she is free. It is this, or these, further requirement(s) and the attendant notion of a higher or better self that chooses worthy actions, it seems to me, that has aroused the concern of theorists of negative freedom such as Isaiah Berlin (1969).

3. Of course it doesn't *follow* that the features that are settled in our uses of the concept of freedom in contemporary English will also be found in the parallel or analogous concepts established in other times and places. It is not impossible that other societies and other cultures have or have had concepts of freedom that are radically different than ours. Determining the similarities and differences among historical instances of this (or any other) concept requires empirical study. But we know enough about the history of the concept of freedom to say that there has been and is a good deal of continuity or positive comparability among its uses. Our confidence in this knowledge is expressed in our ready willingness to say that other societies and cultures do or do not, did or did not, have the concept of freedom. On these and numerous other points I am indebted to conversations with Quentin Skinner.

4. The above remarks rely on Wittgenstein as he has been interpreted by David Sachs (1976).

Chapter Two

1. For a sophisticated argument that all action is brought about by desire, see Brian O'Shaughnessy 1980, esp. 1: lii.

2. For helpful comments on Berlin's discussion, see John Gray 1980a,b.

3. I take this terminology from Michael Taylor 1982, 142.

4. There is of course a wider use of the term "action" according to which such bodily movements are so labeled. Here and throughout I will be reserving the term for what George M. Wilson has called stronger, richer, more full-blooded acts that "import an implication of purposiveness or even intentionality" (see Wilson 1980, 46, and passim).

5. The theory is not always behaviorist concerning obstacles. In some versions, special conceptual and theoretical significance is assigned to obstacles that are placed or left by agents identified as intentional and characterized as acting out of specific intentions.

Here we again encounter questions about deliberate, intentional, knowing deprivations of freedom. Does B make A unfree if B locks A out of A's house by closing a door which, unbeknownst to B, locks automatically on closing; if she does so negligently, for example, by not going to the trouble to find out whether A took a key on leaving? Owing to the fact that B closed the door, A is deprived of a necessary physical component of an action, entering the house through the door, that A would otherwise have been capable of performing. Thus on the strict behaviorist formulation of the Pure Negative Freedom conception, B makes A unfree in all of these cases. This is clearly unacceptable if it is taken to mean, say, that B makes A unfree if the door is blown shut by the wind or if B trips on the doormat and knocks it shut. In these cases A is prevented from entering the house but is not made unfree to do so by B. As we move toward clear cases of knowing, intentional, and deliberate action by B to prevent A from doing X, the case for saying A is made unfree by B gets progressively stronger. It does so because to say this sort of thing is ordinarily to rebuke B. (I am indebted to Paul Brest and David Miller for discussion of these points. Once again, see David Miller [1983], who uses a similar example.)

6. I return to Taylor because the view just sketched will require attention to the, in some respects, more subtle view sometimes called causalism; that is, the view that desires, reasons, intentions, etc. *are* causes and hence that the distinction between movements and actions, if it can be sustained at all, cannot be drawn in the manner I have suggested.

7. In respect to Hobbes there is a further point that accords better with Charles Taylor's views. For a segment of humankind, the *savor* of life comes primarily if not exclusively from overcoming obstacles placed by other human beings and winning out in competitions with other human beings. If, miraculously, we attained to a freedom that was situationless, it would not be "empty" for these prideful ones. It is true, however, that they would find it rather insipid. It is in part for this reason that Hobbes regards such persons as politically dangerous. He harbors an admiration for them, but he is unwilling to depend on them for anything of political importance.

8. As we see below, this is not true of F. H. Bradley's theory.

9. This passage might suggest that the phenomenon which disables the negative theory of freedom is not very widespread or prominent and that the issue between negative and positive theorists is of little practical significance. If most of our desires are import-attributing and second-order, and if it is the occurrence of brute, first-order desires that invalidates the equation of freedom with unchecked desire, then negative and positive theorists will generally agree in their predications of freedom. This inference might also be drawn from another of Taylor's essays in which he distinguishes between "basic," "normal," "paradigmatic," or "happy" actions and what he calls "deviant causal chains." In the former, desires and actions are conceptually and very often empirically inseparable. The desire is "expressed" in (and perhaps only in) the action that it "causes." In "normal" action, "Desire is an intentional state. It is essentially bound up with a certain awareness of what is desired, of its object" (Taylor 1979c, 85). In "deviant" actions, the concept of which is "parasitic" on that of normal action, one or more of several possible kinds of "distortion" occurs so that the agent's awareness of her desires and their objects, and hence of the relation between her desires and her actions, is unclear to her. These distinctions, and the larger argument of which they are

part, will concern us later. For the moment the point is merely that the use of terms like "normal," "basic," and "paradigmatic" might reinforce the impression that brute and unreflected, distorted and deviant, desires occur infrequently. But whatever is Taylor's view about the statistical distribution of brute versus import-attributing and "normal" versus "deviant" desires (taking these two sets of distinctions to at least partly overlap extensionally?), he clearly assigns great practical as well as theoretical significance to keeping them separate in the theory of freedom.

10. In Frankfurt's terms she must also form a "second-order volition," roughly the will to act on one among her desires.

11. Of course agents who form import-attributing desires must also be capable of qualitative evaluations. But for Charles Taylor the distinctions between first- versus second-order desires and brute versus import-attributing desires are separate. He credits the possibility of agents whose desires about their desires are no more than desires composed out of brute desires. This seems implausible, but Taylor insists not only that this is *the* utilitarian and the characteristic negative-freedom view but that the view is correct in the sense that there are actually or actually could be such persons.

12. Although I have primarily followed and responded to Charles Taylor's formulations, the distinctions through which he presents and defends this ascent are, in various terminologies and as a part of differing larger philosophical orientations, familiar from many proponents of positive theories of freedom. Distinctions closely akin to Taylor's are crucial to Rousseau's notion that a moral transformation can (could) be effected by the movement from the state of nature to civil society (Rousseau 1950, vol. 1, esp. vii–viii). Such distinctions are also prominent in T. H. Green (1964), in F. H. Bradley (1927, esp. "The Vulgar Notion of Responsibility," Note C), and in Bernard Bosanquet (1899, esp. chap. 6). For more recent statements, see among numerous others: H. J. McCloskey 1965; Gerald Dworkin 1970; Harry Frankfurt 1971; S. I. Benn (reluctantly and qualifiedly) 1975–76; John Charvet 1981, and esp. John Charvet n.d.; A. J. M. Milne 1968.

13. Frankfurt's position is more complex. He characterizes creatures such as I have just described as "wantons," not persons. He is prepared to endorse the negative conception of freedom to the extent of allowing that in the sense of that conception "wantons" can be free or unfree. But "wantons" have no self-conception on the basis of which to form "second-order volitions" (and perhaps third-order, fourth-order, etc. volitions) and hence they lack "freedom of the will," which is a necessary—but not a sufficient—condition of being a free person. If we reserved "human" to persons, we could say that Frankfurt regards his distinctions and his ascent as essential to a theory of human freedom. But because he seems to have no doubt that there are human beings who are "wantons," the following critical observations apply to his position as well as to the other writers mentioned.

14. Of course it would *not* follow that no events or occurrences in human affairs yield to the analyses under consideration. It may be that such analyses

work well for some of the behaviors or physical movements of psychotics, of drug addicts, of persons suffering from certain compulsions and obsessions, and perhaps even of some deeply habitual behaviors. These further questions, and hence the difficult matter of so-called akratic behavior, will be taken up later. We may note at once, however, that we (or at any rate those of us who are not employees of mental institutions) do not hold psychotics and genuine compulsives morally or legally responsible for what they "do."

15. Here, as in much of my discussion of action, I am indebted to George M. Wilson: "Talk about satisfaction of desire is notoriously liable to conjure up the picture of wanting as the having of a kind of 'mental' urge or impulse— the occurrence of a force or 'inner attraction'. This is encouraged if we hold the idea that satisfying a desire must be the *quelling* of the 'mental' impulse, a *terminating* of the 'inner' force. . . . [I]nsofar as we are searching for an enlightening general conception of the way in which desire and action bear upon one another, . . . [this] model is a philosophical disaster. It seriously distorts the concept of wanting something and wholly falsifies our usual understanding of the nature of the purpose a person's action had when he is truly said to have acted to satisfy one of his desires" (1980, 153).

16. Two caveats concerning these difficult matters. First, the issues here are conceptual, not *terminological*. There is no doubt that we commonly use the term "desire" of infants, neonates, animals, insects, and even the simplest organisms. But just as it is important to distinguish between the concept I have marked by freedom$_1$ and those I have marked by freedoms$_{2-5}$, so it is important to distinguish between desires that are transitive and that involve the elements of expectation and directedness based on experience and reasoning and those that do not. Second, my comments are conceptual as opposed to *empirical*. (They are intended as remarks in philosophical, not empirical, psychology.) I am not a student of infant or animal psychology. The empirical propositions implicit in my examples seem to me to conform to widely accepted understandings of the kinds of creatures to which I refer. But perhaps they do not; or perhaps continued investigation will alter those understandings. If or to the extent that it is established that infants, neonates, fetuses, chimpanzees, dolphins, bees, etc. do form and act on desires as I have analyzed that concept, it will follow that those creatures satisfy one of the conditions necessary to predication of freedom$_2$ and unfreedom$_2$. Such findings would have far-reaching implications for our moral and perhaps even our political thinking and practice. (They would imply, for example, that it would be wrong to say that an infant or a fetus or a dolphin was unfree because it acted on desire.) But such findings would not affect my conceptual claims.

17. In respect to the entire notion that desires and certain primitive kinds of evaluation bring about movements or behaviors over which the agent exercises no control, an excellent antidote is provided by Wittgenstein's numerous discussions of "mechanisms" and of human beings conceived of on the model of machines. See among many highly pertinent passages 1953, pt. I, 157–95, 359–60, 495, 611–34, 689. Of course these passages, and certainly my

discussions here, do not settle the intricate question whether there is or might be an account of "causality" and of "action" that has established or could establish that human actions are to be understood and explained in causal terms. Recent work in the theory of action, especially the work of Donald Davidson, refines the discussion of this matter and enhances the plausibility of such an account. I find George M. Wilson's detailed "neo-Wittgensteinian" criticisms of Davidson's and other sophisticated "causalisms," and his argument for an irreducibly teleological view of action, convincing. Without attempting to recapitulate the detail of his discussion, I will continue to make tacit reliance on his arguments. But the positions taken by Davidson and Wilson are far more subtle and differentiated than those I have been considering above.

18. It should be added that much more might be said about Taylor's explicit and Charvet's implicit treatment of purely quantitative, compositional evaluations. These and other recent attacks on this notion are of course a part of a more general assault on utilitarianism, an assault that goes well beyond the treatment of freedom explicit or implicit in the latter doctrine. My remarks above are restricted to the point that (despite misleading metaphors about "weighing up") quantitative evaluations are not mechanical in any useful sense. Commonplace as they are, inventorying, numbering, calculating, and the like are abstract, refined, and rather intricate operations. In passing over other aspects of recent criticisms, however, I do not intend to endorse the suggestion that quantitative considerations—such as the number of people affected by a decision or action—are somehow irrelevant to moral and political evaluations or systematically inferior to the "qualitative" considerations with which they are, often rather crudely, contrasted in antiutilitarian writing.

Chapter Three

1. For reasons partly stated just below, (1) will require elaboration and refinement in at least two respects. First, further consideration will have to be given to a variety of performances that mix features characteristic of action with the elements typical of movements and behaviors. Second, the notion of prevention, and hence concepts such as interference and impediment, compulsion and coercion, inducement and threat, will need clarification. One can argue (2) in a stronger or a weaker version. The strong version is that desires are integral to all human actions and attempted human actions. Insofar as Hobbes and the classical utilitarians recognized a distinction between action and movement, they advanced a strong version of (2); a strong version is available in O'Shaughnessy (1980). The weaker version is that desires are integral elements in some more or less encompassing subclass of human actions and attempted actions. But the distinction between stronger and weaker versions is not important for present purposes. The important claim is that desires themselves involve the elements of action indicated above. If there are actions that do not involve desires, the elements of action enter in some other way—e.g., as a part of other emotions, of interests, of plans, etc.

2. See also Charles Taylor (1982b) where he again attacks formalism but suggests that Kant himself avoided its worst characteristics.

3. See also G. W. F. Hegel 1977, for instance, pars. 17, 425–28.

4. Bradley insists that the view he is attacking in this essay ("Duty for Duty's Sake") is "not the Kantian view; that view is far wider, and at the same time more confused. As a system it has been annihilated by Hegel's criticism" (1927, 148). But the doctrines he attacks are doctrines that Hegelians have attributed to Kant and Kantians.

5. I leave aside Dworkin's analyses, which follow Felix Oppenheim (1961), of the distinctions among acting freely, being free to act, feeling free, being free, being free with respect to X.

6. In Frankfurt's case they are constituitive elements in the person's freedom of will. As noted in the previous chapter, Frankfurt allows that wantons can be free in the sense of acting freely. But wantons lack freedom of the will and hence their freedom of action is a poorer thing than that of persons. Someone who "enjoys both freedom of action and freedom of the will . . . is not only free to do what he wants to do; he is also free to want what he wants. It seems to me that he has, in that case, all the freedom it is possible to desire or to conceive. There are other good things in life, and he may not possess some of them. But there is nothing in the way of freedom that he lacks" (1971, 17).

7. In this connection see John Charvet's concern that the higher self *itself* will be nothing better than an "arbitrary despot" (n.d., 55ff.).

8. Actually, Hegel allows that habitual conformity to norms can also be Free, but he insists that the habitual conduct must take its origins in education that produces knowing, intentional conformity and that the habits must not become so ingrained and unthinking that the agents have lost all grasp of the reason—the *logos*—for their actions (see 1942, esp. add. 97, par. 151, pp. 260–61).

9. MacIntyre says little about freedom as such, but I take it to be an implication of his analysis that freedom is also impossible in modern societies. What passes for it is, as Hegel put it, "negative freedom . . . [which] when it turns to actual practice, . . . takes shape in religion and politics alike as . . . the destruction of the whole subsisting social order" (Hegel 1972, par. 5, p. 22).

10. For related arguments, albeit from a perspective more individualist than Taylor's communitarianism will allow, see Bernard Williams 1981 ("Persons, Character and Morality") and Harry Frankfurt 1971.

11. The argument for a critical stance toward communal norms is strongest in Taylor 1977a (see esp. sec. II, 3).

12. Taylor's "liberation" is closely akin to Hegel's merely negative and subjective freedom.

Chapter Four

1. This characterization of the positive theory applies best to Taylor's analysis of "brute," "first-order," and merely "import-attributing" desires and to the analogous notions and analyses in the other theories discussed. But something very close to that characterization also holds for Taylor's discussion

of "purely compositional evaluations" and its analogues in other theories. Here there is an assessment of sorts, and hence notions such as "mistake" and "wrongdoing" appear to find a foothold. But the assessment process is described in terms so mechanical as to suggest that the mistakes would not be of reasoning or deliberation but of perception. In "composing" several desires to form a second-order desire, the agent might "misperceive herself," that is, incorrectly assess what Hume called the force and vivacity of one or more of her desires. If so, she might act on a composition of them that she would later regret. Or she might misperceive the external (to herself) circumstances, thereby adopting a course of action that would fail entirely to achieve the desired outcome or that would achieve it with less than optimal efficiency. But because the qualitative appropriateness, suitability, or worthiness of the desires themselves is not evaluated, the range of kinds of mistakes that can be made is severely restricted. It is for these reasons that agents who experience such movements cannot be said to be exercising control over themselves and hence are either unqualifiedly unfree or enjoy no more than an impoverished freedom.

2. If we put Feinberg's suggestion in schematic form, we get something like the following:

FREEDOM

	I Constraints		II Opportunities	
	C Negative	D Positive	E Negative	F Positive
A Internal	lack of: knowledge skill will rationality etc.	psychoses neuroses compulsions cravings habits etc.	presence of items under IAC	presence of items under IAD
B External	lack of: money tools authority etc.	physical and other external impediments to action	presence of items under IBC	presence of items under IBD

Proponents of the negative theory such as Hobbes restrict "unfreedom" to persons and other creatures who are self-activated and whose circumstances put them in IBD; they restrict "freedom" to such persons and other creatures whose circumstances put them in IIBF. Later proponents of this type of theory, such as J. S. Mill and Isaiah Berlin (we might call them "welfare negative libertarians") also give attention to the constraints of IBC and to the opportunities opened up by IIBE. Proponents of the positive theory make IIAF as well as self-activation a condition of freedom and treat IAC as the chief source of unfreedom. They are also prepared to say that the constraints of IBD actually contribute to freedom if they help the agent overcome the limitations of IAC and IAD.

3. See Foucault 1973a, 1973b, 1973c, 1979a, 1979b, 1981; Laing 1969, 1972; Laing and Esterson 1970; Szasz 1968, 1970, 1974.

4. Perhaps even this is too strong. As Paul Brest has suggested to me, there might be an akratic good Samaritan, someone who cannot stop herself from doing good for others at excessive cost to herself. A more moderate, confined, benevolence might be her preferred alternative. As I note in the continuation of the discussion above, however, this conceptualization would be untraditional.

5. Both purely habitual and akratic actions should be kept distinct from actions that are regarded as objectionable in kind but on balance justified or defensible in particular cases. To stay with the same example, it is easy to imagine an Able whose smoking is neither habitual nor akratic. She is well-informed about the consequences of smoking, has reflected carefully about this information, and deliberates about when to smoke and when not to. She knows that smoking has harmful effects on those who do it and on those exposed to the smoke of others. For these reasons she counsels others against smoking and she herself smokes only when alone. But she doesn't regret her smoking. She not only enjoys it but is convinced that stopping would have worse effects than continuing. On balance or all things considered, smoking is her preferred alternative. If there is regret at all, it will be over the fact that she has other characteristics—a tendency to nervousness, to gain weight, or whatever—that make smoking the least undesirable course of action for her. Many human choices and decisions, especially in moral life, have these characteristics.

Chapter Five

1. His distinction between the freedoms of the state of nature and the "liberties of subjects" is not a distinction of kind in my sense. The criteria governing "freedom" are the same and the differences concern the source of the obstacles or impediments to movement and the reliability of the freedom of movement that remains despite them (see 1955, chap. 21).

2. Apparently following Locke, Rousseau thinks that human beings in the state of nature have "ideas" (perceptions) and experience a small number of feelings. These nameless percepts combine, in some manner that Rousseau prudently neglects to discuss, with instincts to produce the movements of human beings in their natural state. He also thinks that by nature human beings have, apparently in latent form, "free-will" and "the faculty of self-improvement." Whereas all other animals can only "submit" to their natural instincts and impulses, the human being "knows himself at liberty to acquiesce or to resist" and dimly senses the possibility of making himself into something

different and better than he now is. Following Descartes, Rousseau regards these capacities as constituting the "metaphysical and moral" as opposed to the "merely physical" and "mechanical" side of mankind (see 1955, 209–10). The discussion of these points is confusing and probably confused. In particular, it is not clear whether these capacities actually operate in the state of nature or whether they are only latent in that state and are triggered into actuality by the onset of sociality and the language that comes with it.

3. The continuation of the passage quoted above shows that Rousseau was motivated in part by a desire not to offend religious sensibilities by seeming to deny that the Old Testament gives the correct history of the "actual origin" of human societies.

4. See Mill 1951, *On Liberty*, chap. 1, and *Representative Government*, chap. 4. For Mill's views on these and other points, see Richard Wollheim 1979; John Gray 1983.

5. Wittgenstein is of course talking about the, in many respects, special case of sensations. But as I am interpreting his argument, the point he is making holds for all referents.

6. "And this language like any other is founded on convention" (*PI*, I, 355).

7. On what seem to be exceptionally quick learners, see his discussion of "calculating prodigies," persons "who get the right answers but cannot say how. Are we to say they do not calculate? (A family of cases)" (*PI*, I, 236). On minimum standards of competency, see especially the lengthy discussion of reading (*PI*, I, 156–71).

8. Their *possibility*, in fact, is conceptually necessary because it is by contrast with them or the idea of them that "ordinary" and "regular," "correct" and "incorrect," are delineated.

Chapter Six

1. On the latter class of exceptions, see Benn and Weinstein 1973.

2. For an explicit defense of a formulation strongly analogous to the above, see Benn 1975–76.

3. For example: "whenever worlds are laid on, underlives develop" (1961b, 305).

4. Goffman's very occasional gestures toward comparative synchronic or diachronic analyses that reach beyond these limits suggest that "Eastern" societies permit, and premodern Western ones permitted, much more of both (see 1956, 245; 1961a, 141). Insofar as it is appropriate to characterize Goffman as a "structuralist," his version of that understanding is primarily culture-relative and culture-determined, not culure-invariant or culture-determining.

5. The best-integrated and hence most confining societies, indeed, diminish the significance of differentiated roles, overriding them with or by an encompassing requirement of identification with the community as such. Goffman claims to have found such an embracing communalism among the

Shetland Islanders he studied in his dissertation research (see 1961a, esp. 101–2).

6. "Universal human nature is not a very human thing. By acquiring it, the person becomes a kind of construct, built up not from inner psychic propensities but from moral rules that are impressed on him from without. . . . The general capacity to be bound by moral rules may well belong to the individual but the particular set of rules which transforms him into a human being derives from requirements established in the ritual organization of social encounters. And if a particular person or group or society seems to have a unique character . . . , it is because its standard set of human-nature elements is pitched and combined in a particular way" (1967, 45).

7. Goffman's analysis of modern societies might be abbreviated by amending one of Thomas Hobbes's most famous remarks: So that in the first place, I put for a general inclination of all mankind, a perpetual and restless desire of maintaining face, that ceaseth only in death. And the cause of this, is not always that a man hopes for a better reputation, than he has already attained to; or that he cannot be content with a moderately good opinion from others; but because such standing as he now has, being by the grace of others, can be assured only by continuous facework.

8. The latter types, of course, being merely "unaware of the situational obligations their conduct sustains" (1963, 226), may *feel* more free than those who dispute societies' demands. But they will scarcely be judged to *be* more free by the steely-eyed social scientist.

9. It is important, however, that he betrays little interest in *political* dissent in any very robust sense.

10. The passage *is* correctly quoted.

11. Even "total institutions" such as prisons and asylums must employ these strategies. Although society generally views the inmates of such institutions as determined by forces beyond their control, those who run the institutions cannot consistently adopt this stance because they must rely upon their wards to direct their own conduct to a considerable degree (see 1961b, 87).

12. "[I]t is just when an individual feels he is sheltered from others' view, and suddenly discovers he is not, that we obtain the clearest picture of what he owes to the gathering" (1963, 41).

13. We might equally say that Goffmanesque selves are empty in the sense of having no fixed or settled character. We might call them "wantons" after Harry Frankfurt except that they have one overweening desire, namely to maintain face, and hence are pushed and pulled hither and yon less by internal forces native to them than by the demands and directives of the society around them. They suffer the likely if not the certain fate of extreme egocentrics. Incessantly concerned with, but unable to control, threats, harms, or slights to itself, the Goffmanesque self "acts" only in response to others, never out of its own dispositions.

14. "Function" and "supportive," I take it, are used in the sense of unintentionally reinforcing the social establishment.

15. Such a stance at this early juncture anticipates the conclusion I will draw in the end, namely, that examining Goffman allows us to formulate and address no more than a simulacrum of the elusive question whether modern sociality as such is the enemy of freedom.

16. Consider his often favorable comments about psychotics. Are they, alone among the inhabitants of modern societies, able to make their own world and hence themselves?

17. A fourth condition is also part of Goffman's view, namely, that the attributes or characteristics that identify me as me must not only be unique to but in some sense originated by me. They cannot, that is, be implanted, infused, instilled, or otherwise produced in me by society. We have already seen that in any very strong form this further condition cannot be satisfied. But it should also be noted that the fourth condition is relevant to the question of distinctive identity and individuality only if it is assumed that society works the same effect on all of its members. If society produced different effects on each of its members, the thesis that we are social products could be true without endangering the notion of distinctive identity. It is likely that Goffman's view, as he intended it, is that we are indistinguishable in the sense that we are all products of our society and in the somewhat more specific sense that we are all devoted to maintaining face. The more uncompromising denial of identity that I am discussing is an inference from his discussions, not an explicit contention of these discussions.

18. See Ludwig Wittgenstein 1953, esp. I, 80ff., 143ff., 167ff., 197ff., 217ff., 235ff. See also Saul A. Kripke 1982. My remarks about identity are also indebted to the work of Derek Parfit (see 1984, esp. pt. 3)

19. Of course these elements also play a prominent role in our uses of the concepts of identity and individuality. A person's patterns of action are ordinarily prominent among the characteristics by which she is distinguished, which constitute her individuality. (In general there is not a sharp demarcation among "self," "identity," "individuality," "agency," and "autonomy.") But because a generalized disinclination to, even incapacity for, action may be an identifying characteristic of a person, and a leading feature of her individuality (Oblomov), the questions of agency and autonomy are distinct from questions of identity and individuality.

20. I am indebted here to S. I. Benn 1975–76, to John Gray 1983, and to exchanges with Gray and with Michael Briand, Peter Steinberger, and J. David Greenstone.

It should be noted that there are stronger versions of "individuality" that carry these and further requirements. For example, in J. S. Mill and the romantic individualists who influenced him there is a notion of "authentic individuality" or "authenticity" which posits an original nature, distinctive to each human being, and restricts "individuality" to persons who achieve consonance between their thought, their action, and their true nature. See, for example, Gray 1983, esp. chap. 4.

21. Oddly enough, there is a sense in which Goffman understood and

agreed with the argument just sketched. At bottom, his complaint about us moderns is that we lack autonomy and hence make dismal use of the freedoms available in civil society. Believing that the "mentally ill" are no worse and (certain rhetorically excessive passages aside) no better than the rest of us in this regard, he was outraged by the fact that those so classified are so often deprived of their freedom in the name of making them autonomous. Insofar as he was correct about the "mentally ill," his outrage was entirely justified.

Chapter Seven

1. This idea is most easily concretized by thinking of actions that require materials or technology or institutional arrangements and ritual forms known to be unknown in some forms of life. Serving beefalo to human beings conceived outside the womb of a human female has only recently become possible. Doing so at a predominantly nonkin, intimate, sit-down, two-wine dinner party will in all likelihood continue to be possible only in a few highly specialized subcultures. Of course there are more recondite views—for example, Quinian radical indeterminacy of translation—according to which each linguistic community has a unique feasible set of actions.

2. That it is not widely shared in our societies, perhaps not even sincerely held by some of those who occasionally announce it, is at least suggested by what might be called the "empty shelves" theme that is so prominent in Western reporting about the Soviet Union and much of Eastern Europe. Although it is acknowledged—if only by silence—that there is little hunger or malnutrition in the Soviet bloc, that one rarely encounters people in rags or without shelter in those countries, the paucity of consumer choices and the dreary, monotonous quality of food, clothing, apartment buildings, and so forth is a constant theme in comparisons between the free and communist worlds.

3. My discussion is obviously influenced by the public law of the United States. I believe it is the case, however, that (what for present purposes are) the major contentions of the discussion are true for modern Western states generally. Some of these states have established religions, and there is variation as to the diversity of religious practices that are tolerated in them. But unlike theocracies such as Iran and what may be called atheocracies such as the Soviet Union, the societies I am calling "modern Western" are alike in breaking the once usual connection between rationality and religious freedom.

4. The above discussion is indebted to comments by David Mapel. Cf. the following remarks of Wittgenstein: "We also say of some people that they are transparent to us. It is, however, important as regards this observation that one human being can be a complete enigma to another. We learn this when we come into a strange country with entirely strange traditions; and, what is more, even given a mastery of the country's language, we do not *understand* the people. (And not because of not knowing what they are saying to themselves.) We cannot find our feet with them. . . . If a lion could talk, we could not understand him" (1953, II, xi, 223).

On the other hand: "suppose you came as an explorer into an unknown country with a language quite strange to you. In what circumstances would you say that the people there gave orders, understood them, obeyed them, rebelled against them, and so on?

"The common behavior of mankind is the system of reference by means of which we interpret an unknown language" (ibid., I 206, 82).

5. In Rawls's system, much of what I have said about the place of rationality in the public-law conception of religious freedom is expressed through a distinction between the Reasonable and the Rational. I discuss this distinction, and Rawls's argument for liberty, in Chapter 9.

6. At the level of political theory, this point of view is found most unequivocally in Hobbes. In the state of nature, a condition entirely lacking in political and social structure, each person lives entirely by her own wits. Because she is always surrounded by competing if not agressively antagonistic others, any freedom of action she maintains is (luck aside) the result of her rational use of the resources she has at her disposal. It is not worse than an exaggeration to say that for Hobbes organized political society is a device for diminishing somewhat the necessity for such individual rationality. Of course Hobbes's confidence in individual rationality was far more robust than the confidence of those who followed him in adopting this line of thought. His clear preference for minimal structural arrangement reflects his belief that most people will be able to cope effectively if the crudest threats and interferences are controlled by the Sovereign.

7. The strains in modern Western thought about freedom that are more emphatically democratic and participatory tend to deride the instrumental and largely defensive rationality of private life and call for an end- or good-oriented substantive rationality of persons performing the public role of citizenship. For reasons already discussed, the version of liberalism with which (in this respect) Rawls identifies (Constant, Tocqueville, Humboldt, Mill, and Berlin are the writers he lists) is skeptical about the notion of rationally delineated collective goods beyond the narrow confines of what Rawls calls the basic structure, and treats participation in public life as no more than one personal good among many. But even this doctrine (opposed in this respect to Hobbes, perhaps to Oakeshott, and certainly to libertarianism) recognizes that reliance on political and social structures to protect individual freedom implies the importance of quite widespread involvement in and rationality concerning public life. Libertarianism presumes a high degree of instrumental rationality in private affairs and assumes that such rationality will itself unintentionally but reliably yield most of the few genuine public goods that there are. By contrast, the Rawlsian line of thought treats as requisite widespread reasonableness about the proper shape of political and social structures as well as instrumental rationality on the part of some considerable number of public officials and other representative agents, assumes but does not require rationality in private life, and values and encourages but does not require widespread rationality in public life.

8. These considerations are one explanation for the fact that many people in the liberal tradition have concerned themselves with the family, the school, the church, trade unions, and so on. Authoritarian, autocratic, and coercive practices in these realms are objectionable in their own right and foster dispositions and patterns of conduct that are pervasively antagonistic to more specifically political freedoms. The persistence of authoritarian thinking and practice in respect to the family and the school, the corporation and the union, in addition to requiring qualification of my no doubt too easy generalizations about the commitment to freedom and equality in modern Western societies, is a source of continuing and deep tension within liberalism. Should, can, liberalism restrict its attention to (or at least concentrate its attentions upon) the "basic structure" or the "civil society" and let individuals take care of their own freedom in other respects? Are we justified in agreeing with Rawls that a society that achieves justice (which means assuring each person's "equal right to a fully adequate scheme of equal basic liberties which is compatible with a similar scheme of liberties for all" [Rawls 1982b, 85]) in respect to or at the level of the basic structure will be, all things considered, an adequately free society? Or must we agree with a legion of critics of liberalism that this stance is self-defeating in the sense that it guarantees the failure of the liberal's project of promoting freedom? Attempts to articulate an intermediate position on this issue are responsible for much of the untidiness of recent liberalism.

The position I have thus far adopted is characteristic of liberalism at least in the respect that it is untidy. I have posited a widely diffused but also diffuse commitment to freedom and equality, treating this as a generalized axiological feature of modern Western culture. I have suggested that a public conception of freedom and more or less elaborate institutional structures have developed a conception and an array of structures that can be seen as implementing the cultural commitment. On this view, the former is importantly dependent on the latter; in cultures lacking a generalized commitment to freedom we find quite different public conceptions and structures. But once in place the public structures give specific content to and serve to promote the generalized commitment, thereby also heightening the significance of that commitment for thought and action that occur in dimensions of social life excluded from the authority of the public structure. Accordingly, there is more or less continuous interaction among the most general features of the culture, the public structure, and what is widely regarded as the private realm.

But recognition that the viability of the general culture and the public structure are influenced by activities in the private realm creates a tendency to expand the activities of the public institutions so as better to protect and implement the public conception of freedom and the generalized cultural commitment. Concern to protect and implement the latter motivates and perhaps licenses interventions in religion, in even the most insistently private aspects of education, in the family, and in the marketplace. These interventions frequently have the character of attempts to enhance both the procedural and the substantive rationality of private activities, thereby putting into question the notion of value-pluralism and the commitment to the associated if not allied belief that a free society benefits from but does not require widespread substantive or even procedural rationality.

This tendency has been a source of distress for a number of notable political thinkers. Writers of great power of mind such as Hannah Arendt, Michael Oakeshott, John Rawls, and (in less encompassing terms) Alexander Meiklejohn have in effect argued that the tendency has destroyed or is in the way of destroying both the distinction and the difference between what is properly public and what is properly private (between public and political life and the social question; between a civil society and an enterprise association; between justice as an attribute of the basic structure and justice in distributions of particular goods among assignable individuals; between public speech deserving the protection of the First Amendment and private speech to be defended, if at all, on quite different grounds).

Given the strength and pervasiveness of the tendency to which I am referring, the views of these writers appear to many to be archaic and irrelevant. This assessment seems to me to be mistaken on both counts. As I have suggested by locating the public-private distinction in the context of a widely received, more rather than less authoritative axiology, the difference between the public and the private has never been and could not be as clear-cut as Arendt, Oakeshott, et al. at least appear to require. If archaic means characteristic of an earlier time, these views cannot be archaic because there is no earlier time in or of which they were characteristic. But they are very far from being irrelevant. This is (in effect) widely conceded in respect to the case with which we began, that is, religious belief and practice; however much we may dispute the details of its interpretation and application, the formula "public protection of privately chosen religious practice" is a fundamental feature of our societies. Analogous formulas such as "public enforcement of private contracts," "public assistance to and protection of private child-rearing, education, medical, and avocational practices" are (as my insertion of the word "assistance" does at least something to indicate) matters of much deeper controversy. But these controversies simply cannot be understood without reference to the belief that the public-private distinction is of great importance.

I further suggest, although this is admittedly an independently disputable point, that this distinction is important because of its connections with the relationship between freedom and rationality. The instrument or device distinctive of action in the public realm is law, that is, rules invested with authority and therefore (typically) binding on everyone in the jurisdiction. In the societies I am discussing, citizens are encouraged to consider the merits of proposed and of already promulgated legislation. It is hoped (among other things) that such consideration will occur in a rational manner and will diminish the extent to which citizens are obliged to obey rules merely because they are invested with authority and despite the fact that in their content they lack, or are regarded as lacking, rational justification. One of the ideas at work in this regard is that laws that are regarded by citizens as having rational justification do not interfere with individual freedom or constitute a less objectionable interference with such freedom than laws that are regarded as lacking such justification. In at least this respect, in the public realm a connection is made between rationality and freedom.

Whatever else we may think of this idea and this connection, an enlargment of the scope of action taken by public authority is likely to strain belief in their practical significance. As the range and detail of legislation increase, it becomes difficult for any substantial percentage of the citizenry to inform themselves concerning, or to engage in reflection and discussion about, the content of existing and proposed laws. Generally shared criteria of assessment do not develop and the likelihood of disagreement and generalized dissatisfaction increases. If so, restricting the public realm, leaving wide scope for activities that do not involve authority and in respect to which, as with religious practices, freedom depends less on shared rationality, can be expected to serve the value of freedom. In this perspective, the public-private distinction has the importance for freedom claimed for it by the writers just mentioned. It has that importance in part because respect for it weakens the dependence of freedom on rationality.

9. Cf. Benn and Weinstein 1971, esp. 314–15. As these authors point out, norms and conventions are subject to challenges which, if successful, lead to changes in what is counted as unfreedom. In their example, when nineteenth-century liberals, socialists, and so forth challenged going assumptions about relations between capitalist employers and workers it became possible to treat work contracts as exploitative and coercive and hence as interferences with the freedom of workers. But it would be a mistake to think that these challengers employed a purely descriptive, normatively neutral concept of freedom. Their challenge, and hence their uses of "freedom" and "unfreedom," were embedded in an economic, moral, and legal ideal alternative to the arrangements they were criticizing. Whatever the content of that ideal, if it was accepted and institutionalized there would then be a new set of norms; acts consonant with those norms would not count as interferences with freedom. For example, in market capitalism modified by collective bargaining, or in socialism, unions and governments importantly restrict actions of workers and owners. But if these restrictions are within the "general framework . . . taken to define the normal conditions of action" (ibid., 315) they count as restrictions on freedom only for those who want to call that framework into question. Of course this does not imply that one cannot challenge the restrictions on grounds other than freedom.

10. See, for example, Benn 1975–76, 109; Benn and Weinstein 1973; Nozick 1969; Steiner 1974–75; Frankfurt 1971, 1973; Day 1977; Weinstein 1963; Ryan 1980; Lyons 1975; Gert 1972; Bayles 1972; Held 1972; Gray 1983; Miller 1983.

11. See Benn 1975–76. Benn's discussion will be considered in greater detail in the final section of this chapter.

12. Note that it is *not* an incentive that it would be unreasonable *to* act upon.

13. There is a question, left undiscussed by Gert, whether B must also be a rational person acting rationally in the circumstances. Presumably B can intentionally or knowingly coerce (attempt to coerce) A only if B is such a person. If B does not know that the incentives she is providing A are unreasonable she cannot intentionally or knowingly coerce A by providing them. But perhaps A could be coerced by B's action or behavior without B intending to coerce A.

14. It is striking that Gert invokes a strong notion of rationality primarily to show that A is coerced by B, primarily to excuse A's inability to cope with B's threats. Little is said about rationality as an asset or strength enabling A to maintain her freedom of action despite B's attempt to deprive her of it. There is a certain tone of passivity in Gert's discussion of freedom.

15. Cf. Gray 1983, 56. On these points see also Pitkin 1984.

16. Of course these remarks are culturally specific. As we have seen, autarchy or freedom of agency would, in Benn and Gray's sense, be an "ideal" for many historical and contemporary cultures—one frequently and emphatically rejected as improper for most human beings. The discussions from which I have been quoting are themselves manifestations of the doubly normative beliefs and values characteristic of Western modernity.

Chapter Eight

1. See Berlin 1969, xxxviii–li; Elster 1976, 1982a, 1982b; Feinberg 1980, 37ff.

2. As usual with Berlin, his full discussion recognizes and takes steps to meet difficulties with his more abstract or programmatic formulations. Consider the following passage: Freedom in the sense of open options "entails not simply the absence of frustration (which may be obtained by killing desires), but the absence of obstacles to possible choices and activities—absence of obstructions on roads along which a man can decide to walk. Such freedom ultimately depends not on whether I wish to walk at all, or how far, but on how many doors are open, how open they are, *upon their relative importance* to my life" (Berlin 1969, xxxix, emphasis added). Up to the italicized phrase, this formulation is vulnerable to my objection above. If the passage is interpreted in the light of this last phrase, and if that phrase is understood against the background of Berlin's larger moral and political views, my objection is largely met (cf. Feinberg 1980, 36–37).

3. Certainly it does not mean tailoring A's interests and desires to "options" imposed upon her by other persons. It is this latter process that is depicted in the novels referred to above. It is a caricature of the Hobbesian position to treat it as consistent with or even implicitly supportive of such processes.

4. Of course all cultures and societies disapprove some interests and de-

sires and entertain and cultivate goods in addition to and in conflict with the prima facie good identified by the liberal principle.

5. See Berlin 1969, Essay II and x–xxxvii; Oakeshott 1975, esp. 36–41. A forceful recent statement is Dennett 1984.

6. The thesis that freedom and determinism are as a practical matter incompatible should be distinguished from two other views on the same set of issues. The first is that determinism is worse than merely incompatible with our normative practices: rather, it is false in its own right, that is, on grounds independent of its relation to our practices. This view *entails* that we are free in the sense that we are not determined. Hence if this view is true, our freedom (as opposed to our being determined) is more than a supposition of our practices; it is a deep fact about us. Whether it is a good or bad thing in the sense of something we should celebrate or lament is an independent question. The second is the view that hard determinism is compatible with our normative practices in that the sense in which our conduct is determined by causal forces is consistent with (or even necessary to) the sense in which we choose and can properly be held responsible for our conduct. On this view, generally known as compatibilism, freedom in a sense that permits of responsibility is intrinsic to our normative practices.

7. For an example of such imaginings, see Nozick 1981, chap. 3.

8. One might argue that we should do our best to articulate the reasons for deep values such as the value of freedom because doing so will arm us against the arguments of challengers and critics. Of course this view, along with its pessimism about the possibility (or perhaps its cynicism about the desirability) of reaching wider agreement, makes the perhaps overly optimistic assumption that the reasons for our set of beliefs and values will prove on examination to be better than the reasons for alternative or opposing sets.

9. As is well known, some arguments of the latter type include the claim that human beings in their true or essential or distinctive nature are not desire-satisfying, interest-pursuing creatures. These characteristics, or at least their present salience, are distortions or perversions; they were not, would not, or will not be present in human beings in their natural, proper, fully developed or realized form. In the classical naturalism of Aristotle, for example, human beings are what they are distinctively fitted to be or to become. We can only discern their true nature by observing them empirically, but in making those observations we must attend to their distinctive (among animate creatures) capacities and what those capacities distinctively enable, not to the behaviors that happen to be prominent among them in this or that time or place. It is instructive that views with this form are now more commonly called perfectionist than naturalist.

10. It is well to remember in this connection that the desires and interests individuals in fact form and attempt to act upon are powerfully influenced by the traditions and conventions, the beliefs and values, norms and rules, of their culture and their society. We can be surprised and even delighted by our fecundity and inventiveness in this respect without falling victim to the sort of

anxiety expressed by expressions such as "God only knows" what desire or interest some maniac might conceive.

I am aware that the Critical Theorists regard these facts as deepening the problem with LP or any principle akin to it. Given that in their view we are participants in a culture (or victims of a culture) that is systematically repressive and distorting of our true human interests, the fact that the interests we form are limited by that culture makes it all the more objectionable to endorse LP. We can endorse LP, but only *after* our culture has been transformed so as to accord with our true nature. Until that time the "toleration" prescribed by LP is "repressive." Because we are not able to "repress" it on our own, it must be repressed on our behalf.

11. Cf. Holmes: "Even today, anti-liberal attacks on self-interest express nostalgia for systems of deference, authority, and condescension" (1984, 253).

12. I believe that the concept acquired its present prominence because of its central place in Rawls's work. See Rawls 1971, esp. 25 and sect. 50. See also Haksar 1979.

13. These all too brief comments on Bentham are principally indebted to Rawls's several discussions of classical utilitarianism. See Rawls 1971, esp. secs. 5 and 30; Rawls 1982a. See also Hart 1982; Lyons 1973. Lyons argues that Bentham's concept of the greatest happiness of the greatest number was "parochial" in that it was to be calculated within existing political units, not for all of humankind. (see 20ff).

14. My brief remarks about Mill are most heavily influenced by Gray 1983 and Berger 1984. In his Chapter 5 Berger reviews major interpretations of Mill's thought concerning these questions.

Chapter Nine

1. A further advantage of taking my bearings from Rawls's method of avoidance is that it allows me to set aside at least some of the details and complexities of *A Theory of Justice*.

2. There is, for example, the question whether it is consistent with the method of avoidance to accord great prominence to philosophers' doctrines such as utilitarianism and perfectionism. Rawls continues to write as if showing the unacceptability of these doctrines amounts to showing that justice as fairness best construes and harmonizes the settled beliefs of our culture.

3. The following discussion is based primarily on Rawls 1982b and earlier writings, but I have tried to interpret these materials in the light of 1985.

4. It should be noted in this connection that the seemingly dismissive or at least skeptical tone of Rawls's phrase "something called 'liberty' " does not betoken doubt on his part about the availability or usability of the concepts "liberty" and "freedom." On the contrary, in *A Theory of Justice* he dismisses disputes about these concepts—for example, those between proponents of positive and negative concepts—as either "merely verbal" or in reality disputes about the value of various freedoms or liberties. He thinks that for the most part they have been the latter and he supports this claim with an

abbreviated conceptual discussion (basically endorsing Gerald MacCallum's analysis [MacCallum 1967]) designed to show that one and the same concept of liberty or freedom is in use in all of the competing positions and theories (see Rawls 1971, 201–2). To my knowledge Rawls has not amended these views in his later writings.

A further word is in order on this matter. I think I am correct in saying that Rawls's conceptual conclusions agree with my own; that is, he briefly defends, and throughout uses, "freedom" in the sense of what I am calling freedom of action or freedom$_2$. In this respect the main difference between us is that he simply does not entertain the claims of theorists of positive freedom that virtue, autonomy, communal solidarity, and the like *are* freedom and that persons and societies who or which lack these qualities are *therefore* unfree. In my own case I have taken up and attempted to refute these claims because they have an initial plausibility and because they have worked a considerable and to my mind unfortunate influence on the theory of freedom. This matter aside, the conceptual agreement between Rawls and myself is essential to the disagreements that will emerge in the remainder of this chapter.

5. Rawls's statement of this position in *A Theory of Justice* can properly be characterized as severe: "The principles of right, and so of justice, put limits on which satisfactions have value; they impose restrictions on what are reasonable conceptions of one's good. In drawing up plans and in deciding on aspirations men are to take these constraints into account. Hence in justice as fairness one does not take men's propensities and inclinations as given, whatever they are, and then seek the best way to fulfil them. Rather, their desires and aspirations are restricted from the outset by the principles of justice which specify the boundaries that men's systems of ends must respect. . . . [I]nterests requiring the violation of justice have no value. Having no merit in the first place, they cannot override its claims" (1971, 31; f. 1982a, 171; 1980, 527).

6. To take one leading example, Rawls says that the choice between private property-owning and socialist regimes is left open by a political theory of social justice. "Which of these systems and the many intermediate forms most fully answers to the requirements of justice cannot, I think, be determined in advance. There is presumably no general answer to this question, since it depends in large part upon the traditions, institutions, and social forces of each country, and its particular historical circumstances. The theory of justice does not include these matters" (1971, 274). As we have already seen, Rawls's most explicit and forceful argument for the limitations on political conceptions is in 1985.

7. An exception of sorts is allowed in the case of the "exchange branch" (see 1971, 282ff. and esp. 331–32).

8. The several passages quoted in the last two paragraphs above are from Rawls 1982b, 82–83.

9. In his more general metatheoretical reflections Rawls endorses this view. See especially his "The Independence of Moral Theory" (1974–75). The objection I am developing is to the "political" argument "he" in fact advances

in his works concerning justice. I am not suggesting that on meta-level or any other grounds Rawls would be closed to the possibility of cogent objections to "his" political argument. It is nevertheless striking that Rawls's theory has always assigned a crucial place to decisions of principle about the most basic features of political society, decisions that are to be binding into the future. There is every reason to expect that Rawls will continue to be open to changes in the formulation of the two principles and in numerous other elements of his theory. It is not easy to imagine him forgoing the claim I am considering. (Presumably this claim has thus far survived examination in "wide," not merely "narrow," reflective equilibrium. See ibid.)

10. See for example Barry 1973; Daniels 1975; Fishkin 1975. In a later paper Fishkin generalizes this objection to apply to all attempts to define an "unbiased . . . perspective or decision situation for the selection of first principles that are to have priority in a liberal state" (1984, 4–7).

11. We might think of Rawls's well-ordered society as a step in this direction, a step toward a society in which more refined judgments could be made and implemented without endangering legitimacy.

12. At the level of a general theory of the conditions of meaning, its defects have in my judgment been most decisively exposed by Wittgenstein. My discussion of his work in Chapter 5 is pertinent here as well, but see especially, Wittgenstein 1953, I, 66–71, 81, 88, 183. With particular reference to "rights" and other concepts especially at issue here, and with account taken of his later adjustments, Hart's "Definition and Theory in Jurisprudence" remains conclusive concerning both the "ideal" and skeptical overreactions to the impossibility of satisfying it. See Hart 1983, 21–49, and 2–6 for the later adjustments.

13. The following discussion draws substantially on Flathman 1984a. The issues in question are frequently discussed as part of the debate over the adequacy of utilitarianism and particularly whether any version of that theory can accommodate and provide an adequately secure place for rights. My discussion in the paper just referred to is in part in these terms, but here, in part because Scanlon's argument is consequentialist but in no clearly identifiable way utilitarian, I avoid any direct comment on that well-rehearsed controversy.

14. For further discussion of civil disobedience and "civil encroachment," see Flathman 1984a, and Flathman 1980, esp. chap. 6.

15. See Ludwig Wittgenstein 1953: "if rule became exception and exception rule; or if both became phenomena of roughly equal frequency—this would make our normal language-games lose their point. —The procedure of putting a lump of cheese on a balance and fixing the price by the turn of the scale would lose its point if it frequently happened for such lumps to suddenly grow or shrink for no obvious reason" (I, 142).

16. In 1971 Scanlon accords a highly significant, even a decisive role, to the value of autonomy. In 1979 he abandons this view. I discuss autonomy in section IX below.

17. It is perhaps relevant in this connection to recall the fate of constitu-

tional and other schemes, however meritorious when considered in the abstract, that have been adopted by or—more often—imposed upon societies to which those schemes are alien or otherwise ill-adapted.

If it seems inappropriate to advert to these instances in discussing Rawls (especially when one has already allowed that the list of rights he proposes comports well with the traditions, practices, and material circumstances of the societies to which he proposes them), this seems to me to be because Rawls himself knows and has considered the kinds of things that Scanlon says participants in foundational reasoning should know and consider. But Rawls's parties must operate without such knowledge and hence must adopt a list of absolute rights without reference to such considerations. Of course it is *we* who as a practical political matter must accept the results of the reasoning that occurs under the constraints of the original position. Using the more encompassing methods of wide reflective equilibrium, we ask ourselves whether those results accord with our considered convictions, convictions that are of course influenced by considerations not available in the original position. But if this dimension of Rawls's thought is emphasized, the original position is at most a heuristic device and might well be regarded as a distraction.

We should perhaps add a word concerning Rawls's claim that a Rawlsian society would be more stable than societies whose basic rights are adopted by an intuitionist method. See Rawls 1971, especially section 76. That argument presumes that the citizenry in fact accepts and acts steadily and conscientiously on the principles of justice. The presumption that they can and will, could and would do so is of course what is at issue.

18. Tendencies of thought in the United States are perhaps relevant to this point. Proposals to call a constitutional convention motivated by the desire to overcome legislative opposition to certain constitutional amendments have aroused exceptionally powerful resistance because they open the possibility (raise the specter would be a more accurate characterization of what many think) that such a convention might reconsider the entire Constitution. Although these tendencies might be regarded as evidence that many people think the Constitution is and should be an agreement binding into the indefinite future, they are better viewed as skepticism about the project of wholesale thinking about the basic structure of society. (I am indebted to conversations with Bonnie Honig on this and related points.)

19. For a closely related argument focusing on justifications for political authority, see Flathman 1980, chaps. 10–13.

20. That it *requires* active, positive governmental promotion of discussion and debate as opposed to protection of them is of course a further and controversial claim. Cf. Fishkin 1984, 15–17.

Chapter Ten

1. For striking examples of such conceptual moves, see Arendt 1961, the essay entitled "What is Freedom"; and Arendt 1959, 29–30, 166–67, 209–11. For the suggestion that Marx made similar moves, see Brenkert 1983.

2. The contrasts here are with the social and economic conditions of freedom championed by Marxism, socialists, and much interventionist or welfare-state liberalism. They are also, and more sharply, with the psychologistic and moralizing views of recent neo-Hegelian proponents of positive freedom such as Charles Taylor, Alasdair MacIntyre, and John Charvet. If we interpreted the latter writers as offering accounts of the conditions rather than the criteria of freedom, the conditions they propose—"responsibility for self," a personality integrated and governed by a higher self, communally established but rational virtue—have even less explicitly political content than the conditions insisted upon by Marxism and the other views first mentioned. True, proponents of neo-Hegelian views commonly argue that virtue and responsibility for self are possible only in a community less fragmented and privatized than the rights-oriented societies they find characteristic of Western modernity. But they have little that is concrete to say about political form or process. Although employing a vaguely Hegelian notion of situatedness, they evidence an unwillingness to accord to political arrangements and practices any very decisive significance.

3. The following discussion of Machiavelli closely follows Quentin Skinner's account. See Skinner 1981, 1983, 1984. I follow Skinner in treating Machiavelli's views as relevantly continuous with contemporary discussions of negative and positive liberty. This procedure ignores the possibility that Machiavelli's treatment of liberty is in a tradition distinct from and incompatible with that which primarily informs the recent debates to which Skinner refers in the works cited and to which I have attended throughout this book. Cf. Pocock 1975, and 1985, especially the essay "Virtues, Rights, and Manners."

4. It is part of Skinner's argument that on Machiavelli's view there can be no such thing as successful free riding by citizens. Citizens who attempt to enjoy the benefits of political life while letting others bear its burdens and absorb its costs invariably lose their own liberties and their own well-being.

5. It is true that Machiavelli was a "realist" in the sense that he accepted people as he found them and tried to instruct them as to how to achieve the objectives they set for themselves. It is not true that he was cynically indifferent to human well-being.

6. Perhaps the generalizations are also "true" or "correct" in the wider, even the unqualified, sense that it is only under circumstances such as those mentioned, and only given a citizenry that practices the Machiavellian prudence, that freedom of action can be maintained. Perhaps we who live under importantly different circumstances must either recast ourselves and our politics in the Machiavellian mold or resign ourselves to unfreedom. This last possibility, decidedly un-Machiavellian in its utopian character, is by no means foreign to the spirit of radically antihistorical thinkers such as Rousseau and Arendt.

7. See above, chap. 5, pp. 37–38, chap. 9, n. 87.

8. This is not to say that such a society operates with an "open options"

conception of freedom. Its members are free or unfree depending on whether others effectively interfere with their attempts to act on the interests and desires, objectives and purposes they in fact have. What is held open is the possibility that their interests, desires, and so forth will change in ways that cannot be foreseen and must not be foreclosed in the strong sense proposed by "fundamental" principles and rules. They foresee the possibility of changes in their interests, not the possible changes in them.

References

Anscombe, G. E. M. 1978. "Rules, Rights, and Promises." *Midwest Studies in Philosophy* 3:123ff.

Arendt, Hannah. 1959. *The Human Condition.* New York: Doubleday.

———. 1961. *Between Past and Future.* New York: Viking.

———. 1977. *The Life of the Mind.* New York: Harcourt, Brace, Jovanovich.

Aristotle. 1953. *Nichomachean Ethics.* Baltimore: Penguin Books.

Austin, J. L. 1979. *Philosophical Papers.* Third Edition. Oxford: Oxford University Press.

Barry, Brian. 1973. *The Liberal Theory of Justice.* Oxford: Clarendon Press.

Baldwin, Tom. 1984. "MacCallum and the Two Concepts of Freedom." *Ratio* 26:125–42.

Bayles, Michael. 1972. "A Concept of Coercion." In J. R. Pennock and J. W. Chapman, eds., *Coercion* (Nomos 14). New York: Aldine.

Benn, Stanley, and Weinstein, William. 1971. "Being Free to Act and Being a Free Man." *Mind* 80:194–211.

Benn, Stanley. 1975–76. "Freedom, Autonomy, and the Concept of a Person." *Proceedings of the Aristotelian Society* 76:109–30.

Berger, Fred. 1984. *Happiness, Justice and Freedom: The Moral and Political Philosophy of John Stuart Mill.* Berkeley: University of California Press.

Berlin, Isaiah. 1969. *Four Essays on Liberty.* London: Oxford University Press.

———. 1981. *Concepts and Categories.* New York: Penguin Books.

———. 1982. *Against the Current.* New York: Penguin Books.

Bosanquet, Bernard. 1899. *The Metaphysical Theory of the State.* London: Macmillan.

Bradley, F. H. 1927. *Ethical Studies.* Oxford: Clarendon Press.

Brenkert, George G. 1983. *Marx's Ethics of Freedom.* London: Routledge and Kegan Paul.

Charvet, John. 1981. *A Critique of Freedom and Equality.* London: Cambridge University Press.

———. N. d. "Positive Freedom Defended." Manuscript, cited by permission of the author.

Connolly, William E. 1983. *The Terms of Political Discourse.* Second Edition. Princeton: Princeton University Press.

Cranston, Maurice. 1953. *Freedom: A New Analysis.* London: Longmans, Green.

Day, J. P. 1970. "On Liberty and the Real Will." *Philosophy* 45:177–92.

———. 1977. "Threats, Offers, Law, Opinion, and Liberty."*Philosophical Quarterly* 14:257–72.

Daniels, Norman. 1975. "Equal Liberty and Unequal Worth of Liberty." In Norman Daniels, ed., *Reading Rawls.* Oxford: Basil Blackwell.

Dennett, Daniel C. 1984 *Elbow Room.* Oxford: Clarendon Press.

DiQuattro, Arthur. 1983. "Rawls and Left Criticism." *Political Theory* 11:53–78.

Dworkin, Gerald. 1970. "Acting Freely." *Nous* 4:367–83.

Dworkin, Ronald. 1977. *Taking Rights Seriously.* Cambridge, Mass. Harvard University Press.

———. 1978. "Liberalism." In Stuart Hampshire, ed., *Public and Private Morality.* London: Cambridge University Press.

Elster, Jon. 1976. "A Note on Hysterisis in the Social Sciences." *Synthese* 33:391–99.

———. 1978. *Logic and Society.* New York: John Wiley.

———. 1979. *Ulysses and the Sirens.* London: Cambridge University Press.

———. 1982a. "Sour Grapes: Utilitarianism and the Genesis of Wants." In Amartya Sen and Bernard Williams, eds., *Utilitarianism and Beyond.* London: Cambridge University Press.

———. 1982b. "Belief, Bias, and Ideology." In Martin Hollis and Steven Lukes, eds., *Rationality and Relativism.* Cambridge, Mass. MIT Press.

Feinberg, Joel. 1980. *Rights, Justice, and the Bounds of Liberty.* Princeton, N.J.: Princeton University Press.

Fishkin, James. 1975. "Justice and Rationality." *The American Political Science Review* 69:615–29.

———. 1984. "Justifying Liberty: The Self-Reflective Argument." Manuscript, cited by permission of the author.

Flathman, Richard E., ed. 1972. *Concepts in Social and Political Philosophy.* New York: Macmillan.

———. 1976. *The Practice of Rights.* New York: Cambridge University Press.

———. 1980. *The Practice of Political Authority: Authority and the Authoritative.* Chicago: University of Chicago Press.

———. 1983. "Liberalism and Authority." In Timothy Fuller, ed., *The Prospects of Liberalism.* Colorado Springs, Colo.: Colorado College.

———. 1984a. "Culture, Morality, and Rights." *Analyse & Kritik* 1:8–27.

———. 1984b. "Moderating Rights." *Social Philosophy and Policy* 1:149–71.

Foucault, Michel. 1973a. *Birth of the Clinic.* New York: Pantheon.

———. 1973b. *Madness and Civilization.* New York: Random House.

———. 1973c. *The Order of Things.* New York: Random House.

———. 1979a. *Discipline and Punish.* New York: Random House.

———. 1979b. *Power, Truth, Strategy.* Atlantic Highlands, N.J.: Humanities Press.

———. 1981. *Power-Knowledge.* New York: Pantheon.

Frankfurt, Harry. 1971. "Freedom of the Will and the Concept of a Person." *Journal of Philosophy* 68:5–20.

———. 1973. "Coercion and Moral Responsibility." In Ted Honderich, ed., *Essays on Freedom of Action.* London: Routledge and Kegan Paul.

Gert, Bernard. 1970. *The Moral Rules.* New York: Harper and Row.

———. 1972. "Coercion and Freedom." In J. Roland Pennock and John W. Chapman, eds., *Coercion* (Nomos 14). New York: Aldine.

Gewirth, Alan. 1978. *Reason and Morality.* Chicago: University of Chicago Press.

———. 1982. *Human Rights.* Chicago: University of Chicago Press.

Gibbs, Benjamin. 1976. *Freedom and Liberation.* London: University of Sussex Press.

Goffman, Erving. 1959. *The Presentation of Self in Everyday Life.* Garden City, N.J.: Doubleday Anchor.

———. 1961a. *Encounters.* Indianapolis, Ind.: Bobbs-Merrill.

———. 1961b. *Asylums.* Garden City, N.J.: Doubleday Anchor.

———. 1963. *Behavior in Public Places.* New York: The Free Press.

———. 1963a. *Stigma.* Englewood Cliffs, N.J.: Prentice-Hall.

———. 1967. *Interaction Ritual.* Chicago: Aldine.

———. 1969a. *Where the Action Is.* London: Alan Lane.

———. 1969b. *Strategic Interaction.* Philadelphia: University of Pennsylvania Press.

———. 1971. *Relations in Public.* New York: Basic Books.

———. 1974. *Frame Analysis.* Cambridge, Mass.: Harvard University Press.

———. 1981. *Forms of Talk.* Philadelphia: University of Pennsylvania Press.

Gray, John. 1980a. "On Negative and Positive Liberty." *Political Studies* 28:507–26.

———. 1980b. "Freedom, Slavery, and Contentment." In Michael Freedman and David Robertson, eds., *Frontiers of Political Theory*. New York: St. Martin's Press.

———. 1983. *Mill on Liberty: A Defence*. London: Routledge and Kegan Paul.

Green, T. H. 1941. *Lectures on the Principles of Political Obligation*. London: Longmans, Green.

———. 1964. *The Political Theory of T. H. Green*. New York: Appleton-Century-Crofts.

Haksar, Vinit. 1979. *Equality, Liberty, and Perfectionism*. Oxford: The Clarendon Press.

Hampshire, Stuart. 1960. *Thought and Action*. New York: Viking.

———. 1978. "Morality and Pessimism." In Stuart Hampshire, ed., *Public and Private Morality*. London: Cambridge University Press.

Hart, H. L. A. 1955. "Are There Any Natural Rights?" *Philosophical Review* 64:175–91.

———. 1973. "Rawls on Liberty and its Priority." *University of Chicago Law Review* 40:534–55.

———. 1982. *Essays on Bentham*. Oxford: The Clarendon Press.

———. 1983. *Essays in Jurisprudence and Philosophy*. Oxford: The Clarendon Press.

Hayek, F. A. 1960. *The Constitution of Liberty*. London: Routledge and Kegan Paul.

———. 1982. *Law, Legislation, and Liberty*. London: Routledge and Kegan Paul.

Hegel, G. W. F. 1942. *The Philosophy of Right*. Oxford: The Clarendon Press.

———. 1977. *The Phenomenology of Spirit*. London: Oxford University Press.

Held, Virginia. 1972. "Coercion and Coercive Offers." In J. Roland Pennock and John W. Chapman, eds., *Coercion* (Nomos 14). New York: Aldine.

Hirschman, Albert. 1977. *The Passions and the Interests*. (Princeton, N.J.: Princeton University Press.

———. 1982. *Shifting Involvements*. Princeton, N.J.: Princeton University Press.

Hobbes, Thomas. 1955. *Leviathan*. Oxford: Basil Blackwell.

———. 1971. *A Dialogue between a Philosopher and a Student of the Common Laws of England*. Chicago: University of Chicago Press.

Hohfeld, Wesley N. 1919. *Fundamental Legal Conceptions*. New Haven, Conn.: Yale University Press.

Holmes, Stephen. 1984. *Benjamin Constant and the Making of Modern Liberalism*. New Haven, Conn.: Yale University Press.

Kateb, George. 1984. *Hannah Arendt: Politics, Conscience, Evil*. Totowa, N.J.: Rowman and Allenheld.

Kenny, Anthony. 1973. *Wittgenstein*. London: Alan Lane.

Kripke, Saul A. 1982. *Wittgenstein on Rules and Private Language.* Cambridge, Mass.: Harvard University Press.

Laing, R. D. 1969. *The Divided Self.* New York: Pantheon.

——. 1972. *Self and Others.* New York: Penguin.

Laing, R. D., and Esterson, A. 1970. *Sanity, Madness, and the Family.* New York: Penguin.

Lyons, Daniel. 1975. "Welcome Threats and Coercive Offers." *Philosophy* 50:425–36.

Lyons, David. 1973. *In the Interest of the Governed.* Oxford: The Clarendon Press.

——. 1978. "Mill's Theory of Justice." In A. I. Goldman and J. Kim, *Values and Morals.* Dordrecht: Reidel.

——. 1982. "Utility and Rights." In J. Roland Pennock and John W. Chapman, eds. *Ethics, Economics and the Law* (Nomos 24). New York: New York University Press.

MacCallum, Gerald. 1967. "Negative and Positive Freedom." *The Philosophical Review* 76:312–34.

MacIntyre, Alasdair. 1981a. *Against the Self-Images of the Age.* London: Duckworth.

——. 1981b. *After Virtue.* South Bend, Ind.: University of Notre Dame Press.

Mapel, David. 1983. "The Basic Structure, Distributive Justice, and the Problem of Pluralism." Ph. D. dissertation. The Johns Hopkins University.

McCloskey, H. J. 1965. "A Critique of the Ideals of Liberty." *Mind* 74:483–508.

Meiklejohn, Alexander. 1960. *Political Freedom.* New York: Harper and Brothers.

Mill, J. S. 1951. *Utilitarianism, Liberty, and Representative Government.* New York: E. P. Dutton.

Miller, David. 1983. "Constraints on Freedom." *Ethics* 94:66–86.

Milne, A. J. M. 1968. *Freedom and Rights.* London: George Allen and Unwin.

Montesquieu, Charles-Louis. 1977. *The Spirit of the Laws.* Berkeley: University of California Press.

Nagel, Thomas. 1970. *The Possibility of Altruism.* Oxford: The Clarendon Press.

Neumann, Franz. 1957. *The Democratic and the Authoritarian State.* Glencoe, Ill.: The Free Press.

Nozick, Robert. 1969. "Coercion." In S. Morgenbesser, P. Suppes, and M. White, eds. *Philosophy, Science, and Method.* New York: St. Martin's Press.

——. 1974. *Anarchy, State, and Utopia.* New York: Basic Books.

——. 1981. *Philosophical Explanations.* Cambridge, Mass.: Harvard University Press.

Oakeshott, Michael. 1975. *On Human Conduct.* London: Oxford University Press.

————. 1983. *On History and Other Essays.* Oxford: Basil Blackwell.

O'Shaughnessy, B. 1980. *The Will: A Dual Aspect Theory.* New York: Cambridge University Press.

Oppenheim, Felix. 1961. *Dimensions of Freedom.* New York: St. Martin's Press.

————. 1981. *Political Concepts: A Reconstruction.* Chicago: University of Chicago Press.

Parent, William. 1974. "Some Recent Work on the Concept of Liberty." *American Philosophical Quarterly* 11:149–67.

Parfit, Derek. 1984. *Reasons and Persons.* Oxford: The Clarendon Press.

Pitkin, Hanna. 1984. *Fortune Is a Woman: Gender and Politics in the Thought of Niccolò Machiavelli.* Berkeley: University of California Press.

Pocock, J. G. A. 1975. *The Machiavellian Moment.* Princeton, N.J.: Princeton University Press.

————. 1985. *Virtue, Commerce, and History.* London: Cambridge University Press.

Rawls, John. 1971. *A Theory of Justice.* Cambridge, Mass.: Harvard University Press.

————. 1974–75. "The Independence of Moral Theory." *Proceedings of the American Philosophical Association* 48:5–22.

————. 1978. "The Basic Structure as Subject:. In A. Goldman and J. Kim, eds., *Values and Morals.* Dordrecht: Reidel.

————. 1980. "Kantian Constructivism in Moral Theory." *The Journal of Philosophy* 77:515–72.

————. 1982a. "Social Unity and Primary Goods." In A. Sen and B. Williams, eds., *Utilitarianism and Beyond.* London: Cambridge University Press.

————. 1982b. "The Basic Liberties and Their Priorities." In S. M. McMurrin, ed., *The Tanner Lectures on Human Values,* vol. 3. Salt Lake City, Utah: University of Utah Press.

————. 1985. "Justice as Fairness: Political Not Metaphysical." *Philosophy and Public Affairs* 14:223–51.

Rorty, Amalie. 1975. "Akrasia and Conflict." *Inquiry* 23:193–212.

————, ed. 1976. *The Identities of Persons.* Berkeley: University of California Press.

Rousseau, Jean-Jacques. 1950. *The Social Contract and Discourses.* New York: E. P. Dutton.

Ryan, Alan. 1965. "Freedom." *Philosophy* 40:93–112.

Ryan, Cheyney. 1980. "The Normative Concept of Coercion." *Mind* 89:481–98.

Sachs, David. 1976. "Wittgenstein on Emotion." *Acta Philosophica Fennica,* vol. 28, nos. 1–3. Amsterdam: North-Holland Publishing Company.

Scanlon, T. M. 1971. "A Theory of Expression." *Philosophy and Public Affairs* 1:204–26.

———. 1978. "Rights, Goals, and Fairness." In S. Hampshire, ed., *Public and Private Morality*. London: Cambridge University Press.

———. 1979. "Freedom of Expression and Categories of Expression." *University of Pittsburgh Law Review* 40:519–50.

Searle, John R. 1983. *Intentionality*. London: Cambridge University Press.

Skinner, Quentin. 1981. *Machiavelli*. New York: Hill and Wang.

———. 1983. "Machiavelli on the Maintenance of Liberty." *Politics* 18:3–15.

———. 1984. "The Idea of Negative Liberty: Philosophical and Historical Perspectives." In R. Rorty, J. B. Schneewind, and Q. Skinner, eds., *Philosophy in History*. London: Cambridge University Press.

Steiner, Hillel. 1974–75. "Individual Liberty." *Proceedings of the Aristotelian Society* 75:33–50.

Strawson, Peter. 1974. *Freedom and Resentment and Other Essays*. London: Methuen.

Szasz, Thomas. 1968. *Law, Liberty, and Psychiatry*. New York: Macmillan.

———. 1970. *Ideology and Insanity*. New York: Doubleday Anchor.

———. 1974. *The Myth of Mental Illness*. New York: Harper and Row.

Taylor, Charles. 1967. "Neutrality in Political Science." In P. Laslett and W. G. Runciman, eds., *Philosophy, Politics and Society*. 3d ser. Oxford: Basil Blackwell. Also in Taylor 1985, vol. 1.

———. 1971. "Interpretation and the Sciences of Man." *Review of Metaphysics* 25, no. 1. Also in Taylor 1985, vol. 2.

———. 1973. "Peaceful Coexistence in Psychology." *Social Research* 40:55–82. Also in Taylor 1985, vol. 2.

———. 1975. *Hegel*. London: Cambridge University Press.

———. 1976. "Responsibility for Self." In A. Rorty, ed., *The Identities of Persons*. Berkeley: University of California Press.

———. 1977. "What Is Human Agency?" In T. Mischel, ed., *The Self: Psychological and Philosophical Issues*. Oxford: Basil Blackwell.

———. 1978. "Hegel's Sittlichkeit and the Crisis of Representative Institutions." In Y. Yovel, ed., *Philosophy of History and Action*. London and Jerusalem.

———. 1978–79. "The Validity of Transcendental Arguments." *Proceedings of the Aristotelian Society* 79:151–65.

———. 1979a. *Hegel and Modern Society*. London: Cambridge University Press.

———. 1979b. "What's Wrong with Negative Liberty?" In A. Ryan, ed., *The Idea of Freedom*. London: Oxford University Press. Also in Taylor 1985, vol. 2.

———. 1979c. "Action and Expression." In C. Diamond and J. Teichman, eds., *Intention and Intentionality*. Ithaca, N.Y.: Cornell University Press.

———. 1979d. "Atomism." In A. Kontos, ed., *Powers, Possessions, and Freedom*. Toronto: University of Toronto Press.

———. 1982a. "The Diversity of Goods." In A. Sen and B. Williams, eds., *Utilitarianism and Beyond*. London: Cambridge University Press.

———. 1982b. "Rationality." In M. Hollis and S. Lukes, eds., *Rationality and Relativism*. Cambridge, Mass.: MIT Press. Also in Taylor 1985, vol. 2.

———. 1983. "Hegel and the Philosophy of Action." In L. S. Stepelvich and D. Lamb, eds., *Hegel's Philosophy of Action*. Atlantic Highlands, N.J.: Humanities Press.

———. 1985. *Philosophical Papers*. 2 vols. London: Cambridge University Press.

Taylor, Michael. 1982. *Community, Anarchy and Liberty*. London: Cambridge University Press.

Walzer, Michael. 1983. *Spheres of Justice*. New York: Basic Books.

———. 1985. *Exodus*. New York: Basic Books.

Weinstein, William. 1963. "The Concept of Liberty in 19th Century Thought." *Political Studies* 13:145–62.

Williams, Bernard. 1978. "Introduction." In Isaiah Berlin, *Concepts and Categories*. New York: Penguin Books.

———. 1981. *Moral Luck*. London: Cambridge University Press.

Wilson, George. 1980. *The Intentionality of Human Action. Acta Philosophica Fennica* 31, nos. 2–3. Amsterdam: North-Holland Publishing Company.

Wittgenstein, Ludwig. 1953. *Philosophical Investigations*. New York: Macmillan.

———. 1967. *Zettel*. Oxford: Basil Blackwell.

———. 1969. *On Certainty*. Oxford: Basil Blackwell.

Index